The
Absent
Stone

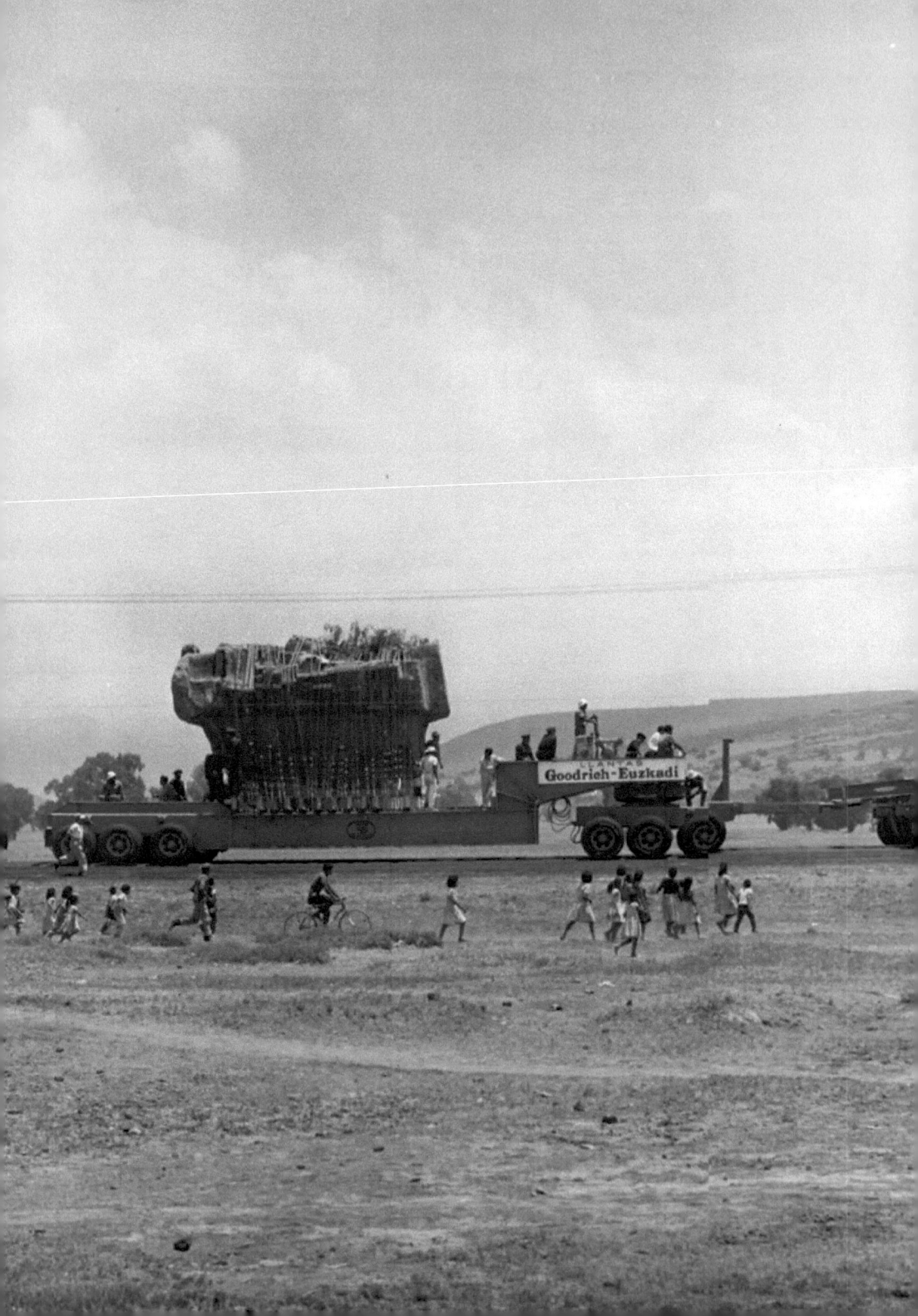

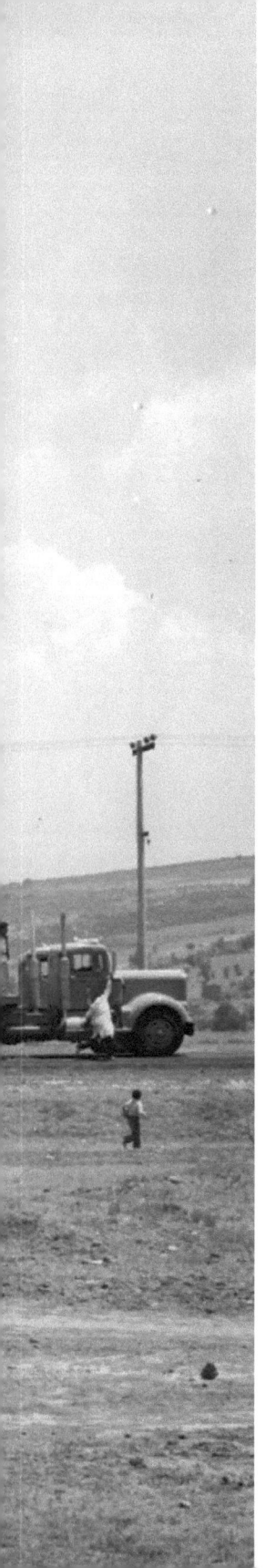

The
Absent
Stone

Mexican Patrimony and the
Aftershocks of State Theft

SANDRA ROZENTAL

Duke University Press   *Durham and London*   2026

© 2026 Duke University Press
All rights reserved
Printed in the United States of America on acid-free paper ∞
Project Editor: Livia Tenzer
Cover designed by Dave Rainey
Typeset in Garamond Premier Pro by Westchester Publishing Services

Library of Congress Cataloging-in-Publication Data
Names: Rozental, Sandra, author.
Title: The absent stone : Mexican patrimony and the aftershocks of state
theft / Sandra Rozental.
Description: Durham : Duke University Press, 2026. | Includes
bibliographical references and index.
Identifiers: LCCN 2025026245 (print)
LCCN 2025026246 (ebook)
ISBN 9781478033127 (paperback)
ISBN 9781478029663 (hardcover)
ISBN 9781478061878 (ebook)
Subjects: LCSH: Museo Nacional de Antropología (Mexico) | Aztec
sculpture—Mexico—Coatlinchán. | Indian sculpture—Mexico—
Coatlinchán. | Aztec sculpture—Mexico—Mexico City. | Indian
sculpture—Mexico—Mexico City. | Tlaloc (Aztec deity) | Aztec gods. |
Mexico—Antiquities.
Classification: LCC F1219.76.S35 R694 2026 (print) | LCC F1219.76.S35
(ebook)
LC record available at https://lccn.loc.gov/2025026245
LC ebook record available at https://lccn.loc.gov/2025026246

Frontis: The stone on the move, April 16, 1964. Photograph courtesy
of Acervo Arquitecto Pedro Ramírez Vázquez.

Cover art: La Piedra de los Tecomates, Mexico City, detail.
Photograph by Sandra Rozental.

Para Vivian, Andrés y Tamara
que me enseñaron a seguir las piedras

Para Ulises, Micaela y Sasha
que son mis brújulas en el camino

Y para la y lo Tlacuaches
que me permitieron acompañarles en su andar

Since we were little, as soon as we learned to walk, my mother took us out to the fields and taught us to look at the ground and find things. Not just potsherds, but stones too. Pretty, polished stones. We would collect them all.

—DULCE GALICIA GONZÁLEZ, in the film *The Absent Stone*

Rocks are in time in a different way than living things are, even the ancient trees. But then, the other thing about rocks is that they are place. Rocks are what a place is made of to start with and after all. They are under everything else in the world, dirt, water, street, house, air, launching pad. The stone is at the center.

—URSULA K. LE GUIN, "Three Rock Poems"

Contents

Introduction

Shortly before midnight, a low-bed trailer carrying a massive, 167-ton, pre-Hispanic stone lurched down Mexico City's avenues under a heavy downpour.[1] Teams of electricians and engineers in hard hats led the way, carefully lifting cables and wires crisscrossing the city overhead to assure the vehicle's safe passage. People lined the route, cheering on the arrival of the convoy. A festive procession of trucks, cars, bicycles, and hundreds more, unencumbered by the rain, followed behind on foot. Under colorful bursts of streamers and confetti, the stone arrived at the Plaza de la Constitución, the city's central square and symbolic heart of the nation.

It was April 16, 1964. For months, the national media had fueled expectations, commenting on every detail of the stone's impending transportation from San Miguel Coatlinchan, a small town barely thirty-five miles east of the capital. Reporters and photojournalists marveled at each stage of the unfolding feat: the excavation on site; the route carefully prepared; new roads being built; old roads repaved, widened, and reinforced to bear the stone's enormous weight. Now the stone headed to the new Museo Nacional de Antropología under construction in the Bosque de Chapultepec.[2]

The volcanic rock chosen as the museum's emblem was born from deep geological time. Later, ancient peoples who thrived in what is now central Mexico carved it into a rough, perhaps unfinished, anthropomorphic figure. For centuries, the stone lay buried in a ravine in Coatlinchan, covered and uncovered by a succession of environmental forces, erosion, and human curiosity. Lacking features that might offer more definitive clues to trace its connection with a specific group or historical period, archaeologists debated whether or not the stone represented the storm god Tlaloc, one of the most important entities in the Mesoamerican pantheon. Its possible attribution was not lost on onlookers who imputed its spectacular and very wet arrival in the city in what was still the Mexican dry season to the abiding powers of ancient deities to tame or unleash the environmental forces that have for millennia governed life and death in the Valley of Mexico.

As the procession was broadcast live on national television, the camera panned the square, revealing the immensity of the crowd gathered to greet the stone. In a solemn and dramatic voice, over the sound of the trailer's deafening sirens, the newscaster announced: "Arriving just now on the Plaza de la Constitución, very close to where a great coup overthrew ancient Tenochtitlan and where Moctezuma's palace once stood, the most gigantic, the most beautiful, and the heaviest effigy sculpted by the people of Teotihuacan, the God of Gods, of mountains, of fertility, and of rain—Tlaloc—has finally arrived in Mexico's capital." In locating the stone's manufacture in Teotihuacan—one of the oldest settlements in the Valley of Mexico—and reminding viewers that Mexico City's central square was once the seat of the powerful Aztec empire, the newscaster celebrated the relocation from Coatlinchan to the capital as the climax of a project begun almost two thousand years earlier. Other media followed suit, compressing centuries of ancient and colonial history, political fragmentation, and conflict to present the stone's movement as "Tlaloc's pilgrimage, five centuries after his empire" (figure I.1).

Lauding the relocation as a national triumph, government officials boasted that both the monument—likely the product of a powerful regime able to harness the labor and manpower to sculpt and eventually move a block of such proportions—and the contemporary low-bed made to transport it were the products of timeless Mexican engineering. This was the same engineering at work building state infrastructures to foster national development all over the country: roads, dams, and public works imagined to connect and modernize but also control the nation's territories. Driven by a Cold War zeitgeist,

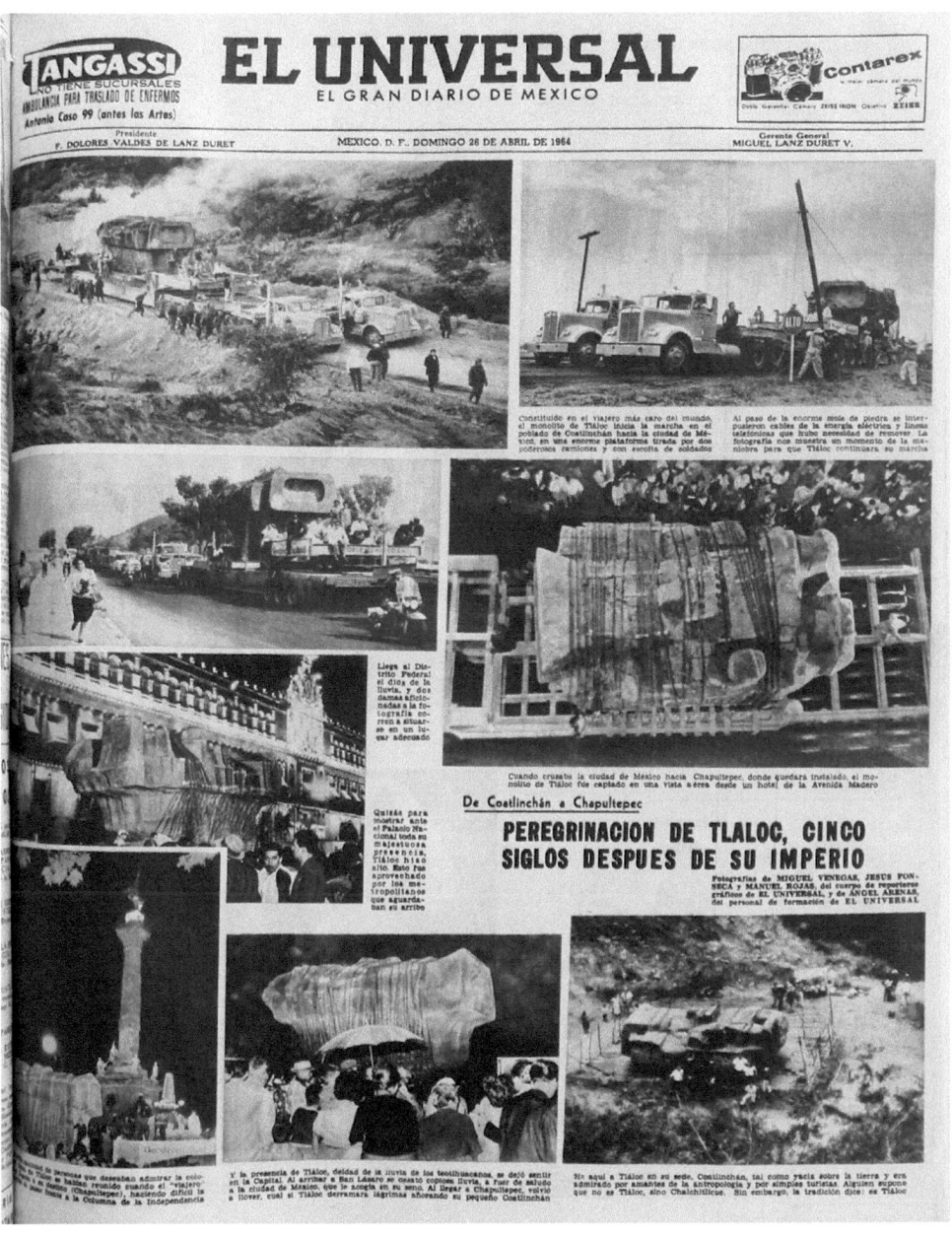

FIGURE 1.1. "De Coatlinchan a Chapultepec: Peregrinación de Tlaloc, cinco siglos después de su imperio" (From Coatlinchan to Chapultepec: Tlaloc's pilgrimage five centuries after his empire). Front page, *El Universal*, April 17, 1964.

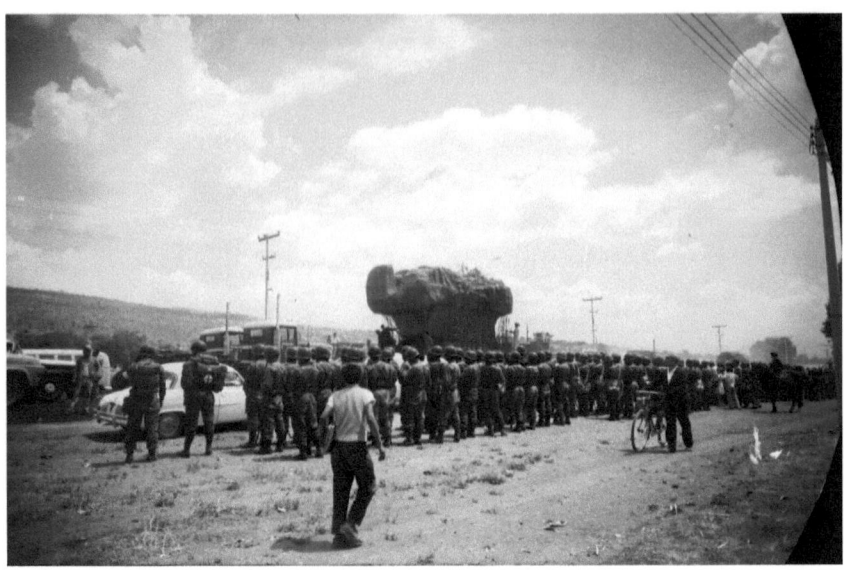

FIGURE I.2. The stone leaving Coatlinchan surrounded by armed soldiers, April 16, 1964. "Tlaloc-Imagen 2," HMA/CRI/19055, Fondo Archivo Fotográfico Hermanos Mayo, Archivo General de la Nación, Mexico City.

the undertaking equated the conquest of space—on Earth and beyond—with power in the international arena, intended to place Mexico on the world political stage. The same newspapers covered the impending relocation's progress alongside reports on the launch of space satellites and the exploits of Yuri Gagarin, famed as the first man to orbit the Earth.

Government officials proclaimed the stone's relocation as a rescue, an operation that would guarantee its conservation as a national heirloom belonging under the care and custody of state patrimonial institutions and experts rather than languishing, exposed and abandoned, in a remote gorge. When town residents tried to stop its removal, these arguments justified the government's use of force and the military's intervention to subdue their opposition. The stone was ultimately removed from Coatlinchan under an escort of dozens of armed soldiers (figure I.2).

The stone's forced relocation and the engineering required to perform this feat were part of efforts to bring together Mexico's ancient past and its progress-oriented present in ways that made it seem as if Mexico as a nation and a political project was as old and monolithic as the ancient basaltic stone. Yet Mexico's "miracle," as this time of state-led modernization financed by recent

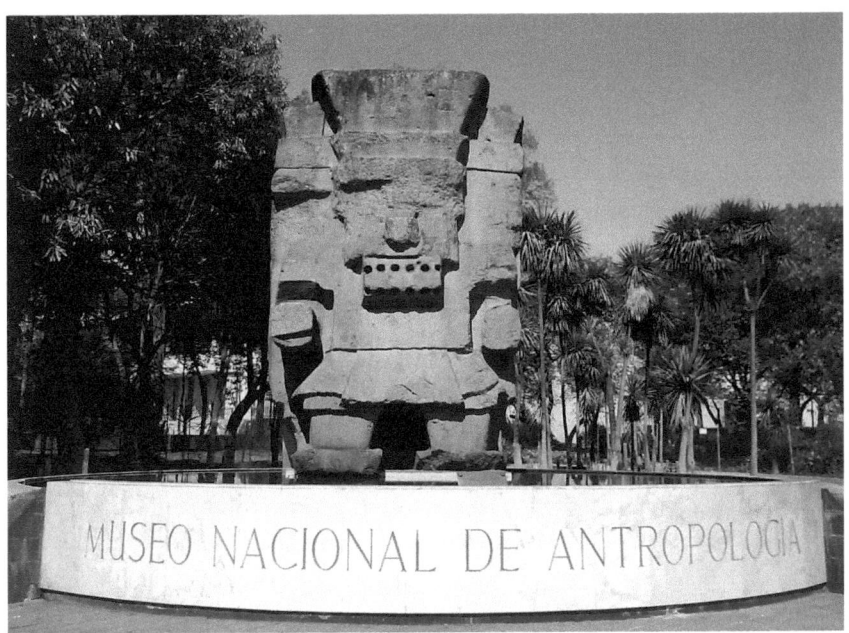

FIGURE I.3. The stone as the centerpiece of the fountain in front of the Museo Nacional de Antropología, Mexico City, 2010. Photograph by the author.

economic growth became known, cannot be dissociated from the postrevolutionary regime's seven decades of single-party rule, including episodes of authoritarianism and repression under the Partido Revolucionario Institucional (PRI, Institutional Revolutionary Party).[3] This culminated in the Tlatelolco student massacre only four years after the stone was forcefully taken from Coatlinchan, when on October 2, 1968, the government violently suppressed a peaceful meeting of students and workers calling for democratization, arresting and killing an estimated several hundred.[4] The dimensions of this state crime are still unknown.

Since 1964, the stone has stood watch over Mexico City as the centerpiece of a circular fountain on the Paseo de la Reforma, Mexico's most emblematic and statue-laden avenue (figure I.3).[5] Although it has a catalog number like the rest of the museum's collections, it is the only artifact placed outside its perimeter. It stands on a busy city street corner, exposed to the elements and the vibrations and emissions of passing traffic. Birds and insects have made its cracks and crevices their home.[6] The stone's placement in public space has become so familiar to city residents who, like me, were born after its epic journey that they rarely stop to question where it came from or how it came to stand in its monumental solitude in front of the museum.

For the first two decades following its relocation, only the words "Museo Nacional de Antropología" were emblazoned on the fountain's white marble base. In 1984, to celebrate the twentieth anniversary of the relocation, the museum added a small bronze plaque inside the fountain's verdant waters. It reads: "This monolith was found in the surroundings of the town of San Miguel Coatlinchan, Estado de México, whose residents generously donated it to this museum in 1964. The monumental statue is unfinished and represents a water deity, a central element in the lifeways of the residents of the agricultural city of Teotihuacan who carved it. Teotihuacan Culture, Classic Period (100 to 850 A.D.)." The tarnished plaque, only legible up close, presents the stone as a generic representation of an ancient deity, reworking its forced dispossession from Coatlinchan, its theft by the state, as a "generous donation." As anthropologist Michel-Rolph Trouillot (1995) argues, the silences folded into historical narratives are revealing of how violence, structures of power, and inequality operate and how they continue to haunt the spaces where those histories unfolded. Through silence and omission, the plaque transformed the stone's place of origin—not even Coatlinchan but its "surroundings"—into a mere detail of its biography, with no mention of the acts of military repression deployed to discipline, threaten, and subjugate its residents who tried to stop its removal and who to this day mourn and live with its loss.

This book, in contrast, documents this stone's theft and the generative effects of its absence in Coatlinchan. In doing so, it unravels the many possibilities of association and attachment that accrue as layers of time and relations condense into and emerge from the stone as place. Here I borrow from Ursula K. LeGuin, who notes that "rocks are place" (see the book's second epigraph). Engaging the stone ethnographically, paying attention to the enduring traces of its absence—the aftershocks of its theft—shows how this stone that was taken from Coatlinchan and converted into a monument by the Mexican state continues to linger, affect, and shape the place it was found in, but also made of, "to start with and after all" (Le Guin 1987, 55).

Desde que se llevaron la Piedra

I first visited Coatlinchan in 2005, arriving on one of the many *combis* that shuttle between Mexico City and this densely populated area of the Texcoco Municipality in the Estado de México.[7] Braving hours in traffic, these minibuses take construction workers, students, and office employees back and forth between their pueblos and the city.[8] Travelers carry bulky bags full of merchandise purchased in city markets or flip through folders of paperwork from banks, hospitals, and government offices, located either in Mexico City or the still more distant state capital, Toluca. Meandering past twisted under- and overpasses, the city slowly gives way to a large stretch of urban sprawl, with warehouses and stalls selling auto parts and scrap metal. Coatlinchan's lush hills, crisscrossed by ravines and dry riverbeds that once flowed into the ancient Texcoco lake, drained over centuries to make way for urban expansion, stand out from what the region's residents pejoratively call "la mancha urbana" (the urban stain).[9] Towns like Coatlinchan, once surrounded by communal forests and agricultural lands where campesinos grew and harvested maize and subsistence crops, have increasingly taken on grayish hues, buried under a labyrinth of asphalt roads and large low-income housing developments.[10]

The combi was full of passengers, so I sat in the front, next to a man whose weight shifted into my shoulder as the vehicle turned onto González, the road that leads into Coatlinchan off the main highway. Apologizing, he asked candidly: "You going to Coatlinchan, huh? You sure? Coat-linchan? *Donde linchan* [where people lynch]?"[11] His play on words was, to say the least, unsettling. Sensing my discomfort, he explained that he was from Papalotla, a nearby town, but his uncle had married a woman from Coatlinchan. "My mother never liked her," he announced. "She always said: 'Never trust a Tlacuache; they will steal from you when you least expect it.' . . . Just be careful. And keep your belongings close!" This was how I first found out that the town I was heading to, to study the effects of state theft, had a reputation for violence and that its residents were known as Tlacuaches, or possums, an animal itself associated with rapacious behavior and theft. This ambivalence would define my time there and my thinking.

Coatlinchan's main square, the Plazuela, marks the entrance to the town. The sixteenth-century church devoted to the town's patron, the archangel San Miguel, and its adjacent cloister, originally built in 1528 and one of the first Franciscan missions in New Spain, flank the square to the west.[12] To the south, a building that used to be an early twentieth-century schoolhouse now serves as the town authorities' headquarters, the Delegación. An array of small businesses dots the square, selling roast chickens on rotating spits, cakes, medicine, popsicles, and cell phone accessories, all to the rhythms of techno-cumbias and reggaeton. Other buildings serve as the private homes of Coatlinchan's wealthier families. These were built looking out to the *monte*, the hillside made up of communal lands and forests that rises toward the Iztaccihuatl and Mount Tlaloc volcanoes, now only discernible on less polluted days.

Strikingly, the first visible traces of the absent stone that I noticed were related to intra-urban transportation infrastructures: a smiling cartoon proudly giving a thumbs-up to a neon sign that read "Coatlinchan" on the windshields of the local combi route, and a little sticker, often crookedly placed, on taxi doors. As I wandered around, I began to see more traces of the absent stone: a bakery and a stationery store named "Tlaloc" and several murals featuring the standing stone painted on old adobe walls. I would later find many more signs, images, and murals depicting the stone as well as myriad replicas and miniatures, both inside people's homes and adorning their gardens and patios. But back in 2005, what caught my attention was how the stone's absence was palpable in town residents' lives and stories, stirring memories, powerful emotions, heated arguments, and much uncertainty and ambivalence regarding its identification, local significance, and how and why it was no longer in Coatlinchan.

On this early visit, I stopped to order a snack at a carnitas stall, where the attendant asked what brought me to town. I said I had heard that "the Tlaloc" (as I then knew the stone) was from here and that I was curious to visit its place of origin. The attendant responded with a complicit chuckle: "Ha! I knew someone would come asking about the Piedra! Just yesterday there was an earthquake. . . . It always shakes when people come asking about her. . . . You know, it isn't Tlaloc, it's Tlala! Tlaloc's partner. It's a goddess, not a god!" A man eating at the stall with his family chimed in:

Tlala? Nobody here calls it that! Not even Tlaloc. Here we know it as La Piedra . . . La Piedra de los Tecomates. Ever since the Piedra was taken, it barely rains. . . . It used to rain nice and hard, the earth was good; now all that remains is dust. It sure rains in Mexico City, though. Floods there all the time . . . and that's because that's where they took our stone. People used to come here from all over the place to see it and to buy *ídolos* [clay figurines], but now Coatlinchan is no longer on the map. Nobody comes here anymore.

I was admiring the man's elegant cowboy boots and *norteño*-style hat when the attendant again interceded: "Everyone knows that the thing they put in Mexico City isn't even the real one. It's a dummy! The real one was shipped off by the government to the land where nobody sleeps . . . where nothing is wasted. It's in Japan!"

An older woman wearing an embroidered apron with a bag of groceries by her side interrupted: "Come on! It's not in Japan! The real one, THE Tlaloc, is up in the monte. My grandfather told me he saw it there. He had a map that showed where it was. The one they took isn't Tlaloc; it's his partner." She then lamented that the stone's removal had brought about many losses for the town: "Since they took the Piedra away, it's been downhill. You know, this town is a mess. Everyone talks about how the government took the Piedra, and that they took the Piedra, and took the Piedra . . . but there isn't any type of solidarity—that is the real reason we lost the Piedra in the first place, and why we are losing everything: our land, our water, what is ours [*lo nuestro*], our town."

Attracted by the fiery conversation, several elderly men hanging out within earshot left their spots under the shade to share their own versions of events, telling me there had been a rebellion when the government first attempted to remove the stone and an ensuing military siege. The oldest man in the crowd raised his voice. Leaning on his walking stick, held in hands calloused by a lifetime of manual work, and removing his straw hat, revealing a white head of perfectly combed hair, he pronounced: "The town authorities sold it to the government—that's what really happened. They took money and negotiated everything. There was never a town assembly, we were never consulted. . . . We've got to tell it like it is! It wasn't the government that took it away. The truth is it was our own authorities. And that is why things are as they are now. They are all corrupt, they are like the government, they steal from the town, from all of us. Vultures! We are guilty of our own fate." The conversation quickly shifted to the town's contemporary ills, framed as both cause and effect of the stone's extraction.

Many of the stories I heard that day were not mentioned again during my following visits or even once I moved to Coatlinchan three years later, nor over the course of the past two decades that I have been visiting my friends there.[13] I even tried to elicit their retelling with no success for the documentary film *The Absent Stone* (2013), which I codirected with Jesse Lerner, filmmaker and scholar of the modern reworkings of all things Mesoamerican, in tandem with the ethnographic fieldwork on which this book is based.[14] Although town residents many times insisted that the "real" Tlaloc was up in the monte, only one other person ever discussed the map that led to it, and the name Tlala and the story about Japan never came up again. However, the phrase "desde que se llevaron La Piedra" (since The Stone was taken away) kept coming up over and over again in conversations. Town residents clearly marked this moment as a tipping point. There was a before and an after of the stone's removal. Even as the phrase conceals the identity of the perpetrators by using the passive voice, it conveys town residents' sense of dispossession, denouncing the stone's removal as a theft, contrasting with the triumphant narrative promoted by the Mexican government and the museum. In Coatlinchan, the stone's absence presses upon the present. In addition to the visible marks left in the town's contemporary landscape and built environment, the stone's absence affects climate and makes the earth shake at its mention. It also generates copies and replicas and even produces other stone carvings, ancient artifacts, and treasure troves that the stone is associated with. Meanwhile, town residents have creatively reworked its absence into their daily lives and environments through a variety of practices that began to reveal themselves as I spent time there and that are the subjects of this book.

Naming the Stone

Over time, the stone has amassed many names, each containing assumptions about where and to whom it belongs, and where and to whom it does not. It is sometimes described through its material and physical attributes as a "monolith": a single, and also separate, block of rock. It is also referred to as a "statue" or a "sculpture," referencing the human interventions that shaped its matter into recognizable form, or as a "monument," alluding to its enormous dimensions and assumed purpose as an upright architectural feature. It has also borne the names of what it has been thought to represent: an "idol" in viceregal times, or a specific deity associated with water in the Mesoamerican pantheon, such as Tlaloc, or Tlaloc's female counterpart Chalchiuhtlicue, in the modern era. Most of these names were given by outsiders as they sought to engage, study, describe, and make sense of its shape, features, and location: archaeologists, collectors, government officials, engineers, and curious travelers, all captivated by its enigmatic history. Its unique proportions and its relative isolation in Coatlinchan, far from other pre-Hispanic structures and ceremonial complexes, sparked much interest and speculation.

For the residents of Coatlinchan, my main interlocutors and teachers, who sometimes refer to the stone affectionately as El Tlaloc or La Chalchi, the stone is mostly known as La Piedra (The Stone) or La Piedra de los Tecomates, after the Nahuatl term *tecomatl*, which translates as "vessel" or "orifice."[15] This name alludes both to its material and to the carving's most salient formal features: two rows of six aligning round cavities, or *tecomates*, sometimes described as the stone's "mouth" or "teeth." Town residents also use humor, referencing the stone's formal resemblance to figures drawn from comic books and popular animations, calling it El Mono or Monigote (terms used for dolls), King Kong, or even SpongeBob SquarePants.

It took me time to understand the theoretical valence of these names beyond their material and formal designations. Their proliferation points to the difficulties of fully encompassing why the stone matters to people in Coatlinchan in language. At the same time, they show that town residents are deploying humor to both make sense of and contest its theft. Naming the stone remains challenging. One of the central arguments of this book is that this is because it is not separate from the place and people with which it coexisted and which it continues to be related to and affect even after its relocation. The stone's ungraspability in a name is symptomatic of the complexity of the relations in which it is embedded and entangled and in which it continues to actively participate. I decided to use La Piedra throughout the book, not to settle on a single name but because this is the way town residents mostly call it. I have also learned that in calling it a "stone," they resist understanding it as a solidification of something else. For them, it is not a representation of a powerful being, an ancient deity to be revered and feared, or an ancestor with vital qualities and agentive capabilities—or at least not only. It is a stone because it is made from, part of, and constitutive of the material elements but also the geologic and environmental forces and human and nonhuman bodies that make up territory and guarantee its reproduction.

As scholars across fields and disciplines have shown, stone, despite its hardness, solidity, and alleged permanence, is also energetic and generative of relations, calling into question strict boundaries between the animate and the inanimate, the solid and the fluid, the organic and the inorganic.[16] Stone's geological qualities are in fact changing, made up of ruptures and discontinuities—unconformities—that complicate its association with fixity, wholeness, and endurance.[17] In Coatlinchan, beyond its geological characteristics, La Piedra is related and connected to people and place in ways that cannot easily be broken, even if the stone itself was physically moved, stolen, or repurposed.[18] Despite its physical absence, then, and perhaps even through the force of this absence, the stone from Coatlinchan continues to be inextricably bound to and related to the territory it was made in and from, and where it retains presence and the possibility for action.

Aftershocks

Those who witnessed the stone's arrival in Mexico City in 1964 describe the earth reverberating under their feet as the low-bed's enormous weight passed by, comparing the sensation to the region's frequent earthquakes. The following day, *El Día*, a popular Mexico City newspaper, published a cartoon showing the arriving convoy buried in mud with a little rain cloud hovering above (figure I.4). The image was accompanied by the following commentary: "Soon the crowd congregated, mesmerized by Tlaloc's passage in the midst of a downpour that fell so symbolically upon the deity. The cries of 'Bravo! Long

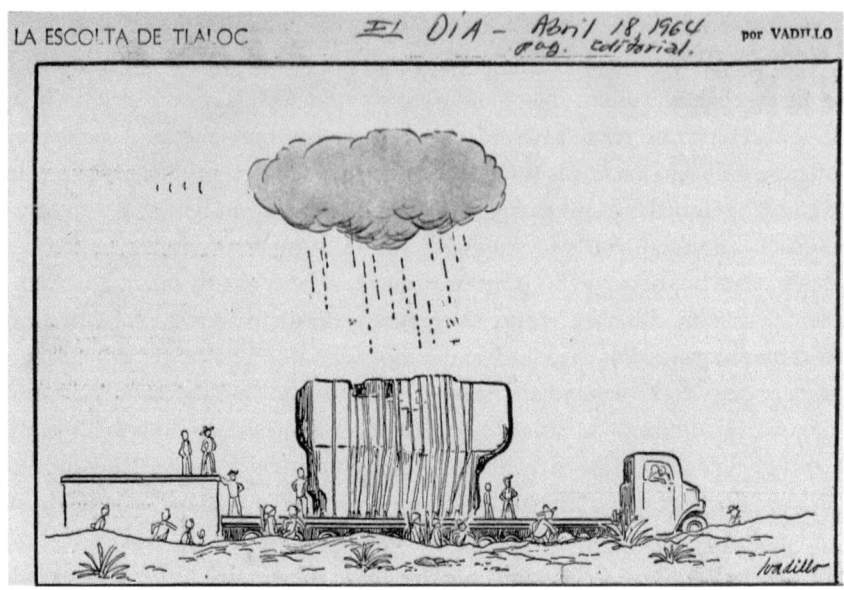

LA ESCOLTA DE TLALOC   *EL DIA - Abril 18, 1964 pag. editorial.*   por VADILLO

FIGURE I.4. Leonardo Vadillo, "La escolta de Tlaloc" (Tlaloc's escort), *El Día*, April 18, 1964.

live Tlaloc!' on young people's lips as they clambered up buildings and public monuments made the anthropologist Luis Aveleyra, who was involved in its transfer, exclaim: 'This is the Mexican's telluric character!'" Aveleyra (1926–2001), an archaeologist professionally trained to excavate the ground, and also the previous museum's director, was then in charge of coordinating the new museum's collections.[19] His exclamation as well as witnesses' sensory memories can be read as more than momentary hyperboles.

In Spanish, as in other romance languages, *telluric*, from the Latin *tellus*, is translated interchangeably as "earth," "soil," "ground," "floor," "land," "place," and "country," as if these terms were synonyms. But what if *the telluric* were understood as bundling these concepts together? Such a combination would involve connecting what is above and below the earth's surface, linking the substances, bodies, and networks that bind earth (ground, floor, land) to the materials that it contains (soil, organic matter, but also water) and to that which it produces (plants and trees but also human and nonhuman beings), as well as more abstract concepts describing human attachments to the earth, like "place," "territory," and "country."[20]

In ancient cosmologies, Tlaloc, a telluric entity, embodies such a bundling. In Nahuatl, the name for the deity, and for its most important ceremonial site, the mountainous region known as Tlallocan, located in the same mountain range and very near Coatlinchan, translates as "of the earth" or "covered by earth." The deity associated with water and rain, thunder and lightning, was also venerated on mountaintops and volcanic craters as well as inside underground caves and sinkholes. Tlaloc, in fact, was thought to control precipitation as well as the forces emanating from the Earth's core that provoke earthquakes. In this way, Tlaloc embodies the connections between the ground and what lies above and under it: climate and atmosphere as well as water flows and telluric forces, enabling or hindering human and nonhuman survival on its surface.

In Nahuatl-speaking Mesoamerica, the term *altepetl*, which has been translated as "territory" or "settlement," also describes how the telluric binds people, places, and the environment.[21] Made up of *atl* (water) and *tepetl* (mountain), the concept very literally brings together specific sites located in landscapes and the people who live off, inhabit, and cultivate these landscapes, as well as the environmental forces that make them thrive. Accordingly, the altepetl glyph in sixteenth-century codices is represented by a topographical feature, a mountain from which underground streams emerge, with the toponym of a specific town or people hovering above. This representation makes visible the connections between communities and the earthly configurations they inhabit and sow as well as the above- and belowground dimensions of those configurations. The concept of the altepetl has important political implications because it holds these elements—people and the environments they live on and from— together as the core of sovereignty. In this guise, it has been taken up by contemporary Nahua thinkers and activists for a politics that challenges corporate and state-sponsored forms of extractivism threatening present-day communities and their territories (Quintero Wier 2020).[22]

In order to underscore these relations, and following these Nahua activists and thinkers' lead (rather than an essentialist, timeless, or ontological argument), I frame the stone's relocation from Coatlinchan, an ancient altepetl as well as a contemporary town, as a telluric phenomenon. This is also why I have come to think of its enduring effects and affectations as "aftershocks," a term used mostly in the earth sciences, especially seismology, to describe the lasting and lingering vibrations that follow earthquakes after the actual seismic event.[23] Mexico, and particularly the central valleys where both Coatlinchan and Mexico City are located, is an area known for frequent earthquakes that make human and deep time coincide and collide in recurrent and palpable ways (Denizen 2018, 2019; Reddy 2023; Summers 2023, 2025). Built on a former lake bed, the Valley of Mexico is not only prone to telluric movements caused by the tectonic fault lines that crisscross the earth's core underground. It is also subject to a very particular phenomenon linked to the consistency of its ground and to its historical relationship to water. Its soft and moist soils, made up of lake sediments, absorb the Earth's movements, projecting and reproducing the resonances of seismic waves beyond actual quakes (Cinna Lomnitz 1988, 1990; Cinna Lomnitz and Castaños 2006). Seismologists suggestively describe this phenomenon for lay audiences as a "jello effect" (Cruz Atienza, Singh, and Ordaz 2017).

In Spanish, the word for these reverberations is *réplica*, denoting a kind of turbulence that lingers and amplifies, repeats and replicates, well after a telluric phenomenon occurs. *Réplica* comes from the Latin *replicare*, combining the prefix *re-* (back, again, or anew) with *plicare* (to fold), and translated as "folding back," "folding over," or "bending back." In seismology, *réplica* describes the folding over of the earth that reverberates in ways that make a telluric event ripple, even if steadily decreasing in intensity and frequency according to a consistent pattern. Réplicas in their telluric form, then, recall but also reproduce and repeat the effects of a seismic event.

Thinking of the effects of the stone's relocation as aftershocks is particularly insightful given the multiple meanings of its Spanish equivalent. Like the word in English, *réplica* is also used to designate copies that duplicate matter through iteration, folding back the singular and the original by opening it up, allowing for multiplication and ultimately, perhaps, for substitution or replacement. Even as replicas reproduce what was there before, to replicate is also always generative. Replicas unsettle processes of reproduction because they are both the same and different at the same time, producing something new even if the result looks and maybe feels exactly the same as an original.

The term *réplica* has a third meaning in Spanish, associated with the power of language to "fold back" and "make anew" through the act of answering back. Its verb form *replicar* means "to protest." It can, then, also involve replacing by contesting, refuting, or refusing. In Coatlinchan, replicas of the stone in all shapes, materials, and sizes, but also of the event of loss and dispossession itself, continue to produce rumblings that extend aftershocks into the present. These replicas are continually reclaiming and reproducing the stone as well as responding to, even contesting, its theft by the Mexican state. Replication often takes on the form of humor as a politics of contestation, calling attention to how humor and parody can be deployed as alternative aesthetics to unsettle and subvert the status quo and stand against power (Boyer and Yurchak 2010; Trnka 2011; Bernal 2013; Boyer 2013; Goldstein 2013; Haugerud 2013; Petrović 2018; Rehak and Trnka 2019). Humor in Coatlinchan is a politics in itself that speaks back to power (Marcus 1988; Bakhtin 2010), counteracting, responding to, and refuting state theft.

The stone's aftershocks, its réplicas in Coatlinchan and beyond, also reveal territory to be composed of copresences, interactions, and attachments that tie and intertwine humans and nonhumans to the *tellus*, the "earthly," as well as to the elements, substances, and forces that sustain it. Although territory tends to be understood as a portion of land under the jurisdiction of a political agency (Brighenti 2006; Foucault 2007), ethnography has proven a rich instrument to unsettle and enrich this definition, showing how territory can sometimes not easily be located in a single place or how various territories can overlap, layered onto one another, coexisting simultaneously, "elastically" altering surfaces and creating relations (Verdery 1994, 2003). Territory can, for example, be constituted through temporally and spatially discontinuous pathways that link places to the deep histories of the people who inhabit and sustain them over time (Abercrombie 1998). It can contain and hold memories of habitation and affect as well as material vestiges that persist well after forced displacement (Navaro-Yashin 2012; Richard 2018). It can be reconstituted through emergent surfaces built to traverse terrains even if transit is forbidden (Kernaghan 2022a) or renew landscapes when remaining in place becomes threatening and dangerous (Khayyat 2022). Territory, in other words, depends on the three-dimensional materiality of the ground that makes places into lived terrain, transformed through human experience, action, and perception (Gordillo 2018, 2020, 2021). Given this complexity, territory is not necessarily synonymous with the acts of demarcation and boundary drawing prevailing in many conceptualizations, including those of the state itself.

In some cases, as in Coatlinchan, territory exists and is in fact reproduced elsewhere than, or in ways no longer recognizable, on the surface. Coatlinchan's residents have lived off their land for generations, growing maize and other subsistence crops, or gathering firewood and other resources from the community's hills and forests.[24] Their social and ritual lives have been organized around agricultural cycles and festivities that in turn structure the calendar year. The stone was intricately connected to these cycles, rooted in and constitutive of the substances and relationships that make up and sustain the town both above- and belowground. These substances—land, water, crops, plants, but also ancient artifacts—have historically been coveted by outsiders, including the Mexican state and its representatives. Town residents equate the stone's removal with both these entrenched forms of extractivism and more recent examples of dispossession. At the same time, they continue to experience the aftershocks of what has been taken from their territory in ambivalent ways: even as they mourn their loss, they also contest dispossession through its generative effects and multiple forms of replication. Like scars, the enduring effects of repeated thefts are often painful, but the absence of stolen things also produces new capacities for healing, survival, and regeneration. Even when forcefully taken, these things cannot be fully detached from territory, nor from the networks of relations that secure its existence. In Coatlinchan, the absent stone is absent and present at the same time, bound and related to the ground, even if far away. Its theft might have hindered, but did not break, its relations.

The Grass of a Lake

Shortly before his death, Pedro Ramírez Vázquez (1919–2013), the architect commissioned by President Adolfo López Mateos (1958–64) and Jaime Torres Bodet (1902–74), then secretary of education, to design and build the Museo Nacional de Antropología, described the stone's relocation as one of the most important achievements of his career as well as of modern Mexican history (Ramírez Vázquez 2008).[25] The architect celebrated its transportation from Coatlinchan to Mexico City as an engineering marvel as well as a salvage operation that rescued an object of national *patrimonio* belonging to the Mexican people as a whole and to the institutions charged with caring for and preserving their heritage.

Mexico is one of the countries in the world, along with perhaps Greece, Egypt, and Israel, where ancient things have held a central place in modern nation making.[26] Premised on the ideology of *mestizaje*, making ancient Indigenous artifacts excavated underground into the nation's patrimony became central to the Mexican postrevolutionary state's technologies of national reconciliation and territorial consolidation following decades of political fragmentation and turmoil.[27] Although this process began with late nineteenth-century collecting practices that justified the extraction of ancient monuments and their relocation to the nation's capital and to the Museo Nacional to prevent their looting and export (Bueno 2010, 2016; Garrigan 2012; Achim 2017), it gained its force from the 1917 Constitution, which bundled subsoil resources, like oil, mineral ores, and water, with ancient artifacts into a single law rendering these inalienable as state property.[28] This law, Article 27, regulates patrimonio as the nation's inalienable possessions as well as its telluric foundations and roots, located literally inside and under the country's ground (Cottom 2008; Azuela 2011, 2019).[29]

In Spanish, *patrimonio*, a term related to kinship, is used in Mexican state discourses and laws in ways that condense its common English equivalents, "patrimony," "heritage" and "inheritance," while also indexing patriarchal power relations and forms of sovereignty.[30] The concept of patrimonio implies the *patria*, or fatherland, binding people to territory and to one another while also giving the Mexican state authority and political control over them (Claudio Lomnitz 2001).[31] Such patriarchal claims exceed legal definitions when it comes to the pre-Hispanic, making this time period and its material vestiges the nation's origin and core, its "soul" (López Hernández 2018). Through laws and practices of patrimonio, therefore, the state regulates and controls how and who can excavate and study (Vázquez León 2003; Holley-Kline 2025), restore and conserve (Salas Landa 2018, 2024a), and, more importantly, own and keep such objects and sites, always under the vigilance of state-sanctioned experts, national museums, and institutions assumed to be their proper caretakers (Achim, Deans-Smith, and Rozental 2021).[32] The state has used the power it derives from patriarchal conceptions of care to cordon off, relocate, and control these objects and sites, sometimes resorting to violence in the name of their preservation.

Yet patrimonio laws also connect ancient artifacts to other substances and materials related to enduring forms of sovereignty that exist parallel to that of the nation-state (Ferry 2005).[33] Patrimonio is in fact mired in ambivalence because, even as the concept and its laws imply the power of the state over certain objects and substances, they assume that these simultaneously belong to and constitute everyone that makes up the national community but no one person, people, or community specifically (Breglia 2006). Article 27 is in fact the same law that maintains, even if it does not fully recognize, forms of inalienable property and distributed sovereignty that are also connected to territory, preserving corporate bodies such as landed communities known as ejidos (Claudio Lomnitz 2001).[34] But for the residents of Coatlinchan, and I suspect for many communities like it, territory exceeds landed property, even communally administered land, as a form of relating to the ground that they inhabit and thrive on, including the objects and substances that lie underneath that ground and that might be extracted from it. Hence, even as artifacts from the pre-Hispanic past are legally owned, administered, and managed by the Mexican state and its official heritage institutions, they also exist as sites that contain and sustain communities' own forms of sovereignty and the stuff that allows for their endurance and reproduction in specific places.

Nevertheless, patrimonio as a legal regime and state praxis continues to be premised on an artificial divide between objects and the places, communities, and environments they are located in, reproducing an assumed nature/culture binary (Rozental 2017b). In Coatlinchan, as in other contemporary communities in Mexico coexisting with vestiges of the pre-Hispanic past, ancient artifacts operate within multiple and dynamic arrangements that resonate more with how feminist scholars have imagined human and nonhuman relationality (Strathern 2005), forms of "intra-action" and "the mutual constitution of entangled agencies" (Barad 2007, 33). These challenge patrimonio's patriarchal tenets by focusing attention on conceptions of care based on interconnection and mutuality. Philosopher Isabelle Stengers (2005) insists on thinking through an "ecology of practices" to underscore the ways in which humans and nonhumans are intertwined in ways that make them indissociable from the world around them. By focusing on how patrimonio could be part of such an ecology, we might extend what Marshall Sahlins (2011, 2) discusses as the "mutuality of being" that defines kinship to nonhumans that exist as "earth beings" capable of political action (Myers 2001; Cadena 2015, 2018; Povinelli 2016) or to telluric entities that, like the Coatlinchan stone, are inextricable from and generative of the earth, people, and environments in and with which they coexist.[35] Removing them from territory, even if for the purpose of their conservation, encapsulates them as bounded things, limiting their participation in such networks. At the same time, their removal and displacement stimulate new attachments, relations, and replications.

Despite its generative aftershocks, the legal extrication of patrimonio that justified the stone's removal from Coatlinchan ignores the ways that objects, sites, and, of course, people are embedded in each other's existence. It also allows the Mexican state to violate, deny, and even criminalize local claims, property rights, and other kinds of affective, political, and even ecological attachments to ancient things on the part of the people and communities that coexist with them. Engaging ancient vestiges outside this nature/culture divide resonates with how people and communities like the residents of Coatlinchan experience them: as connected to and enabling not only social reproduction but that of bodies and territories, and of the organic and telluric forces that—like rain and soil—guarantee survival.

In publications as well as during numerous public appearances and interviews, and during my own conversations with him, Ramírez Vázquez underscored that the stone's extraction was negotiated with and accepted by Coatlinchan's residents, who understood and supported, even celebrated, its national significance and place as national patrimonio in the museum. He highlighted the festive spirit of the event: "Yes, it became a party. In Mexico, we make everything a party!"[36] The architect, who kept a vast archive of documents related to all his projects, forbade the reproduction of photographs showing soldiers in Coatlinchan and insisted that the stone was not removed by force. Instead, he highlighted that, at the time, it was crucial for him, but especially for President López Mateos, who was then finishing his term in office, for town residents to agree and support its relocation. Ramírez Vázquez told the same anecdote many times: on his request, town representatives called an assembly during which he explained the importance of the museum and the pride town residents would experience at having their ancestors' contribution featured there. After his speech, a local teacher intervened to defuse villagers' opposition. The architect referred to this teacher as a "maestro Nahua," indigenizing his identity. In his recollection of the event, the teacher said: "Look, muchachos, the stone is like the grass of a lake: the grass at the edge and at the center of the lake is all grass from the same lake" (Ramírez Vázquez 2008, 67). Ramírez Vázquez used the word *laguna*, referring to bodies of water that, like the ancient lake of Texcoco, were shallow wetlands, seasonally fluctuating and making clear borders separating its waters from its banks difficult to discern. Following what the architect described as a "common Nahuatl formula," the nation was metaphorically rendered a single body with no clear boundaries and with homogeneous and generic, therefore interchangeable, vegetation.

Metaphors, especially when state power is naturalized as a biological phenomenon like grass growing in a lake, are deeply political.[37] According to the architect, the teacher had convinced his peers that "everything was Mexico" (Ramírez Vázquez 2008, 67) and, therefore, their stone—the equivalent to grass on the edge of the lake—belonged to the center in Mexico City. By setting this in Nahua cosmologies, he further naturalized the nation and the state's claim on ancient artifacts for its museum. The parable made the legal regime of patrimonio, inherited from colonial laws and developed in the nineteenth century to consolidate the newly independent nation, into an Indigenous category.

Over the past three decades, many of the academic literatures on heritage worldwide, and on archaeological heritage specifically, have focused on the uses of ancient things and sites with clear political agendas (Kohl and Fawcett 1995; Abu El-Haj 2001; Meskell 2008).[38] In Latin American contexts, and in Mexico specifically, community museums have become sites where patrimonio has been reconfigured in ways that creatively adapt idioms of museum display to local narratives and needs (Camarena and Morales 2006; Hoobler 2006; Rufer 2014, 2017).[39] Yet, in these museums, artifacts and monuments considered patrimonio continue to be understood as separate objects, existing as distinct and bounded things that might be connected to people and communities because they are key to fostering and extending kinship but not actual participants in the production and reproduction of the necessary conditions of a community's existence. By confining objects to museum spaces, even those that are situated, curated, and administered locally, these projects continue to separate things from the environments and the people that sustain them, maintaining the preservationist logic of state patrimonio that conceives of objects' care as conservation and not connection.

To Rob a Thief

I now turn to another metaphor drawn from the natural world that serves to rethink how we might understand communities' ties to ancient things claimed by the Mexican state as national patrimonio. People born and living in Coatlinchan are known as Tlacuaches, after the small marsupial endemic to the Americas. The animal has many surprising abilities: it is immune to certain predators' venom and can deceive others by playing dead in moments of danger. The *tlacuache* is also key to maintaining ecosystems, fertilizing soils, and helping distribute seeds. Nevertheless, its nocturnal habits as well as its parasitic penchants for occupying ready-made burrows and stealing food from other animals, including humans, have given it a bad reputation. The animal's rapacious behavior is premised on its unique physiognomy. Its pouch, but also its hands and feet with opposable thumbs (the only non-primate with this feature), are what allow it to scavenge and survive. According to Mesoamerican myths and stories, this physiognomy is the direct result of its thieving but also of its cunning and adaptive abilities: its characteristic prehensile, albeit hairless, tail is thought to have been scorched when it snuck down to the underworld to steal fire from the gods and share it with humans (López Austin 1996). In myth as well as in evolutionary paradigms, tlacuaches, then, have not only endured cataclysm and threatening circumstances; they have been scarred, marked, and transformed by their work to better human existence, proving that they are fundamentally interspecies collaborators as well as creative survivors.

Whereas other towns in the region proudly bear nicknames associating their residents with charismatic creatures or with skills in specialized crafts, Coatlinchan's moniker has historically associated its residents with the animal's negative qualities: theft and deception.[40] Town residents themselves complain about the animals, who notoriously steal eggs from chicken coops or the sweet *agua miel* from magueys before the liquid can be fermented to make pulque. They also joke about tlacuaches' gusto for the beverage, building up their own reputation as festive but also overindulgent drunks. Ultimately, town residents wear the nickname with a combination of humor and reservation, sometimes referring to it with pride when discussing their ability to get away with something but also with defensiveness, hoping to dispel rumors that the moniker's origin lies in town residents' own rapaciousness, or at best living parasitically off the backs of others. They emphasize that the creature's positive qualities—its abilities and dexterity—outweigh the negative: in ancient codices, tlacuache warriors are shown as trusted keepers of knowledge and territory.[41]

And yet theft and what anthropologists describe as negative reciprocity (Sahlins 1963, 1972) do not always, or not only, have negative effects. Emphasizing the negative valence of a relationship often obscures its generativity, even in its destructiveness. Theft also works to create relations, building ties that bind and connect people and communities. Sometimes, theft sustains webs of domination and subservience within power structures that exist parallel to and in collaboration with the state (Claudio Lomnitz 2005; B. Grant 2009), and sometimes theft might even foster local forms of collaboration and solidarity that resist and speak back to the state and its own modes of institutionalized violence (Poole 1987). In documenting Coatlinchan's residents' relationships to ancient things and other materials and substances taken from their territory, this book contributes to showing Tlacuaches to have been creative survivors of theft rather than its instigators or passive victims. And this theft, committed by the Mexican state and justified through legal registers and state practices of patrimonio, was premised on a questionable distinction between nature and culture, and between people, objects, and environments with which they coexist. The state's exercise of patrimonio politics and its alleged salvage of the stone was in fact based on a fundamental misrecognition of theft. Denouncing the stone's removal as state theft also shows the generative effects of this action and the relations that came into being in the wake of dispossession.

Saqueo, derived from the Latin *saccus*, is used colloquially in Mexican Spanish to refer to any act of looting, taking, or collecting ancient things that is not undertaken by the state, its heritage institutions, or sanctioned experts.[42] In this sense, as stipulated by patrimonio laws and practices, any form of owning, relating to, coexisting with, keeping, or taking ancient objects outside of institutional contexts is criminalized as illicit theft. The Instituto Nacional de Antropología e Historia (INAH, National Institute of Anthropology and History), constituted in 1939 to care for and administer national monuments and sites under the rubric of patrimonio, is charged with sanctioning individuals and communities who do not turn objects over to the state. This same logic criminalizes those who replicate patrimonio without official institutions' permission, even if these replicas, "monos" (Zepeda 2000) or "original interpretations" (Lerner 2001), are not necessarily made to deceive, nor to be sold as forgeries (Pasztory 2002; Brulotte 2012).[43]

The INAH recently ran a campaign to familiarize the public with how to handle patrimonio that exemplifies how criminalizing saqueo as theft is central to its mandate. Using the heading "What do I do if I find archaeological pieces?" (this term is used in the museum and art world assuming such objects as separate and valuable collectibles), the infographic offered bullet-point

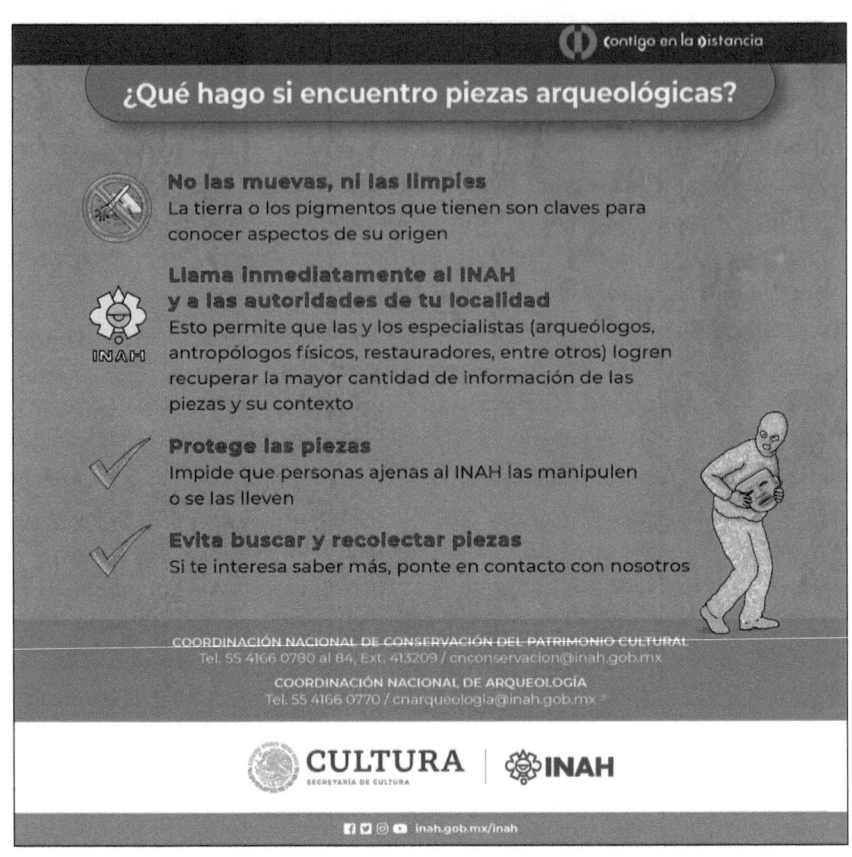

¿Qué hago si encuentro piezas arqueológicas?

No las muevas, ni las limpies
La tierra o los pigmentos que tienen son claves para conocer aspectos de su origen

Llama inmediatamente al INAH y a las autoridades de tu localidad
Esto permite que las y los especialistas (arqueólogos, antropólogos físicos, restauradores, entre otros) logren recuperar la mayor cantidad de información de las piezas y su contexto

Protege las piezas
Impide que personas ajenas al INAH las manipulen o se las lleven

Evita buscar y recolectar piezas
Si te interesa saber más, ponte en contacto con nosotros

COORDINACIÓN NACIONAL DE CONSERVACIÓN DEL PATRIMONIO CULTURAL
Tel. 55 4166 0780 al 84, Ext. 413209 / cnconservacion@inah.gob.mx

COORDINACIÓN NACIONAL DE ARQUEOLOGÍA
Tel. 55 4166 0770 / cnarqueologia@inah.gob.mx

CULTURA
SECRETARÍA DE CULTURA | INAH

inah.gob.mx/inah

FIGURE I.5. "¿Qué hago si encuentro piezas arqueológicas?" (What do I do if I find archaeological pieces?). Infographic published by the Instituto Nacional de Antropología e Historia, 2023.

instructions alongside an illustration of a person fully masked like a bank robber and carrying off an iconic Teotihuacan mask similar to those in the Museo Nacional de Antropología's collections (figure I.5):

1 Do not move or clean them: dirt or pigments on them are essential to knowing aspects of their origin.
2 Immediately call the INAH and local authorities: experts (archaeologists, anthropologists, professional conservators, and others) succeed in recovering the greatest information about the pieces and their contexts.
3 Protect the pieces: stop anyone that is not from the INAH from manipulating or taking them.

4 Avoid looking for and collecting pieces: If you are interested in know-ing more, contact us.

On Christmas Eve 1985, the Museo Nacional de Antropología was itself fa-mously the subject of theft, a few months after a massive earthquake shook the country.[44] And looting has been documented all over Mexico, where there is a thriving black market for ancient things commercialized as valuable artworks.[45] According to patrimonio laws, as can be seen in the INAH's recent campaign, these forms of theft and other kinds of manipulation or attachment to ancient artifacts are equally criminalized as saqueo. The ways in which people in Coatl-inchan and other places understand and experience these objects and their per-manence as constitutive of community and territory, as well as their efforts to replicate things that have been stolen from it, call this logic into question. In fact, these approaches reverse the relationship between the licit and the illicit as well as between theft's victims and its perpetrators.

In other parts of the world, cases of forced dispossession like Coatlinchan's have been denounced as theft linked to colonial violence, inspiring Indige-nous communities, First Nations, and former colonies to file legal demands for restitution and repatriation.[46] Legal frameworks for repatriation have been critiqued as partial and incomplete means to translate cultural claims over ar-tifacts and human remains (Brown 2003, 2004; Rowlands 2004), yet, as many have suggested, they have served both in practice and in context for communi-ties and postcolonial nation-states to reclaim sovereignty over things and foster cultural renewal in the wake of dispossession (Coombe 1998; Barkan and Bush 2002; Fine-Dare 2002; Peers 2017; Fforde et al. 2023).

In Mexico, national legislation does not formally recognize separate sovereignties, Indigenous or otherwise, that could legally claim substances, ob-jects, or monuments defined as national patrimonio, making legal claims and demands for return by any individual or local community untenable. Objects made before the arrival of Spanish colonizers continue, then, to be legally construed as being out of place and illegally held anywhere, or by anyone, that is not a state-run and sanctioned heritage institution. To return to Ramírez Vázquez's phrasing, patrimonio laws and practices assume that the objects and sites that it encompasses are the indistinguishable and, therefore, inter-changeable grass of a national lake. And yet, as I hope this book shows, pre-cisely because of how such objects are connected to humans and nonhumans who inhabit and constitute specific territories, their severance is always partial and incomplete. Their absence leaves vibrant traces and powerful aftershocks. Even as the stone was taken away and repurposed as a monument miles away, it continues to be present in Coatlinchan. Its theft did not thwart its ability to remain connected, participating in networks and associations that sustain the place, people, and territory where it once lay. At the same time, its removal continues to produce replicas: new objects, actors, and relations that allow the stone to multiply, contesting its theft as it also shapes myriad relations both above- and underground.

Structure of the Book

The chapters that follow are structured around the story of the stone: first as it was made into a separate object from the place where it was found and then as it lingers, multiplies, and reproduces in Coatlinchan despite—and also because of—its absence. Part I, "The State of Patrimonio," relies on archival sources as well as interviews with key participants who orchestrated and lived through the stone's relocation to show how scholarship, legal regimes, engineering, and finally state theft participated in severing it from the territory where it was found.

Chapter 1, "A Curious Thing," focuses on how late nineteenth- and early twentieth-century scholars used scientific methods and arguments to make sense of the stone in relation to the ravine where it was found. They hoped to solve what they understood as an inherent contradiction: why was the largest ancient stone effigy found to date in the Americas lying in what they considered an isolated and insignificant place? Their interpretations of the stone's features, material qualities, possible identification, and gender ultimately served to prove that the site was arbitrary and thus unrelated to its makers' intentions and ancient uses. Their work consolidated the stone as a self-contained and therefore potentially portable monument, long before it was physically removed.

Chapter 2, "Engineering Transfer," uses interviews, published accounts, media, and archival sources to analyze the role that technology and engineering played in actually moving the stone and repurposing it as a standing monument for the Museo Nacional de Antropología in the 1960s. These efforts were very much in line with a developmentalist national state project that imagined public works and state-of-the-art infrastructure as a continuation of an ancient civilization's quest to control the environment—specifically water.

Chapter 3, "Theft," places archival sources and ethnographic fieldwork in Coatlinchan in conversation to trace the tensions and negotiations between state agents claiming to "rescue" the stone as national patrimonio and town residents who sabotaged their efforts, trying unsuccessfully to stop its relocation.

These tensions show how the stone was rooted in what town residents consider "lo nuestro" (what is ours), a telluric concept used to describe the stuff that makes up community and grounds it in a specific place.

Part II, "Aftershocks," analyzes the ways in which, after more than six decades, the stone's absence continues to vibrantly mark and affect Coatlinchan's present. Based on over twenty years of continued ethnographic fieldwork, these chapters problematize the distinction between objects, communities, and the places and environments they are embedded in, showing how the stone and other vestiges from the ancient past are constitutive of relations that produce and reproduce territory over time.

Chapter 4, "Scars," looks at the visible marks and material traces that emerged in the stone's wake, especially in the ravine that once contained it. As "aftershocks," these traces replicate and amplify the stone's absence, acting on and affecting town residents' daily life and experiences. These scars mark Coatlinchan's landscape in tangible ways as they also bind town residents to each other and to territory. They serve as both painful reminders of past violence and temporally open-ended processes of reproduction, regeneration, and healing.

Chapter 5, "Treasure," explores how the absent stone is entangled with other substances and objects such as gold, sand, water, and other ancient artifacts that town residents consider "lo nuestro." Once bountiful and self-replenishing, treasure remains fragile, hidden in Coatlinchan, continuously under threat of extraction and appropriation. Understanding ancient things, including the stone, as treasure complicates state discourses that focus on the material qualities of such objects as separate, authentic, and singular vestiges from the past that require isolation, protection, and intervention to ensure their care and conservation. As treasure, these things remain embedded in territory, guarded by humans and more-than-humans, as they generate wealth, abundance, and well-being and continue to sustain and replicate the community and the territory on which it thrives.

Chapter 6, "Replicas," explores how the stone's physical removal allowed it to multiply, producing reproductions and miniatures of different shapes, materials, and sizes. These replicas resonate with how processes of replication, iteration, and itinerancy—namely of saint images—have historically been involved in the production of territory in Mexican and other Latin American contexts.[47] By paying attention to how replicas work—their materiality and scale, what exactly they reproduce, as well as the humor with which they are arranged and moved across space and time—this chapter shows how the stone continues to generate new objects and networks of relations amid the residents of a community known for its loss.

Chapter 7, "Watershed," analyzes how Coatlinchan's residents experience the stone's removal as both cause and effect of drought and environmental disruptions like climate change. Their understanding frames the stone and other objects claimed as patrimonio as central to telluric processes that guarantee rainfall and access to water and therefore life on Earth and in the specific place they inhabit. Through their own collecting practices, Tlacuaches are responding to state theft and working to restore a damaged ecology. In this way, they challenge legal regimes and state practices that justified the stone's extraction from Coatlinchan and reframe it as a site of connection, care, and renewal.

The conclusion discusses town residents' recent efforts to return the stone to Coatlinchan, situating their work within a worldwide movement to return museum collections to source communities and appropriate or remove statues and monuments that embody and perpetuate violent histories. In conversation with these actions and debates, as well as with recent Mexican feminist activism, their call for restitution invites a politics of patrimonio that takes into account how certain objects and sites cannot be separated from the places and communities they are embedded in and constitutive of. Theirs is not only an effort to right a historical wrong. Ultimately, their call for the stone's return is premised on the ways in which it remains connected to and interacts with telluric forces crucial to their town and the region's survival, collective well-being, and environmental restoration.

Coda

Throughout the book, I cite many conversations I had with architects, engineers, archaeologists, artists, museum curators and staff, and others who are public figures and have themselves given interviews or published accounts of their participation in this history. I also refer to many conversations and exchanges I witnessed and participated in over a very long period of time in Coatlinchan. Some of my interlocutors there asked me to use pseudonyms, but most wanted their real names in this book. Like the engineers and workers who participated in moving the stone, many town residents told me that they had been interviewed many times by journalists, scholars, and media makers but were rarely given credit for the information they provided. Some have authored their own books, designed websites, or used social media to tell their own versions of this history and make their knowledge public—which I cite. In anthropology, we have often assumed that giving our sources pseudonyms protects them. Sometimes this practice also dispossesses people of their stories and histories. Since some of my friends and interlocutors in Coatlinchan also engage in collecting ancient artifacts, a practice still criminalized under Mexican law, I often use only their first names, a strategy that credits specific people's stories and experiences but also ensures that the information they provided cannot be used to incriminate them. This is the best solution I could come up with, although I realize it, too, is imperfect.

PART I

The State of
Patrimonio

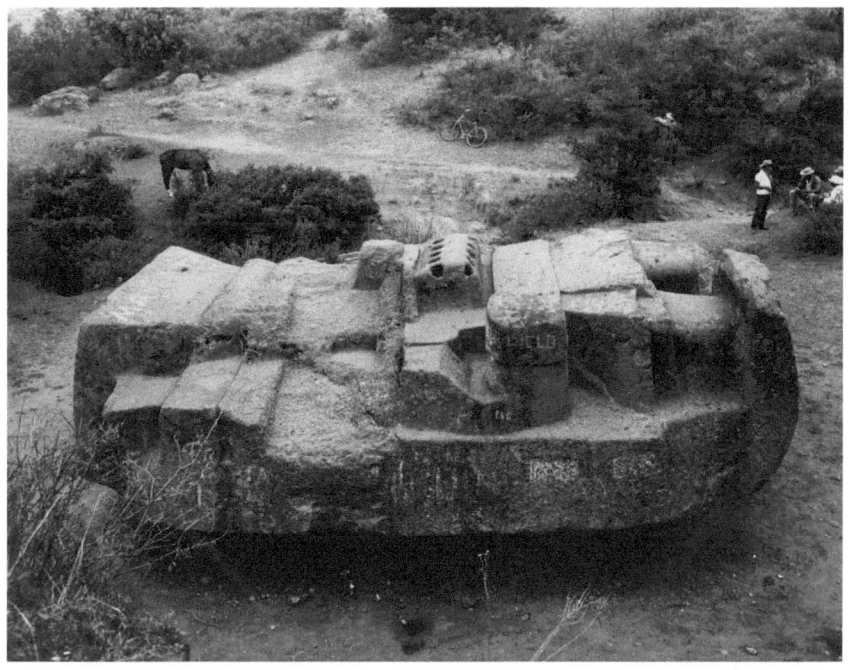

FIGURE PI.I. The stone in Coatlinchan, 1963. Photograph courtesy of Acervo Arquitecto
Pedro Ramírez Vázquez.

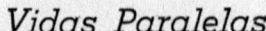
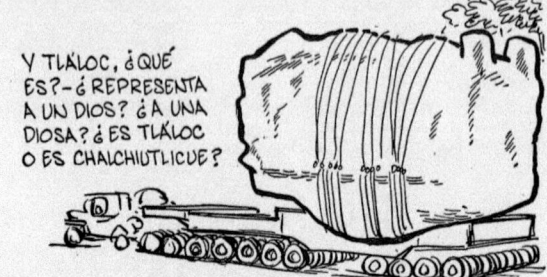
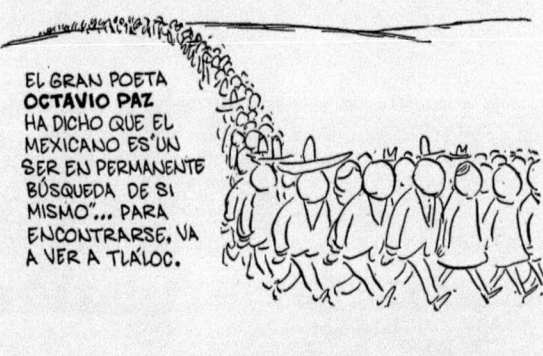

FIGURE PI.2. Abel Quezada, "Vidas Paralelas" (Parallel lives), *Excélsior*, April 23, 1964. The text of the cartoon translates as:

Why do Mexicans go see *Tlaloc*? Because Tlaloc is the same as Mexicans. Mexicans are the center of controversy: Are they Indians? Spaniards? A mix of the two? Neither?

And what is Tlaloc? Does it represent a god? A goddess? Is it Tlaloc or Chalchiuhtlicue?

Like Mexicans, Tlaloc has lost their [*su*] original physiognomy and, like Tlaloc, Mexicans are surrounded by mystery.

The great poet *Octavio Paz* once said that Mexicans are "in permanent search of themselves [si mismo]" . . . Maybe, to find themselves, they go to see Tlaloc.

And they do find themselves! Tlaloc is the *same* as them. Nobody knows exactly what or whom it *is*, and even so, it *is* Tlaloc.

I

———

A Curious Thing

Long before the stone was taken from Coatlinchan, late nineteenth- and early twentieth-century historians, antiquarians, artists, and engineers were puzzled by its location. They saw an inherent contradiction between the stone and the place where it was found. On one hand, its dimensions—it was and remains the largest monolithic sculptural work found in the Americas—signaled its ritual and political significance in ancient times. On the other hand, it lay alone, prostrated, and heavily eroded in a remote gorge, far away from other ancient structures, settlements, and known ceremonial sites. Given its isolation and poor state of conservation, there were few clues available to identify what the stone was as well as what or whom it represented and, more importantly, why it was and had remained in Coatlinchan.

Using historical and scientific methods and arguments as well as a certain amount of speculation, these early scholars analyzed the stone's material qualities—its mass, weight, composition, features, and even its possible gender—in relation to its location. Through their work, the stone went from being a geological feature embedded in landscape to a distinct entity, referenced as a human-made object: an "idol," a "statue," a "sculpture," a "carving," a "monolith," a "monument." Each of these appellations entailed different assumptions determining what the stone was as well as where and to whom it belonged. Ultimately, these scholars concluded that it ended up in Coatlinchan because of a series of unfortunate events and telluric accidents that were not tied to its makers' intentions nor to its ancient uses. In establishing the stone and the site in Coatlinchan as separate, related only by chance and not intention, their work produced the stone as singular, self-contained, and distinct from the place where it was found, readying it for extraction, much before it was physically relocated to Mexico City.

Challenging the modern obsession with making things separate has been central to much of the scholarship emerging from science and technology studies (STS) in recent decades (Callon 1986; Latour 1987; Law 1987). Philosopher of science Bruno Latour (1993) historicized the practices that worked to divide the world into separate realms through scientific processes of "translation" and "purification," in ways that produced nature as separate from society and humans as separate from nonhumans. Reconstructing the painstaking efforts by various scholars to "purify" the stone by making it separate from Coatlinchan offers a window into how this work of separation resulted from complex negotiations and contested claims that did not always coincide but had important political consequences. For Latour, purification, in fact, was never fully successful as it only eclipsed the ways in which the world has always been constituted of relations and networks that make such severances ultimately impossible. Unraveling the processes by which the stone was constituted as a distinct and "curious thing" also points to how it might have resisted this separation, remaining attached and related to Coatlinchan.

What Could It Be?

In 1882, Juan W. Butler (1851–1918), a US-born Methodist missionary working in Texcoco, published the first known account of the stone in a Mexico City newspaper.[1] With the enigmatic title "What Could It Be?," he wrote: "For a while now, the brothers from one of our foreign congregations have been inviting us to accompany them to visit a carved stone in the mountains. . . . After an hour on horseback, we arrived at the location and were amazed by the curious thing we had in view. There, there is a stone idol that is 8 varas tall by 3 varas wide [a vara is about a yard]. It has arms and feet. It has a head with a nose, and traces of teeth." Having described its features, Butler tried to explain the stone's placement in the remote gorge: "This idol must weigh around sixty tons. It is the opinion of some of the residents from the neighboring towns that this idol was at some point located at the summit, and that, with the rains or an earthquake, it fell to the foot of the mountain where it now lies. Its head is carved, somewhat in the style of Egyptian idols, and the local indians describe it as a vessel intended for sacrificial blood."[2] The missionary used the word *idol* in his description, a term common in Mexico at the time and even today to designate figures associated with pre-Hispanic cosmologies and ritual, signaling the enduring legacies of colonial iconoclasm. He also called it a "carved stone" and a "curious thing," offering an estimate of its weight and using local accounts to question its origin in Coatlinchan. In this very first and brief description, Butler presented the stone as already separate and even misplaced, having been moved and dragged there accidently by environmental factors (rain) and telluric movements (earthquakes).

Jesús Sánchez, then the curator of the Museo Nacional, read Butler's report and decided to study the stone more in depth. He was the first to designate it as a "sculpture" representing an ancient deity (Sánchez 1886). Like Butler, Sánchez believed the stone had ended up in Coatlinchan by accident and thought it should be relocated, but he accepted that it was too heavy to be moved with the technology available at the time. In his report "Estatua colosal de la diosa del agua" (Colossal statue of the goddess of water), published in the Museo Nacional's official journal, he related that he sent a team of experts on site to inspect and study it, as well as the museum's draftsman, and later Mexico's most famous landscape painter, José María Velasco (1840–1912).[3] The museum's study, and especially Velasco's depiction, were central to separating the stone from Coatlinchan (figure 1.1). Like Butler's initial description featuring body parts, Velasco's image anthropomorphized the stone even further and presented it as a lone bipedal figure. Echoing many scientific imaging practices at the time, this rendition presented the huge mass that lay partially immersed in the ground as a stand-alone object.[4]

The stone's translation through miniaturization onto paper allowed it to become portable and able to circulate beyond its actual location, making it available for intervention without considering the broader body or bodies it might have been attached to.[5] Before Sánchez's publication, other images of the stone were also in circulation. A postcard based on a glass-plate negative showed the stone embedded in a lush gorge (figure 1.2). The photographer included a human figure next to the sculpture to give the viewer a sense of scale. A caption named the stone as "Xicaca" and identified it as a female water deity.[6]

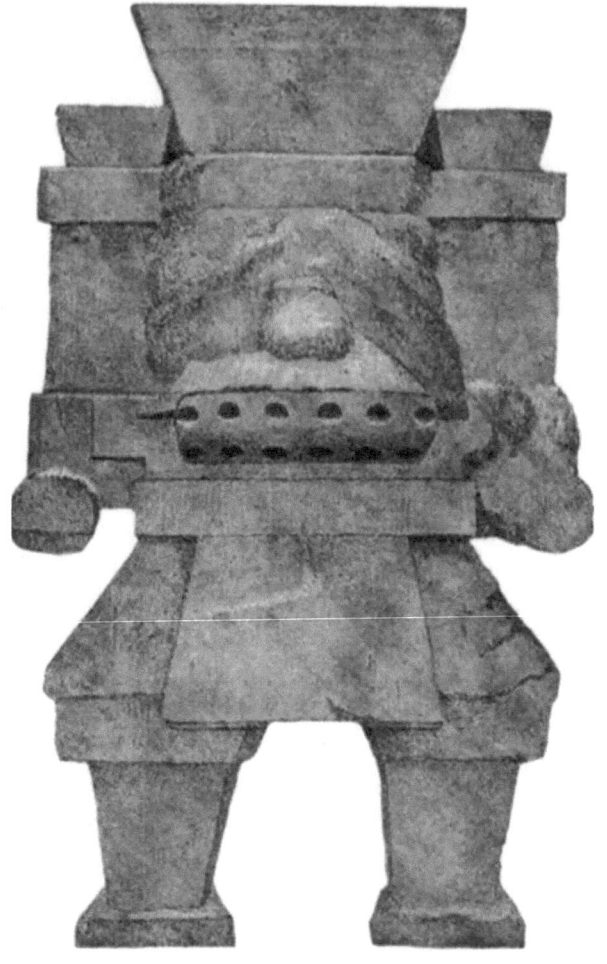

FIGURE 1.1. "Estatua colosal de la diosa del agua" (Colossal statue of the goddess of water), drawing by José María Velasco. From Sánchez 1886, 31.

The stone's enormity was captured through tight framing and by way of the person's hand gently touching its surface. The image showed the stone as an integral part of its surroundings. By contrast, Velasco's rendering represented it as a single mass floating on a white sheet of paper, completely separate from the place where it lay.

In the following years, the sense that the stone did not belong in the ravine and that it required relocation became palpable in publications that speculated on its possible weight, the slope of the terrain, and the technological means that might transport it to the Museo Nacional in Mexico City, considered its rightful place. For example, in 1903, Luis G. Becerril, an engineer interested in geology, wrote: "One only has to walk 3 kilometers with a slight and uniform

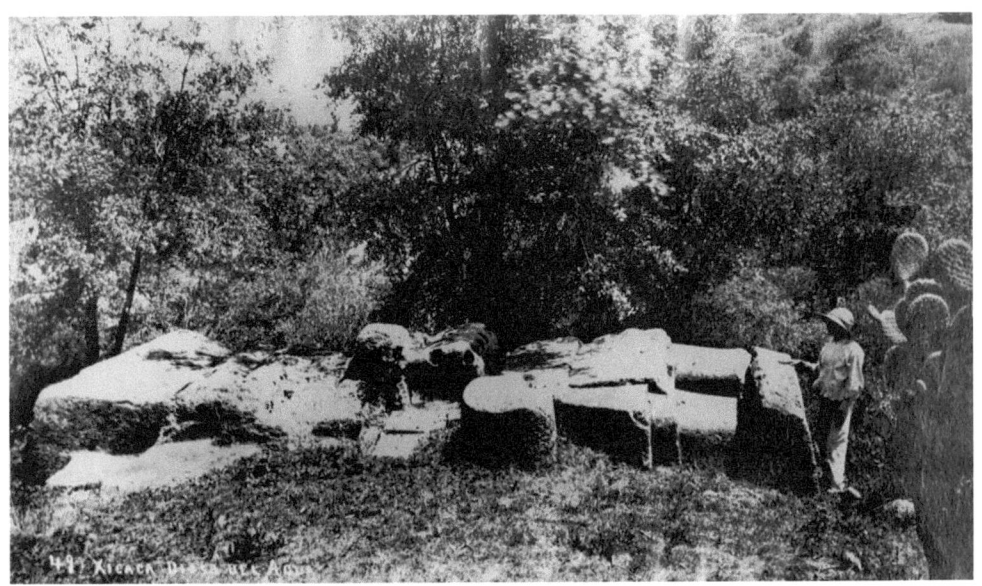

FIGURE 1.2. "Xicaca Diosa del Agua" (Xicaca, goddess of water), postcard, ca. 1880. Courtesy of Fototeca Nacional, Fondo Teixidor, catalog 428406.

slope, making it possible of course to suppose that the idol's transport would be easy and cheap. . . . If this monolith is successfully brought to our museum, it would undoubtedly get everyone's attention because of its shape, size and the nature of the rock, until this day the largest idol manufactured by Indians in the entire American continent" (1903, 71). Becerril's emphasis on topography and conclusion that the stone's movement would be relatively uncomplicated assumed it might, therefore, be imminent. He also used the term *monolith* to refer to the stone, assuming it was a single and self-contained block of rock that could be separated and transported elsewhere if only the means to do so became available. This name would endure and become part of the stone's biography as scholars began to refer to it as "The Coatlinchan Monolith."

Excavation

Archaeology as a practice, and its main method, excavation, were soon deployed to physically sever the stone from the ground and ready it for extraction. Leopoldo Batres (1852–1929), a scholar of ancient Mexico who served as the inspector of monuments during Porfirio Díaz's government, conducted the only field archaeological dig ever undertaken on site.[7] For him, unearthing the stone

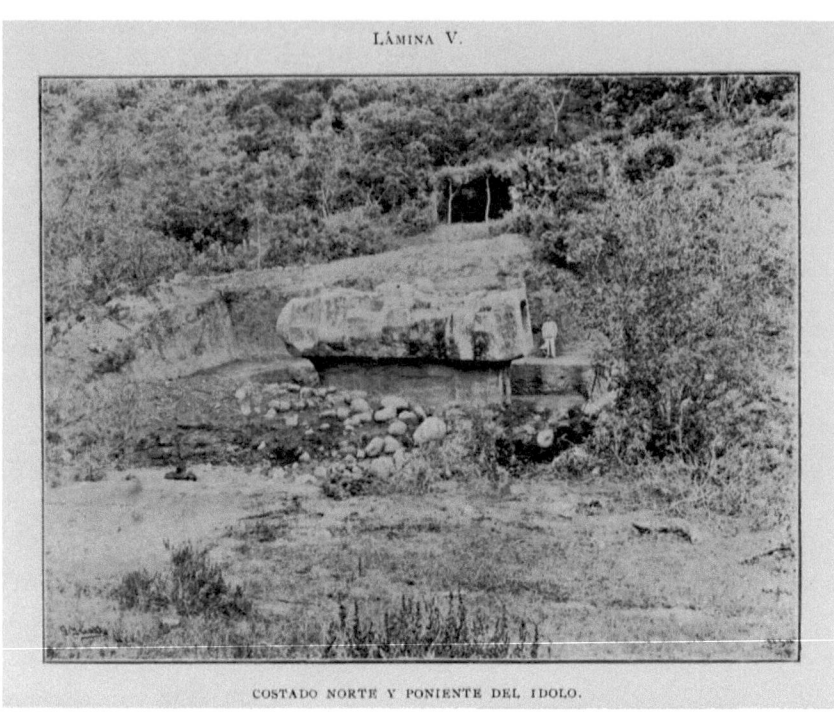

FIGURE 1.3. "Costado norte y poniente del ídolo" (North and west side of the idol). From Batres 1903, plate 5.

was the only way to make it visible in its entirety for its identification. This endeavor eventually facilitated its removal from Coatlinchan since designing its transport required accurate measurements.[8] Images were crucial to this work. Batres included plates and photographs documenting each step of the excavation process. One of these photographs showed a thatched-roof hut and a man standing next to the stone that gave viewers a sense of scale in human terms (figure 1.3). The dig exposed the various layers of dirt and rocks removed to fully unearth the stone from the ground. Yet the stone's back appears still deeply entrenched in the earth.

Batres included drawings with precise measurements attributed to architect Guillermo de Heredia, rendering the stone a single three-dimensional mass for the first time (figure 1.4).[9] These drawings anticipated the stone's extraction from the ground, showing parts and angles that would not have been visible when it lay partially buried in the ravine. Batres, nevertheless, documented the stone's location in the ravine, mapping its position in relation to a stream, which he identified as Santa Clara, that ran parallel to its flanks and then down

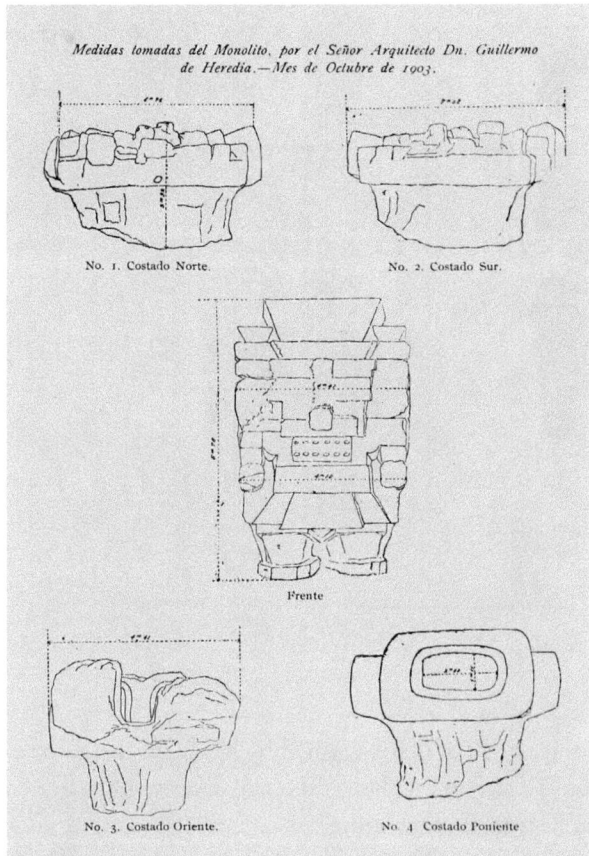

FIGURE 1.4.
Guillermo de
Heredia, "Medidas
tomadas del monolito"
(Measurements taken
from the monolith).
From Batres 1903.

the hillside to Lake Texcoco. Although he included a plate that showed the position of the stone vis-à-vis this body of water, he did not comment on its relevance for the stone's identification (figure 1.5).

For his study, Batres reworked the photograph of the stone lying in situ that had earlier circulated as a postcard, using the same visual cues but portraying the stone upright, "as it would have stood when it was worshipped" (1903, 6) (figure 1.6). He also included a human figure to give the viewer a sense of scale, this time dressed in contemporary campesino attire, staring reverently upward. Batres used the plate to restore the stone to the position he imagined it would have had in ancient times, as a sculptural feature standing on, rather than integrated within, Coatlinchan's territory. The local landscape now simply served as its background and context. Like Sánchez, Batres concluded that the stone was too heavy to be moved. He believed, regardless, that it was in danger in

FIGURE 1.5. "Posición del ídolo respecto al arroyo de Santa Clara" (Position of the idol in relation to the Santa Clara stream). From Batres 1903, plate 2.

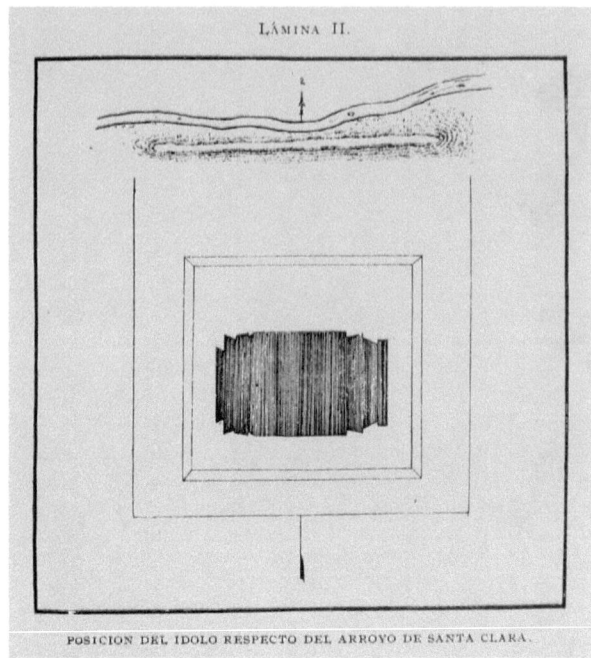

LÁMINA II.

POSICION DEL IDOLO RESPECTO DEL ARROYO DE SANTA CLARA.

Coatlinchan because it was at risk of being harmed by locals. As inspector of monuments, he appointed a guard to watch over the site along with the nearby ruins of Huexotla, where he was also excavating.[10]

Following Batres's work, the stone's ultimate relocation was discussed in ways that sought to guarantee its proper place as well as its appropriate publics. In 1912, a government official from the Secretaría de Instrucción Pública y Bellas Artes requested that the Museo Nacional again explore the possibility of moving it, this time not to the museum but to a public square in Mexico City. The museum's experts, ultimately concerned with the stone's conservation, reported that it was too heavy to move but definitely in need of protection.[11] Because it was located on arable land, they thought it was at risk of being desecrated by local residents who "did not understand its value and importance" or that it might be harmed by the currents that flooded the ravine during the rainy season. Echoing Batres's recommendation a decade earlier, they suggested that the stone be surrounded with a barbed-wire fence and raised on a pedestal to avoid further deterioration.[12] Perhaps because this too required a major investment, the stone was not raised and the pedestal was never built. The stone remained prostrated in the ravine, imagined as a vulnerable object and therefore available for new forms of intervention.

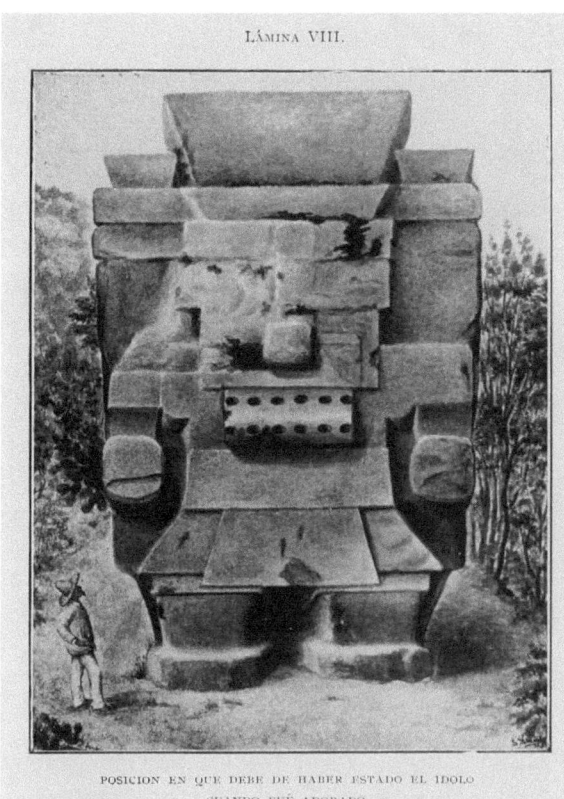

LÁMINA VIII.

POSICION EN QUE DEBE DE HABER ESTADO EL IDOLO
CUANDO FUÉ ADORADO.

FIGURE 1.6. "Posición en la que debe de haber estado el ídolo cuando fue adorado" (Position of the idol as it would have stood when it was worshipped). From Batres 1903, plate 8.

Speculations on what the stone was and might have been continued for many decades. During this time, Coatlinchan began hosting a steady stream of visitors interested in Mexico's ancient vestiges. By the mid-1910s, the town was featured as a destination in travel books and tourist maps. One such travel book, published in 1935, included a folding map of Mexico City's surroundings showing sites of interest along highways and rail infrastructures (figure 1.7). Quaint Indigenous villages with local charm, the canals of Xochimilco and donkeys carrying food sacks, majestic colonial churches, and ancient pyramids like the ones at Teotihuacan were portrayed amid the region's most salient topographical features (Mackie and Dick 1935). Unlike nearby towns like Huexotla and Texcoco represented by their colonial churches (of which Coatlinchan also had a fine example), Coatlinchan was marked with an image of the prostate stone.

The stone soon became a landmark and tourist attraction. Some of the most knowledgeable scholars of ancient Mexico went to Coatlinchan to visit it, noting that its excavation had led to little certainty regarding its possible

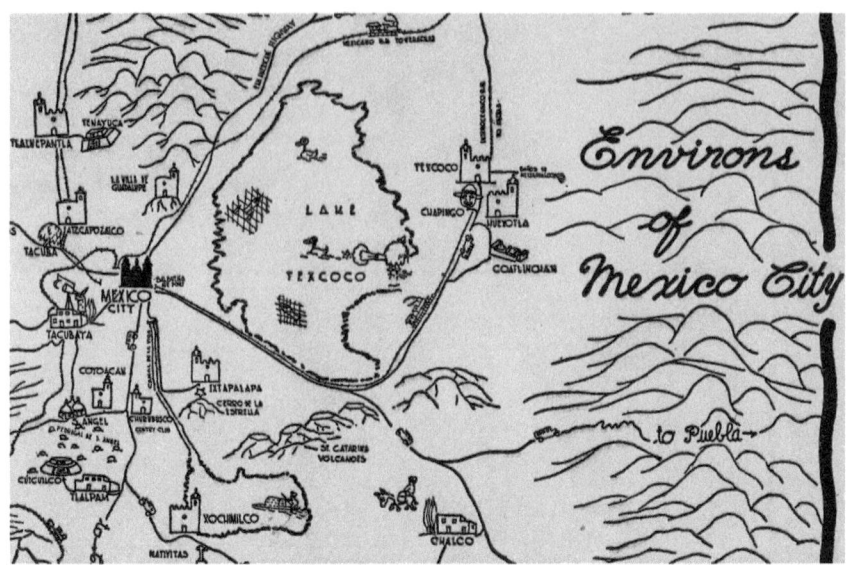

FIGURE 1.7. Detail of "Environs of Mexico City," foldout map. From Mackie and Dick 1935.

identity and ancient uses.[13] Decades after Batres's study, the travel writer Norman Pelham Wright wrote in *Mexican Kaleidoscope*: "I feel that I should mention a lone, enigmatic idol, known as the idolo de Coatlinchan. . . . This rather grim monolith lies deep in a remote gorge. . . . The figure is horizontal, foreshortened, stylized, and grotesque. . . . No one will venture an opinion as to the age of this grim and puzzling figure, nor attempt to identify the culture to which it owes its origin" (1947, 89). In other words, the stone remained an impressive yet mysterious vestige that contrasted with the grandiose ceremonial complexes located only a few miles away in Teotihuacan and Mexico City that the writer recommended as being more visit-worthy.[14] As his account shows, over the course of almost a century, the stone remained in Coatlinchan awkwardly, as a "rather grim and puzzling figure," isolated and remote in ways that continued to stir up a great deal of anxiety.

Gendering Place

Debates over the stone's possible identity were grounded on interpretations of its place in the ravine as well as on the ravine's own position within the local topography. In order to determine what the stone was and what or whom it represented, scholars centered on whether or not it was from, made in, and intended to remain in Coatlinchan. In this process, the stone became gendered and also gendering, as its proximity and relation to geological features like mountains, rivers, and lakes and to water in general determined if it was male or female. As a female entity, it was considered to be more attached and related to the place where it lay, whereas as a male, it became independent from the site and therefore available for relocation. Gender binaries, and their implied associations with power, attachment, and relationality as well as with water's life-giving potential, were activated to determine whether or not the stone belonged in Coatlinchan and were ultimately used to justify its relocation.

For the Museo Nacional's curator, Jesús Sánchez, the stone's location in the ravine was key to its identification as a female water deity. He described the landscape as "beautiful" and "lush," channeling water from the peak of the mountain named after the storm god, Tlaloc, to the basin of Lake Texcoco. In the "Cañada del Agua [as the residents of Coatlinchan call this particular ravine]," he wrote, "lies a gigantic stone statue representing a woman dressed in the fashion common to Aztec idols, lying on her back with an unfortunately completely disfigured face and without hands" (1886, 28). Sánchez interpreted the stone's disfigurement as a combination of the effects of erosion and colonial campaigns against Indigenous idolatry. Because it was defaced, he believed that the statue's placement in a ravine where water flowed was the only clue to determine its identity. Given its size and that it was found in a gorge associated with water, femininity and fertility, Sánchez was certain that the statue represented Chalchiuhtlicue, the female Aztec water deity. He cited Bernardino de Sahagún and Fray Juan de Torquemada, sixteenth-century friars who meticulously wrote about Indigenous lifeways and described the cult of Chalchiuhtlicue as the goddess of horizontal bodies of water such as rivers and lakes. By contrast, the preferred location for sites associated with Tlaloc, the male rain deity, was on elevated mountaintops where clouds formed and rain first touched the ground. Sánchez (1886, 30) ultimately supported his claim with the coinciding opinion of his contemporaries, Gumesino Mendoza (1829–96) and Alfredo Chavero (1841–1906), the leading experts on ancient Indigenous societies and religions at the time.

Alfredo Chavero had earlier published Velasco's image as the illustration for his entry "Chalchiuhtlicue" in the volume on the pre-Hispanic past that he authored for the widely read encyclopedic work on all things Mexican, *México a través de los siglos* (Mexico through the centuries) (1887–89).[15] This entry made the stone in Coatlinchan into the quintessential representation of that specific deity. Like Sánchez, Chavero believed that the stone represented the female deity Chalchiuhtlicue because of the place where it was found: "There were rivers that flowed from the mountain to fertilize the ancient lands of the kingdom of the Acolhuacan. These were then conducted through aqueducts to mount Texcutzinco. . . . These flows were symbolized in Coatlinchan where, in the Cañada del agua, on this side of the valley, a ravine formed between two mountains carrying water from the high peaks—mainly Mount Tlaloc, whose water flows toward Lake Texcoco. That is where the colossal statue of Chalchiuhtlicue can be found" (1887, 662). Chavero went on to discuss the statue's measurements and human-like features as well as Chalchiuhtlicue's genealogy in relation to other water deities in ancient Mexico. By comparing the stone's attributes with the formal qualities of other ancient statues that were either clearly female or somehow associated with water because they bore objects that he considered instruments to measure its levels, he concluded that it represented the water goddess.[16] Although the statue itself did not have iconographic elements associating it with the liquid (with the exception of the reservoir at the top of its headdress), its location in a ravine channeling water, and in Coatlinchan specifically, was what finally made Chavero certain that it was Chalchiuhtlicue. He lamented its poor state of conservation, which he attributed to its location, which had ironically brought it in contact with water's destructive forces: "Unfortunately, its hands and face are destroyed, as it lies, cast in the ravine, mistreated by the very waters of which at another time it was a deity" (1887, 663).

Chavero believed the stone was not just carved in Coatlinchan but also intended to be worshiped there. He speculated poetically on what its cult might have looked like:

When the waters came down—after long periods of drought following the rainy season—the fields were burnt and the canoes would scrape the bottom of the lake; the torrents were merely piles of rocks and the rivers were empty. Everything was thirsty: nature and mankind. And then the Mexicas made a great feast for the water and rain gods, with many child sacrifices. The peoples of the valley contemplated the mountains anxiously, from the Iztaccihuatl to Mount Tlaloc, which they believed to be a great water depot. They went hurriedly to the Coatlinchan ravine where the water that fed the lake, watered their lands, and quenched their thirst came from. (1904, 26)[17]

He ended his vivid description with a reconstruction of a Nahuatl song allegedly recorded by colonial chroniclers:

And so the communities went to ask the deity of Coatlinchan for water. They contemplated it with angst . . . and suddenly water started sprouting from the goddess's mouth. For these indians, it was the water that had been held prisoner in the mountains that finally flowed freely to quench their thirst and give them life, water their fields, produce crops, and fill their sacred lake. From all their tongues came a tremendous clamor that echoed throughout the whole valley; they all threw their arms toward the goddess; and all their voices sang Mexica hymns: Malinalla nomactemi, açan teumilco chicauaztica motlaquechizca. Otlacatqui çenteutl, atl, yayaui cani tlaca pillachiualoya chalchimichuacan, yyao, yantala, yatanta, a yyao, ayyaue tlil yao, ayyaue, oayyaue. (1904, 26)

Chavero's rendition connected the stone to the elements and to agricultural cycles intimately related to the region's topographical features and to ancient rituals designed to domesticate them. In his view, the stone was placed in the ravine in Coatlinchan because it was on the path taken by water flowing from Mount Tlaloc, down to Lake Texcoco. And this was the place where the deity's telluric powers were invoked and animated to guarantee fertility and sustenance.[18]

Chavero got into a heated argument with Batres about the stone's possible gender identity shortly after the latter's excavations (Batres 1904a, 1905). Their disagreement hinged on the stone's measurements and identifying features as well as on its location in Coatlinchan and the place's topographical associations with water. Batres was the first to identify the stone as the male Aztec rain deity Tlaloc, although he enigmatically titled his study ¿Tlaloc? (1903), leaving room for doubt. Despite the question marks, the stone's identification as a male entity was central to how Batres understood its misplacement in Coatlinchan and its need to be relocated elsewhere. According to Batres, the stone represented Tlaloc (generally portrayed with fangs and goggle eyes) and not Chalchiuhtlicue (usually rendered wearing a jade skirt and characteristic headdress) as Chavero argued. Batres was critical of Chavero's methods because Chavero had never himself been to the site where the carving was found, relying on others' texts and drawings to build his argument.

Velasco's drawing was at the heart of the two scholars' debate. According to Batres, Chavero had used iconographic speculations and Velasco's sketch to make his claims. Yet Velasco, who had in turn used Sánchez's calculations, had drawn a deformed version of the stone, misleading Chavero to think that the figure was wearing a skirt rather than a *maxtli*, the loincloth associated with masculinity. Batres contrasted this with the scientific character of his own work, justifying the intervention of official archaeology: "The monolith remained largely hidden until the official pickax came to finish uncovering it, revealing its true shape and size" (1903, 3–4). Of course, it was his own pickax he was referencing.

Batres's excavations led him to believe that the stone was part of an altarpiece for an important pre-Hispanic shrine devoted to the Aztec male rain god, built on top of nearby Mount Tlaloc, and that it had been dragged to Coatlinchan by a mudslide—another telluric force. He based his interpretation first on the material evidence unearthed on site: objects and pottery sherds, in addition to human skeletal remains, that he believed belonged to small children, a common ritual offering in ancient cults to Tlaloc (1903, 18). He also cited the writings of Torquemada, the sixteenth-century Franciscan friar who mentioned a statue of Tlaloc carved out of dark basaltic rock located on Mount Tlaloc that, just like the Coatlinchan stone, lay partially broken: "The Acolhua lord Nezahualpiltzintli, monarch of Texcoco, had a larger monolith made, carved out of a very dark and very large stone; a very hard stone so that it would last many years. So he took the pumice one away from its place and substituted it with the new one. However, a thunderbolt fell upon the new monolith the very same year of its replacement and broke it into many pieces" (Batres 1903, 11). Torquemada reported that locals believed that a supernatural entity was responsible for this and quickly restored the previous statue to the site: "The Acolhuas were frightened and believed that the electric discharge had been a manifestation of Tlaloc's anger because it was not his will that his white image be replaced, so they brought the white monolith back to its first site and took away the one made by Nezahualpiltzintli, placing it in the provisional location where the white one had been" (Batres 1903, 11). This act of restoration and replacement became linked to future extractivist and racialized practices ingrained in the colonial project: "As they moved the large and hard black statue, an arm was broken off, which they tried to solder using three nails made out of gold. Once Christianity was in place in these lands, the bishop Zumárraga cast down the diabolical stone, as the missionaries called it, and had the arm broken off in his presence, simultaneously taking the rich gold nails" (1903, 12). According to Batres, the stone's ultimate desecration, its mutilated left arm and leg, as well as its dark stone matter confirmed that it was the very same statue of Tlaloc now in Coatlinchan.

This evidenced not only that the statue's location in the ravine was aleatory but that it had been partially responsible for its destruction following double iconoclastic gestures: the ancient stone deity's wrath following its intended substitution by another sculpture during the reign of Nezahualpiltzintli, and Bishop Zumárraga's intentions to topple ancient Indigenous cults and seek colonial wealth (I return to this story about gold in chapter 5). The stone's location in Coatlinchan and its current state were, then, not its origin but the result of telluric events and desecration resulting first from supernatural vengeance (notably one associating lightness and whiteness with power) and second from colonial extractivism related to its misplacement. Furthermore, Batres's interpretation dated the statue to the Postclassic period. This had the pragmatic value of glossing its placement in Coatlinchan as recent as well as arbitrary, the result of the whims of the elements and telluric accidents rather than the purposeful planning and ritual considerations of its ancient makers. Given these findings, Batres concluded that the stone did not belong in the ravine and should therefore be rescued from there.

Like many scholars studying the stone in these early years, Batres mentioned local residents' accounts of what the stone was but dismissed them as mere hearsay or as residues of Indigenous idolatry that ultimately misunderstood the stone for a powerful deity. He began his monograph stating that many of the misunderstandings surrounding the stone's identification could be traced to how scholars had been "inspired" by lay archaeology enthusiasts and "by the fantasies of simple peasants from the town who called it 'Zocaca,' 'La Esquila' (bell), or 'La Piedra de los Tecomates'" (1903, 3). Batres recorded the names, including "Piedra de los Tecomates," still in use in Coatlinchan today but was not interested in them, instead seeking "truth" in colonial sources. He did not view local accounts and naming practices as reliable forms of knowledge.

Others mentioned local interpretations only to underscore the stone's aleatory position in Coatlinchan and justify its removal. The engineer Luis G. Becerril, mentioned earlier, reported his conversations with locals. He described them as "ignorant because they believed the stone was an enchanted woman, rather than an inert statue" (1903, 70). Becerril was convinced these were "legends" told by "superstitious people" who expected the petrified being inside the stone to come to life at any moment (I come back to this story in chapter 7). He assured his readers that the stone was nothing more than a man-made artifact, insisting that even in pre-Hispanic times it was not a deity to be worshiped but a decorative architectural feature: he argued that the headdress and perforations were part of an intricate system that made rainwater collect in the reservoir and flow through the orifices of the standing statue (1903, 70). In other words, the stone was no more than a premodern fountain.

Unlike some of his peers, Chavero argued that the stone carving represented a female deity partially because of these local accounts, which he understood as a kind of archive that was perhaps more reliable than the speculations of so-called experts. He related a conversation over coffee with several well-known scholars who had, in his view, erroneously assumed the stone's identity as Tlaloc instead of taking local accounts seriously:

We were having coffee on the roof terrace of Zelia Nuttall's house, the old residence of conquistador Pedro de Alvarado, as was our tradition.[19] She had invited me for lunch, as well as Dr. León, in the company of Mr. Bowditch, the wise archaeologist from Boston, his distinguished wife and his lovely daughter. In one group, we admired the beauties of the horizon that extended on the rough stony ground, behind the trees and gardens, up to the gigantic Ajusco. In another, Mrs. Nuttall and Mr. Bowditch were discussing their next visit to Teotihuacan. "When we return," said Mrs. Nuttall, "we will stop by Texcoco and we will go see the great knocked-down Tlaloc near Coatlinchan." (1904, 3)

Chavero was surprised that Zelia Nuttall and others present assumed that the figure represented the male deity. He quoted the villagers who, unlike the experts present at the luncheon, knew the statue as a female deity: "the indians believed the idol was the goddess of water" (1904, 3). We can perhaps infer that Chavero's insistence that the stone represented Chalchiuhtlicue and that it was worshipped in the ravine was based not merely on iconographic interpretations and site specificity but also on local people's identifications and forms of knowledge.

The debate regarding the stone's gender and its place in Coatlinchan continued through another series of articles published by Chavero and Batres during the next two years and at the 1904 Americanist Congress held in Mexico City, where the two publicly rejected one another's hypotheses. Despite Chavero's many attempts to prove that the sculpture represented Chalchiuhtlicue and belonged in Coatlinchan, Batres's insistence that it represented Tlaloc and that its location was an accident prevailed (Batres 1905). The stone's possible identity remained an ongoing subject of debate. In 1905, Léon Lejeal, a scholar at the Collège de France, concluded: "There is tremendous uncertainty around the problem of findings relating to the sexes! Direct observations of the monument do not tell us anything about how it was made. . . . How do they want us to give our opinion if we have not seen it? The monolith that has caused so much awe is certainly a deity of fertilizing humidity. But we don't know anything more about it. Tlaloc? Chalchiuhtlicue? Cruel enigma!" (1905, 195).

Nevertheless, the stylistic similarities between the Diosa del Agua, a monument that Batres famously transported from Teotihuacan to the Museo Nacional in 1889 (Bueno 2010, 2016), and the stone in Coatlinchan continued to draw scholars' attention well into the mid-twentieth century. Because of their iconographic similarities and the well-preserved features of the Teotihuacan monument whose skirt bore water-related symbols, the Coatlinchan stone was believed to represent the same female deity. The two statues were considered to have been part of a triad of megalithic effigies of Chalchiuhtlicue intended for Teotihuacan, along with a third much smaller statue still found at the site to this day (Carballo and Robb 2017). Even as this scholarship gendered the stone in Coatlinchan as female, its proponents implied that it did not belong in the ravine—this was the place where the stone was quarried and carved but not where it was intended to remain. Once finished, it would have been transported to Teotihuacan, a ceremonial and political center, where it would have been erected as an architectural or ritual feature. This hypothesis reinforced the stone's need for relocation as a form of rescue and restoration, including its repositioning as a standing monument.

An "Erratic Block"

Beyond what the stone was and whom or what it represented, debates surrounding whether or not it belonged in Coatlinchan hinged on the materiality of the stone itself and whether or not it was physically attached to the ravine and to its matrix rock. Becerril, who was also an active member of the Sociedad Mexicana de Geología and the draftsman for the Comisión Geológica Mexicana since 1888, had early on insisted that geology, and not archaeology, was the appropriate science for studying the Coatlinchan stone. He cited geologist Juan de Dios Villarello, who presided over the Universidad Nacional's Instituto de Geología (National University's Institute of Geology) and was a specialist in topography, hydrogeology, metallurgy, and mining, and who "determined the stone's nature and density and measured its volume with the most intricate calculations" (Becerril 1903, 71). Becerril dismissed the work of scholars like Batres and Chavero because it was reliant on historical reconstruction and iconographic interpretation rather than "hard science" that might allow "the idol to be known in a different way than it had been known by lay people, as well as by admirers of merely large and curious things" (1903, 71). He trusted data directly deduced from the stone's physical properties. He declared that it was made from a hornblende andesite, an intermediate volcanic rock whose density, not merely dimensions, had to be taken into consideration to calculate its weight "founded in science" (1903, 71). Moreover, geology's insight on the material qualities of the stone proved that it was unquestionably from Coatlinchan because such large boulders of porous and, therefore, easy to carve volcanic rock were common in that specific area.

These rocks were of such proportions and mass that George Vaillant (1901–45), an archaeologist and curator at the American Museum of Natural History, believed that the stone had remained abandoned in Coatlinchan because its carvers had miscalculated its weight, an error that he associated with the unfortunate fate of Indigenous people in the Americas:

> The statue was never finished. It lies still anchored to its matrix of living rock in a ravine near Texcoco. Larger by far than the Goddess of Waters [from Teotihuacan], battered by the elements, the deity of Coatlinchan cannot fail to impress the modern visitor. Its concept is grandiose, but the engineering skill was lacking to cut the sculpture free from its base. Prometheus in his chains may symbolize the tragedy of European thought, but to me, this goddess, still an integral part of the land that made her, represents the paralysis of indian civilization. (Vaillant 1950, 61–62)

If for Vaillant the stone's attachment to the ravine served as a symbol of "paralysis," for others, it led to speculation about whether or not it was a finished work at all. Rather than having succumbed to erosion, telluric events, or purposeful iconoclastic defacement, this hypothesis centered on its makers' intentions as well as their artistic and technological capacities. In a posthumous publication from 1957, Miguel Covarrubias, a well-known Mexican artist and ethnographer, wrote:

> Over 23 feet high, nearly 15 feet wide, and about 13 feet thick, the "Tlaloc of Coatlinchan" is a statue that remains attached to the matrix rock, apparently abandoned before it was completed. It is difficult to visualize the manner in which this enormous mass could have been carried down the mountain, had it been finished. The position of the statue, its unfinished condition, and the erosion it has suffered through the centuries preclude defining with certainty what it represents beyond that it is a male figure with a short skirt and a massive headdress and that it was intended to have a strange mouth mask, perhaps justifying its identification as Tlaloc, the rain god. (1957, 133)

In other words, the stone's permanence in Coatlinchan provided an engineering problem that could not be overcome by its makers. Covarrubias concluded that it was left "unfinished" in a site it was not actually destined for since its makers' intention was to eventually transport the finished sculpture to a ceremonial site, even if this might not have been feasible at the time.

In 1963, a year before the stone's relocation to the Museo Nacional de Antropología, geology, once again, became essential for determining the stone's origins, provenance, and ultimate destination. US-based geologist Howel Williams (1898–1980) and archaeologist Robert Heizer (1915–79), interested in ancient heavy transport, conducted a study that showed that both the Diosa del Agua and the Coatlinchan stone were made from the same rock and, therefore, came from the same quarry (Heizer and Williams 1963, 95–98). By analyzing thin sections of both stones using a microscope, they argued that they were carved in the same ravine, where torrents had dragged the large andesite lava boulders from the same volcanic source.

Coatlinchan was then scientifically determined to be a quarry for raw material emerging from the Earth's core, ideal for carving deities. Heizer and Williams explained the stones' large size: "the boulders in the alluvial fans that descend to Coatlinchan and Texcoco are unusually large because they were derived from a very thick flow of massive lava on the steep slopes of Mount Tlaloc, a high eroded Pliocene volcano whose summit lies 13 km east-southeast of the unfinished monument" (1963, 95). Their findings, based on geologic events in deep time, supported Batres's and others' hypothesis that the stone came from elsewhere and had accidentally landed in Coatlinchan. In this interpretation, the stone's location was not explained by human decisions, nor the wrath or favor of ancient deities, but by even more ancient telluric forces. Coatlinchan was simply where a volcanic rock large enough to carve into a monumental ritual effigy had landed after a prehistoric eruption.

It was Heizer and Williams's opinion that it was politics, and not the lack of technological abilities, that made the stone's makers unable to finish and move it to its intended location. In a later publication, they speculated: "This statue could have been dragged down to the shore of Lake Texcoco, placed on a raft, and carried north by water to a point where land transport was again resorted to. Alternatively, it could have been dragged overland on a sledge from the source to the city [Teotihuacan]." Technology was not the problem, since "even the Coatlinchan statue . . . could presumably have been moved if the Teotihuacanos had seriously wanted to do so" (Williams and Heizer 1965, 58). Based on other events of heavy transport in different parts of the world, their calculations showed that, at the time of its carving, given the available technology, between 1,833 and 4,025 men would have been required to move it (1963, 97; 1965, 58). They speculated that ancient Teotihuacanos simply could not harness the manpower necessary to move the stone at a time that coincided with the political decline of the city, leaving them no choice but to leave it unfinished in its quarry. This also explained why the object's form was rough and unpolished, having been abandoned and discarded, left to history as a perpetual work in progress.

By the mid-1960s, when the stone was chosen as an ideal monument for the Museo Nacional de Antropología then under construction, engineers and government officials were once again faced with conflicting interpretations of its physical properties and relationship to the place and ground where it was found. This time, the conversation shifted to whether or not it was physically part of Coatlinchan and attached to bedrock. This was also a legal concern since, following Mexican patrimonio laws, if it was attached to the matrix, the stone could not be severed or removed. According to these laws, there is a distinction between moveable things considered distinct monuments and ones that are immovable, either because they are embedded in archaeological sites or monumental structures or because they are physically part of landscape and/ or geological features. Like petroglyphs, carvings made from rocks attached to bedrock, even if stipulated as *patrimonio nacional*, are legally considered immovable (Cottom 2008). Detaching the stone to ready it for its removal, then, first involved proving that it was physically separate from the ground in which it lay and only then could it become legally subject for extraction.

In a video interview, architect and archaeologist Ricardo de Robina (1919–2001), who headed the 1964 museum's design team, explained that this concern led to much uncertainty as to whether the stone could be moved at all (Aguayo et al. 1997). Before commissioning engineers to design the technological details for its transport, he was commissioned to prove that it was in fact a bounded and separate thing. He, in turn, delegated archaeologist Luis Aveleyra and museum designer Mario Vázquez (1923–2020) with conducting the necessary examinations. In 2007, sitting in the library on the second floor of the museum where he spent every Tuesday until his death, Mario Vázquez, known for his humor, generosity, and well-tempered character, giggled when I asked him about the study: "Well, 'study' is a big word. . . . We got on our hands and knees and dug with our hands until we were able to pass a wire under the stone and only then could we ascertain that it was a distinct monument lying on the ground, not actually part of it." Vázquez stressed that the stakes were high but also found it humorous that he and Aveleyra had improvised this technique. Without disclosing the study's methods, in his official report now in the museum's archives, Aveleyra concluded: "Even before it was carved, the idol from Coatlinchan was a simple isolated block of rock that was never part of the region's matrix. . . . Expert geologists have attested to the absolute integrity of the rock, the consistency and health of its mass, as a precaution given the possible tensions the monolith might endure during the procedures of transporting, discharging and erecting it."[20] Even as the study was based on improvised methods, its author validated that the stone was indeed a single and separate object, demonstrating that it was severable from Coatlinchan, just as they made sure of its physical integrity to prepare it for extraction.

In 1964, coinciding with the year of its relocation, Eduardo Noguera, an established archaeologist who also served as one of the curators of the new museum's archaeology halls, wrote an article in the journal *Anales de Antropología*. This is astonishingly the most recent work to date on the stone published in a disciplinary journal in the field of archaeology. There, Noguera surveyed the existing scholarship on the monument, advancing his own position regarding long-standing debates on its identity, gender, and location. He concluded that its back showed that it was probably not, as many had argued, an unfinished work but had been eroded by the elements over time; that it most likely represented a female deity; and that it was carved in Coatlinchan and then abandoned there (1964, 134). Probably writing before the stone's weight was calculated by engineers working on its potential transfer to the new museum, Noguera used geologists Heizer and Williams's estimate at 197 tons.[21]

The main reason for Noguera's return to the stone as the subject of academic interest was to disclaim archaeologists', in his own words, "erroneous assumption" that it was attached to bedrock. The article, written by a professional archaeologist, reinvested the work done by Mario Vázquez and Luis Aveleyra as a scientific archaeological dig: "recent excavations have proven that this is one of the many erratic blocks in many places in the locality and within the same ravine, just that this one is of much larger proportions" (Noguera 1964, 135). For Noguera, the stone was a larger than usual "erratic block" whose nomadic wanderings happened to bring it to Coatlinchan. The archaeologist also believed the stone could be made portable and even partible, proposing that for its transport, it be separated from its "stem," the "unnecessary protrusion" on its back. Cut away from this section, the stone would weigh only 125 tons, making its transport much less challenging (1964, 135). In Noguera's opinion, given the carving's Teotihuacan slope and panel style, severing it from its "stem" was not an act of destruction but a way of completing the work since it was surely meant as an architectural feature that could stand upright or flank a building. Separating the sculpted part of the stone from its "stem" and thus part of the rock in its rough, natural form, was, in his eyes, a way of concluding the work begun but left unfinished by its ancient makers.

Even as Noguera suggested the stone be partitioned, he expressed doubts regarding its identification and its relationship to Coatlinchan's territory. Echoing Chavero's late nineteenth-century conclusions, Noguera believed that the place where the carving lay was central for its identification as the female deity Chalchiuhtlicue, associated with lakes and rivers. He was also one of the very few to express ambivalence about whether the stone should be moved at all: "perhaps the monolith was never meant to be moved from the site where it lies, the site it was assigned to by its makers with precision" (Noguera 1964, 138). A few sentences later, he continued: "despite the known ingenuity, ability and resources of pre-Hispanic peoples, they did not have the adequate means to move this colossal sculpture, nor perhaps did they ever intend to do so since it is likely that they wished it to remain in the place where it was carved to fulfill its functions as the goddess of water flows" (141). The article's last paragraph brings forth Noguera's ambivalence:

> In any case, although in other moments of history the stone could not be removed from the site where it has lain for many centuries, if it were to be removed today (even though its authors' wish was that it remain precisely in this site to be revered) using extraordinary mechanical resources, it could be exhibited in the new Museo Nacional de Antropología, but to very different ends than the ceremonial and religious purposes it served in those times. Placing the monolith in the museum will display the works of pre-Hispanic peoples in the first moments of our era that are still the subject of our admiration today. (1964, 142)

Noguera's intervention validated the stone's relocation as a separate and therefore portable monument, while acknowledging that moving it to Mexico City and exhibiting it in the museum might not coincide with its makers' wishes, nor with the stone's ancient ritual uses. Removing it from Coatlinchan and taking it to the newly built museum was, in his view, part of a different project that repurposed and harnessed its powers as an ancient water deity now in the service of the modern Mexican state.

2

Engineering Transfer

Following decades of speculation regarding how and why the stone came to be in Coatlinchan, and whether or not it was intended to remain there, it was finally transported to Mexico City on April 16, 1964. Given the weight and size of the load as well as the stone's designation as national patrimonio the Mexican government and its engineers custom-built the largest low-bed trailer ever made at the time to transport it to its new urban abode, boasting a combination of ancestral and homegrown technological skills and legacies. The thirty-five-mile journey, at an average speed of three miles an hour, took almost nineteen hours. The bright orange finish of the enormous steel rig contrasted with the rugged texture and uneven shape of the dark basaltic rock, strapped to the vehicle under a mesh of ropes and steel cables like an ancient Gulliver.

The stone's relocation coincided with a moment in Mexican history characterized by the widespread construction of public works, notably dams and highways. This was a time when Mexico, like many countries of the world, invested heavily in infrastructure as a means to both connect and power nations toward progress, development, and economic prosperity. As Timothy Mitchell has shown for Egypt's own application of engineering technology for such projects around this same time, these public works didn't just extend but actually produced and replicated nation-states on the ground (2002, 44).[1] The stone's relocation to the museum became such an "infrastructural technology" (Harvey and Knox 2015), extending the reach of the Mexican state through a network of public works made to control territory as well as the elements, especially the turbulent willfulness and energetic potential of water. This substance and its force were critical to producing the energy necessary to power Mexico's development, relying on the construction of huge dams and hydroelectric plants.[2] The same engineers building these hydraulic infrastructures to control the currents of myriad rivers and reservoirs were commended with moving the stone, inadvertently reinvesting it as a modern incarnation of an ancient water deity. These engineers harnessed the deity's powers to divert and control the liquid for political ends by way of technical expertise, custom-built technology, and the power of the Mexican state to control the elements. As scholars in various fields have argued, moving an object conceptually, physically, and geographically always radically transforms it, even if the intention behind this movement is conservation.[3] In this case, moving the stone transformed it into the water deity Tlaloc.

Recent anthropological work has highlighted how infrastructure needs to be understood beyond function and form (Mrázek 2002), even as a "poetics" that is open-ended, always in the process of becoming (Larkin 2013). Time is central to this work, as infrastructure unavoidably connects the past, present, and future through claims of modernity, promises of attainable futures, and inevitable ruination (Anand, Gupta, and Appel 2018), tied to its materiality and its own processes of decay within the environments in which it is built (Uribe 2017). In the case of the stone's relocation, these overlapping temporalities were all the more explicit. It was by moving a stone, transformed into an ancient deity, that the contemporary Mexican state produced itself as modern and effective but also deeply rooted in the country's pre-Hispanic past. In this process, state-of-the-art technology and engineering—disciplines bound to a promised future, and not exclusively those associated with the past like archaeology and history—became the relocation's main protagonists. Throughout the process, the language of engineering also transformed the stone, enhancing the archaeological details and arguments used to justify its extraction.

For many of the engineers involved, the stone's transportation implied enormous stakes, partially because of the technological challenges set by its size and weight but also because, as national patrimonio, it had to be handled with special care, making it portable without subjecting it to vibrations that might compromise its integrity and preservation. These challenges and the complicated means designed to solve them made the engineers charged with its transport feel central to the nation's bid in the human conquest over the environment. The stone's telluric powers were not lost on them as they actively participated in subverting its ability to control the elements and water in favor of the modern nation-state. Their sense of pride endured late into their lives: two of the engineers, as well as other technicians who worked directly on transporting the stone, enthusiastically shared their stories and their carefully kept personal archives with me. Others, no longer alive when I did the research for this book, published their own accounts on how participating in the project marked their lives. By framing their work as a "transfer," the term they most often used as well as the term preferred by government officials, architects, and museum staff to describe the stone's relocation, they naturalized its repurposing as merely a movement of a mass from here to there, further disassociating the stone from the ties and relations that bound it to the ground, to a specific territory, and to the people who inhabited and sustained it. Their accounts are the main sources for this chapter.

Moving Tlaloc

I first met Enrique del Valle Prieto (1937–2020) in 2011 at an IHOP near his Houston home. He told me:

> You came to the right person. Once I was sitting in my car listening to the radio, and some guy was claiming that he had done all the calculations. He was making the whole thing up! But then the phone rang just like that, and the architect Pedro Ramírez Vázquez went on the air. He said: "I have no idea who this person is, he never worked for me, nor on the project. The only engineers who worked on the transfer, who did all the complicated calculations and can talk about the process, are the engineers del Valle Prieto." My father and me.

Del Valle Prieto had for many years been employed alongside his father, also Enrique del Valle Prieto, by Construcción Urbana Francisco Alonso Cué (CUFAC), a Mexican construction company. In the early 1980s, he had moved to Texas to work for a company that manufactured air compressors. "I just kept on moving huge things," he said with a chuckle. In a more in-depth exchange over a coke in one of the lounges of the Woodlands Golf Club, where he was an energetic player, the engineer, then in his late seventies, reminisced: "I moved

Tlaloc! Well, my dad and I did, but I am the only one left to tell the tale." His eyes lit up when he recalled: "It was truly magnificent, a spectacular project. Something like that will never be done again. Every detail, every step had to be precise, carefully calculated. It was a huge responsibility and . . . What a challenge!" The engineer smiled as he reported: "Every time I pass by Reforma when I go back to Mexico City, I say hello to my old buddy Tlaloc. Of course, I say hello! I say hello there! There is my friend Tlaloc! Hello! Goodbye! One of my father's friends even nicknamed me 'Tlaloquito' [little Tlaloc, also a pun that sounds like *está loquito* (a little crazy)]. We have a bond, you see."

This bond hinged on the engineer's deep knowledge of mass and matter. His job had been to estimate the stone's weight based on the size and kind of rock it was carved out of. Using these calculations, he designed the technological means for its transport. Del Valle Prieto kept evidence of his work as treasured personal mementos in his home in what he referred to as his "personal Tlaloc archive": a cardboard box filled with dozens of folders full of translucent green and blue paper worksheets and a worn photo album with polaroids and large prints documenting different stages of the process (some reproduced here). He flipped through the folder of pages filled with equations. "People have published books where they discuss these results, but they could never prove how they did it. They would need all these intermediate steps, and I am the only one who has them. Of course! I am the one who did them!"

Del Valle Prieto showed me a worn copy of the book *Cómo llegó Tlaloc a Chapultepec* (How Tlaloc arrived at Chapultepec) (1993), published by another engineer, Alfonso Tovar Santana, that contained a fold-out page with a drawing representing the process to calculate the stone's weight (figure 2.1). The book had been given to him by a friend. It greatly upset him because it didn't credit his work: "First we had to measure the stone's surface. I used string to surround the Tlaloc every twenty centimeters on a wooden frame. So, I divided it into twenty-two sections and added up section by section to calculate the total contour." The image made the stone into an amalgam of transversal slices of each of the sections accompanied by their measurements, but none of the process to calculate these figures was mentioned. Del Valle Prieto emphasized his authorship over the calculations. Like Mario Vázquez, the museum designer who, along with the archaeologist Luis Aveleyra, determined the stone was not attached to the matrix by using a wire (see chapter 1), the engineer took great pleasure in revealing that his calculations were the result of the use of a simple household item, an unlikely instrument for such a complicated endeavor.

Tovar Santana's book, by contrast, framed these calculations as precise measurements relying on complex mathematics and specialized instruments, in

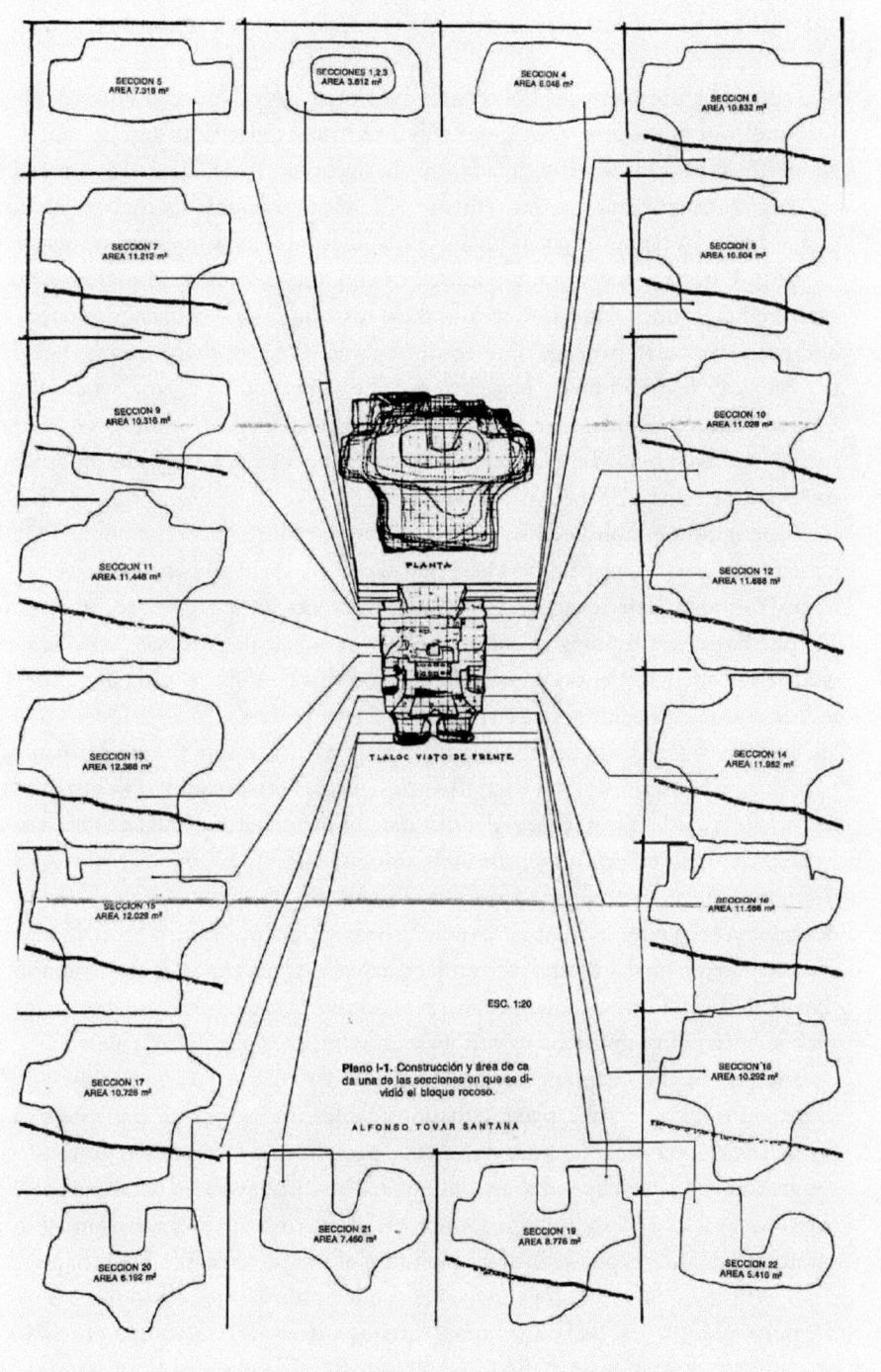

FIGURE 2.1. Contour of the stone, measured by section. From Tovar Santana 1993.

a similar tone to reports given by the authorities at the time. Published as part of the commemorations marking the museum's thirtieth anniversary, the book was edited by the Instituto Politécnico Nacional (IPN, National Polytechnic Institute), one of the most prestigious public technical universities in the country, where Tovar Santana was full-time faculty. In the book, Tovar Santana compared the feat to other historical movements of ancient monuments that required technological intervention in both ancient and more recent times, from ancient Egypt to European metropolitan museums and public squares. In so doing, he inscribed the stone's relocation within these historic engineering feats to rescue and preserve world heritage. For Tovar Santana, the case that best paralleled the Mexican feat had taken place around the same time in Egypt, where the United Nations Educational, Scientific and Cultural Organization (UNESCO) had sponsored moving Nubian temples to spare them from a watery burial amid the flooding caused by the Aswan Dam.

The engineer established a connection between contemporary engineering's efforts to preserve ancient monuments by relocating them and ancient societies' ability to move these structures across vast distances using archaic technology. Despite having no training in ancient history or archaeology, Tovar Santana included a chapter in the book that emphasized this continuity, situating Coatlinchan as one of the important city-states that ruled over the Valley of Mexico in ancient times, as well as a discussion on the place of the stone in the pre-Hispanic pantheon. The engineer even tried to settle debates between archaeologists and historians regarding the stone's identity, date of manufacture, and ancient uses. Eulalia Guzmán (1890–1985), the archaeologist famous for the discovery and defense of the authenticity of Cuauhtémoc's bones, wrote the book's prologue, denouncing the relocation as state theft.[4] The engineer positioned himself, nevertheless, as the final arbiter of the project, explaining it as a nationalist triumph that guaranteed the monument's conservation and gave continuity to its ancient makers' intentions, thwarted by conquest and centuries of colonial rule.

The rest of the chapters in the book used visual cues, foldout drawings, illustrations, photographs, plans, equations, tables, and graphs to translate to a lay audience technical language and the specialized procedures required to weigh, transport, and upend the monument. The author offered details on how the route was traced and planned, the work done to prepare the terrain, with photographs and maps to illustrate each step of the process. The final chapters dealt with the steel structure and harness built to lift the stone and place it on the purpose-built low-bed trailer as well as the tractors and trucks that provided the vehicle's horsepower. A final section provided readers with an itemized budget of the project's cost, totaling 2,011,320 pesos, a significant amount for the time. Tovar Santana didn't provide sources for all this data beyond his own experience working on the project, without specifying in what capacity. The reader was left, notwithstanding, with a sense of the immensity, precision, and expense of the ordeal.

In late October 2009, more than twenty years after the his monograph's publication, Tovar Santana sat across from me at the noisy Café La Habana, a classic hangout for writers, left-wing intellectuals, and revolutionaries in central Mexico City.[5] He lived nearby in the Tlatelolco complex, another alleged wonder of Mexico's modernizing infrastructures built only a few years before the stone's relocation.[6] He was friendly and obviously quite thrilled to discuss "moving Tlaloc," as he referred to the process. He nevertheless made sure to tell me that he had reconsidered some of his earlier claims and triumphant appraisal of Mexican engineering as a means for heritage preservation. He now distanced himself from the project and, in line with Guzmán's prologue, had become quite critical: "The government should have built a site museum there in Coatlinchan. They should never have taken it. It was not right. For me it was a job. I wasn't making any of the decisions. I was neither Ramírez Vázquez nor López Mateos! I was just an employee doing what I was paid to do."

In his early nineties when I again spoke to him in 2020 over the phone (it was the beginning of the COVID-19 pandemic), he happily volunteered the information missing from his book: he had been hired by the Mexican company Fervi S.A. de C.V. that belonged to structural engineers José Antonio Fernández Paz and Vicente Villaseñor, who specialized in steel structures. Fervi was in charge of designing the steel structure with cement foundations that the stone would hang from before it was lowered onto the vehicle. After working for Fervi, Tovar Santana was hired by CUFAC to trace the route from Coatlinchan to the museum. He was responsible for reinforcing the sewage pipes that ran under Mexico City's streets and highways so that they would not succumb under the low-bed's weight. He discussed how he had to find ways to get around difficult areas where there were no bridges allowing easy crossing, like the San Lázaro train station and the steel bridge in Ecatepec. The engineer reminisced extensively on the logistics involved, making his ingenuity and ability to surmount seemingly impossible obstacles the driving force of his narrative.

Both Tovar Santana and del Valle Prieto relied on their expertise in telluric materialities, studying the ground and its substances, consistencies, and capacities to ensure the endeavor's success. Tovar Santana worked to prepare and transform terrain to facilitate the stone's transportation, whereas del Valle Prieto performed topographical surveys and calculated the stone's weight using features from the local landscape for his estimations. Del Valle Prieto confessed: "We used what I like to call the good old engineer's calculometer. The stone was still on the ground when I measured it, so there was no way to actually measure its entire surface. I couldn't just place it on a scale, could I? So, I had to be creative and try to guess as best I could." The engineer estimated the length of the string he could not physically place around the parts of the stone that were in contact with the ground. He also used a rock that he found lying close by that appeared to be made of a similar kind of volcanic basalt. It was this rock that he submerged in water to calculate the stone's total volume. "That pebble weighed 2,300 kilos per cubic meter, so we just multiplied that by the square meters we had measured with the sections of string, and that is how we got the 167 tons."

Del Valle Prieto showed me a picture of his younger self with a theodolite, wearing overalls and a hard hat, working in the ravine (figure 2.2). "See, more proof that I did all the measuring!" He also showed me a typed document that he wrote in 2004 for the museum's fortieth anniversary on Ramírez Vázquez's request. He added: "this is a sort of memoir, an effort to write down how I became involved in one of the most impressive engineering projects of modern Mexican history." In the document, which Ramírez Vázquez also kept in his archive, del Valle Prieto describes how, having just graduated from the engineering school of the Universidad Nacional Autónoma de México (UNAM, National Autonomous University) in 1962, he began working for CUFAC on topographical surveys in Chapultepec Park, the place that would become the site for the new museum. At the time, neither he nor the company knew what the survey was for; they only found out months later when they were granted the concession to build the museum. Having completed the survey, the young engineer went to Chiapas to build highways and bridges. He returned to Mexico City in 1963, once CUFAC was commissioned to relocate the enormous stone from Coatlinchan to Chapultepec. By the time he returned, a road, around six meters wide, leading from Coatlinchan's main square up to the site where the stone lay, had already been built. The route traced by Tovar Santana from the town to the museum was being prepared and the plan to transport the stone by low-bed trailer was already in place. Now del Valle Prieto was hired to estimate the weight of the stone and come up with a way to transport it safely to the museum.

For many of the engineers involved, including Tovar Santana and del Valle Prieto, what made the transfer so difficult was not so much the stone's weight but the fact that it was considered a priceless piece of Mexico's patrimonio. Any impact or disturbance could fissure the porous basaltic rock. So the challenge was to successfully transport the heavy artifact while actually moving it as little as possible. This required all kinds of logistics. Del Valle Prieto highlighted the contradiction faced by the team: "What we did was move this enormous thing

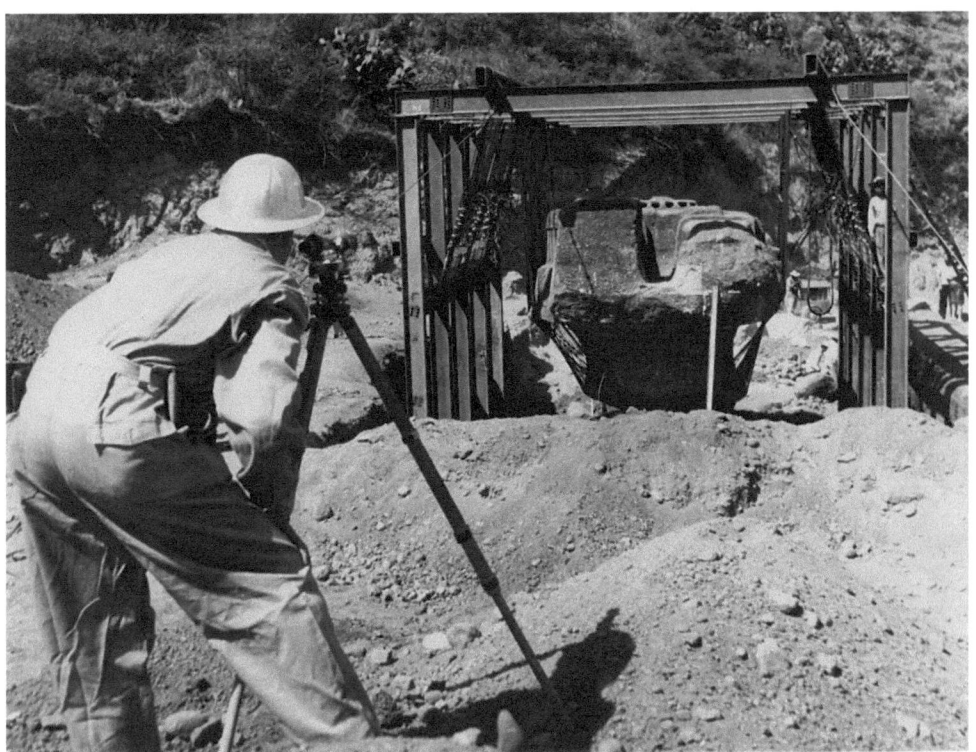

FIGURE 2.2. Measuring the stone in situ, 1963. Photograph courtesy of Enrique del Valle Prieto.

from one place to another, quite a distance! And yet we did everything so that the monolith itself would never move." He explained that, for the stone to remain in one piece, he and his team built a structure around and over it made up of five steel frames and two beams (figure 2.3). This structure allowed engineers to excavate under the stone without disturbing it, hanging it from a sort of "hammock." The cables were fixed from its extremities toward the stone's center following the pattern of the dig, making sure that its weight never shifted. The engineer designed the structure with deep cement foundations dug into the ground so that the frames could support the weight evenly without bending. Once it was freed from the ground, hovering from the structure in a kind of "cocoon," it could be lowered onto the low-bed. The cables could then be removed from the frames and tied to the vehicle, fastening the stone in place. The low-bed was equipped with a fresh cement base. Protected with thick plastic wrapping, the mixture hardened around the stone, cushioning, stabilizing, and

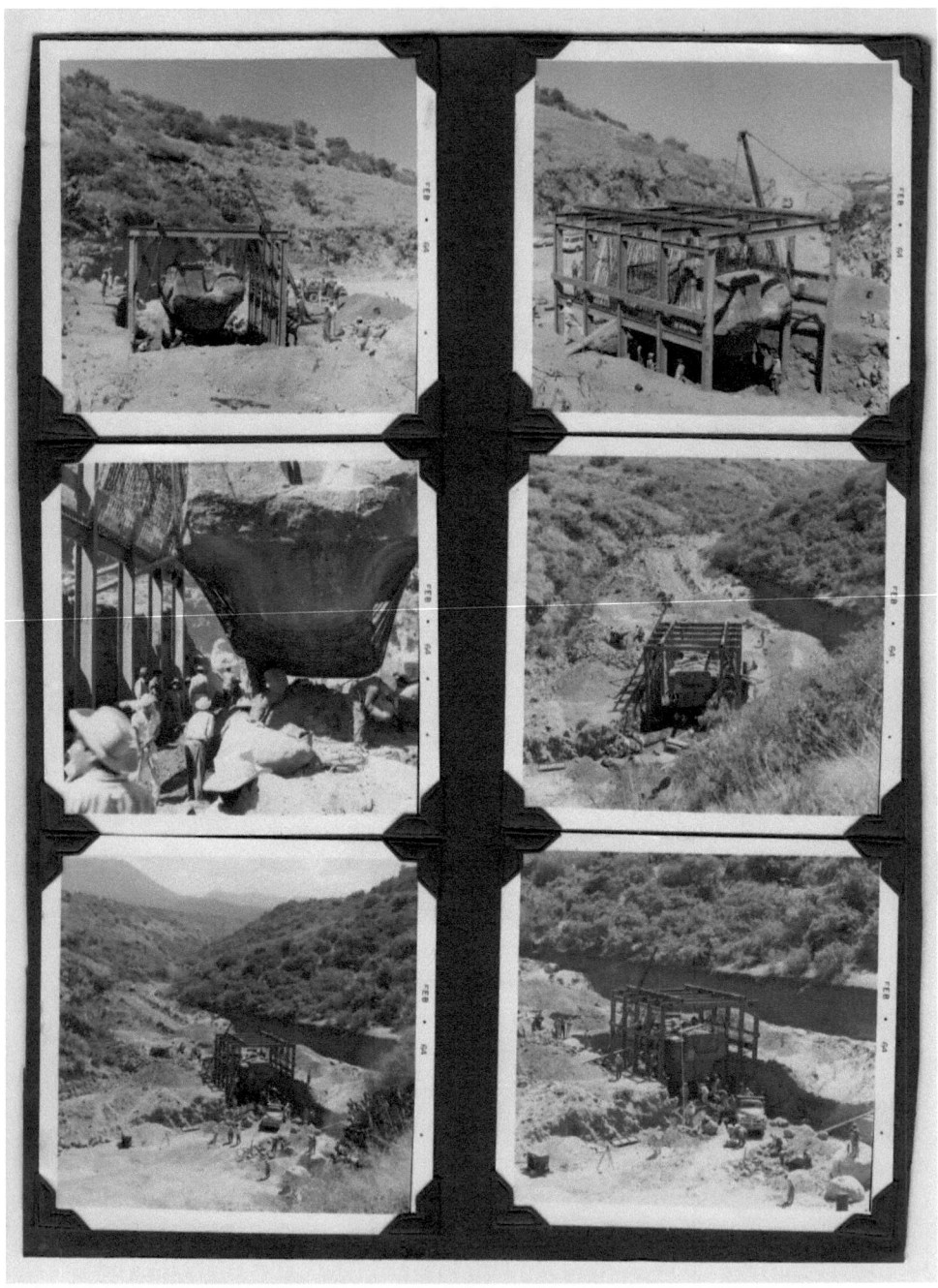

FIGURE 2.3. Contact sheet with images of the steel structure built to suspend the stone, 1964. Courtesy of Acervo Arquitecto Pedro Ramírez Vázquez.

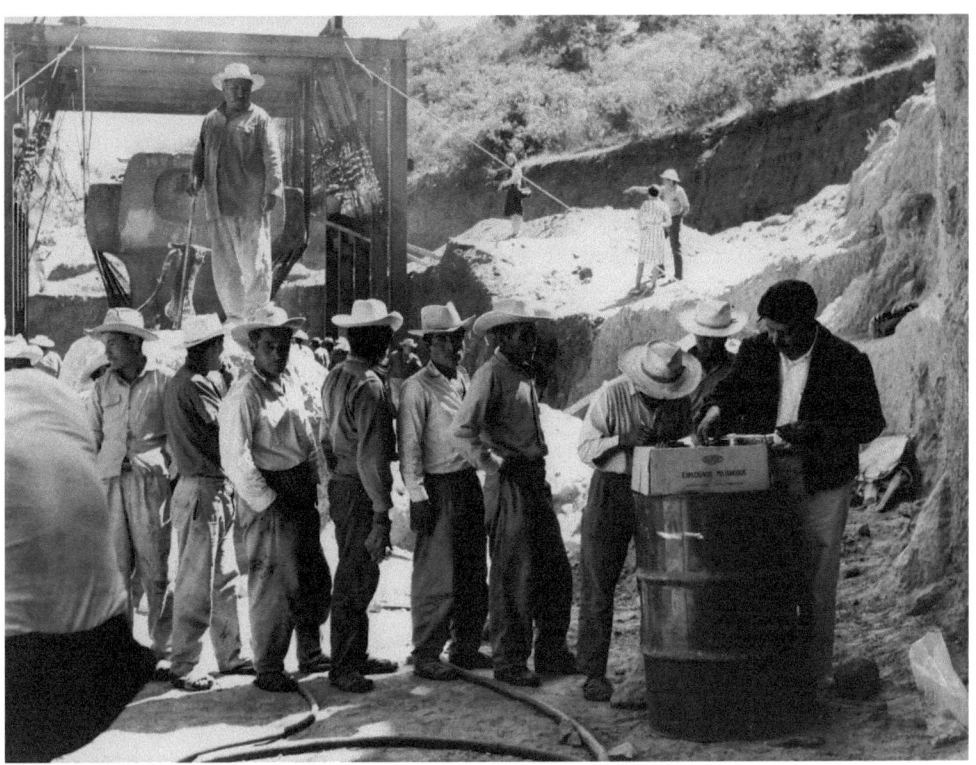

FIGURE 2.4. Local workers in the payment line, 1964. Photograph courtesy of Acervo Arquitecto Pedro Ramírez Vázquez.

distributing its weight evenly on the steel beams so that it would not be affected by the bumpy ride that lay ahead.

The construction company hired laborers in Coatlinchan for the excavation as well as for the construction of the road leading to the ravine, supervised by another engineer who took up residence in the town for several months and coordinated the work.[7] According to del Valle Prieto, local labor was key to the project's success because much of the work had to be done by hand.[8] Heavy machinery and other perhaps more efficient means of excavation could generate vibrations that would cause irreparable damage to the stone. In his description of the costs of the project, Tovar Santana emphasized that much of the budget was used to pay daily salaries to thousands of "peons" (figure 2.4).

The trade journal *Construcción Mexicana* featured a story on the complicated engineering procedure given the stone's status as patrimonio: "There wasn't a trailer-truck in Mexico that could meet the requirements. . . . There wasn't any transport vehicle that could transfer the stone without taking any risks because the stone, sculpted by pre-Hispanic hands, had priceless historical and artistic value. The complicated and time-consuming maneuvers to suspend it from 42 steel cables so that it could be secured on the trailer were a testament to its quality as an irreplaceable object. No precaution was spared to transport the largest single-stone sculpture in America" (1964b, 33).[9] In another article, the journal praised the ingenuity of the engineers that combined innovative techniques and "primitive" methods, code for manual labor:

> Geologists, archaeologists, architects, all imposed exceptional security conditions that the engineers were required to fulfill: the sculpture was not to be disturbed in any way as it was mounted onto the vehicle that would transport it; during the maneuver, it could not be submitted to any effort different from what it had endured for centuries; thus, in order to excavate it, and even given that the ground surrounding it in the ravine was made of rock, no explosives could be used, nor could they be used in a one-kilometer radius where engineers were also working to make a road on which to transport it to the nearby village of Coatlinchan. . . . The primitive procedures of hammer, chisel and wedge became necessary. Given these conditions, it took two months, during which vertical planes had to be formed and 10 digs undertaken. (*Construcción Mexicana* 1964a, 18–19)

Del Valle Prieto also insisted that the biggest complication was the restriction on the use of explosives, even though boxes of explosives can be seen in several photographs documenting the procedure (see fig. 2.4). Local workers spent more than a year digging under the stone (figure 2.5), clearing the rocks, and compacting and smoothing the terrain to build a road and clear the area. So, although technology was key to successfully moving the stone, it was in fact work done by hand provided by Coatlinchan's residents that made it budge. Del Valle Prieto was proud of this and of his own work "lifting Tlaloc" (figure 2.6).

Later, government officials and Ramírez Vázquez mentioned that locals had provided the labor force for the undertaking to reinforce that town residents were in agreement with its relocation (see chapter 3). Even with all these precautions and planning to keep the stone in one piece as national patrimonio, del Valle Prieto confessed that during the procedure, a small part of the stone broke off. "I picked it up and for many years, I kept my little piece of Tlaloc," del Valle Prieto said with an impish expression. "The small piece of rock was probably part of its foot. I have no idea how it broke off, but I kept it as my little piece of history. Then one day, during one of my moves, I packed it in a box, and then it was lost. I have no idea where it ended up."

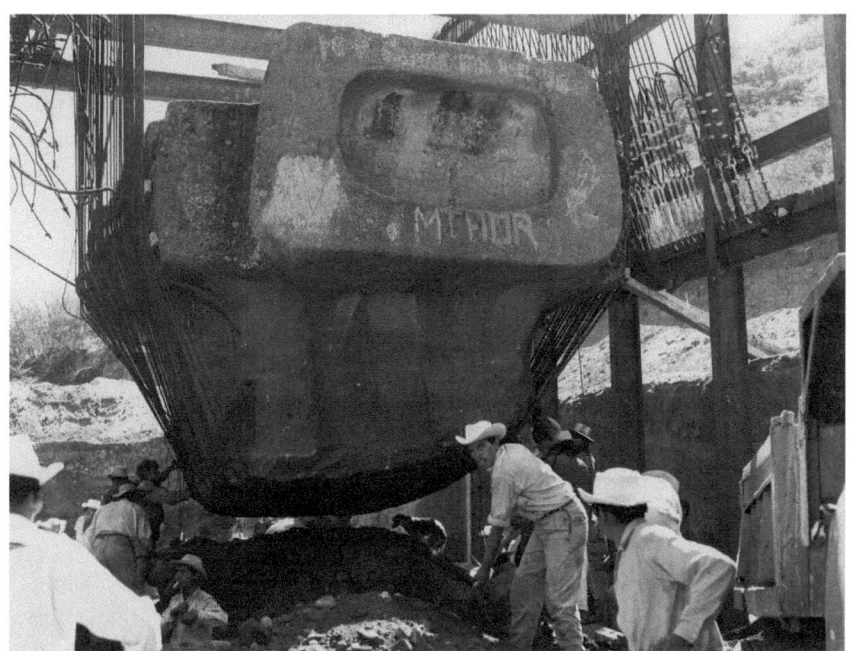

FIGURE 2.5. Workers excavating the stone, 1964. Photograph courtesy of Acervo Arquitecto Pedro Ramírez Vázquez.

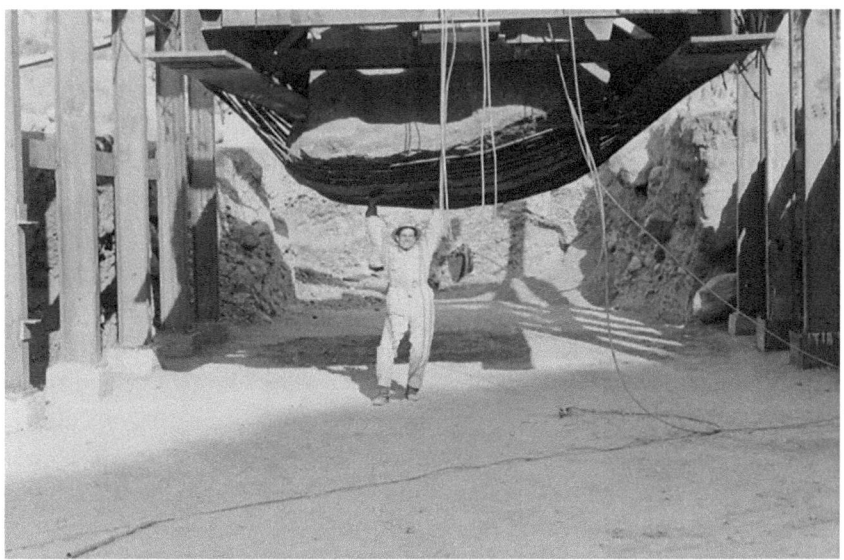

FIGURE 2.6. Enrique del Valle Prieto under the "hammock," 1964. Photograph courtesy of Enrique del Valle Prieto.

Made in Mexico

As they were planning the maneuver, engineers speculated on the type of vehicle required since there were no traction devices big or powerful enough for the job in existence in Mexico or abroad. Given the stakes of the project for the Mexican government, officials wanted a national company to design the vehicle as a strategy to promote Mexican-made technology on a world stage. Even though the project ultimately relied heavily on foreign manufacturing and expertise, the government, as well as the engineers hired for the task, flaunted the achievement as the product of purely Mexican engineering and even framed it as a continuation of ancient autochthonous technology. Moving the stone was animated by the engineers and other participants' fervent nationalism whereby homegrown technologies, materials, and labor were instrumentalized, even if this was not entirely the case. Participating in the stone's relocation became directly linked to consolidating the nation, using engineering and local technology to produce Mexico as an integral territory and homogenous political formation.

The contract for the trailer truck was given to the Mexican firm Trailmobile de México, a subsidiary of a US-based manufacturer with access to foreign technology and capital. Even in its Mexican headquarters, the company was heavily reliant on consultants who had prior experience with heavy transport in the United States. These engineers worked for the US truck manufacturer Fontaine Truck Equipment, located in Birmingham, Alabama, known for designing low-bed trailers with extreme resistance for the United States army. Fontaine Trucks are to this date the US military and NASA's main suppliers for transporting tanks, fighter planes, and space shuttles. In the 1960s, the company's base in Alabama also immersed the stone's transport in the politics of Mexico's northern neighbor: the low-bed trailer's construction was affected by the civil rights movement underway in the United States. Since Mexican steel mills didn't have the capacity to make beams of the size required for the vehicle, these were manufactured in workshops in Birmingham. Ramírez Vázquez told me that the stone's relocation was almost canceled because of the escalating violence and strikes that had closed down factories in the Southern United States. Yet the low-bed trailer had to be ready in time for the museum's opening in September 1964, commemorating the anniversary of Mexican independence. A devout Catholic, the architect appealed to a contact in the Mexican church who in turn asked Martin Luther King Jr. to intervene and guarantee the beams' timely completion on behalf of President López Mateos.[10]

The engineer assigned to oversee the design for the beams and the low-bed was Salvador García Ramos, the production manager for Trailmobile de México.

Like Tovar Santana, he, too, published his own book, *Tlaloc: El dios de la Lluvia* (Tlaloc: The god of rain), in which, like Enrique del Valle Prieto, he described his participation in "one of the most important accomplishments of recent history" (1982, 12). He narrated how he became involved in the project, mostly drawn by the engineering challenge of "historical proportions":

> One day, toward the end of 1962, the company's general manager, the engineer Augusto de Yta, called me into his office, and said to me "Salvador, how would you like to design and make the biggest low-bed trailer of its kind anywhere in the world?" For a moment, as we chatted, a series of questions came to my mind: What capacity would the largest trailer in the world have? What was it going to transport? Just a few months before, we had designed a trailer that was able to carry 120 tons for a project undertaken by the Comisión Federal de Electricidad. (1982, 14–15)

Trailmobile was one of the preferred companies hired by the Mexican government for its public works in the 1960s, especially related to transforming water into energy to power the country's development. García Ramos was likely referring to the Infiernillo dam underway in southern Mexico, another product of the "Mexican Miracle" that funded massive infrastructure projects requiring the transport of heavy turbines to distant and inaccessible areas.

The engineer was lured by the possibility of breaking new technical ground and by how making a truck that would carry the stone to the museum would also ensure the company's reputation: "The project itself was fantastic, first because of the prestige it meant for the company to have been the first to build the biggest trailer in the world; and secondly because, for both the technical and administrative personnel, it was an honor and an opportunity to collaborate on this magnificent event; and finally, for me, as a technician, it meant the satisfaction of designing and directing the making of something so special and interesting" (1982, 15). He understood and relished the stakes: "The trailer could by no means fail. The reader has to imagine what would happen if the trailer was destroyed or simply failed on its way to the museum. Yet, what animated the whole process was our desire to take advantage of the opportunity to demonstrate Mexico's technological development, our ingenuity and capacity to succeed in such important endeavors!" (1982, 15). García Ramos claimed that the trailer was entirely designed and made in Mexico, integrally manufactured and assembled on Mexican soil in Trailmobile's headquarters in San Pedro Xalostoc, Texcoco, not far from Coatlinchan. He never mentioned Birmingham or its steel mills. The whole procedure was framed as an operation proving that technological futures could be made in Mexico. The low-bed in

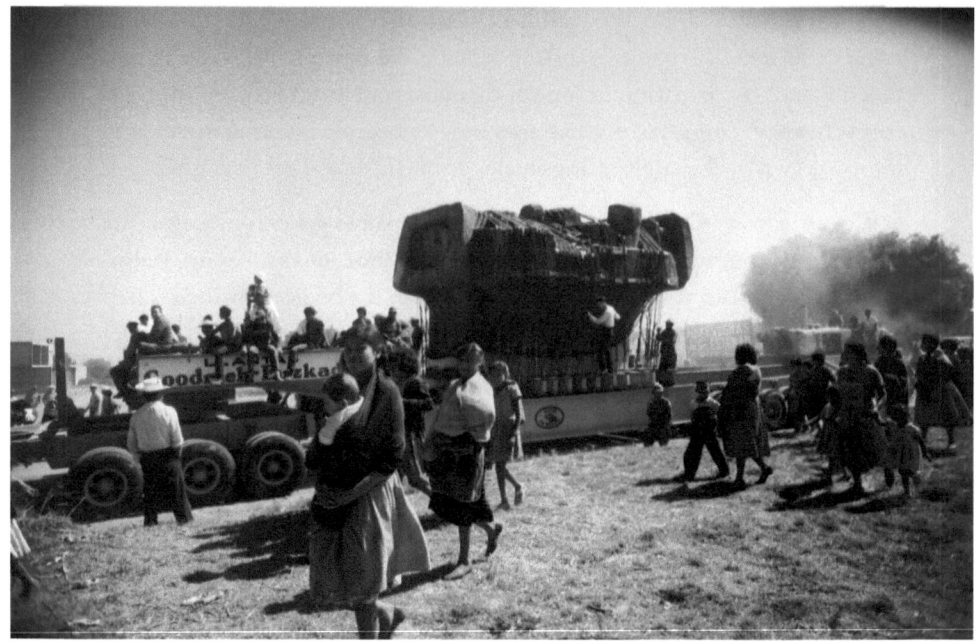

FIGURE 2.7. Low-bed with "Hecho en Mexico" logo carrying the stone, 1964. "Tlaloc-Imagen 7," HMA/CRI/19055, Fondo Archivo Fotográfico Hermanos Mayo, Archivo General de la Nación.

fact sported "Made in Mexico" logos all over its US-manufactured steel beams (figure 2.7).

Making the vehicle in Mexico had other costs and obstacles. For example, it had to abide by Mexican laws that specified the weight that could be carried on Mexican highways and streets. For the engineers, these requirements were a hassle and raised the cost of the entire endeavor. Despite their US colleagues' recommendation to build a trailer with far fewer tires, they had to design ways to distribute the weight evenly to fit these limitations using a dolly and many more tires than might otherwise have been necessary. García Ramos offered the following specifications:

> The low-bed trailer was made up of 3 longitudinal type I loading joists, with a 92 cm slope and a 42 cm rim; 6 sections of U-shaped specially pre-fabricated steel, placed upside down and longitudinally; 18 transversal beams to distribute the load, welded to the joists and longitudinal sections. The suspensions were the most important mechanical parts; there

were 18 pivot-type suspensions total, made out of special steel, each with both longitudinal and transversal workings. It had 36 double tires, made up of 72 tires of 11 × 20–14 layers. The dolly also had a special mechanical part, a rotating round table, attached to the trailer with a tension rod, as well as the capacity to turn 180 degrees so that it could turn both left and right without any obstruction. The rotating table had both longitudinal and transversal movement for shock absorption and the ability to adapt to the terrain. It is important to understand that a rigid structure in motion that is carrying a heavy load can easily break. This is why it was necessary to give the trailer as much flexibility and resistance as needed. Once the dolly was attached to the trailer, the whole measured a total of 20.3 meters. (1982, 25)

I quote at length to show how, like Tovar Santana, García Ramos used figures and technical details to explain why certain elements were used that were not necessarily the most effective but would abide by Mexican regulations.

Most of the reporters who covered the relocation's progress zoomed in on one specific figure that marked public opinion as one of the most cited features of the entire process: the seventy-two tires that rolled the stone from the ravine in Coatlinchan to Mexico City. The tires were provided by Goodrich-Euzkadi, a Mexico-based company founded by Basque immigrants who teamed up with B.F. Goodrich to produce the first Mexican-made rubber tires in the 1930s. The newspapers that covered the transfer mentioned Goodrich-Euzkadi and published photographs of the trailer in motion sporting the company logo. With this campaign, the company hoped to show that its tires—Mexican tires, made with Mexican rubber and B.F. Goodrich's engineering expertise—could transport the most precious and heaviest of loads: a 167-ton ancient rain deity.

Once the stone was repositioned in front of the museum, the company, whose all-time slogan was "Duran más" (Long-lasting), advertised its tires with images of the ancient stone on the low-bed under the heading "The past arrived in the present via Goodrich Euzkadi" and a text explaining that the transfer was successfully undertaken with the same "security and ease with which Goodrich Euzkadi tires transport you on all of Mexico's roadways" (figure 2.8). The campaign was run by a Mexican advertising agency, Edelman and Associates. One of Edelman's top executives told me that the idea was to show that "if our tires can move Tlaloc, they can move you!"[11]

One of B. F. Goodrich's executives based in the United States came to Mexico specifically to cover the event and publicize the company's participation. Under the heading "Tlaloc to Wall Street," the company's internal magazine boasted:

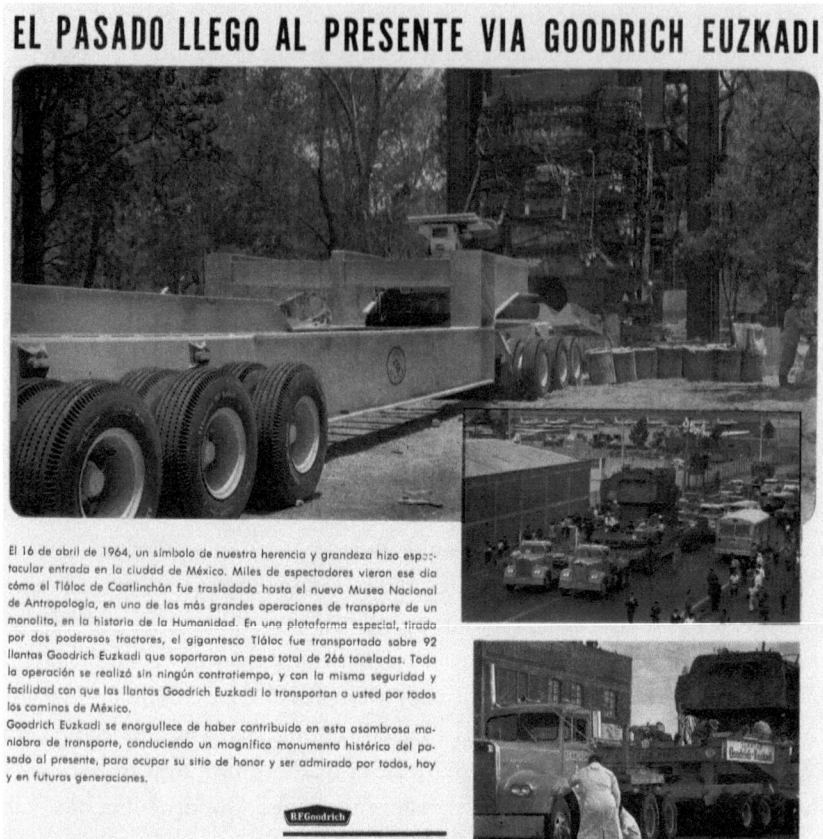

FIGURE 2.8. "El pasado llegó al presente via Goodrich Euzkadi" (The past arrived in the present via Goodrich Euzkadi). Advertisement on the back cover of *Artes de México*, special issue on the Museo Nacional de Antropología, 1965.

"The most modern resources and Goodrich's most advanced technology were used to rescue a 14-century-old Mexican cultural expression. . . . Soon, thanks to Mr. Mentzer, the head of B.F Goodrich Co who came to witness the event, the news will get the attention of Wall Street."[12] The company highlighted how its know-how "rescued" Mexico's ancient and ancestral heritage again in 2004 when, marking the fortieth anniversary of the stone's relocation, Continental AG, the multinational corporation that took over Goodrich-Euzkadi in 1998, commemorated its participation in the historic event in its monthly magazine: "The proven quality of Euzkadi tires guaranteed the safety of the delicate maneuver. And this is how Euzkadi tires contributed to Mexico's development and greatness in a new and significant manner."[13]

Donaciano Suárez was the person who worked on the stone relocation on behalf of Goodrich-Euzkadi. In 2009, in his home in the Polanco neighborhood in Mexico City over a cup of tea and delicious cake, he proudly recounted his participation in the feat and attributed Euzkadi's involvement to his own divine-inspired idea. "God illuminated me," he said. "And so, when Ramírez Vázquez came to the company asking merely for an estimate of how much the tires for the trailer truck would cost, I took a huge risk. I said, look, arquitecto, the tires will not cost you a cent." According to Suárez, the architect was very astute: "So he stared at me and asked, in exchange for what? . . . I wasn't as smart. And then, out of divine illumination, I said, in exchange for the publicity!" Suárez had serious doubts that the architect, but also the company's executives, would agree. He finished the story with glee: "By the time I left his office, my legs were shaking. I thought I would get fired, but luckily my boss thought it was a good idea." Suárez was then put in charge of Euzkadi's new client, coordinating a team of technicians specializing in pneumatics and engineers working for Trailmobile and CUFAC. Like the architect and the engineers, he kept his own mementos of his participation: a large-format photo book with the title "Operación Coatlinchan," the official code name for the procedure, written in funky sixties psychedelic typographic design.[14]

Pointing to one of the photographs showing the low-bed trailer surrounded by a team of engineers wearing hard hats, he exclaimed: "That's me! There! Telling everybody what to do! Making sure the vehicle could easily roll on the dirt road and then on the highway pavement. It was marvelous! Beautiful! I headed the entire procession and there were electricians that disconnected and connected telephone lines and electric cables as we passed. It really was a thing of beauty!" Echoing del Valle Prieto's emphasis on the aesthetics of the maneuver, for Suárez, moving the ancient stone was both a technical and ritual performance: a "procession," a "thing of beauty." Suárez kept an archive with news clippings and articles published by the company magazine over the years commemorating Euzkadi's participation in the historic transfer. His most treasured possession was the large album with printed photographs of the event that the company had made as a Christmas present for its most valued customers. The large glossy images showed Euzkadi technicians hard at work, testing and checking the tires. Like the low-bed, all Euzkadi personnel wore armbands sporting a "Made in Mexico" logo. As he flipped through the album, Suárez showed me one picture of himself crouched next to the tires (figure 2.9). He confessed: "things didn't go as smoothly as planned behind the scenes." The

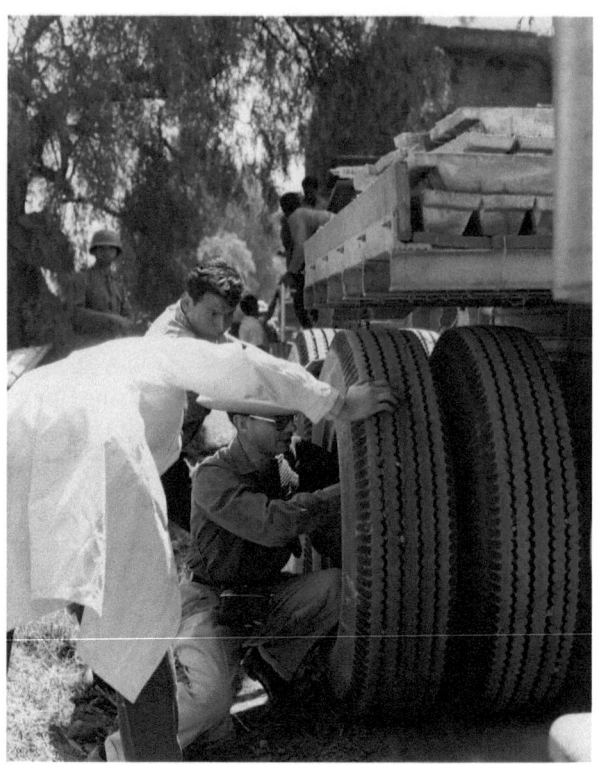

trailer had to stop on several occasions because of miscalculations and technical glitches. He had never told anyone because the company didn't want the
press to find out, but he had even had to change a flat tire!

Many of the people who personally witnessed the stone's relocation recall
the tires and assumed that they were purpose-made. The advertising campaign
that placed Goodrich-Euzkadi at the forefront of the endeavor and the media's
fascination with the vehicle that required so many tires transformed the ordinary rubber pneumatics into valuable artifacts, despite the company's insistence
that these were just ordinary tires. For Goodrich-Euzkadi, this was in fact the
whole point of the campaign: their run-of-the-mill tires, accessible to any con-
sumer, could move an ancient deity and the heaviest and largest pre-Hispanic
monument in the Americas. During our conversation, Suárez made fun of this.
He was also concerned about the data. "For some reason the press kept insisting that there were seventy-two tires and even Ramírez Vázquez has written
that there were seventy-two, but there were ninety-two! I should know—I put
them there." He pointed to several advertisements and documents in his archives that had, like the advertisement in figure 2.8, the correct figure in print.

He laughed. "There was even this big-deal truck entrepreneur who was set on buying all ninety-two tires from me because the guy thought that they were somehow special, that they had been made solely for the historic maneuver." Suárez's face lit up telling this story. "But the tires were just standard tires; there was nothing special about them. There were just a lot of them! If only I had pretended and sold them, I would now be a rich man!"

Goodrich-Euzkadi was not the only company that spun the fact that the stone's relocation was the product of quality Mexican technology and engineering for its own publicity. Trailmobile de México published ads in trade magazines saying, "Our company feels great pride to have manufactured the rig that made it possible for Tlaloc, God of rain and of fecundity, to now be present in all his majestic grandeur next to the new Museo Nacional de Antropología, the temple of our cultures and legitimate pride of Mexico." Meanwhile, Delta Industrial Mexicana (DIMSA), a company that manufactured copper valves used to build the museum's sanitary installations, printed ads saying its products were "destined to endure, just like this great work," alongside images of its valves juxtaposed with the stone. Other companies, unrelated to construction, like the Mexican watch brand Haste, proclaimed, "Mexico's time is progress and Haste is Mexico's time," alongside their Fairline wristwatch covering part of the stone, with Mexico City's modern skyline as a backdrop (figure 2.10). Briomica, a company that manufactured decorative plastic laminates, publicized that its products were as solid and long-lasting as the ancient sculpture and the means developed to transport it to Mexico City. Ford made an ad for its luxurious top-of-the-line Galaxie car, with a sharply dressed couple posing by the car in front of the stone standing upright on Reforma.

Ultimately, the stone's relocation was made possible by a vehicle made up of different elements: steel beams manufactured in Alabama, a dolly made in San Pedro Xalostoc, truck motors designed to move the contraption with their potent 320 horsepower provided by a US military supplier, ninety-two tires made by a Basque company with a local Mexican franchise, and the stone itself, identified as a pre-Hispanic rain deity recast as national patrimonio, strapped onto the low-bed and imprinted on its cement bed. I was able to piece together how this assemblage came into being through the stories told by the engineers and technicians who provided the details and shared how the experience impacted their lives. I met most of them through chance encounters and contacts: Pedro Ramírez Vázquez's secretary had kept Enrique del Valle Prieto's contact information and shared it with me, Tovar Santana answered an email I sent to his faculty email at a public university, a friend of a friend happened to know Donaciano Suárez. Some of the procedure's participants had also considered

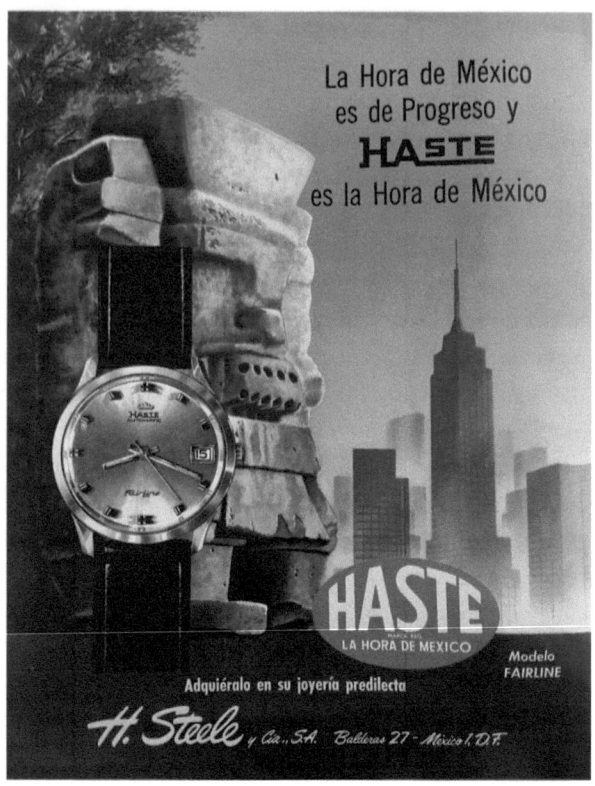

FIGURE 2.10. "La Hora de México es de Progreso y Haste es la Hora de México" (Mexico's time is progress, and Haste is Mexico's time). Advertisement, *Life* magazine, 1965.

their work and insider knowledge interesting enough to write their memoirs or even publish books on the process. My research also coincided with the advent of social media, so, when a group of Mexico City photography and history enthusiasts who ran the Facebook page La Ciudad de México en el Tiempo published a photograph of the stone's relocation, I was able to follow the comments stream, in which Noe Rivas, also an archaeology enthusiast, wrote a post about his uncle, Nemesio Becerril Rivas, one of the two truck drivers who had driven the vehicle. In an email exchange following the post, he told me that his uncle was eighty-four and eager to talk about his participation in "el traslado," so I scheduled a visit to San José el Vidrio, a small town in the Estado de México, about two hours from Mexico City, where his uncle, who normally lived in Querétaro, spent time visiting his family.

Becerril Rivas sat down on an elegant wooden chair next to the fireplace in his family's living room. He lamented: "Everyone remembers the day Tlaloc arrived in the city, and the rain, and the rain, but who remembers the people who actually brought him there? It was me! I was the one who drove the truck, well, the low boy, that's the right name for the *plataforma* . . . well, me and Alfredo Rocha, who was the other driver hired for the job." He mentioned several names: Miguel Quintana had hired him; Mr. Guillermo Vildosola was the manager at Kenworth, the company that made the truck cabs; and several engineers participated—Carlos Lazo, Jorge Ronda, Manuel Rocha Alfaro, and Héctor and Luis, whose last names he couldn't recall. He hadn't kept in touch with any of these people and thought that, since many were older than him at the time, most were probably no longer alive. "When we arrived in front of the National Palace, they were taking photos of everything, but not of us, but in the end, by chance, I appear in some of them. It was totally silly—they made us wear hard hats, overalls and boots, and god knows what gear . . . but we were just driving a truck!"[15]

He went on to describe that, even though he had driven many trucks, it took him a little while to get used to the custom-made transmissions and to feel confident maneuvering the trailer. "Yes, it rained heavily that day, but the hardest part was navigating the city streets. . . . We had to cross the railway tracks near the Tecamac hospital and that took many hours, and then there was that iron bridge near Ecatepec where we had to stop and lower the air in the tires so that they could handle it. And then the rain, boy did it rain!" He paused and kept silent for a while. When I pressed him to say more about how being a part of the event had affected him, Becerril Rivas kept going back to stories of his life, getting to know every corner of the country through years of driving trucks all over Mexico: Tijuana, Zacatecas, Querétaro, Acapulco. I insisted and asked: "Yes, but how was driving *this* truck different from the other trucks you drove?" He answered with conviction, "Nah, the truck was like any other truck. Tlaloc was just another load, just a damn heavy one."

Once it was used for the stone's relocation, the "Made in Mexico" truck that Becerril Rivas had driven was allegedly divided and repurposed as several vehicles to serve in new infrastructure projects. Donaciano Suárez told me that the trailer, including "his" tires, was taken apart and made into four separate low-beds that were given to the Ministry of Education, specifically to build schools for the Comité Administrador del Programa Federal de Construcción de Escuelas (CAPFCE, National Program for School Construction Administrative Committee), the agency that Ramírez Vázquez happened to be in charge of. Ramírez Vázquez, on the other hand, insisted that the cost of the whole procedure was compensated to the Mexican people because the trailer was taken apart and made into three low-beds sent to move heavy turbines for the Infiernillo dam in the Balsas River that would produce 1,120 megawatts of electrical charge distributed all over the country. Whether it was reused to build dams or schools, the custom-built vehicle was made to be disassembled and repurposed in a way that multiplied its use for the heavy transport and infrastructural needs of the Mexican state.[16] For the engineers, technicians, and Ramírez Vázquez himself, moving the stone was a nationalist enterprise because it was about rescuing an object of national significance but also because it was inscribed in a larger project to develop and connect remote areas through public works and, specifically, dams built to generate electricity that could service the whole population.

Tlaloc Anew

The connection between 1960s infrastructure projects using state-of-the-art engineering and ancient Mesoamerican civilizations was a constant reference in how the Mexican state imagined its interventions at the time. Most notably, public works were imagined as giving continuity to technological endeavors designed by pre-Hispanic societies to transform the environment and control the elements. These pioneering hydraulic technologies had rerouted water from rivers and lakes, using canals and aqueducts as well as elaborate sewage systems, as central components of both urban planning and expanding empire.[17] The Secretaría de Recursos Hidráulicos (Ministry of Waterworks), under López Mateos, set up its work as a continuation of these hydraulic endeavors that had been truncated by conquest. In drawing these parallels, the 1960s Mexican state connected contemporary Mexican engineering to its pre-Hispanic equivalents, while also reinvesting ancient deities—namely Tlaloc—as the patron of its efforts.

Alfredo E. Colin Varela, an engineer who worked for the Secretaria de Recursos Hidráulicos, published a monograph the same year as the stone's relocation in which he dwelled on the connection between the ancient past and Mexico's progress-oriented present. He explicitly tied the regime's hydraulic policy to the realm of the supernatural and the power of ancient water deities through what he described as a common "hydraulic imaginary." The cover of *Tláloc, López Mateos y la SRH* (1964) featured a gold emblazoned representation of the pre-Hispanic water deity taken from one of the murals from the Tepantitla complex in Teotihuacan. The book opened with an image of the Coatlinchan stone still in situ and a "Mythological Semblance" in which the author extended the power of Tlaloc, the ancient rain deity, into the Mexican postrevolutionary state's ambitious waterworks as a means for progress and social change: "How real and human are these concepts from ancient Mexico! And how contemporary these preoccupations and desires when we understand the revolutionary government's interest in forcefully and valiantly solving the chronic problems faced by the people to guarantee their livelihood through agriculture. . . . This is why we can establish an interesting likeness between the figure of Tlaloc for pre-Hispanic cultures, and modern science and technology that are fighting to control the elements to make them docile and subservient to the needs of all mankind" (Colin Varela 1964, 9). The engineer imagined continuity between the ancient societies' cult to Tlaloc and the deity's contemporary iterations that took the shape of hydraulic engineers, pipes, and dams, all working together for the nation's prosperity:

> The monuments that were built in honor of Tlaloc have, in contemporary Mexico, become gigantic structures erected with pride to dominate water's fury and tame it according to the will of men. The destructive force of lighting has been transformed, thanks to the most advanced technology, into a useful force for humanity. Hydraulic engineering, like a modern Tlaloc, will give peasants the abundance and prosperity they have so desired. This new Tlaloc, as powerful as the one from Aztec mythology, is represented by an enormous army of men and machines at his service who work incessantly to win the battle for the "greatness of Mexico." (1964, 10)

Colin Varela's image of Tlaloc as an alloy of men and machines working together to tame water and make it available for the Mexican people recalls a project completed only a few years prior that brought together Mexico's most famous muralist, Diego Rivera, and the engineers who in the 1950s designed a complex system of hydraulic infrastructures to channel water from the Lerma River Basin to ever-expanding Mexico City. Not far from the Museo Nacional de Antropología, Rivera sculpted another modern Tlaloc to receive these waters and distribute them to a thirsty populace. The work, designed by Rivera using different color rocks and mosaic, lies inside a fountain just outside the Dolores sump (Cárcamo de Dolores) that was completed in 1951, after almost a decade of construction work. In an underwater mural, *El agua, origen de la vida* (Water, origin of life), painted inside the reservoir where this water was stored and distributed, Rivera animated the mighty pre-Hispanic deity using perspective to paint two enormous hands providing water, and life, to all Mexicans. These hands were painted next to the engineers and planners who designed the pumping sump and the system that would bring water to the city as well as disinfect it to make it potable. Together, Tlaloc and the engineers materialized the work of the Mexican welfare state and its redistributive policies: water was brought equally to quench the thirst of the bourgeoisie, the urban poor, and the campesinos whose fields provided nourishment for the country as a whole.[18] Rivera and Colin Varela's rendition of Tlaloc as the patron of Mexican waterworks coincides with the way the postrevolutionary government imagined itself as a life-giving force that would remedy Mexico's economic and social inequalities through agrarian reform and water infrastructures.[19]

As then secretary of education and the museum's prime instigator, Jaime Torres Bodet, emphasized in his memoir, the stone's relocation also reinstated Tlaloc as the agent of Mexico's progress and forward-looking modernity where water and its uses were being repurposed to ensure development: "Omnipotent Tlaloc: that great stone mass, that pre-Hispanic deity, that ruler of rain.... From now on, few eyes can look upon it with indifference or disdain. Tlaloc reigns over Chapultepec and presides over the great cultural spectacle that is the new Museo Nacional de Antropología, upright and most dignified" (Secretaría de Educación Pública 1964, 380). The politics and triumphant undertones of the stone's relocation became evident as Tlaloc seeped into the realm of the supernatural. The torrential downpour that accompanied the stone's entry into Mexico City is to this day remembered as the Mexican state's success reawakening the deity's meteorological powers, aligning Tlaloc with its own work to control the elements. The Coatlinchan stone's relocation became the perfect event to disseminate the importance and ingenuity of Mexican engineering when unforeseen events were tackled in the spur of the moment by Mexico's most competent technicians. Its meteorological powers as a water deity were time and again referenced, many times by the very engineers who had been to Coatlinchan along with Ramírez Vázquez and asked to convince town residents that it was not a rain-making deity. Ironically, these very engineers kept coming back to the stone's identity and its powers over the elements that had to be cared for but also assuaged and appeased. These engineers all highlighted the downpour that Nemesio Rivas Becerril recalled and that greeted the convoy as the low-bed trailer arrived in Mexico City. The following day, the Mexican press stressed that the two events—the stone's relocation and the rain—were cause and effect. When I last spoke to del Valle Prieto in 2017, he, too, hinted at the stone's supernatural qualities, namely its ability to control rainfall. Suspecting I would be incredulous, he said, "I know what you are thinking, but I swear to you, it rained in front and behind Tlaloc. Not one drop touched Tlaloc!"

In the months that followed the stone's relocation, and under the auspices of the Secretaría de Educación Pública (SEP, Mexican Ministry of Education), the popular comic book series *Aventuras de la vida real* (Real-life adventures) published *Una deidad en el asfalto* (A deity on the asphalt) (Cardona Peña 1964).[20] The issue told the story of the stone's relocation, with special emphasis on the engineering details involved in planning the procedure, and on its quasi-supernatural meteorological effects (figure 2.11). The comic book devoted several pages to townspeople's efforts to keep the stone in Coatlinchan but framed

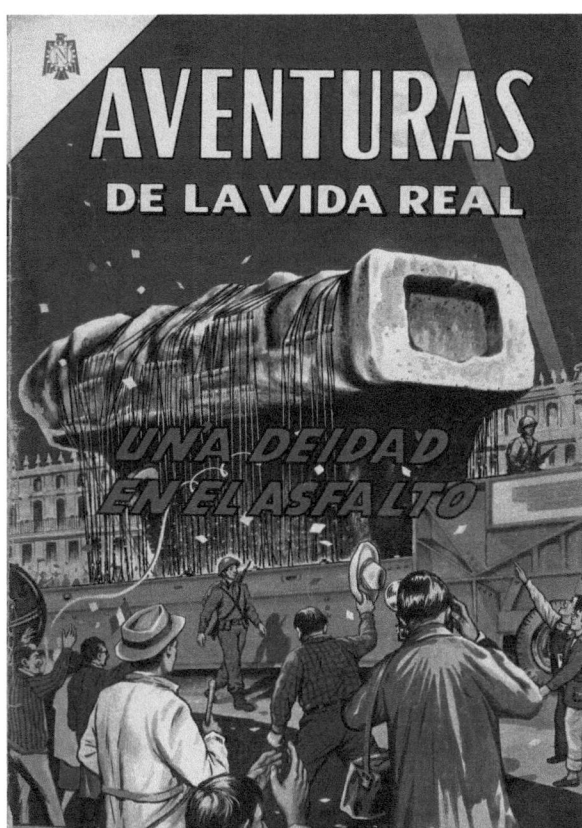

FIGURE 2.11. Cover of *Una deidad en el asfalto* (A deity on the asphalt), in the series *Aventuras de la vida real*, 1964.

these as the result of deep-seated, almost irrational, or at best misplaced beliefs in the stone's rainmaking powers. Townspeople represented early in the narrative as peaceful campesinos wearing white manta clothes and straw hats as they nonchalantly drove their tractors and worked the land, watching from a distance as the engineers prepared the stone for its transport, suddenly became dark and sinister, with bulging angry red eyes and racialized, almost grotesque features and expressions. They were portrayed using sickles and other agricultural tools to violently break the steel cables that fastened the stone to the lowbed, smashing the truck's windshield and puncturing its well-advertised tires (figures 2.12 and 2.13).

The genre of the comic book, circulating broadly in Mexico at the time and often used by state dependencies as a pedagogical tool (Rubenstein 1998), was used to justify the military's intervention as a civilizing mission: state officials, including architects and engineers but also the local priest and a man in military uniform, were shown going to Coatlinchan to negotiate with town residents

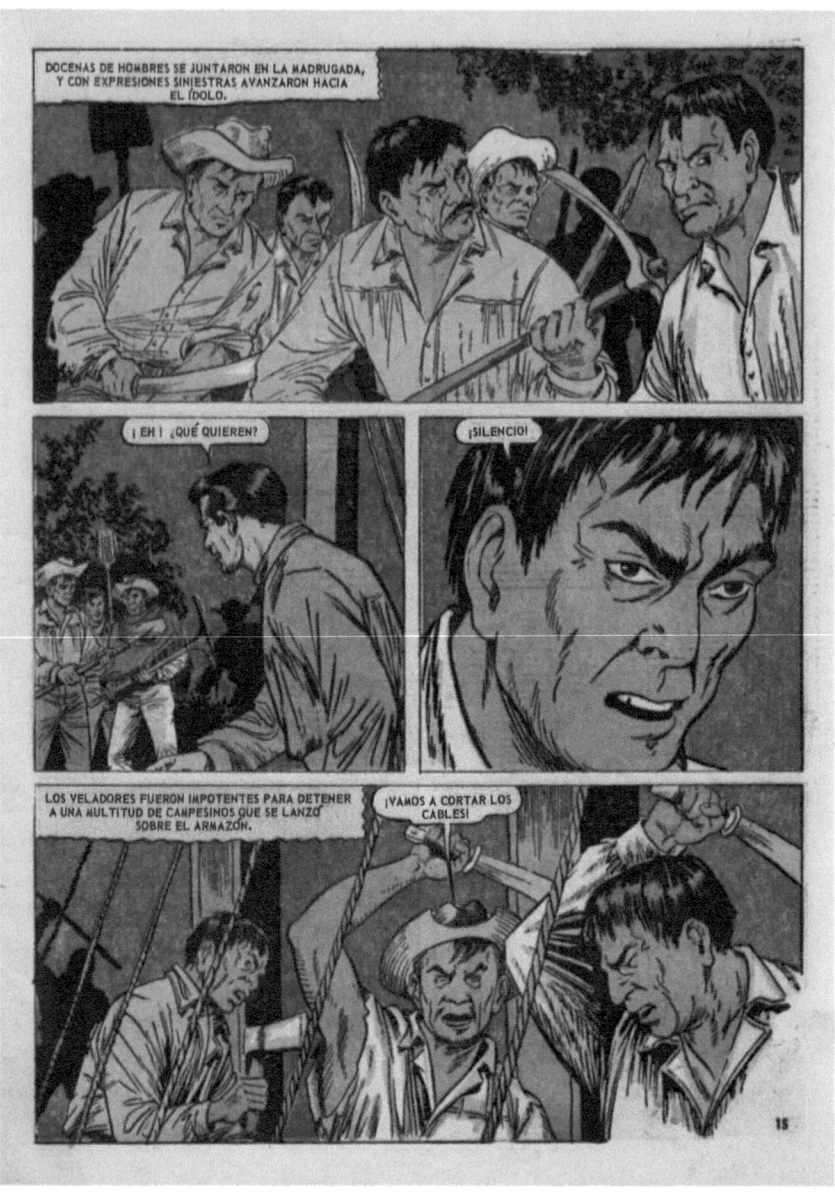

FIGURE 2.12. *Una deidad en el asfalto*, 1964, p. 15.

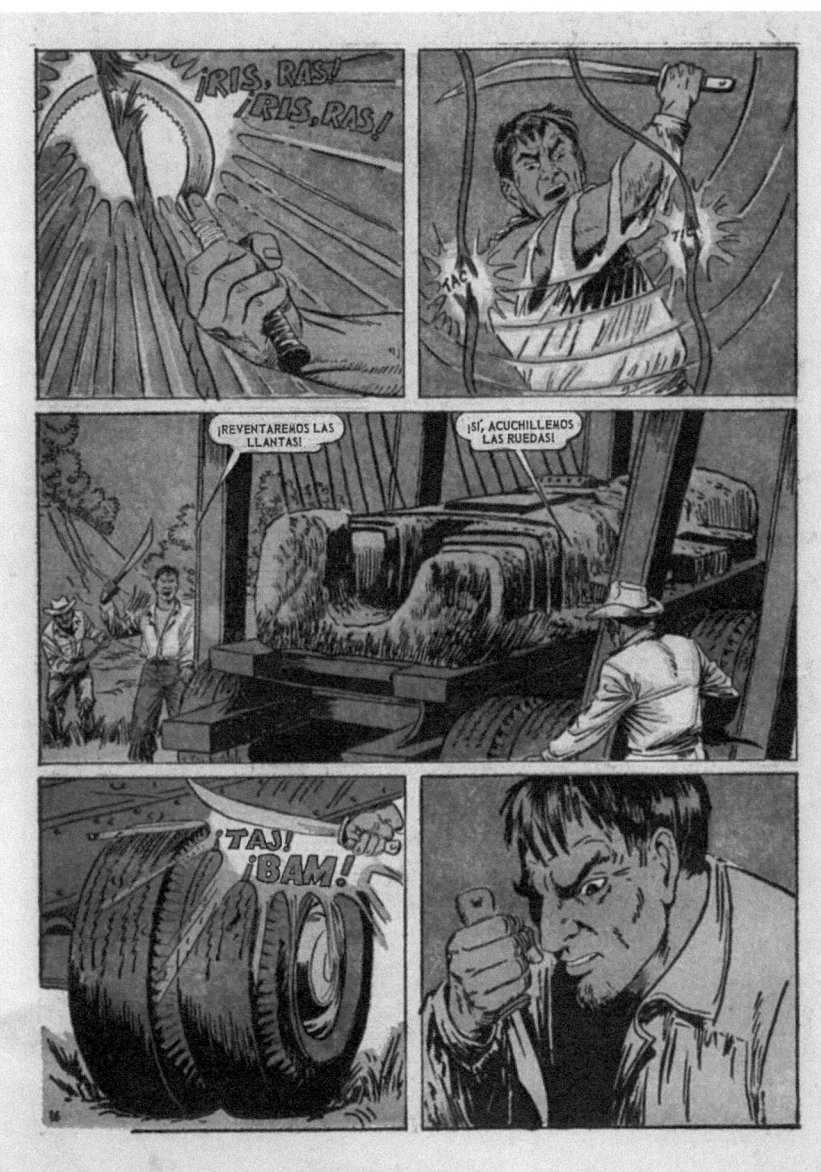

FIGURE 2.13. *Una deidad en el asfalto*, 1964, p. 16.

FIGURE 2.14. Cover of ¡Siempre! showing the stone with a sign identifying it as "Tlaloc (?), God of Rain," June 3, 1964. Because the stone has not been set upright, the god has not provided relief from heat and drought.

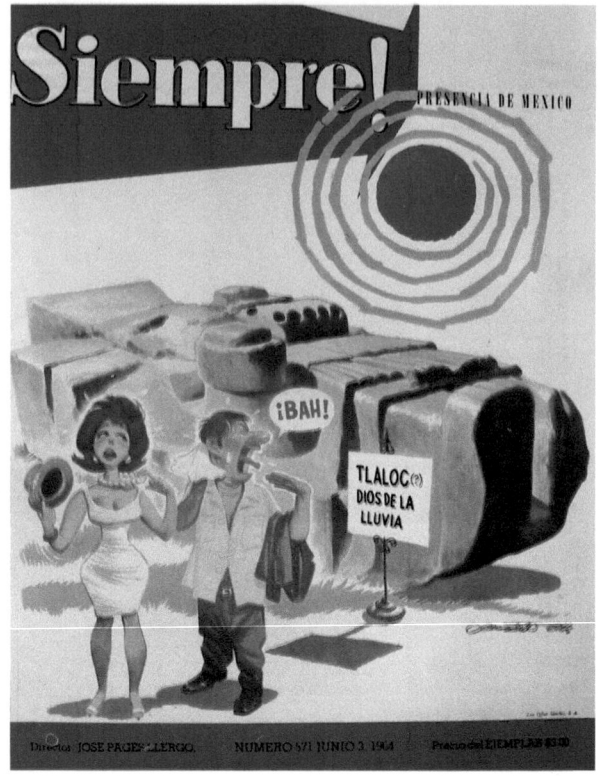

and convince them that the stone was not a deity with powers to be revered or feared but a secular monument that belonged in a museum. According to the comic book, most of the town ultimately understood the stone's "national value" and agreed to the transfer. Town residents were portrayed watching sadly as the stone left Coatlinchan, while a woman, dressed in 1960s fashion, representing Mexican modernity, celebrated the stone's relocation with confetti. Ironically, the comic ended with a sequence attributing the torrential downpour on the day of the stone's arrival to the deity's actions as the incarnation of the all-powerful Aztec storm god, Tlaloc.[21]

The overall sense that the stone's relocation was responsible for rainfall, or the lack thereof, endured for several months after its arrival in the city when a terrible drought affected the areas surrounding the capital. Water scarcity was attributed to the deity's wrath because it had taken several months for engineers to raise the stone to its new standing position, assumed to be the position intended by its makers and desired by the deity it represented (figure 2.14). The procedure took time because the engineers had to dismantle and reinstall the

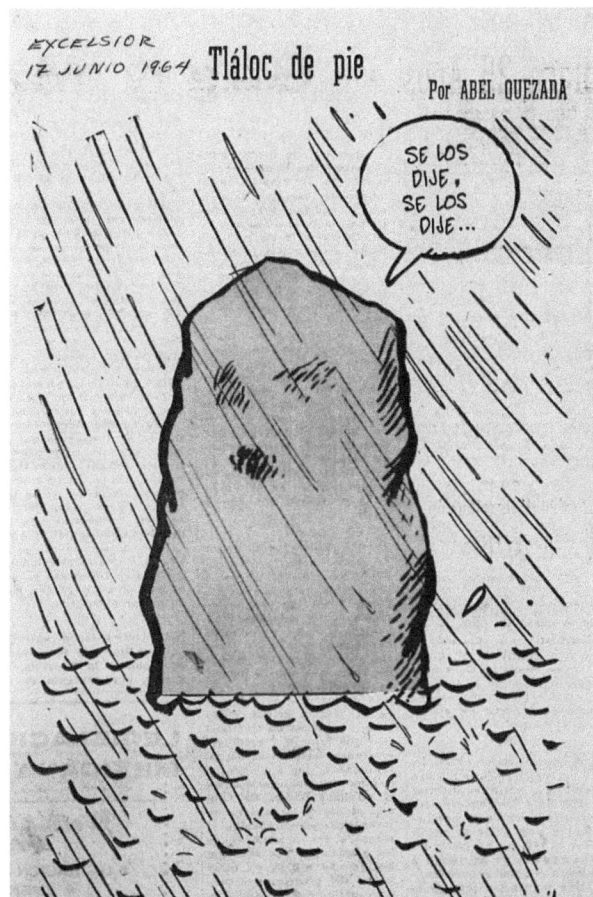

FIGURE 2.15. Abel Quezada, "Tláloc de pie" (Tlaloc standing), *Excelsior*, June 17, 1964.

same steel structure that had carried it from Coatlinchan and repurpose it with a crane to raise it in front of the museum. The end of the drought in mid-June coincided with the moment when the stone was finally placed upright. Once again, newspapers depicted the ancient water deity, finally appeased, rewarding Mexico City with the precious liquid. In a cartoon by Abel Quezada, a "standing Tlaloc" hidden under a rain cover tells passersby: "I told you so, I told you so ..." (figure 2.15).

Many of the engineers who worked on the stone's relocation also participated in building replicas for some of the most important dams being built all over Mexico. These replicas were designed as monuments commemorating the completion of the Mexican state's ambitious public works and honoring the country's ancestral patrimonio. They were strategically placed to guarantee abundant water for the dams' reservoirs that would in turn move the turbines and generate power. Many of these dams were located on the border with the United States, geographically removed from a Mesoamerican context, transporting the emblematic water deity as well as the tentacles of the modern Mexican state from the center to the northern periphery. These replicas connected all of Mexico through a single patrimonio but more importantly through a common belief in the powers of progress, technology, and public infrastructure brought to life by Tlaloc's proven ability to control water.

In 1960, President López Mateos signed an agreement with US President Dwight D. Eisenhower to build a massive dam on the US-Mexico border. In 1969, the Presa de la Amistad was built to seal the friendly relations between the two nations. A reproduction of the stone that had been relocated to the Museo Nacional de Antropología only five years earlier was built on the reservoir of the dam in Ciudad Acuña, Coahuila. This replica was made using many stones fixed together to reproduce the monument's imposing shape and size with a caption that identified it as "Tlaloc, God of Rain." Designed to commemorate the dam's completion, the replica was also a means to propitiate water for the massive embankment dam (figure 2.16).[22]

The replica in Coahuila was not an isolated incident. Guillermo Garnier Villagrán, an engineer who worked for the Comisión del Río Fuerte, was commissioned in 1966 to make a monumental replica of the stone carving for another dam project underway since 1953, the Presa Miguel Hidalgo in the northern state of Sinaloa. He designed the replica to stand on top of a new wall built to contain the dam. In an interview for a local magazine, the engineer explained that during its construction, torrential rains halted the wall's completion. The engineer in charge of the dam called Garnier in and said: "Please put a hood on that creature of yours so that it will stop raining." Garnier obeyed his boss and covered the monument with a huge plastic tarp. The engineer recounted that the rains immediately stopped and his team was able to complete the wall.[23] In both Sinaloa and Coahuila, replicas were built to signal projects pioneering engineering technology, yet their makers did not overlook that the deity they were replicating was associated with the precious liquid whose power they sought to harness. These replicas brought to life the López Mateos regime's "hydraulic imaginary" enunciated by Colin Varela and its investment in water infrastructure and dams as almost mystical and divine interventions.

Along the same lines, the Mexican comedian Cantinflas produced a 1970s animation in which his emblematic character, Amigo, calls upon Tlaloc's renovated rain-making powers outside the museum as a defense mechanism against US imperialism.[24] After a North American tourist mocks a tour guide's explanation that the stone monument personifies the ancient rain deity Tlaloc, Amigo

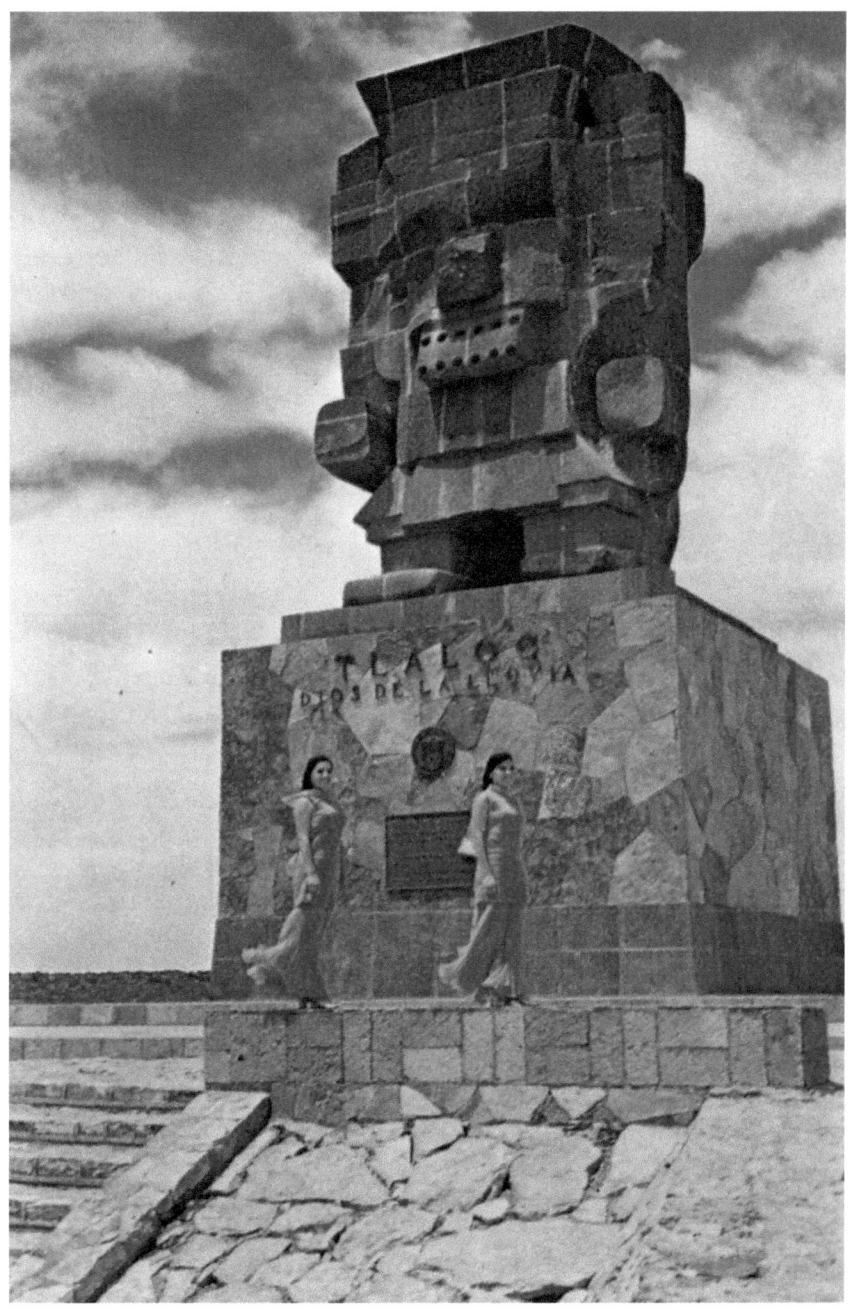

FIGURE 2.16. Postcard from Presa de la Amistad dam, 1960s.

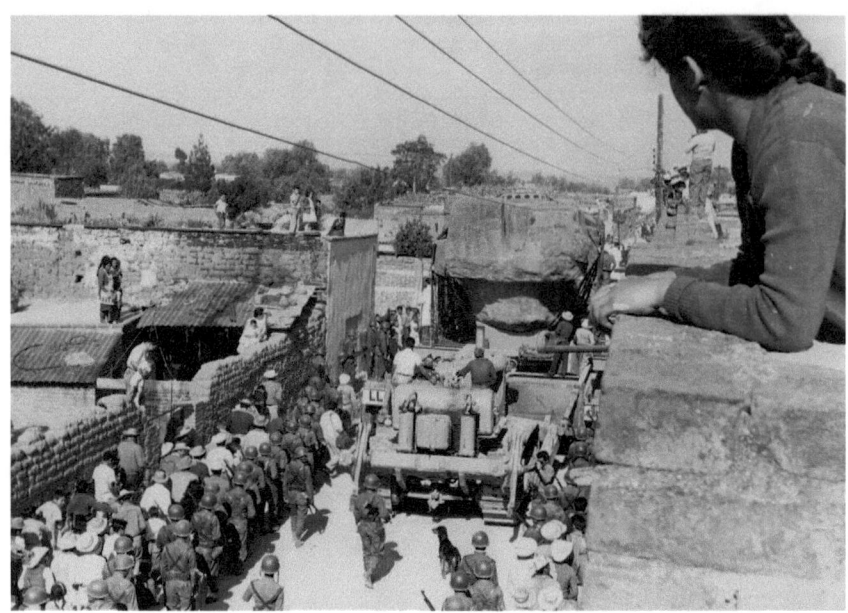

FIGURE 2.17. Leaving Coatlinchan, April 16, 1964. Photograph by Prometeo Courtesy of Acervo Arquitecto Pedro Ramírez Vázquez.

asks the deity to show him otherwise. The earth begins to shake—more telluric activity!—and the deity comes to life, gushing water from its mouth, drenching the tourist. Amigo, lying playfully on the rim of the fountain, pokes fun at American popular culture, referencing a mainstream film: "So, you didn't believe, Chiquito? How did it go for you 'Singing in the Rain'?" As these examples show, the stone from Coatlinchan was made into a modern-day Tlaloc, available for extraction as well as replication as a stand-in for the Mexican state's power over water, while consolidating the nation and guaranteeing its progress. However, creating this new and invigorated Tlaloc was premised on state-enforced violence and theft. Only a few months before the stone's relocation, the same national newspapers that presented the transfer so triumphantly and indulged its rain-making abilities had reported on the state's failed attempt to remove the stone from Coatlinchan due to community resistance. On February 22, as the trailer arrived on schedule in Coatlinchan to take the stone away, town residents sabotaged the procedure, throwing rocks at its windshields, puncturing its tires, and filling its gasoline tanks with dirt. They stormed the site where the stone hung from the hammock-like steel structure and cast it down to the ground. The state responded by sending the military to quash the rebellion and placed the town under surveillance, imposing a strict curfew for several months. Engineers returned to Coatlinchan, this time setting up camp in the ravine with a round-the-clock military presence as they worked to raise the stone anew and ready it once more for transport. In April, the stone was once again separated from the ground and readied for relocation, this time escorted by dozens of armed soldiers. Town residents had little choice but to watch silently from the street or peering from windows and crowded rooftops as the stone was forcefully taken from their territory (figure 2.17).

Decades later, town residents describe this moment as a form of theft, reversing the relationship between the legitimate owners and perpetrators of looting or saqueo stipulated by Mexican patrimonio laws: "It was the morning of April 16th 1964 when the enormous stone made its way down from the ravine, escorted by soldiers and archaeologists who guarded and stroked it like vultures: they were stealing Coatlinchan's greatest treasure."[25]

3

Theft

When town residents tried to stop the stone's removal in February 1964, the newspaper *Novedades* reported on events in Coatlinchan as a "mar de fondo," a kind of groundswell or telluric backlash following a storm or earthquake.[1] The architect of the museum, Pedro Ramírez Vázquez, quoted in the article, borrowed the metaphor of the earth's unpredictable movements to express his surprise at the unfolding of events. He claimed not to understand why town residents had taken action. In his view, they had no legal right to claim the stone since it belonged to the Mexican people as national patrimonio. And, in any case, locals had been consulted and agreed to the stone's extraction, and were even complicit with it, since they provided the labor for its transportation. Ramírez Vázquez underscored that government officials and the museum team had worked to garner their support and that they freely and generously donated it to the museum. The architect considered that town residents should have been thankful and proud to have an object made by their ancestors rescued, preserved, and displayed so prominently on the national stage. He insisted that this particular stone was especially at risk because it was in a remote location where it was exposed both to the elements and to the potentially destructive practices of local residents, whom he believed were ill-equipped to adequately care for it. Like Ramírez Vázquez, museum and government officials framed the stone's relocation as a rescue: placing it under state care and protection in the museum would guarantee its preservation for posterity.

But if the stone belonged unquestionably to the Mexican state and the institutions responsible for patrimonio's care, and at a time of authoritarian one-party rule, why did government officials try to get townspeople's consent and negotiate its extraction at all? And why did they, in turn, need to prove town residents were in agreement with its relocation and willingly gave it up for the museum? And once faced with opposition, why did they decide to send in the army to remove it? These questions show that, even for government officials at the time, the state's jurisdiction over the stone was far from clear. For more than a year prior to the planned relocation, they mobilized legal registers and negotiated with local residents to support their salvage efforts. This work reveals that, despite being cast as a risk factor, town residents' attachment to and custodianship of the stone was, if not fully recognized and valued, at least deemed worthy of consideration. At the same time, legal instruments and the language of gift giving and exchange worked to usurp town residents' sovereignty and delegitimize their claims and actions to keep the stone in Coatlinchan.

Ultimately, the state's preservationist and patrimonial logic that conceived the stone as a separate monument that needed to be preserved in the museum, and that could become the subject of an exchange or even a gift to the nation, clashed with the ways Tlacuaches experienced it as embedded in the town's territory, which they participated in sustaining over many generations. The stone's attachment to Coatlinchan can be reconstructed through their stories, childhood memories, and the traces left by those who experienced it firsthand in the ravine and who, as the years go by, are fewer and fewer. Their narratives challenge the nationalist discourse of the 1960s that framed the stone's relocation as a mere "transfer" undertaken to rescue a monument using homegrown engineering technology. For most Tlacuaches, this was not a rescue, a transfer, or an exchange. The stone's removal was undoubtedly a theft. This and the work done to legitimate it begs the question of what constitutes state theft and how legal discourses of patrimonio and its need for rescue, conservation, and care were deployed to make such theft licit.

During the museum's opening ceremony, Jaime Torres Bodet, then secretary of education, declared it a "Monument of Monuments," highlighting the building's use of contemporary architecture and exhibition design as well as the exemplary quality of its collections, many allegedly rescued in various parts of the country from imminent decay and possible disappearance.[2] This appellation became the title of a feature film produced in tandem with the museum's opening to document its construction.[3] *Monumento de monumentos* (Hernández Bravo 1964) used tight frames and modernist shots to highlight the museum's almost pharaonic proportions, showing hundreds of laborers painstakingly plastering cement, laying steel bars, and installing thousands of artifacts in glass cases.[4] The film underscored the museum's work rescuing collections in the name of conservation. Archaeologists were shown diligently working in digs and museum conservators busy cleaning and mending broken pots and statues, readying them for display, while artists worked on murals, dioramas, models, and sculptural works to enhance the museum's immersive qualities.[5]

Just after the opening credits, the film begins with the Coatlinchan stone's relocation. The narrator, Agustín Barrios Gómez, who was then also Mexico's most famous newscaster, discussed the titanic efforts needed for its transport, as images of various bodies of water and rain immersed the viewer in Mexico's aquatic landscapes ruled by the powers of Tlaloc, the ancient rain deity awoken during the process. The sequence focused on workers using their hands as well as drills and other machinery to excavate the stone, first digging it out of the ground and then lowering it onto the vehicle that would transport it to the museum. Positioned directly on the low-bed, the camera metaphorically received the stone while Barrios Gómez described its extraction as a rescue operation with military undertones:

> For centuries, this enormous third-century monolith slumbered in a ravine. Housing treasures of art in adequate spaces and museums has become a major concern for all peoples. In this context, it was decided that the Tlaloc needed to be transferred to the new and gigantic Museo Nacional de Antropología through what came to be known as "Operación Coatlinchan." The formidable archaeological wealth of our country is proof of its autochthonous culture, great originality, and inspiration. The new Museo Nacional de Antropología was born as a necessary and ample enough space to guarantee its rescue and classification.

Barrios Gómez implied that the stone's rightful place was not in Coatlinchan, a small and peripheral town, but in a public museum in the nation's capital

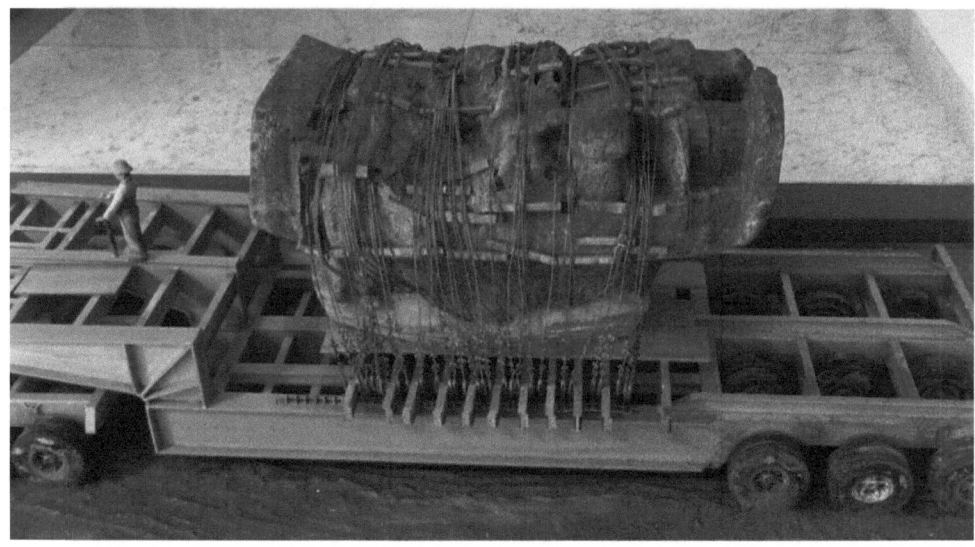

FIGURE 3.1. The model in Pedro Ramírez Vázquez's office. Film still from *The Absent Stone*, directed by Jesse Lerner and Sandra Rozental, 2013.

where it could be kept and admired by all. Taking it from a location where it was not only misplaced but ultimately at risk was the state's responsibility. In other words, the end justified the means.

In the summer of 2009, almost fifty years had passed and Pedro Ramírez Vázquez, already in his nineties, maintained a similar perspective. He was then working on his memoir, surrounded by framed photographs and plans of his most well-known buildings, many of which still serve as important government offices, public museums, and recreational infrastructures. Sitting at his desk, he reminisced about the stone's relocation as one of the most noteworthy achievements of his career.[6] Even as the museum as a whole had brought him international acclaim, it was "bringing the Tlaloc," as he referred to the process, that was to his mind one of his greatest accomplishments.

The feat's importance materialized in the vestibule of his firm, where a glass case containing a detailed model of the stone strapped to the low-bed trailer still greets visitors (figure 3.1). This was one of the architect's most prized possessions. He proudly boasted: "It is such a perfect rendition, every detail, every cable. It is a precise copy of one of the most magnificent events in Mexican history." The model also triggered vivid memories: "When I see it, it takes me back to the day we finally were able to move the immovable. It was like nothing I have ever experienced—thousands of people lined up waiting for us, calling

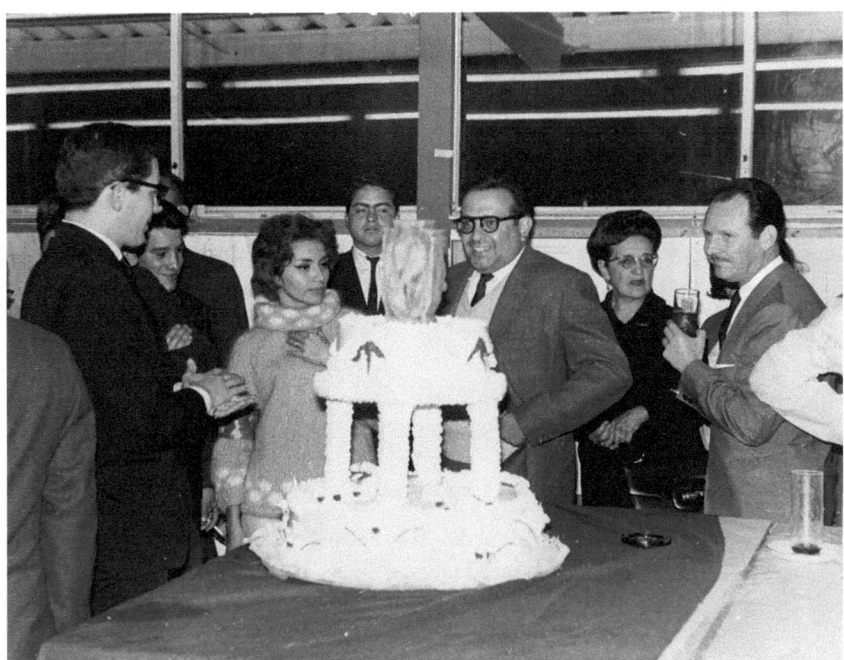

FIGURE 3.2. Pedro Ramírez Vázquez celebrating his birthday, April 16, 1964.
Photograph courtesy of Acervo Arquitecto Pedro Ramírez Vázquez.

Tlaloc! Tlaloc!—and it was the middle of the night. And then, the rain!" For the architect, the downpour was an unmistakable sign that his own work to rescue the stone and bring it to the museum was aligned with the forces of nature as well as with the deity's will.

During an event held at the museum in 2014 honoring Ramírez Vázquez posthumously, his son Javier Ramírez Campusano stood at the podium and emotionally told the audience: "For my father, that monument was very special. He planned the Tlaloc's transfer to coincide with his forty-fifth birthday, April 16, 1964. He then died that same day, on April 16, 2013. He and the stone were strangely connected." There is a photograph in the architect's archive that visually captures this calendric happenstance: surrounded by people toasting and clapping, the architect looks with delight onto a large birthday cake, covered in icing and crowned with a miniature of the stone standing upright (figure 3.2).

The architect admitted many times that bringing the stone to the museum was not his idea. Early on, the committee overseeing the building's construction under his leadership discussed the need for some sort of sculptural element

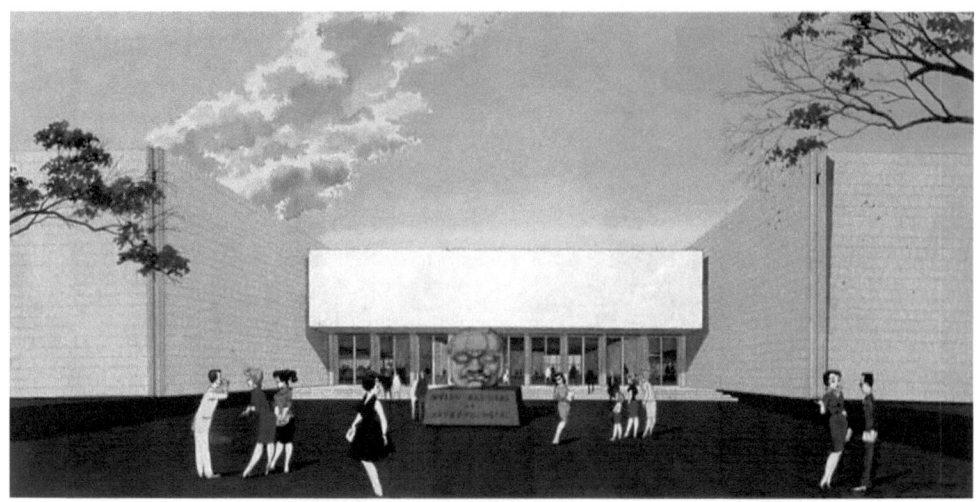

FIGURE 3.3. Watercolor architectural sketch by Pascual Castañon, circa 1960s. Courtesy of Acervo Arquitecto Pedro Ramírez Vázquez.

from the pre-Hispanic past as a central architectural feature.[7] He was keen on the Aztec Calendar Stone as a possible candidate, but the committee decided that it would instead be the centerpiece of the Sala Mexica, the climax of the museum's curatorial layout.[8] Another possibility was one of the colossal Olmec heads found in Veracruz in the 1950s. Sketches and watercolors in the architect's archive show such a head placed on a pedestal guarding the museum's entrance, just like the ones that famously traveled to Houston and New York in the 1960s (figure 3.3).[9]

Architect and archaeologist Ricardo de Robina, who headed the museum's design team, explained that he had to convince Ramírez Vázquez that, next to the museum's monumentality, the Olmec head would look like a "ping pong ball."[10] President López Mateos also opposed Ramírez Vázquez's selection, comparing the Olmec head to a "golf ball."[11] These analogies to sports and games show that those working to make the museum, including the president, had a different scale and tone in mind. The artifact chosen as the museum's defining monument had to be on par with its dimensions, reinforcing the regime's grandiloquent political ambitions and nationalist ideals.

Ramírez Vázquez's next choice was a six-meter-tall stela from Edzná, a Maya site in the southern state of Campeche. This stela was supposedly ruled out because it was made of limestone, a material that would suffer from long-term exposure to the elements (Ramírez Vázquez 2008, 66).[12] The architect recalled that, after much consideration, he decided to shelter the stela in the museum's Maya Hall. However, the monument had mysteriously disappeared by the time government authorities came to remove it (Ramírez Vázquez 2008). For the museum's twentieth anniversary, the politically left magazine *Proceso* revisited this story given that none of the other archaeologists consulted, including de Robina, Aveleyra, and Román Piña Chan, in charge of the Edzná archaeological site, recalled the stela or its mysterious disappearance (Ponce 1985). Hoping to dispel rumors that it was stolen, years after his death, Ramírez Vázquez's firm insisted that it was in fact not a stela but a tower and that it had collapsed by the time the museum's envoys went to survey how to bring it to the museum. This monument's mysterious story exemplifies how state theft and the tensions between the licit and the illicit appropriation of ancient monuments underlay the museum's collecting project much beyond the Coatlinchan case.

In an interview, de Robina explained that he had visited Coatlinchan in his youth and was impressed by the stone's enormous size. In his eyes, this was the only object in all of Mexico large enough to reinforce the museum's monumental ambitions. Ramírez Vázquez narrated the choice of the Coatlinchan stone somewhat differently, stating that it was its basaltic material, known for its hardness and resistance, that ultimately made it an ideal candidate to stand outdoors as an architectural feature. He also framed the decision as a presidential decree at a time when Mexican presidentialism was at its climax. According to the architect, it was President López Mateos, known for being an avid hiker, who stumbled on the colossal stone in Coatlinchan. Considering it abandoned in a remote ravine, he suggested bringing it to the museum.[13] Ramírez Vázquez reported that, having consulted leading archaeologist Alfonso Caso, who believed that it was too heavy to move, López Mateos, true to his faith in the power of the Mexican state and its engineers, instructed the architect: "Is there anything that we can't do with today's technology? Just bring it!"[14]

During one of our many conversations overlooking his garden where two albino peacocks and a family of Vietnamese pigs roamed happily, Ramírez Vázquez further elaborated: "López Mateos told me about the monolith and said that it had stayed in Coatlinchan, a place that was only ever meant to be its workshop, because it was never finished given that its makers lacked the technology to move it to a ceremonial site. But we had the technology! We could finish what our ancestors had started."[15] In other words, bringing the stone to Mexico City as a monument for the new museum—a contemporary ceremonial center of sorts—was a way for the Mexican state to complete what national ancestors had left unfinished. The fact that the stone was thought to have been made for Teotihuacan, the site imagined as one of the birthplaces of

Mesoamerican civilization, would also allow the museum to harness the symbolic force of this national origin myth.

During another conversation in his office in 2010, Ramírez Vázquez belittled the stone's importance for Coatlinchan's residents. The architect insisted that it only figured on the fringes of Coatlinchan's economy because it was essentially out of place there, left incomplete by its ancient makers and undervalued by the area's contemporary residents: "It was an unfinished piece so there wasn't much tourism, only a handful of Sunday visitors. These visitors were the most the stone ever gave the town in terms of development. The only real benefit went to a single woman who sold sodas. Townspeople who did not see or use the monolith as a source of income suddenly realized that the government had come to claim it as one of Mexico's treasures and decided that they wanted to exploit that value for themselves." For the architect, the stone's value for townspeople was minimal in terms of both money and development until it was coveted by the museum. Their dispossession of a stone would result in the conservation of a national monument for generations of Mexicans.[16] He incredulously commented: "Just imagine, they wanted us to build a museum there in Coatlinchan! But who would go to a ravine in the middle of nowhere to see the Tlaloc? In Chapultepec, all of Mexico and the world would be able to see and admire Tlaloc!"

Coatlinchan's residents were, however, perhaps not the only ones who thought the stone could stay on site and still be exhibited as a national heirloom. Carlos Pellicer, the acclaimed poet who built a regional archaeology museum and the La Venta Park in his native Villahermosa, Tabasco, as well as scholar of Nahuatl language and philosophy Miguel León-Portilla, also opposed the stone's extraction (Pomar 1963). They argued that it should remain in Coatlinchan, where it could be part of a tourist route linking different sites in the region associated with the Mesoamerican cult of Tlaloc. The "Tlaloc Museum," as they called it, would be the first "specialized museum" in Mexico, showing the connections between contemporary rain petition rituals among the region's Indigenous communities and ancient sites linked to water and its uses, like the nearby ruins and aqueducts at Texcotzingo. This plan would also promote tourism in the area and offer people from Coatlinchan alternative sources of income. Alberto Beltrán drew a sketch to accompany their proposal, showing the remaining structures and water reservoir belonging to Tepetitlan, Coatlinchan's colonial hacienda only a mile away from the ravine, transformed into a recreational water park (figure 3.4).

Ramírez Vázquez, regardless, believed that the stone could not stay in Coatlinchan because he was convinced it was at risk there. During our exchanges, the

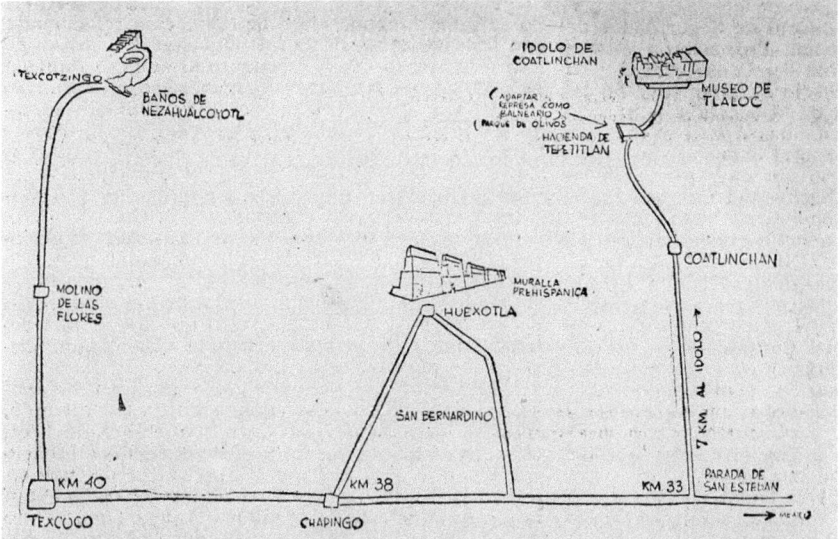

PLANO DE ACCESO A Coatlinchan. Se llega al lugar por el kilómetro 33 de la carretera México-Chapingo-Texcoco. El camino que se ha construido única-mente para transportar la escultura prehispánica más grande de las conoci-das, y que quedará abandonado después, puede servir para conducir a los pa-seantes hasta el lugar donde se construiría el Museo de Tláloc, que enriquece-ría el caudal cultural de la región.

FIGURE 3.4. Alberto Beltrán, "Plano de acceso a Coatlinchan" (Plan of access to Coatl-inchan). Drawing of Carlos Pellicer and Miguel León-Portilla's proposed tourist route. From Pomar 1963.

architect was sometimes defensive. He insisted that town residents were harming the stone, desecrating it with graffiti: "They didn't look after it because it didn't have value for them. When we arrived to begin work there, the whole stone was covered with scribblings. Imagine, an object of that value and importance!" In his eyes, these markings, commented on by scholars as acts of vandalism made by both locals and visitors since the early decades of the twentieth century, were irrefutable proof that the residents of Coatlinchan were a threat to the stone; they were therefore not its adequate custodians.[17]

People in Coatlinchan, however, are quite proud of having carved their ini-tials on the stone's surface. Many, in fact, actively dismiss rumors that the graf-fiti was done by outsiders or by tourists who came on weekend excursions. They flaunt how they or their kin carved the "EM" on the Piedra's "nose," the "D" above its mouth, or the "MR" on its arm.[18] One of Coatlinchan's schoolteach-ers and my host for several months, Guadalupe Villarreal, or Maestra Lupe, as she is affectionately known, is certain that her father carved the "SA" inside the headdress but was unable to finish his full name, "Salvador," because the engineers arrived and cordoned off the site to begin preparing the stone for extraction. The teacher's father was from Monterrey and had married a woman, her mother, from one of the town's prosperous families. Maestra Lupe thought he had wanted to carve his name precisely because of the value that the stone had for town residents. He wanted to show that he, too, was attached to Coatlinchan, that he had grown roots there, even if this was not his birthplace: "He told me many times that he wrote those initials there one night when he was going to graze goats in the nearby hills. He told me that he felt at home in that spot, that the Piedra reminded him that, even though he wasn't from here, he was home." Other town residents also claim authorship of the same letters, reminiscing of adolescent lovers etching their initials—Susana and Antonio, or Anastasio and Selena—making their affections live on in time through these acts of inscription. These etchings were, then, maybe not acts of vandalism by people who didn't value the stone, as Ramírez Vázquez believed. Perhaps they might be understood as adding to layers of care and affection, incarnating and preserving community ties and relationships in this particular place, inscribing it as home.

Tlaloc for Development

José Chavarría Mancilla conducts the band that plays at Coatlinchan's community events and festivities. His father, José Chavarría Zamora, had been the town's best-known composer. Three of his songs were about Coatlinchan, and two of them told the story of the stone's relocation. "Tlaloc se fue" (Tlaloc left), a danzón written in 1964, repeats a chorus that marks the stone's removal as a state-sanctioned theft:

> Tlaloc se fue a Chapultepec
> Tlaloc está en Chapultepec
> Tlaloc se fue a Chapultepec
> Se lo llevó Torres Bodet.

> (Tlaloc left to Chapultepec
> Tlaloc is in Chapultepec
> Tlaloc went to Chapultepec
> Taken by Torres Bodet.)

The tune is strangely joyful for a song that denounces dispossession, playfully using the linguistic happenstance whereby the then secretary of education's last name has the same meter as "Chapultepec," the stone's new urban abode.

With a melody strikingly similar to a military march from the early twentieth century, the second song, "La marcha de Tlaloc," was written as both an ode
and a farewell to the stone:

En Coatlinchan tristeza hay
Ya el resguardo alerta está
Todos se ponen a marchar en pos de Tlaloc que se va
Tlaloc se va y no volverá
El pueblo entero va con él
Le tiran flores, le gritan ¡viva!
Y hasta los niños van también
Marchemos al compás
Marchemos todos en unión
Porque la unión es paz
Y el progreso de la nación
Con gran resignación
Y bajo el sol arrasador
Marchando el pueblo va, para decir adiós, adiós.

(In Coatlinchan there is sadness
The guard is on alert
Everyone marches behind Tlaloc, who is leaving
Tlaloc is leaving and will not return
The whole town accompanies him
They throw him flowers, they yell out "viva!"
And even the children follow
Let's march to the beat
Let's all march united
Because union is peace
And the nation's progress
With great resignation
And under the blistering sun
The town marches away, while saying farewell, farewell.)

Coatlinchan's authorities originally commissioned the march to accompany
the stone as it left the town on its journey toward the museum. However, don
Chavarría Mancilla told me with a somber expression: "There were so many
problems, they ended up sending soldiers and people in town were banned
from participating. So the march was never played. It was forgotten." The composer's son himself only remembered some of the lyrics and melody, but on

my request and excited about the possibility of assuring his father's legacy, he interviewed elderly musicians who had worked with his father to reconstruct the score and lyrics. He dreamed of conducting a marching band to perform the song in Coatlinchan for the first time more than five decades after his father wrote it.[19] The lyrics' juxtaposition of nationalist slogans and images of sadness and resignation, however, puzzled don Chavarría Mancilla. He, nevertheless, tried to explain town authorities' and his father's intentions at the time: "I think they wanted to show that the town was sad but also that they had no choice but to be proud." He looked away and said no more. The song's lyrics, written before town residents tried to stop the stone's extraction and Coatlinchan was placed under military curfew, already hinted at their coerced acceptance of its removal.

Since the stone's intended relocation was announced in May 1963, government authorities visited Coatlinchan, seeking local authorities' consent to ensure the procedure went smoothly. The press reported on these meetings in which Secretary Torres Bodet as well as Eusebio Dávalos Hurtado, then the director of the INAH, and Ramírez Vázquez, accompanied by Benito Bustamante, Texcoco's municipal president, met with a commission of town residents that included their elected representatives (*delegados*) as well as the headmistress of the local primary school (who happened to be Maestra Lupe's aunt). In an article published by *El Universal*, these authorities were said to have expressed their "complacencia" (willing agreement) with the government's intention and even offered "their help to take on this important task" out of "patriotic interest."[20]

Pedro García, an experienced welder and active community member who passed away in 2024, spent most of his time in his family home that doubled as his workspace, with wires and metal assemblages scattered all over the courtyard. Back in 2010 and before his health deteriorated, he liked receiving guests, serving them pulque, which he flavored with his favorite fruits: prickly pear, strawberry, and tamarind. I visited him often as he was mostly retired then and keen on telling stories about "the good old days." Don Pedro was an avid collector, displaying all kinds of objects that caught his eye on the shelves that lined the walls of his home. He meticulously kept documents and old photos, having been one of the first in town to have a camera. Among his "archive," as he referred to the many folders he kept in a cabinet, he stored a photocopy of a contract, along with the deed to the plot of his house, and his and his wife's birth certificates.

He showed the three fading pages to me with certain reserve. The photocopies had been entrusted to him by a man who had long ago served as part of the Comisariado Ejidal, the collective body that manages Coatlinchan's communal lands. The document was a copy of a contract, signed in 1963 by Benito

Bustamante and more than sixty town residents who had ejido plots, many who had inked their fingerprints, signaling that they were probably not literate. Even if at that time and until today, many town residents who are heads of households are not necessarily ejidatarios, the ejido assembly serves, nevertheless, as the legitimating process to secure the town's consent.

"You know," don Pedro pondered as he flipped through the pages, "people say the government took the Piedra by force, but they took it with all the rights guaranteed by the law [*con todas las de la ley*]." He went on: "People here are full of crap [*dicen pura tontería*]! It's about time they owned up to their mistakes. See here, everyone agreed—this is a contract and it is signed by all the ejidatarios from the assembly. I am not proud of it, but here is my father's signature. They all signed because they all agreed. What could they do? They wanted the town to develop [*progrese*], they wanted to be modern and have all the services." Don Pedro showed me the contract as evidence that the stone had been legally, even if not entirely willfully, relinquished. He concluded: "The stone seems like a small price to pay for progress, for your children to succeed [*superarse*], don't you think?"

The document was written in familiar bureaucratic form, setting up the terms of an exchange among equal and voluntary parties. I transcribe it here:

> In the town of Coatlinchan, Texcoco Municipality, state of Mexico, at twelve o'clock on the 22nd of April of 1963, all the residents [*vecinos*] gathered in the building of the Delegación Municipal, in the presence of citizen Benito Bustamante Buendía, Constitutional Municipal President of Texcoco, discussed the following matters:
>
> 1 The town accepts to surrender [*entregar*] its idol to the Federal Government with the intervention of the state Government.
> 2 The idol will be surrendered in exchange for the Federal Government, through the Ministry of Education's, agreement to build a full-fledged primary school adjusted to the needs of the town, as well as the donation of the plumbing and electrification equipment to complete two wells that already exist in the ejido lands of San Pedro and La Presa, and a clinic [*centro de salud*] with the participation of the Ministry of Health, and as an indispensable component, the pavement of the highway to the town over a four-kilometer distance, including its dependent roads.
> 3 Before the authorities and given the unanimous will of the Assembly, the Committee Pro-Construction of Material Works for the Town constituted by [names of the community representatives].

The following will be reported to the citizen Governor of the state for his respective agreement, adjourning the present session minute, signed as proof thereof.

Benito B.

The next two pages featured the ejidatarios' signatures and fingerprints as well as the stamps of the Association of Heads of Family based at Coatlinchan's Rural School, Coatlinchan's Delegacíon Municipal, and the Municipality of Texcoco, validating the document as an officially sanctioned contract.[21]

Salvador Suárez Hernández, known as don Chava, was with me that day. A carpenter by trade, he was the town's official *cronista*, or local historian.[22] He was the one who introduced me to don Pedro, his good friend and compadre. Much of what I know about Coatlinchan and its history was shared by don Chava, who welcomed me in his home near the centro de salud several afternoons a week, telling me stories and showing me documents, maps, and his carefully organized collection of encyclopedias, history books, and magazines. Sitting next to Pedro that day, he seemed very surprised when his friend placed the yellowing photocopy on the table for us to inspect: "I didn't know about this," he said. "But . . . We never agreed!" He was silent for a while and then exclaimed: "It is a fake! The main document is on one page and all the signatures are on two blank pages. This was how the government fooled and took advantage of us in those days." After a few minutes, he went on: "My grandfather told me that they had an assembly with a teacher who was one of the few people who knew how to read and write. He told everyone that the contract was to stop the government from taking the Piedra, and so they all signed. That is what this document is, it's a lie!" For Chava, the teacher, a state employee after all, had likely partnered with the authorities to dupe his fellow townspeople. In the weeks following, Chava became keen on proving that the document was a fraud.

He introduced me to don Miguel, then in his late nineties, who sat with us on his porch while his wife helped interpret his barely audible voice. When Chava asked him about the negotiations that led to the stone's removal, he corroborated that the exchange had taken place but hinted that town representatives, including himself, a delegado at the time, had not been entirely in agreement but felt obligated within local power structures into acquiescing to its terms. Chava showed him the contract and his signature on one of the pages. "I am ninety-six years old. I don't remember how many of these contracts [*actas*] I signed in my lifetime. This one is just like all the others. Who knows if it is real or fake. Who knows?" He scoffed and continued, "In any case, the government never fulfilled its side of the bargain." His wife intervened: "The damn road was never paved, the wells were only powered decades later using community funds and labor, and even the school and the clinic were deficient. They were built using materials, labor, and even land donated by us!"

Don Miguel interjected that he was the one who had donated the plot for the clinic, after the municipal president of Texcoco had asked him personally for it. He knew he could not say no. He added: "Government officials came to take their picture, to cut ribbons, but they only fooled us," he said. "There were no medicines or doctors in the centro de salud and the school had no teachers nor educational materials. They were just buildings. Empty shells. Built by us, on our lands, with our materials, with our hands." Miguel, as well as many elders who lived through these events, described them using terms that recall the language of bellic aftermaths: they had to "surrender," "give up," or "relinquish" the stone to the powers that be.

The most common story I heard from elders was that government officials came to Coatlinchan, offering to take the stone in exchange for a paved highway, the electrification of two wells, a school, and a clinic. In other words, the state offered the town infrastructures, promising development and better opportunities for its residents. Yet these were the same infrastructures that were being set up all over the country at the time, reinforcing the state's commitment to public education, universal health care, and modernization. The school and the clinic are still in use in Coatlinchan today. Both buildings are iconic of a particular moment of the Mexican state's consolidation and its expansion into previously inaccessible territories in the 1960s and 1970s through public infrastructures. They were designed using the modular architecture conceived and implemented by Ramírez Vázquez himself before he was charged with building the museum, when he worked for the Ministry of Education as the head of the CAPFCE. The clinic and the school exchanged for the stone, even if deemed deficient, are, to this day, the only public institutions that service town residents.

Rumors of corruption surround many of those elected to administer the town's collective bodies. "That is the definition of being an *autoridad*," I overheard a man at a town meeting say to his neighbor, "to steal from the pueblo and become rich alone." The relationship between being a community authority and corruption is crystallized in stories surrounding the stone's removal in 1964, narrated by many as the result of illegitimate negotiations between government officials and a handful of town residents that were at the time its representatives.

On our way to the market that sets up in town every Tuesday, Gabi, a stylist who caters to local weddings and festivities, pointed to a series of grandiose and fairly new three-story houses: "You keep asking about the stone . . . You really want to know where it is? Well, there you go. There! In those houses, in their pickup trucks and new cars. That is where it is!" Gabi was angry about the stone's theft decades before she was born, but she was even more upset by what she saw as its transformation into the private fortunes of a new local elite who used their position as community authorities to finance their luxurious living. Gabi was convinced, like many others, that town authorities at the time of the stone's relocation had received bribes and favors in exchange for collaborating with the government. "They never got the town's consent," she said. "They didn't run an assembly; they just signed off what was ours and got rich for it." Gabi was referencing the traditional forms of collective decision-making that took place through town assemblies and that had not been respected when the stone was taken.

Elders in Coatlinchan remember the stone having been coveted by Mexican state agents long before the 1960s. When I rented a room in his home a block from the cloister of the church, don Panchito often told stories about his father, who had worked as a guide taking people to see the stone in the 1920s and 1930s; he told me there were tourists and scholars but also engineers who came to survey the terrain and measure the distance to the closest railroad station only a few kilometers away (figure 3.5).[23] Don Panchito's father had assured him that even the notorious dictator Porfirio Díaz had personally come to Coatlinchan because he wanted to take the stone away and display it in his home in the Castillo de Chapultepec. However, townspeople had stopped even the "great caudillo." Like Panchito, many elders insisted that, despite being poor and disenfranchised, town residents would not have allowed anyone to take the stone, even if the right technology had been available. In 1964, they tried to stop its removal. They had done what they could to sabotage the procedures, but the army was sent in and crushed their efforts.

In February 1964, the national press widely covered the uprising that took place in Coatlinchan. Newspapers published images showing the stone barely hanging from the broken and twisted steel structures made to prepare it for transport, surrounded by soldiers. Most of this coverage attributed townspeople's actions to their stubborn and progress-adverse beliefs in the stone's supernatural powers, justifying the state's use of military might to quell their actions and take the stone by force. *Impacto*, a broadly read weekly, for example, clamored in a headline, "Mutiny in the Town of Coatlinchan in Defense of Its God Tlaloc" (figure 3.6). Accompanied by photographs of the destruction following the events and the town overrun with soldiers, the article described town residents' "violent attitude" and quoted them saying: "If they

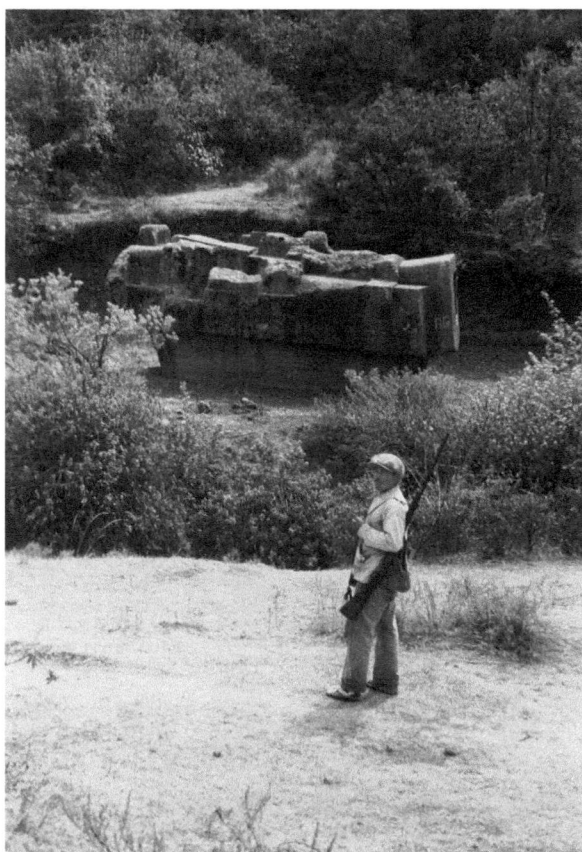

FIGURE 3.5. A local guide in Coatlinchan, 1937. Photograph by Martin Horst. Courtesy of Museum für Völkerkunde Dresden, F 1977-2/300.2.2.

take it, it will stop raining here and our crops will be lost. We cannot allow it to be removed."

Although most of the Mexican press explained town residents' actions as the result of persistent and misplaced beliefs in the powers of ancient deities, a common trope explaining Indigenous idolatrous practices since viceregal times, *La Prensa*, a left-leaning daily, featured the story "Coatlinchan decidido a conservar su Tlaloc" (Coatlinchan determined to keep its Tlaloc) to make sense of the stone's attachment to Coatlinchan in different terms. The reporter (identified as R) asked town residents directly why they had opposed the stone's removal. He quoted two elderly residents who assured him that "the monolith is something that cannot be separated from the town."

R: Do you think that if they take Tlaloc away it will stop raining?

ELDERS: No sir, the one who gives us bread, water and life is in heaven.

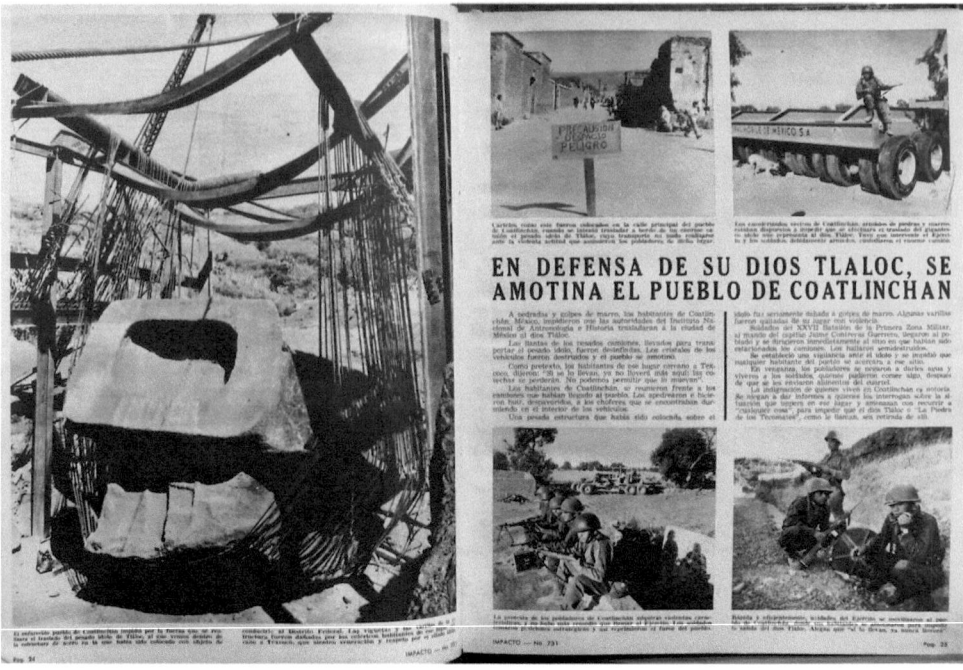

FIGURE 3.6. "En defensa de su dios Tlaloc, se amotina el pueblo de Coatlinchan" (Mutiny in the town of Coatlinchan in defense of its Tlaloc god). *Impacto*, March 4, 1964.

R: Why then are you opposed to the monolith's transfer?

ELDERS: We all want/love [*queremos*] the place where we have always lived. We are fond and attached to our surroundings. And so, we became accustomed to seeing and loving the Tlaloc. Also, people come to see him and this is good for our town that is poorer and poorer every day.[24]

Father Zenón López González, still remembered as one of most active priests in recent memory for his efforts to strengthen communal associations, including founding Coatlinchan's credit cooperative, was also quoted in the article. He reiterated that town residents had rebelled because of sound economic calculations. They were devout Catholics who worshiped San Miguel and not "idolatrous indians" who believed the stone was a god. Town residents would suffer a loss of income because the stone would no longer provide a tourist attraction in Coatlinchan. In other words, in taking the stone, the state was in fact also usurping the town's possibility for economic prosperity.

Borlote

Nowadays, Tlacuaches describe that day using many terms: some say it was a "rebellion." Others insist that it couldn't be described as such because it wasn't a premeditated mobilization but a spur-of-the-moment reaction. They call it alternatively the "borlote" (row), "ramalazo" (lash), "alboroto" (ruckus), or simply "el lío" or "el desmadre" (the mess, chaos, or the term's slang equivalent). Regardless of how they name it, people I spoke with insisted that the town acted to defend the stone because it was rightfully theirs, "nuestra." Like for the elders quoted by the *La Prensa* reporter, the stone was indissociable from the town, its people and their territory broadly configured. Whether or not it was physically attached to the matrix rock was not how they understood this attachment. It belonged to and in Coatlinchan because it was integral to it, and that was why town residents fought to keep it there.

Antonio López, a welder by trade, is known for his abilities in his craft and because of his extraordinary condition and stamina: well into his eighties, he is an avid cyclist and often participates in long-distance pilgrimages to shrines all over Mexico on his shiny red bicycle. He was also the only person I met who openly admitted to having been involved in the actions to thwart the stone's removal. All other known participants were said to have passed away or had conveniently left town. Don Antonio assured me that town authorities back then engaged in the exchange solely because they, like everyone else in Coatlinchan, including himself, believed that the stone was in fact immovable. As I sat with him in his workshop, surrounded by pieces of tin, broken appliances, and disorganized reels of cable and wire, he re-created the events that led up to the "borlote," as he referred to the event. He emphatically recounted:

> My grandmother lived to be 115. She told me many times that people knew the stone wasn't from here; that it had rolled down from the mountains. Her grandparents were going to bring it to be an idol for us, for the town— they had made stone rollers to roll it on, but they hadn't been able to because the stone was bewitched [*encantada*]. They would dig and it would sink, and dig again, and it would sink again. It might have been because of its weight, but people believed it was bewitched. Who knows . . .

He insisted that the stone was rooted in the ground and that town authorities knew this and, therefore, had intended to dupe the government, and not the other way around. They had negotiated the exchange as a ruse, thinking that they would end up with both the wanted infrastructure and the bewitched, rooted stone.

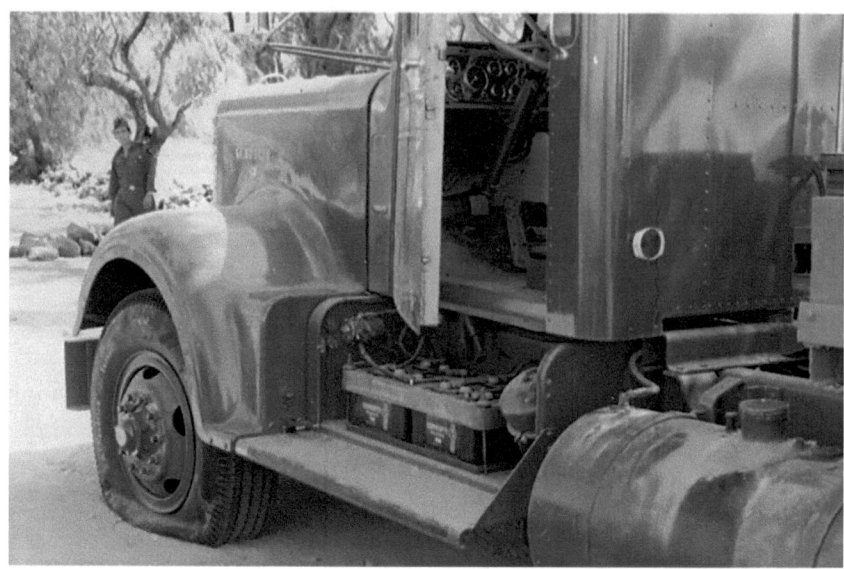

FIGURE 3.7. The damaged truck, February 1964. Courtesy of Enrique del Valle Prieto.

Don Antonio told me that everyone was surprised when the engineers were able to lift the stone out of the ground. On the day the trailer arrived, they realized its removal was imminent: "Nobody bothered with it until they came to take it away. I didn't believe they could remove it either. But that was the problem, and it was rough. We had to hide away. We went to see it, we cared for it, and we decided we didn't want anyone to take it away." Don Antonio underscored that even the town representatives who had negotiated with the government were certain that the bewitched stone would resist displacement on its own and sink back into the earth, but when it didn't, they decided to take action.

He told me that town residents took advantage of the fact that the vehicle had gotten stuck on the way—a miscalculation of the road's width on the part of the engineers—to stop its removal. They threw stones at its windshields and chased away the two truck drivers and the engineers (figure 3.7).[25] Then, they all went to the site where the stone hung from steel beams and decided to cast it down, loosening the cables. With its weight no longer evenly balanced, the heavy stone fell to the ground, twisting the structure into an unrecognizable shape. Don Antonio was very proud that he had worked faster to loosen the bolts and that's why the stone had fallen lopsided. He giggled under his breath as he said: "I kept several of the bolts for years! Who knows where they are now, maybe somewhere in my mess."

Amado Sánchez, who passed away in early 2023, was one of many town residents hired by the construction company CUFAC to build that structure. Other family members were hired for the project. His brother, who was the night watchman at the ravine the night of the rebellion, had witnessed the events (don Amado wanted to make sure I wrote down that he had only been a bystander, not an active participant). He had told him that those who stormed the ravine wanted to put del Valle Prieto's car under the stone before setting it loose from the cables but that it fell much faster and more suddenly than they expected, leaving no time for "pranks." The prank, Amado explained with a laugh as he recounted the story, would have "taught them all a lesson." Instead, townspeople stole the engineers' tools, hoping to use them for their own projects: "wheelbarrows, picks, shovels, everything, even the dynamite. The only thing that was spared was the engineer's level." Don Amado made fun of the press, which reported at the time that town residents had broken the cables using sickles and machetes (this story was portrayed in comic book form; see figures 2.12 and 2.13). "They were steel cables!" he exclaimed. "It is ridiculous that they said we broke them with sickles!"

Don Antonio related that, fearing local violence, the government called in the army to suppress the "ramalazo" and, more importantly, to ensure the stolen dynamite was not used against officials and engineers. "The plan was not to use it against people!" he underscored, but to blow up the stone. He looked determined as he spoke: "¡Ni con dios, ni con el diablo!" (Neither with god nor with the devil). If the stone couldn't remain in Coatlinchan, it would not belong to anybody or go anywhere else. "We wanted to blow it up rather than to watch it be taken away." In other conversations, he offered a different explanation: He was the one who had stolen the dynamite, just one box, to use in his fields. He and others in town had learned to use explosives to blow up heavy boulders to clear terrain when they were hired to build the road that the trailer would pass through. "I figured I could use it to blow up some stones on my land that were a nuisance."

The stolen dynamite was never used. Don Antonio confessed: "We kept the dynamite in my barn, under heaps of hay so that the authorities wouldn't find it." His speech accelerated as he gesticulated with his hands and arms for dramatic effect: "The next day, the whole place was full of soldiers, from González [the main road] up to the ravine. It felt awful. We were all scared that there would be more violence, so we gave in." He continued: "But I often ask myself, what did they imagine? That we would try to blow up soldiers? With one box of dynamite? How many soldiers could we blow up? One, two, three . . . ? We wouldn't have been able to kill all of them even if we tried. We wanted to use it in our fields, but for them, we were dangerous." On the contrary, don Antonio emphasized, townspeople were the stone's caretakers and, after its relocation, this care was relinquished: "It's strange, we used to go and see the stone all the time. And then they took it away and that was that. Everything changed. I didn't see it again until almost thirty years later when I went on a bicycle race to Mexico City. And there it was. I told people, you see that stone, it's from over there, it's from my town. I tried to stop its removal but hey, such is life. Now it's in a place that people pass by in cars, on bikes, nobody cares."

Maestra Lupe was interviewed by a reporter in 2014 for the fiftieth anniversary of the stone's removal. She told the reporter that the town had rebelled because of a misunderstanding: they had been told that the government was going to take Tlaloc, but they knew the stone was not Tlaloc, that it was a female deity. The reporter quoted her account:

> When they took the stone away I was studying at the Normal de Maestros and I remember arriving here at about four o'clock in the afternoon. This was a sacred place and I saw the largest low-bed trailer in the world. It was the last days of February. The church bells were ringing. The people had already organized and demanded those who came to leave, because they were not going to take the stone, that this was not Tlaloc. They said that if they wanted Tlaloc, they should go and get him, to see if they could find him. Boys, girls, young men and women, elders . . . the whole town was in the Plazuela! Some to destroy it and others to throw it down! It was 12 o'clock at night and people began to destroy the low-bed. The stone was on a swing and townspeople had no other weapons than the tools they used for agriculture. All night long the people kept hitting and hitting the low-bed. At about five o'clock in the afternoon the stone fell. The earth rumbled and shook. At 10 o'clock in the morning—I have the photos—the army went up to the town. The soldiers began to scatter like cockroaches. Locals hid the dynamite, and warned that if they took Chalchiuhtlicue with them, it would be better to make it explode. We had the army against us; the soldiers were very rude; in the end they took the stone away on the specially made low-bed. It was pushed by two bulldozers and dragged by four trailers. People were crying. Some who heard it was happening ran to see if it was true. The soldiers were shouting that the people should turn back. (Cruz Bárcenas 2014)

Over our own conversations about the events that followed, Maestra Lupe and others told me that the soldiers who were posted in Coatlinchan during the months it took to prepare the stone once again for relocation were ruthless. She said they demanded food without paying for it, got drunk at the *pulquerías*, and there were many rumors that they took advantage and even raped local women.

Like for don Antonio and Maestra Lupe, many Tlacuaches are convinced the stone was attached to their territory and to its people through forms of recognition and care that were violently harmed by its removal. Literally and figuratively embedded in territory—rooted—the potential of its extraction might even demand an act of sacrifice via the object's destruction. Don Antonio explained that this is why it was a "borlote." It wasn't a "rebellion," he insisted. "It wasn't planned or thought out." His expression denoted a certain sadness as he told me: "We just did what we could, what we had to do. We didn't know what we were doing; we just had to do it." He then told me about what he described as the scariest days of his life. He and several others were arrested and kept for several days in jail for questioning. The police reported they were drunk and violent, dismissing and delegitimizing their actions. He was still upset that they had been criminalized because of the missing dynamite imagined as a potential weapon against government authorities and soldiers who in town residents' eyes were in fact the perpetrators of violence they were trying to stop.[26] The stone was ultimately removed from Coatlinchan under duress, with armed soldiers flanking the convoy on all sides. The Mexican press celebrated "Tlaloc's arrival" while also showing its reliance on the repressive presence of the army. Photojournalists captured this presence with striking images that made it look almost like the soldiers, and not the carefully engineered low-bed trailer, were carrying it away (figure 3.8).

From Our Mexican Hearts

Two days after the stone's arrival in Mexico City, a small ceremony and luncheon were held at the museum that included some of Coatlinchan's representatives. *La Prensa* published an article illustrated with photographs showing a young girl handing a document to Torres Bodet, with Ramírez Vázquez in the background. My friends in Coatlinchan identified the girl as the daughter of one of the delegados who was also present. The story appeared under the headline "Coatlinchan Bids Farewell to the Idol: A School for a Village That Shows Gratitude Toward the Authorities in an Official Act."[27] The reporter quoted extensively from the delegado's speech that day, capturing some of his ambivalence and likely censored opinions:

> This object [*pieza*] was taken by government orders and because it is national property [*bienes de la nación*], and in my town there has been a misunderstanding by individuals dreadful in orientation and culture. . . .

FIGURE 3.8. "Ya está aquí Tlaloc" (Tlaloc is here). Front page, *La Prensa*, April 17, 1964.

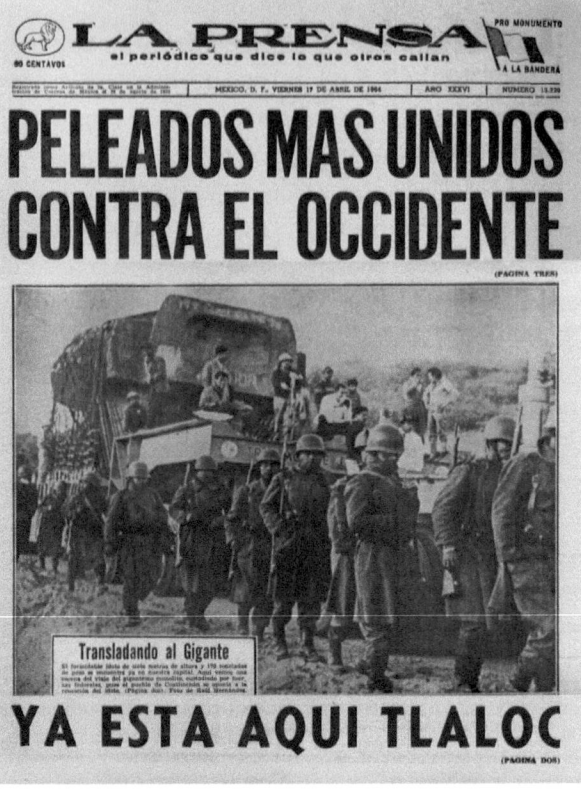

Once again I tell you that these are *bienes de la nación* and that nobody has sold the *piedra* for so many millions, despite what people are saying... that they divided the millions, the value of the given monolith. I would like all the people who have given this wrong version of the story to come out and say this here because it has caused unruly behavior against our social and cultural well-being.

He combined justification with nationalist sentiment:

We must thank the Tlaloc monolith for all the benefits it has brought from the bottom of our Mexican hearts: we now have a school, a shrine to education for our children of today and of tomorrow. We must know, compañeros, that if we want our patria to be great, it will only be so if we create a cultured, moral and civic sentiment for it. The nation requires that our children be educated and not exploited as labor since their early youth, this is why, a few people of citizenship age, one could say illiterate, disturbed the well-being of the people. We must thank Secretary Torres

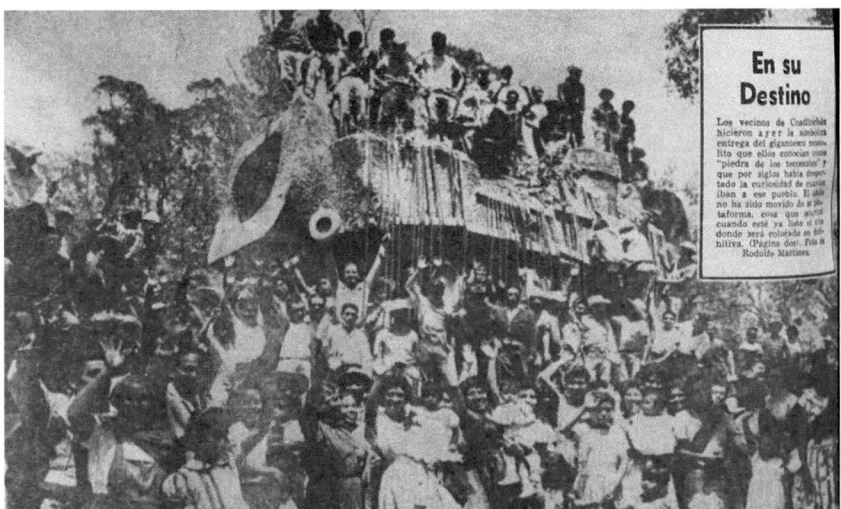

FIGURE 3.9. "En su Destino" (In its destiny/destination). Back cover, *La Prensa*, April 18, 1964. Photograph by Rodolfo Martínez.

Bodet, who has been inspired to give so much to our pueblo by building us a school, as well as architect Pedro Ramírez Vázquez.

The reporter concluded: "Finally [he] recalled that, just as they had previously requested, they [the community members] asked for the town's pavement, pumping equipment for irrigation of ejido lands and other benefits in exchange for Tlaloc. He also asked president López Mateos's forgiveness for the anomalies that had taken place in the past months when townspeople got fired up because of what was ultimately a misunderstanding."

In the reporter's transcription, the delegado, in representation of Coatlinchan's residents, thanked the government for educating villagers in exchange for the stone, legitimizing the community's dispossession through civilizing nationalist discourses and belittling townspeople's efforts to stop the stone's removal as a "misunderstanding."

According to the reporter, Torres Bodet replied that the presence of Coatlinchan's residents "eloquently bore witness to the deep human sentiment of national unity in Mexico." The article ended with Torres Bodet's words of reconciliation: "From the place where [the stone] lay dormant for centuries, you decided to accompany your eminent neighbor all the way to Chapultepec, not so as to bid it farewell, since he will continue to be yours, as well as of all Mexicans, but to publicly show the civic and understanding spirit with which you

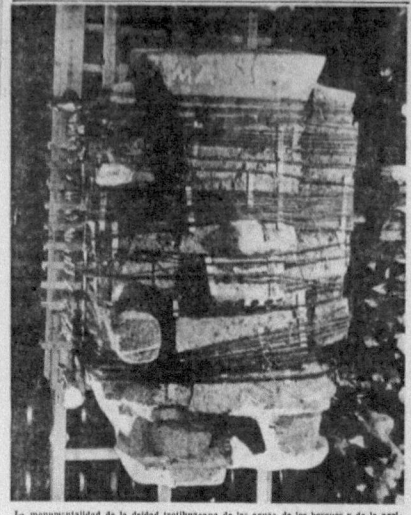
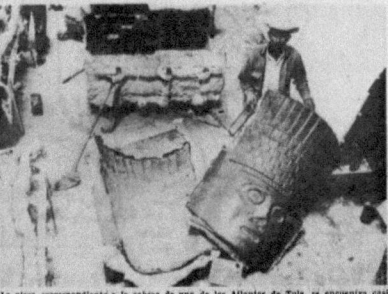

FIGURE 3.10. "Si nos descuidamos hasta a Tláloc se llevan" (If we lower our guard, even Tlaloc will be taken). *El Universal Gráfico*, April 17, 1964.

have allied yourselves with President López Mateos's government project, animated by wanting to give Tlaloc an appropriate place worthy of the grandeur of the magnificent collections of the Museo Nacional de Antropología." Echoing Ramírez Vázquez's grass metaphor, Torres Bodet allegedly continued: "The patria is a collective work [*es obra de todos*]. It belongs to all of us. Conscious of its responsibilities toward the future, the country of today is proud to pay homage to the glories of its past."

The back cover of the newspaper featured a festive image showing town residents, like the comic book woman throwing confetti, posing with smiling faces and their hands up in the air after having officially handed over the stone. The caption read: "En su Destino" (in its destiny/destination) (figure 3.9).

The day following the stone's arrival in Mexico City, *El Universal Gráfico*, another important newspaper, published "La Tournée de un Dios," a play-by-play of the stone's journey side by side with another article discussing how ancient artifacts from Mexico were under threat of being stolen. Ironically, referencing the stone's enormous weight, the headline read: "Si nos descuidamos hasta a Tlaloc se llevan" (If we lower our guard, even Tlaloc will be taken).[28]

The article alerted readers to the alarming destruction and looting taking place in Tula, an archaeological site in the nearby state of Hidalgo, famous for its stacked-stone Atlantes, many now dismembered and whose parts had recently been lost, destroyed, or simply disappeared, likely taken to feed the international trade in antiquities and museum collections (figure 3.10). To remedy the situation, the article reported that Mexican authorities were making replicas to stand on site as part of Tula's renovations as well as to send to museum collections abroad. Faustino Sánchez, credited with "discovering the formula for making replicas of millimetric precision," used molds cast from originals. He was commissioned to produce replicas of Mexico's most important "archaeological jewels" as a solution for stopping their theft. At the time, thinking of the stone from Coatlinchan's relocation by the hand of the state as theft and the possibility of leaving the stone in place and making a replica for the museum seems to have not been imaginable.

PART II

Aftershocks

———

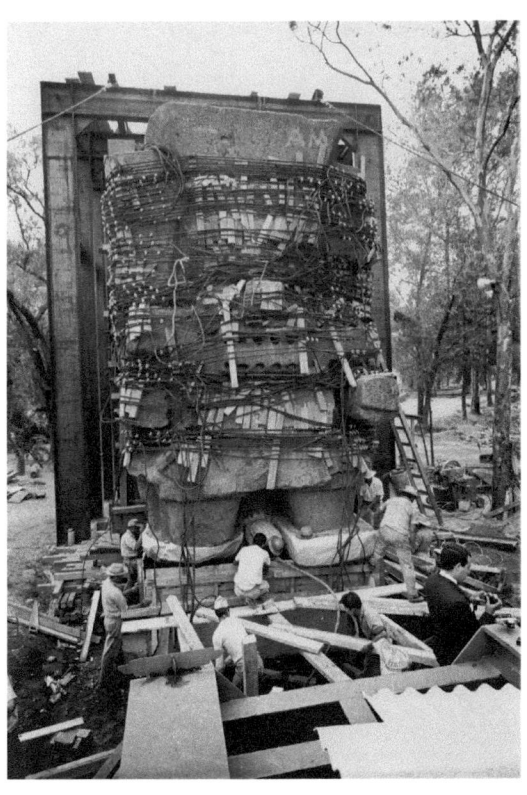

FIGURE P2.1. Installing the stone in front of the museum, 1964. Photograph courtesy of Acervo Arquitecto Pedro Ramírez Vázquez.

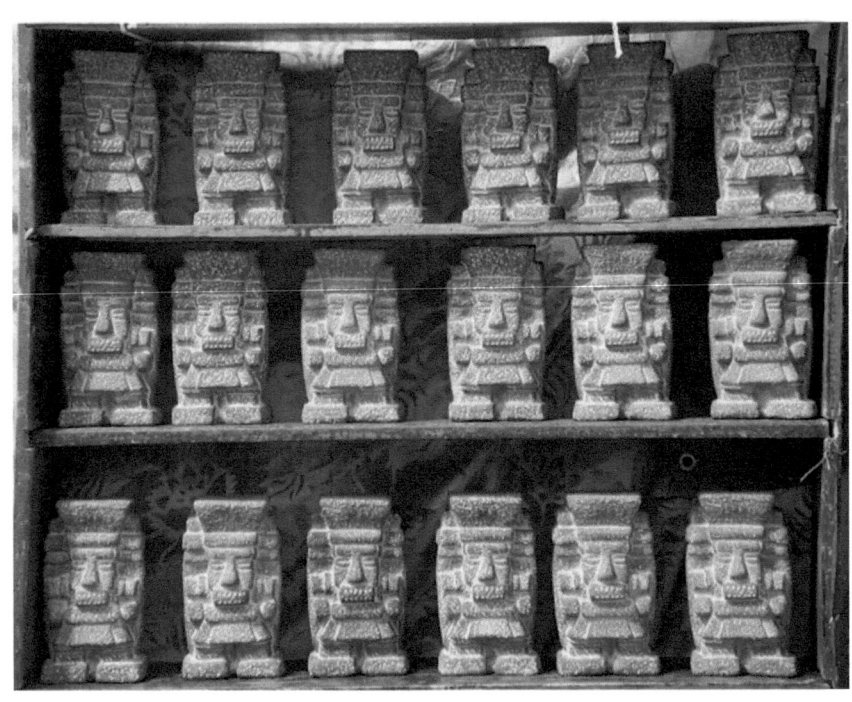

FIGURE P2.2. Stone souvenirs for sale in Coatlinchan, 2010. Photograph by the author.

4

Scars

Don Chava, the town's *cronista*, was not living in Coatlinchan in 1964; he was in Mexico City, where he had gotten a job as a carpenter making cabinets for Singer sewing machines. He came home on weekends and would listen to his friends and kin talking about the back-bending work they were doing: building the road to the ravine, spending more than a year clearing rocks and brush by hand. Chava insisted this work left more than bodily aches and pains among Tlacuaches. Several of his friends and neighbors were forced to destroy parts of their own family homes lining the town's main street because it needed to be widened for the low-bed trailer's passage: "People might not have agreed, but they needed the money and this was salaried work at a time when people only lived off maize." He paused and told me: "Even if you can't see the road just like that, even if you need to look for it, we see it. We know it is there. For Coatlinchan, the road is a constant reminder of the wound from when they took the Piedra away. It's like a scar, even so many years later. It has only partially healed, the skin has grown, and the wound has closed, but you can still see the mark where the damage was done. It still hurts. It can never be completely erased." Don Chava's framing of the road built for the stone's extraction as a kind of lingering and painful wound transformed the town and its territory into a metabolic organism that was perhaps healing but, like a scar, continued to bear the visible and sensory marks of past violence.

Whether in the ravine where it once lay or in Coatlinchan's built environment and surrounding landscape, the stone's absence lingers through such visible marks and traces that continue to act on and affect town residents' daily life and experiences. Like don Chava, Tlacuaches sometimes describe these marks as "scars," a term that irrevocably calls out harm's enduring presence and lasting effects. Even as physical wounds heal, scars become tangible records that preserve injuries, incorporating the violence of the past into the present (Rufer 2023). But scars also constitute events in themselves. They are temporally open-ended processes of material regeneration, replacement, and replication. Physically made up of the same matter as the skin that they replace, scars grow to occupy the place of wounded tissue, but they are always different. This difference is palpable in the flesh. Scar tissue cannot sustain sweat glands or hair follicles and the skin also feels different: it is more fibrous, less flexible, more prone to shearing; it can also itch or scratch (at least for a while), an uncomfortable reminder of pain long after it subsides. Scars, then, are a form of replica, made up of similar, but never quite the same, somatic matter as that which they replace. And yet, in this difference, scars, like replicas, are not always lesser, nor necessarily negatively experienced. As other forms of bodily inscription, they generate materializations of boundaries but also of relations, between selves and the social and material worlds they inhabit.[1]

From the earliest ethnographies of scarification rituals to more recent work by medical anthropologists interested in the effects of surgeries in a variety of contexts, anthropologists have shown that scars can be valued, even flaunted, because of what they reveal about their bearers' lives, their trajectories, and the status and positions they occupy in the world.[2] Scars can therefore be both painful reminders and valued traces that mark and bind. And scars are never stagnant: they change, expand, and compress with time. Ultimately, scars materialize the body's capacity for healing. The analogy that Tlacuaches make between the stone's removal and a scarring wound as well as their work to heal from this injury call for careful attention to the kinds of physical marks that emerged in its wake and how these marks act on the present. As scars, they point to a different way of understanding the stone, not as a distinct object but as part of a body that was harmed and that is still in the process of recovery.

Tlacuaches refer to this body as "lo nuestro," a telluric concept that implies a kind of binding of people to each other and to the earth as well as to other things and substances that it is made up of and contains. Lo nuestro is what constitutes the body of the community in this place.

Tecomates

Nowhere are the scars produced by the stone's removal more visible than in the specific place that once contained it. Known as Santa Clara, the ravine was once incorporated into the lands that belonged to Tepetitlan, the hacienda that dominated the region.[3] This name and a cross still maintained on the highest point of the surrounding hillside are a testament to the area's colonial history when land and bodies of water were distributed among specific saints and incorporated into Catholic forms of devotion. Tlacuaches mostly refer to the ravine as "La Cañada del Agua," an appellation that materializes its relationship to water and to its topographic configuration within a system of rivers formed on the peaks of mountains flowing into the Basin of Mexico. Many also know the site as "El Paraje de la Piedra" (the stone's place or spot), identifying it by way of the stone that it once hosted. I have also heard people refer to the ravine simply as "Tecomates," short for "Piedra de los Tecomates," but also equating the place itself with absence and emptiness: the ravine is itself an empty vessel, a tecomate, carved into the landscape by a river that contained and channeled water. For many Tlacuaches as well as for scholars who identified the stone with the female deity of rivers and lakes, Chalchiuhtlicue (chapter 1), this was also why the site was chosen by its ancient makers. The empty ravine is now doubly deprived of the contents by which it is defined: water and the carved stone.

Doña Luz, in her eighties when I met her, was always happy to chat while she tended to her family's butcher shop. She offered a third explanation linking the ravine to emptiness, this time in the form of ecological decay. It was her understanding that the name didn't refer to the shape of the site, nor to the stone at all, but to a shrub whose fruit, a kind of gourd, is also called tecomate. This plant grew abundantly in the ravine in the past and the gourd was used by campesinos to carry water before the advent of metal and plastic bottles. However, tecomates had mysteriously disappeared around the same time that the stone was forcefully taken from Coatlinchan. Doña Luz was convinced that this was not a coincidence: the shrub required high levels of humidity and rainfall that the stone's removal had diminished. Elders like doña Luz still remembered times when a river, one of several that flowed from Mount Tlaloc, passed through the ravine.[4] This river was abundant within living memory,

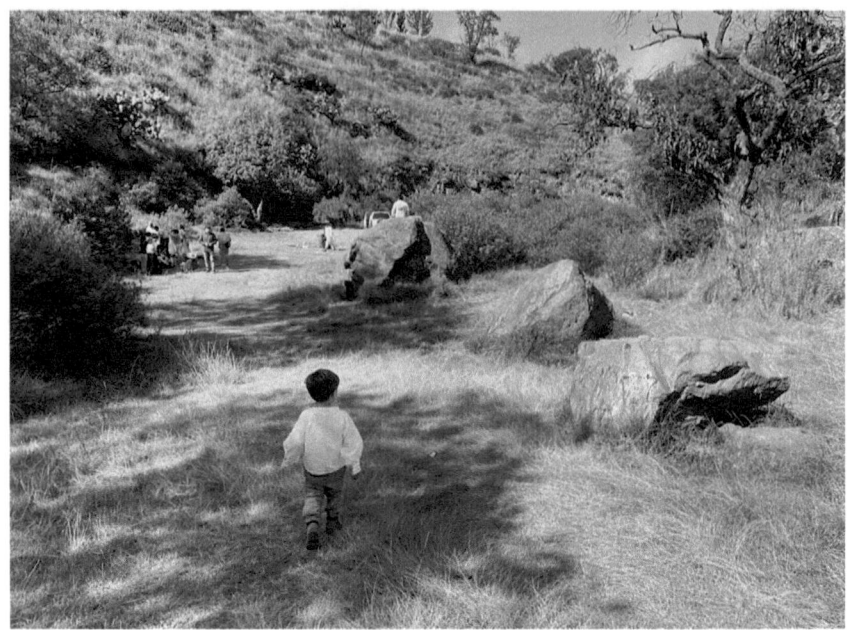

FIGURE 4.1. The Santa Clara ravine, 2023. The stone used to lie where people are gathered. Photograph by the author.

even flooding the area during storms. Nowadays, only a small brook trickles intermittently from the surrounding hills during the rainy season, passing just behind where the stone once lay. Sometime in the 1970s and 1980s, the town received a government grant to install several small dams to control the stream for local irrigation projects. Town residents told me that these dams, in addition to prolonged droughts, had made the river dry up. The site is now barren, with very little vegetation. Three large boulders lie on the rim of the gorge, covered in spray paint, tags, and graffiti (figure 4.1).

The place's most striking feature is barely discernible on the ground, overgrown with weeds. Through Google Earth's panoptic lens, a wide straight line becomes visible amid the brush, contrasting with the winding dirt roads and pathways carved into the landscape by campesinos' and monteros' footsteps. The straight road, the one don Chava referenced, extends from Centenario, Coatlinchan's main and widest paved road, becoming an intermittent dirt road the width of a two-lane highway. This road, buried under dust and brush during the dry season, is almost entirely erased by mud, puddles, and tall grass during the rainy months. It is also a dead end, terminating abruptly in the empty ravine. The *comisariado ejidal* (the ejido's representative) uses it occasionally to survey boundaries separating Coatlinchan from colliding towns. Sometimes, on weekends and holidays, Tlacuaches drive motorcycles and four-wheel-drive vans and pickup trucks to reach the ravine, setting up family picnics and afternoon drinking fests, or sometimes attending a Mass during Holy Week when the town priest visits the site.

Without any signage, I got lost many times trying to follow directions to El Paraje de la Piedra. Not long after moving to Coatlinchan, I visited the site with one of the community's representatives, who offered to drive me in his pickup truck. We arrived in the ravine but only after taking two wrong turns and getting momentarily stuck in the mud. As we drove up, the man told me that, like many of the men his age (he was in his late sixties, a contemporary of don Chava), he had been hired as a day laborer by the construction company that had taken the Piedra away. "Funny," he said with a sneer. "I practically built this damn road and now I can't even find it."

Coatlinchan's contemporary residents, notably the younger generations with access to online resources, are well aware that debates surrounding the stone's identification partially hinged on whether or not it was physically attached to the ravine and to its bedrock (chapter 1). Some have even tried to uncover tangible traces of this attachment. César, who was studying architecture at the IPN at the time, told me: "Well, you know that the stone was part of the matrix, right? The government broke the law by taking it! They stole it! There is evidence in the ravine. There, there is a huge scar. My friends and I found it." He then described how they had used picks and shovels to dig in the ravine. As they shoveled the earth, they suddenly heard a "thump" when the metal instruments reached a hard material less than five feet underground. César vividly recounted how they kept digging and little by little uncovered a rocky surface shaped like a mirror image of the stone's back. César and his friends' exploration was fueled by their desire to prove that the government had committed a crime. He lamented that his friends had decided not to make their finding public and had reburied the evidence. But this "scar" was a form of injury and César told me he would someday expose the truth. César was not the only one looking for visible traces of the stone's violent detachment on its back. Don Félix, an elderly Tlacuache who passed away several years after I interviewed him and whose family owned one of the town's largest *tortillerías*, looked through photographs of the stone upright in front of the museum on my laptop and pointed to visible grooves on its rocky surface: "You can see the scars of the sledgehammers on its back if you look closely."

César's and don Félix's stories coincide with many town residents' take on the controversy of whether the carving was in fact separate from the ground it lay in. Some of the residents who were hired by the construction company and engineers recalled that they had spent months trying to excavate the stone but were never able to wholly dig it out of the ground: "It never ended," don Amado told me. "It was impossible to find its bottom. They must have used a jackhammer or something because that thing kept going and going deep!" To this day, townspeople claim to have heard the rumbling of mechanical tools and dynamite explosions in the hillside late at night, audible proof that the engineers severed the rock from the matrix in secret. During our conversations in 2010, I asked Enrique del Valle Prieto, the engineer in charge of calculating the stone's weight, about these rumors. He insisted that no explosives could have been used because any reverberation could have caused the basaltic rock to crack, threatening its integrity: "We couldn't use dynamite. Are you kidding? Don't forget, the Tlaloc is patrimonio! The most important thing was to get it to the museum in one piece." Of course, the engineer meant unbroken, but perhaps also as a monolith, singular bounded stone that was not attached to the place where it had lain for centuries. Despite the engineer's insistence that dynamite was not used in the process and his own admonition that the stone did in fact not make it to the museum in one piece since he kept his own "little piece of Tlaloc" (chapter 2), town residents point to tangible marks in the landscape that they believe indicate otherwise. Walking the path that leads to the ravine over the years, town residents of all trades and ages have pointed out to me small cylinder-shaped cavities in the rocks that line the road, coinciding with the shape and size of dynamite sticks.

Holes

In 2014, to mark the fiftieth anniversary of the stone's removal, artist Ulises Figueroa asked town authorities for permission to produce an art installation evoking its absence. With their consent, he installed binocular viewers at different points surrounding the ravine, each containing a slide that he had photographed using handmade model reconstructions speculating on different moments of the stone's history: when it was being carved in ancient times, being defaced under the orders of colonial priests, clambered and photographed by early twentieth-century tourists and boy scouts, and finally, lying fastened to the truck that would transport it to Mexico City in 1964. Each slide also featured text by way of intertitles, explaining these moments of destruction and decay, ultimately leading up to its removal in 1964. Peering into the devices, viewers were confronted with the stone's absence as these images became superimposed over the empty ravine's contemporary landscape (figure 4.2).

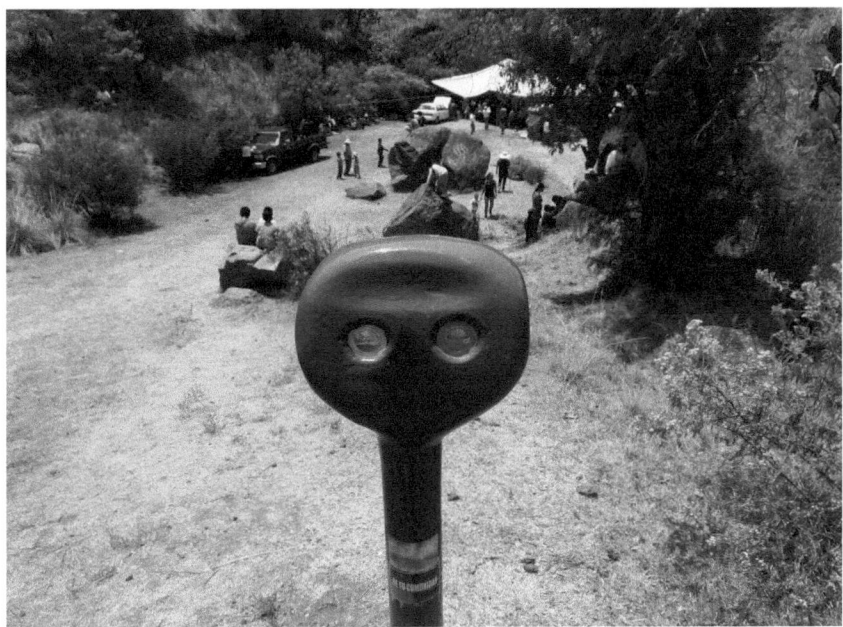

FIGURE 4.2. Ulises Figueroa's installation, 2014. Photograph by the author.

Figueroa had grown up in nearby Ecatepec and heard about the stone's theft since he was a kid from his grandparents, who, like many in the region, used to visit Coatlinchan and the ravine on family and school outings. They, too, attributed the entire region's changing ecology and drought to its forced relocation. Inspired by projects in different parts of the world using digital media and visual technologies to repatriate objects from museum collections to source communities, Figueroa had originally proposed to use the viewers to superimpose a single image of the absent stone and the empty ravine, hoping to "bring it back," while confronting people with the violence of its loss.[5] However, the project changed as town authorities intervened to make the installation more didactic.

Isrrael Pixihua, who goes by both his birth and Nahuatl names, belonged to groups interested in local history and culture, the Grupo Cultural Coatlinchan and its subsequent offshoot the Calpulli Makoyolotzin (which I will return to), and had just been elected as a community representative when Figueroa contacted him. His account of the negotiations with the artist privileged local needs: "Our youths have heard about the Piedra, but they don't know its history, its importance, its essence. Those who knew it on site, who really knew the

Piedra, are elderly and will soon be gone. This was an opportunity to transmit some of their lived experience to the younger generations." For Isrrael Pixihua, the installation was a way of marking the stone's theft as well as restituting an intimate knowledge of Coatlinchan's importance in ancient political and cosmological configurations. By making the stone visually present in various moments of the town's history as an important settlement in ancient times and then a tourist destination, he hoped that younger generations would stay and invest in Coatlinchan. He also hoped they would take on cargos in the communal bodies that administered community lands and resources. By the same token, outsiders would become aware of the historical importance of the place that they had come to visit or live in and would respect it.

The installation was well received by town residents who flocked to the ravine for a Mass held by the local priest during Holy Week, coinciding that year with the fiftieth anniversary of the stone's removal. During the event, children sat around picnic blankets as older family members told stories of their own encounters with the stone in the ravine as kids, and younger folks related their parents' and grandparents' accounts of day trips to visit the Piedra as schoolchildren. People liked to climb and sit on its belly, the stone slightly warmed by the sunlight (figures 4.3 and 4.4). This was overall a festive event as well as a very successful detonator of multigenerational storytelling.

When a few months later I accompanied Isrrael Pixihua back to the ravine, three of the viewers and the large cement blocks that anchored them to the ground were gone. A single viewer was still standing, but the lenses were broken and the slides had been partially torn out. Isrrael Pixihua told me that he and the town authorities, anticipating that they might be vandalized or stolen, had put stickers on the devices that read: "Take care of me, I am the history of your community." He was puzzled that, despite this, the installation donated by a local artist to restore something stolen from Coatlinchan had in turn been stolen and harmed. He decided that only outsiders could have been responsible: "I can almost guarantee you that it wasn't anyone from here who threw it down. Townspeople respect, they know the essence, all that past that is a part of us. The outsiders who have moved here—that's another story. They live off the town, drink our water, and they destroy everything that is ours [*todo lo nuestro*] because they don't understand its importance. They don't know our history, they don't see themselves as being a part of it." For Isrrael Pixihua, the installation's destruction was tied to the reasons that had made town authorities enthusiastic about Figueroa's project in the first place. The work was imagined as a tool for community building at a time when many residents felt the community was being threatened by outsiders who did not understand

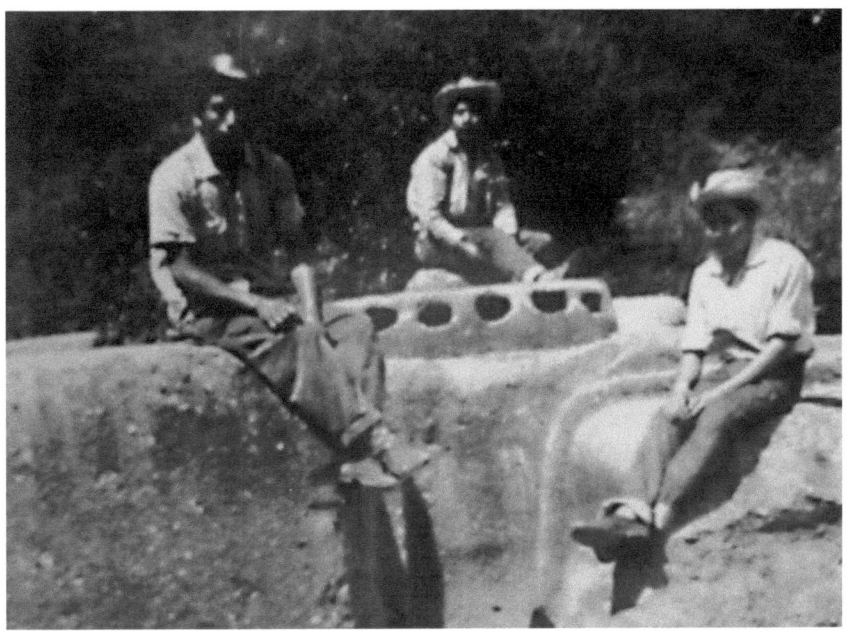

FIGURE 4.3. Bruno Morales, Leonardo Cadena, and Rogelio García sitting on the stone, 1950s. Courtesy of Bruno Morales.

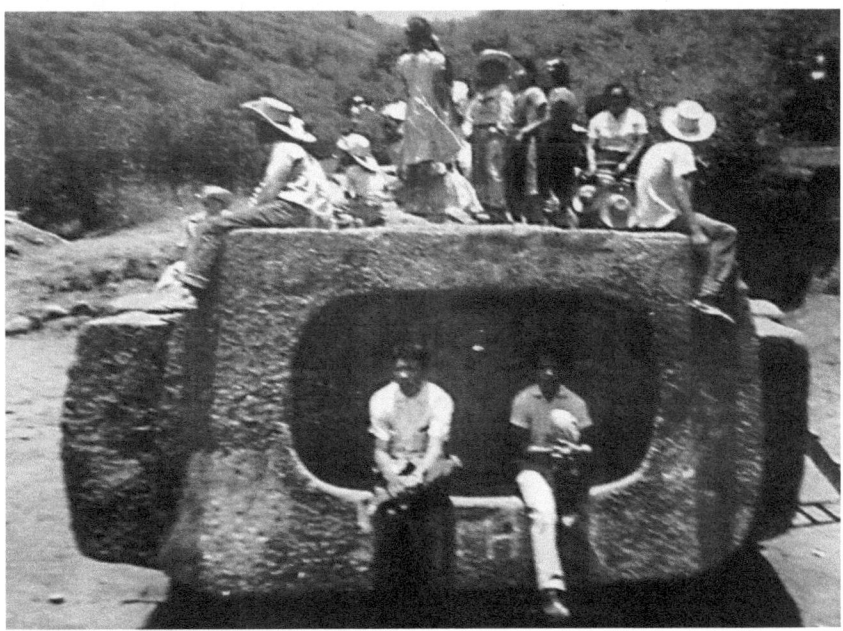

FIGURE 4.4. Tlacuaches posing on the stone, 1950s. Photograph courtesy of Pedro García.

the town's history, nor respect it, who only sought to profit from its resources, leaving little for younger generations to stay, invest, and live there for. Most of Isrrael Pixihua's own siblings and his adult children had themselves looked for work opportunities elsewhere and left Coatlinchan.

Figueroa was not aware that his work had been dismantled since he had not been back to Coatlinchan since. Personal circumstances had made him move to Pachuca and he had been busy with his family and work life. In 2022, I sought him out and told him that the visors were no longer in the ravine. He reacted calmly:

> Well, I knew they wouldn't last forever. They were printed on material that would eventually decay with exposure to the elements. Maybe six months, a year, that is all they were going to last. . . . I like to think that if someone took them it was because they liked them, because they wanted to see the stone, I don't know . . . in their own homes or backyards. That just gives the piece a new life. I am kind of into that. Doesn't seem to me like they were destroyed; maybe they are just serving new purposes elsewhere.

This "elsewhere" turned out to be in Coatlinchan, and in Isrrael Pixihua's home. As soon as he saw what had happened to the installation, he had removed the last visor standing and, in his words, had "rescued" the device, restoring the broken slide with scotch tape and taking it to his basement "for safekeeping," along with Figueroa's models, which the artist had also donated to the town. Isrrael Pixihua was hoping that both the models and the visor would eventually be part of a community museum that he and other town residents had been planning to build for many years. This museum was part of a larger set of projects designed by community authorities and local groups and activists hoping to draw attention to local history and rekindle the town's sense of community. Many of the objects that Isrrael Pixihua imagined would be in this museum were stored in his basement, including a large model of ancient Coatlinchan that he and his peers had made.

The precariousness of the space seemed at odds with these things' intended conservation. Every rainy season, the whole family worked to keep the basement from flooding, controlling the humidity and saltpeter that corroded its foundations. In a way, this basement was another kind of scar of the stone's removal. Having been educated in the community's primary school installed by the government in exchange for the stone and given access to transportation routes built in connection to its removal that made travel easier, in his twenties, Isrrael Pixihua was faced with the scarce opportunities in his hometown and had decided to brave his luck crossing the border. He spent years living undocumented in Pomona, California. There, he had been hired to work in construction and had fallen in love with basements, promising that upon his return he would build one himself, the very first and only basement in Coatlinchan. His basement became an architectural effort to materialize his experience of living in the United States and bring back a piece of what he called "the American way of life." Given the conditions of the local soil made up of sands connected to ancient riverbeds, maintaining this feature was an incredibly arduous task. And still, it was a place that he and his family cherished and kept up as a repository of things that were under threat but that could be salvaged underground to both represent the community and guarantee its future.

The relationship between the underground and its harboring of valuable things did not just take shape in Isrrael Pixihua's basement. The architects and engineers who were sent to Coatlinchan in the 1960s had also surveyed what lay below Coatlinchan's ground. During their prospecting, coinciding with vertiginous urbanization in and around Mexico City, they found that the soil near the ravine was rich in good quality sand that could be used for construction. As a result, several sand mines and rock quarries were dug out in Coatlinchan's territory, not far from the ravine, their contents exploited and sold by the ejido, providing a large part of its members' income. Since this was quite a large sum of money, far exceeding the income generated by agriculture, the sand mines became one of the main sources of tensions as well as corruption within the ejido and outside of it.

The largest of these mines, Las Joyas (The Jewels), a rather poetic name describing the value of its sandy contents, was abandoned in the 1990s after having been exploited for decades. The enormous hole, very close to the empty ravine and to the only privately owned ranch in the eastern part of the town, Tecuac, has become the subject of much speculation, as townspeople associate its emptiness with danger and risk. I overheard many conversations about how it was being used as an illicit dumpsite for hospital waste. Others said it was used to bury some of the bodies of the thousands of disappeared persons in the wake of the country's recent war against drug trafficking. There were also less alarming rumors about the possibility of transforming the old mine into an artificial lake as an ecotourism project that might help deter its illicit uses, recalling the 1963 proposal by Carlos Pellicer and Miguel León-Portilla to build a waterpark in Coatlinchan (chapter 3). In 2017, when the construction of the new Mexico City airport was underway nearby, town residents circulated flyers decrying that the mine was going to be used as a dump for toxic muds removed from the former lakebed to make way for the airport.

The people in charge of the ejido are drafting a contract to fill Las Joyas with "toxic muds" from Lake Texcoco. The contract will last 10 years despite the grave damage this would cause to the environment, aquifers, flora, fauna, as well as agricultural lands. This will bring us illnesses like cholera, diphtheria, gastrointestinal sickness, different types of cancer and genetic malformations, to mention only a few.

This text was accompanied by an illustration showing the aftershocks of this contamination both above and below Coatlinchan's ground, making the town ultimately toxic and uninhabitable (figure 4.5). The flyer carried the question "Will you allow this to happen?"

Water was especially fraught in contemporary town life. The three wells administered by the Comité de Agua Potable "Tlaloc," the communal body in charge of making drinking water available for local households, pumped water from underground aquifers into pipes and reservoirs. The appropriation, theft, or pollution of this water was tied to the stone's removal in very literal ways. The stone served as the logo for the Comité, featured on its stationary, members' T-shirts, and other paraphernalia, pointing to the stone's relationship to the liquid's availability as a life-giving source for the community (figure 4.6).

Margarito, the oldest of the water pipefitters (*fontaneros*) who serviced the potable water system, told me that the *comité* was formed in the late 1950s to dig and administer wells since the prior source of community water, a natural spring in the monte, mysteriously dried up. Margarito understood the town's water scarcity as a direct consequence of the stone's removal: "There was almost no water left only a few years after the Piedra was taken, so you can draw your own conclusions," he told me. Margarito went on: "When I was a kid, this place was known for its abundance in water. People from the nearby villages were envious of our rivers, perpetual streams of fresh, clean water, of our gardens." Margarito took a moment to list all the fruit and flower trees that used to grow in Coatlinchan and describe how fresh and perfumed the air smelled when they were in bloom. He elaborated: "We had so much water, we even gave up some of our springs at Tula and lent them to Tequesquinahuac [the neighboring town], and then the *ojo de agua* dried up. And then we started making holes in the earth and pumping water from the ground, and building the system, the tunnels and pipes. Now people have drinking water in their homes, but their gardens are dry. The spring is dry and, since they took the Piedra, it stopped raining too. . . . We were left dry." Margarito associated the system that allowed townspeople to

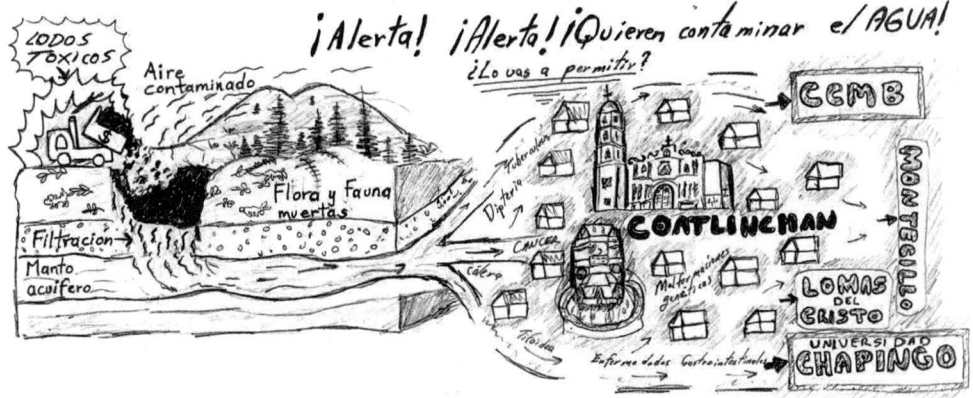

FIGURE 4.5. Image from flyer distributed by Coatlinchan residents, 2017.

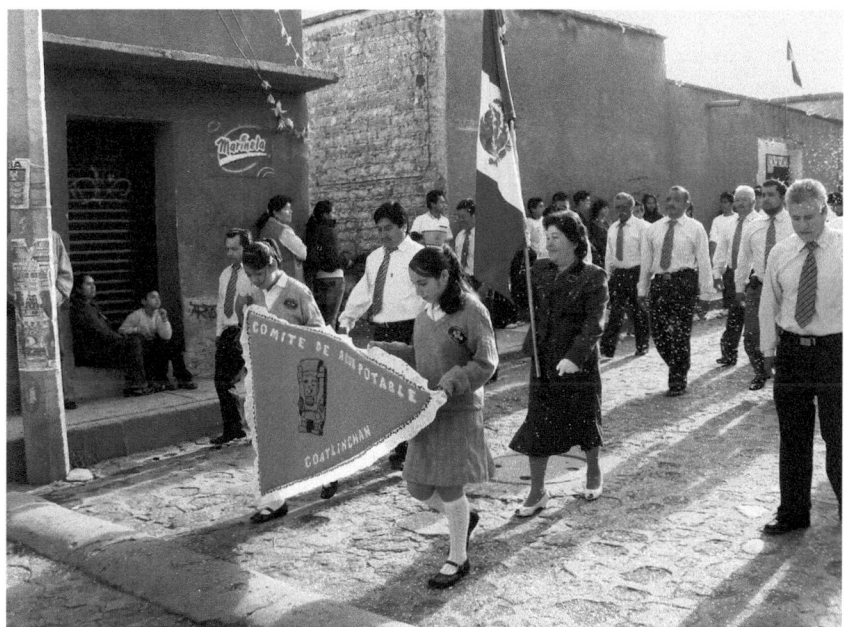

FIGURE 4.6. Parade for Independence Day in Coatlinchan, 2009. Photograph by the author.

have running water in their homes with dryness and scarcity. He was frustrated: "Everyone doesn't have water. Half the town can't get water most of the time, we have to manage the liquid so carefully, six hours here, seven hours there, three hours off, four hours on. Me and the other *fontanero*, we go around managing the system all day long so that as many people as possible have water, but the fact is they don't—there just isn't enough."

Water intermittency and increasing scarcity is much discussed in present-day Coatlinchan, as more and more residents have to follow tight schedules that ration the provision of drinking water; many have bought or built reservoirs in their homes to store the liquid privately. Elders nostalgically recall a past of water abundance, not just in the rainy season but year-round. That water flowed in open-air canals lining the town's streets built using community labor.[6] In addition to quenching their thirst, they sustained plentiful gardens and orchards in residential compounds. Tlacuaches bring up recent water scarcity as the main reason to limit the numbers of newcomers settling in their territory. In the meetings of the Comité de Agua Potable, heated debates and confrontations hinge around engineering ways to charge new residents extra for water use or to close down their water outlets and control differentiated access to drinking water.

Lo Nuestro

In 1963, just as engineers and architects were busy measuring, weighing, and suspending the stone in the ravine, a team of anthropologists came to Coatlinchan, commissioned by the Organization of American States (OAS) to evaluate the effects of the Mexican Revolution's agrarian reforms on campesino communities (Martínez de Verburg and Verburg Moore 1964). These reforms and, specifically, ejidos were framed by the Mexican state as a form of restitution, giving back lands to communities thought to have been dispossessed by conquest and subsequently by the liberal reforms that dismantled community property as well as the agricultural haciendas that thrived well into the late nineteenth century (Zendejas 1994; Azuela 2011, 2019; Kouri 2017, 2020). Coatlinchan was chosen as a case study because it had been reconfigured as an ejido thirty years before and was easily accessible from Mexico City.[7] The study focused on the fragmentation and inequality in community members' land ownership patterns and concluded that the reorganization of Coatlinchan's lands had created factions and fractures in the town.[8] However, focusing on landed property and resources did not acknowledge the ways in which, for town residents, community was constituted and sustained through relations linking people to what lay both above and below the earth's surface. Locally, people understood these relations as "lo nuestro."

The OAS study was published in 1964, the same year that the stone was forcefully removed from Coatlinchan. Yet its authors did not mention the stone or the state's intentions to take it to Mexico City; nor did they mention other elements that I heard town residents time and again describe, as they did the stone, as "lo nuestro." The study focused solely on land as a measurable surface that could be divided, owned, worked, and exploited to provide sustenance and profit.[9] Its authors detected corruption among authorities who allegedly signed off several land plots to themselves.[10] They concluded that Coatlinchan's ejido did not result in economic self-sufficiency since town residents had to seek out salaried income.[11] They determined that Coatlinchan's ejido was, therefore, an active agent of development projects in the region that were politically complicit with US imperialism and de facto working in ways that called into question the ideals of the revolution (Martínez de Verburg and Verburg Moore 1964, 85).[12]

The OAS anthropologists were not interested in documenting a much longer history of conflict and disruption pertaining to various forms of extractivism that had historically dispossessed Coatlinchan of what its residents considered "lo nuestro." They did not describe the many large stone masonry houses dating from the late nineteenth and early twentieth centuries that even today dot the town's main streets. These solid, often two- or three-storied houses contrast with the relatively modest adobe and cement block constructions that make up most of Coatlinchan's built environment, hinting at internal hierarchies and prior histories of inequality. Inside some of the larger adobe houses, it is common to find architectural features taken from the haciendas: large stone masonry incorporated into the walls; cantera stone archways; elegant multicolored tiled floors garnishing kitchens and internal courtyards; bits and pieces of gilded frames and intricate ironwork adorning windows, doors, and balconies (figure 4.7).[13] These fragments and their incorporation into the town's built environment can be seen as another kind of scar, remnants and markers of older forms of extractivism and violence repurposed to heal historical wounds.

According to most of the people I got to know in Coatlinchan, it was the stone's removal, and not agrarian reforms, that unsettled the core of the community and altered residents' relationship to "lo nuestro." This event was remembered as a kind of wound inflicted by the state's hand with the complicity of many of the community's own representatives. What was taken was not only the stone but an essential component of what made up the community, sustained through local forms of government, solidarity, and cooperation but

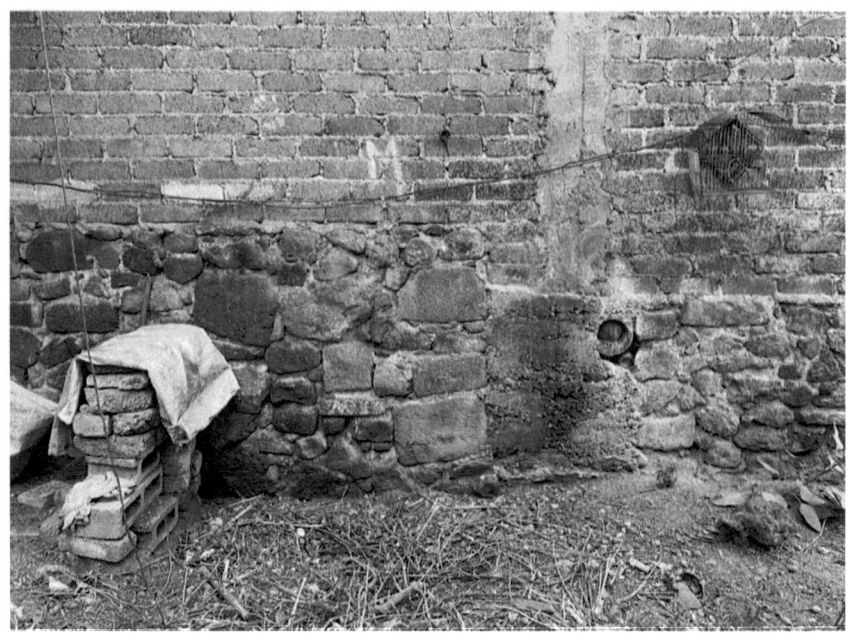

FIGURE 4.7. A wall, likely from the old Tepetitlan hacienda, 2009. Photograph by the author.

also through substances and features connecting its people to territory both above- and belowground. The state had, therefore, not only stolen the stone; it had failed to recognize, undermined, corrupted, and harmed the very body that it had put in place as the core of the postrevolutionary project's mission to restore communities.

Nowadays, the definition of Coatlinchan's territory as communally held land continues to be a site of contention. As the OAS study showed, even back in 1964, plots within the ejido were already sold, rented, and exchanged through local practices. Following the 1992 constitutional reforms that made the sale and disaggregation of ejido lands legal, town residents are worried that the ejido and collectively owned resources that make up "lo nuestro," notably water, are increasingly vulnerable.[14] Over informal conversations, Coatlinchan's ejidatarios expressed fear that their peers might seek personal ownership over their plots or decide to sell them. Yet Coatlinchan's ejido has for the most part not yet been sold. There have been ongoing discussions on land sales given that many of the state of Mexico's infrastructure projects have been built nearby; most notably a new Cultural Center that opened in 2011 and a highway, the

Circuito Bicentenario, connecting the region to the state of Puebla. These projects are seen as a threat because they have driven up land prices and harbored projects that could potentially expropriate communal lands or warrant access to ejido-owned roads.

These infrastructure projects sparked many conversations about what would happen if individuals decided to sell to the government at differing prices and sought personal profit over the collective good. The tension surrounding these threats escalated because Coatlinchan's neighbors, most famously the ejido of San Salvador Atenco, also part of the Texcoco Municipality, resisted selling their lands for the construction of Mexico City's new airport in 2002 and 2006 and actively participated in finally halting its construction in the former lake bed following a referendum in 2018.[15] Nevertheless, in Coatlinchan, town residents are much more concerned with other forms of expropriation and extraction that articulate their sense that territory cannot be reduced to landed property but is made present through substances, objects, and networks of relations that make up "lo nuestro," a body that exists above and below the earth's surface and that, as such, can be wounded or harmed. Such an understanding meant that the loss of territory and its scarring could exist beyond its surface registers.

One October morning in 2009, Coatlinchan woke up to the church bells ringing, summoning town residents to the streets. Within the hour, a crowd stormed the entrance of Tecuac, the privately owned ranch made up of lands that had once belonged to the old Tepetitlan hacienda that dominated the area before the revolution. The large colonial hacienda was partitioned sometime in the nineteenth century into the hacienda that kept its name to the south and the large Tecuac ranch to the north. Both belonged to the same owner until the revolution, when Tecuac was given to a revolutionary general.[16] The crumbling adobe and stone structures are in ruins, with a live-in guard to deter possible squatters. Just before I moved to Coatlinchan, the guard who had worked there for many years had been beaten and chased away. He was quickly replaced, and nobody seemed to know much about what had happened. Some speculated that he had been bought off by people from Texcoco who wanted to buy the property. For decades there have been rumors that the owners want to sell the ranch and make it into a luxury hotel, but no such project has materialized.[17] Yet, that day in 2009, people had been talking for several weeks about how the ranch was going to be taken over by squatters organized by Antorcha Campesina, a political organization associated with the PRI and well-known for its land encroachments. The church bells were tolled after town authorities detected a caravan of pickup trucks going up toward the old ranch at the crack of dawn and small groups of people carrying bags of cement and setting up piles of their belongings just behind the hacienda's old olive grove. Town residents carried ropes, a recognizable threat to lynch invaders.

As I followed the crowd up Centenario, the town's main road that extends into the monte and leads into the ravine where the stone once lay, I came across the comisariado ejidal whom I had interviewed a few weeks before. He exclaimed: "See, this is exactly how it was when they took the Piedra! When we hear the bells, we know there is trouble. We leave whatever we are doing and come out to protect the pueblo and lo nuestro. We did it then, and we are doing it now." The comisariado was not the only person who made the analogy between town residents' actions that day and their forebearers' efforts to sabotage the stone's removal in 1964. A woman in the crowd who had a loudspeaker yelled at the squatters: "*Chinguen a su madre* [Fuck you]! You think you can just take what is ours. They took our stone, but we won't be fooled now, we are stronger, we won't let you take *lo nuestro*!"

I was puzzled by the analogy. The stone was technically communal property as it had been removed from the ravine that was on ejido lands that had been expropriated from the Tepetitlan hacienda and given to the community, whereas the Tecuac ranch was privately owned by a family that did not even reside in Coatlinchan. Why, then, was the town mobilizing around its possible seizure? When I asked the comisariado, he explained that town residents were not defending the ranch or its owners but "lo nuestro." He further explained that townspeople were upset, and rightly so, because if the ranch's lands were seized and developed, new residents who were not native to Coatlinchan would move there and demand to use the town's water supply, drawing the already scarce liquid away from local households. This was all the more alarming because Tecuac was on the northern side of the town, on higher lands and closer to where the water wells and reservoirs were located, favoring water flow by gravity. Defending the ranch was not about the land as a measurable and delimited surface but about its position within a broader network that connected water flows and other substances above and below the ground. The comisariado told me that as more and more outsiders were buying and squatting on previously arable lands, water scarcity had become the town's most pressing problem. In his rendering, the church bells and the town's mobilization were not just formally similar to the episode in 1964; these actions were also similar because they were about defending what made up and sustained the town and its territory. "Lo nuestro" had to be defended from harm and encroachment.

Although it was the principal hacienda for much of Coatlinchan's history, the ruins of Tepetitlan that Tecuac once belonged to are harder to locate. Few

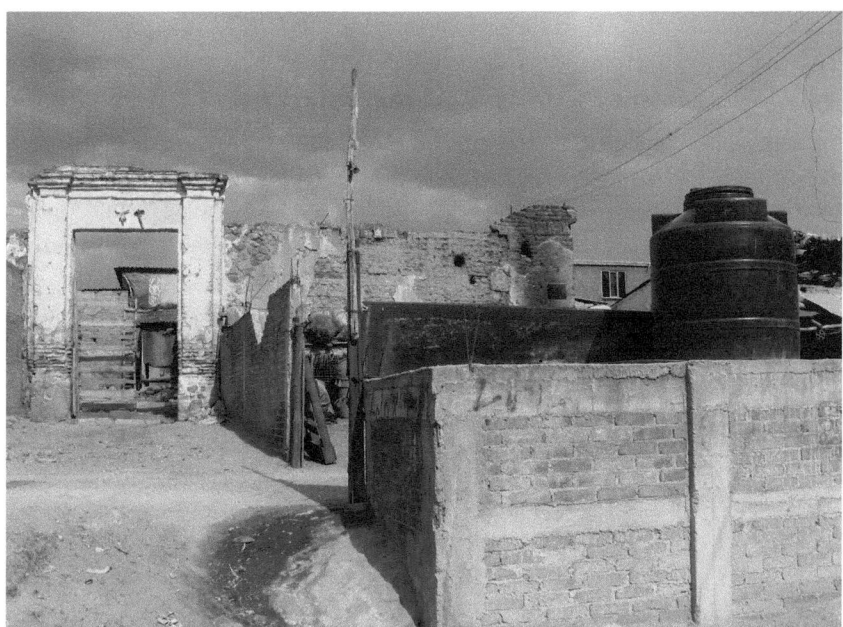

FIGURE 4.8. Ruins of Tepetitlan, 2009. Photograph by the author.

people, especially of younger generations, even know where the hacienda was, and, although many of my acquaintances gave me directions, it took me several walks in the area to find its visible traces. In contrast to Tecuac, Tepetitlan's lands were fully incorporated into the ejido, both as individual *parcelas* and as communal pastures and *bienes comunales* (community lands). Most of its old adobe and stone structures were dismantled to make way for more recent constructions. The remains of one of the main building's archways is still visible under a makeshift compilation of concrete block and tin roofs crowned by a black plastic Rotoplas water tank (figure 4.8).

Parts of the hacienda's chapel can be made out amid piles of stone and adobe blocks looming in a field where the last surviving of the town's sheep livestock, once part of the prevalent campesino lifestyle, are taken to graze. Large carved stone masonry that surely made up its walls can still be found recycled as part of contemporary walls and fences, noticeably in a recent building that functions as a high school. When, in 2012, I visited the area with don Chava, he pointed out that some of these walls' foundations looked like the classic *talud-tablero* style of pre-Hispanic architecture. He speculated that the hacienda was likely built over a *tlatel*, an ancient stone mound, like others that peppered the town center.[18] Chava pointed to the geometric stones still visible among the rubble to show the group that the wall's builders had probably repurposed ancient stones as construction materials. The old hacienda, therefore, was embedded in a layered history of colonial extraction and appropriation of "lo nuestro." These fragments were then also scars marking historical violence and loss.

Unlike the center, where people worked mostly at home or in their shops, making them easy to find and available for conversations, the area around Tepetitlan was desolate during the day. Residents left early in the morning and came home late at night after a day's work in the town center, in Texcoco, or in Mexico City. In this part of town, its southernmost point, residents are mostly poor and recent immigrants from various parts of the country. Many of the men work as masons and handymen and the women provide domestic help for homes in Coatlinchan's center. These families rarely participate in community events. They are referred to as "avecindados" or "vecinos," signaling their recent arrival and, therefore, their lack of legitimate membership in the community that might guarantee their access to community land, water, and resources as well as other rights and duties. They are often discriminated against as "foreigners" and even "invaders," disdained for their roots in Indigenous communities in Oaxaca and Yucatán. Rumors circulate that they squatted on the old hacienda lands illegally. For years, community authorities have wanted to evict them and restore what is left of the old hacienda to build a community center or museum. Older residents complain about these new residents as a symptom of how the town is changing, expelling younger generations who are losing interest in working the land, leaving room for outsiders, referred to derogatorily as "vampires," to invade abandoned plots or buy land at depreciated prices. These outsiders are suspected of sucking the town dry of increasingly scarce communal resources.

Despite town residents' efforts, the town's sovereignty over territory and its resources are considered to be under threat. In addition to recent immigration, new sources of wealth have become the subject of gossip among residents who denounce the transformation of "lo nuestro" into private and individual property, while at the same time admiring their neighbors' home renovations, new pickup trucks, and expensive brand-name clothes. The town's newest elites are rumored to have made their fortunes by having been former town authorities who allegedly stole from the community, or, alternatively, they are rumored to be involved in the drug trade, Mexico's more recent hypercapitalist economy. Recent wealth is also understood as resulting from the appropriation of communal resources. The relatively recent industry of cattle farming is seen as a form of theft of "lo nuestro" through bulls' bodies, purchased as calves, fattened, and subsequently sold to the meat industry. In other parts of Mexico, raising cattle is a capital-intensive industry with expensive inputs. In addition to paying for the calves, cattle farmers have to sustain and nurture the animals' growth for many months before they are old and large enough for sale. Tlacuaches, however, have turned cattle into an extremely profitable business by using communal resources, especially water, emanating from territory into the main input for sustaining fairly large herds.[19] Through such enterprises, a few families in Coatlinchan are transforming "lo nuestro" into private capital. In these ways, the harm endured by Coatlinchan following the stone's theft and other appropriations of "lo nuestro" is ongoing. Yet town residents are creatively repurposing theft and its aftershocks, working to heal and restore that which makes their town and its territory endure.

Healing

In his late thirties when I first met him in 2005 and a graphic designer by trade, Marcelo, who prefers his Nahuatl name Tlakuanikoatl Ocelotl Xicome, was, like Maestra Lupe, don Chava, and Isrrael Pixihua, an active member of the Grupo Cultural Coatlinchan, a group made up of teachers, activists, and young professionals who shared an interest in protecting and promoting local history and culture. In 2009, he and other members of his generation founded the Calpulli Makoyolotzin, working specifically to reactivate Coatlinchan's ancient Indigenous legacies through language revitalization and ritual. The Calpulli Makoyolotzin is an offshoot (the name is a nahuatlization of the term *macollo*, used in botany to refer to the bud or offspring) of its "parent" organization, the Grupo Cultural, which was largely focused on historical research and preservation. Like many groups associated with La Mexicanidad, a movement that began in the Valley of Mexico at the height of Indigenismo in the 1940s and that has since expanded all over the country and beyond, the Calpulli's designation as a "calpulli" rekindled the kind of localized political, religious, and economic collectivity defined by the altepetl, the region's main unit of social and territorial organization in ancient times that was made up of several calpullis.[20] In contrast to the Grupo Cultural, Calpulli members referred to their practices in ritual terms, describing their work as a way to study and preserve local history but also to restore and reactivate ancient Indigenous cosmologies, lifeways, and forms of knowledge. They envisioned their work as a kind of healing following centuries of colonial and more recent forms of violence. Theirs is a very particular theory of cultural continuity that perceives the pre-Hispanic past neither as fully past nor as having resisted or survived in linear

FIGURE 4.9. Coatl-
inchan map, sixteenth
century. Courtesy of
Mediateca INAH, Insti-
tuto Nacional de Antro-
pología e Historia.

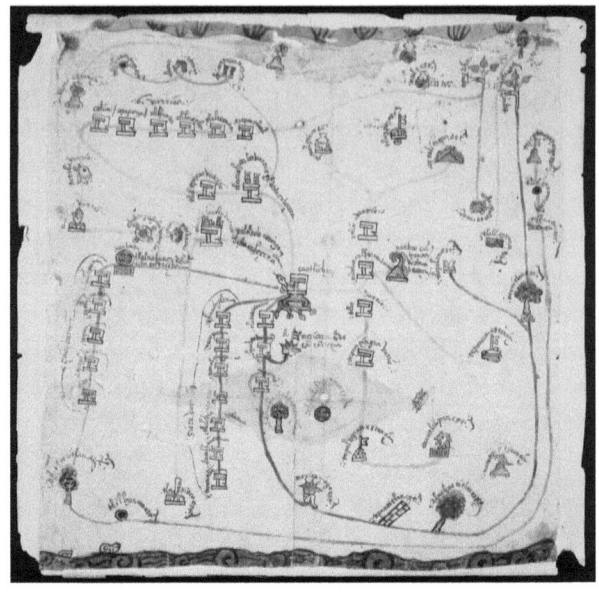

time. For Calpulli members, this past lies dormant in territory ready to be unearthed, reawakened, and restored with the right kinds of research, uses, and
understandings.

In 2002, Tlakuanikoatl Ocelotl Xicome came across a facsimile of Coatlinchan's oldest cartographic representation displayed in a bookstore window.[21]
This was a reproduction of a sixteenth-century painted manuscript known
alternatively as the Mapa de Coatlinchan or Coatlichan (as the toponym is
spelled in the map). This document is now in the INAH manuscript collection,
stored in a vault on the second floor of the Museo Nacional de Antropología,
not far from where the stone now stands (figure 4.9).

The map immediately caught Tlakuanikoatl Ocelotl Xicome's attention
because it showed the town's pre-Hispanic glyph as an ancient altepetl, surrounded by other glyphs and toponyms that were familiar to him. He describes
his find as "oro molido" (powdered gold). This metaphor anticipated the ways
in which the document and what it shows about Coatlinchan as an ancient
altepetl would be activated by the Calpulli as a kind of treasure map.[22] Using
homegrown research methodologies, the group repurposed the document to
explore and map the town's contemporary territory while also revealing traces
and hidden forms of knowledge left behind by ancient ancestors.

The map combines pre-Hispanic glyphs and pictograms with Latin script
glosses and European-style illustrations depicting the sites, flora, and fauna of
Coatlichan (an alternate spelling for ancient Coatlinchan), an altepetl that

flourished in the Acolhuacan region during the late Postclassic period (Mateos Higuera 1945; Bittman Simons 1978). Six spiraling color lines emanate from the central glyph showing a snake emerging from a *calli* (house or construction) atop a mountain gushing water. The lines connect the Coatlichan altepetl, the largest glyph, to its six dependent calpullis, each with its own satellite towns, estancias, and barrios—hinting at an ancient system of political, social, and territorial organization based on small-scale kin-based collectivities sharing and controlling territory and the environment. The map set ancient Coatlichan as part of a political and telluric configuration linking settlements to places through their connection to topographical features, bodies of water, and human and nonhuman life located within territory. Because of its hybridity, the map has been used as an example of Indigenous resistance to conquest, expressed through the endurance of Nahua forms of spatial representation.

In the 1990s, the map figured among a collection of glossy poster-style life-size facsimiles published by the Benemérita Universidad Autónoma de Puebla and the INAH, alongside scholarly interpretations, in this case by an expert of ancient Central Valley maps, Luz María Mohar Betancourt (1994). This was the edition that caught Tlakuanikoatl Ocelotl Xicome's eye and pocket. Enthusiastic about the map, Calpulli members found Mohar Betancourt's predominantly linguistic analysis problematic. Tlakuanikoatl Ocelotl Xicome was an especially outspoken critic: "Scholars write from a distance. They don't even come here to experience the place. The map could be about anywhere." For him and for the group, it was not enough to decipher glyphs and translate place-names from Nahuatl; an intimate, embodied, and multisensory relationship to territory was necessary. In order to make the map truly legible, Calpulli members spent several years walking Coatlinchan's territory, searching for documents and land titles in institutional and personal archives, and conducting interviews with family members and town elders about the sites represented and named on the map. Through this research, they matched places now named after Catholic saints and liturgy to their Nahuatl toponyms and glyphs (Rozental 2020). They found that although only a handful of these Nahuatl place-names were still in use, many were common knowledge only one or two generations ago, remembered by elders or figuring on nineteenth-century and early twentieth-century title deeds. The older generations who grew up in Coatlinchan when it was a small agricultural town didn't speak Nahuatl but spent their days traversing its territory to tend to their fields, pasture sheep, or gather firewood. Their intimate knowledge of territory and named places helped the Calpulli identify topographical features such as rocks, caves, and bodies of water marked on the map. Elders also showed the group the remains of several tlateles that were marked on the map but had been largely destroyed. For much of the early twentieth century, tlateles were well-known to town residents because they provided supplementary income: known as "idoleros" (idol people), outsiders would regularly come to dig for or buy pre-Hispanic figurines easily found there. Now that tourists and collectors so rarely come to Coatlinchan, many consider tlateles mere cumbersome piles of rocks and have dismantled them to make way for local agriculture or construction. Using the map, Calpulli members located their collapsed structures, many fading from local memory, excavating and rebuilding them to the best of their abilities. They also used this information to build the model of ancient Coatlinchan that Isrrael Pixihua stores in his basement. Through these efforts, they hoped for more than preservation. The Calpulli incorporated tlateles and sites identified on the map into a ritual itinerary taking them to different locations over the course of the calendar year, performing rituals following the colored pathways marked on the document as a collective effort to restore relations to territory and to their ancestors.

Historical maps, and especially ones made for land title cases, are extremely valuable for residents of towns like Coatlinchan who have diligently stored them in local repositories or sought them out in both state and national archives.[23] In Coatlinchan, however, the map is used beyond its possible sustenance for land claims. Calpulli members activate this and other traces from ancient times located in territory to access knowledge from another time that can in turn be used to sustain that territory in the present and well into the future. In this usage, the map has a performative quality that, when read in tandem with multisensory and intimate knowledge of territory, works to uncover ancient traces and vestiges that are latent in and also necessary for its production and reproduction over time. As Tlakuanikoatl Ocelotl Xicome liked to remind me, the group's use of the map echoes the ritual work undertaken by pre-Hispanic calpullis who themselves enacted elaborate stagings, drawing on the force of images and territorial representations to ensure their altepetl's endurance. For the Calpulli, pre-Hispanic materials and ancient objects like the stone, tlateles, and the map offer the possibility of restoring the past as a form of knowledge that is part of "lo nuestro" that can be accessed, manipulated, appropriated, and revived through spatial and ritual practices. "For us, the past is not a closed chapter but always here, lying under our feet, latent. It is our essence; we just have to work hard to find the pathways to access it," Juan Manuel Tochintecutli, one of the Calpulli's founding members and the owner of a small sporting goods store, told me during one of our many conversations. "We disagree with scholars who just see maps and stones, dead objects. For us, these things are not dead at all. They are breathing; they tell us stories. We just have to learn how to listen to what they have to say."

For several years, every Sunday at daybreak, Calpulli members met in Coatlinchan's Plazuela and embarked on multihour walks. Their preparation was similar for each expedition: they got together the night before to study the map and discuss a specific landmark in relation to their research and knowledge of the place. The walk itself had to be done while fasting; no food or water could be consumed. Calpulli members considered these walks a form of sacrifice—an offering of the body's energy to the guardians of ancient sites. During one such expedition in 2011, Rosa, a strong and joyful woman in her fifties, explained: "This is about committing ourselves, our essence, our labor through our bodies and our souls. We don't want to pretend to be what we are not. We are not Indians [*indios*]; we can't go back in time. But we can learn from our ancestors, feed their essence to create a balance, using our bodies to offer them our energy and our strength." Other Calpulli members shared Rosa's sense that it is by living in and with territory that Coatlinchan's essence, harmed by various forms of extractivism, could be restored and sustained.

Upon arrival at a site, the Calpulli performed both a literal and a ritual cleansing. They first changed from jeans and T-shirts to white cloth pants, loincloths, and blouses for men and embroidered huipiles for women, replacing sophisticated hiking boots with homemade leather sandals. They lit copal in an incense burner, scanning each participant's body, purifying themselves and others with the scented smoke. Saluting the four cardinal points and their associated elements in pre-Hispanic cosmologies, they asked permission from the site's ancient guardians. They then placed an offering: incense, fruit, flowers, pulque, a variety of seeds from local crops, and rainwater as well as water from the town's potable water system and samples from each of its wells. A replica of the stone was also offered to the site's guardians in return for safeguarding their territory. The final element in the offering was each participant's bodily energy: a dance to the rhythm of *ayoyotes*, rattles, and drums, all handmade by Calpulli members.[24]

Daniel Ayatitlicui was charged with teaching Calpulli members the dance steps. During one of the group's meetings in 2009, he explained that the dances were "not for show." "It is part of the work we are doing, an offering of ourselves, a sacrifice. No need for choreography and somersaults." He once said that ancient spirits visited him in his dreams and showed him the steps. He derided other *danzantes* like the ones who congregate near Mexico City's Templo Mayor, who "jump around" while donning elaborate colorful yet industrially made costumes that, he said, were "probably made in China." He insisted that both the attire—the handmade clothes and accessories crafted from local materials—and the dance steps had to be invested with town residents' bodily energy to actually produce "essence" that could then be gifted to Coatlinchan's ancient guardians. Town residents' bodies, nurtured by local crops and water, were then part of what sustained the community and its territory.

Having finished the ritual, each participant cleared brush, removing overgrown weeds and trash. This was a common practice when they visited the ravine where the stone once lay, used by community members and outsiders for picnics and recreation. "People come up here to drink or dump their garbage; they don't realize these places are sacred, that they contain our essence," Daniel Ayatitlicui lamented, as he and his wife, also a Calpulli member, picked up empty liquor bottles and beer cans. "So, we come and clean, trying to appease the anger of the guardians who care for these places when most of us don't." The couple was then expecting a baby and had decided that the ravine would be where they would conduct the child's birth ceremony, which they described as "the pre-Hispanic equivalent to baptism." Daniel Ayatitlicui clarified: "Except it isn't about inscribing the baby in the book of life and linking its soul to God, but to territory, our territory." He referred to the ritual, which is a common practice in Mexico and one that many believe originated in pre-Hispanic societies, as a *siembra* (planting) because the umbilical cord that linked the baby to its mother was interred in the ground. This ritual linked the person to the earth, binding them for their lifetime and beyond (Báez 1998). In 2022, as Tlakuanikoatl Ocelotl Xicome turned fifty-two, the equivalent of a century in ancient Mesoamerican temporal cycles, the Calpulli held another ceremony reviving an ancestral practice in the ravine. The group dug a metaphoric tomb for him to be buried in, covered with sand from the barren brook and offerings, only to emerge restored and renewed, welcomed into his new life cycle under a shower of local flowers and rose petals. Like the siembra, this ritual was premised on a conception of persons being related to but also emanating from the earth, living according to its cycles, growing from but also being renewed by it.

Calpulli members use the term *faena* to refer to the work they collectively perform in different parts of Coatlinchan to upkeep and care for territory, borrowing the term from local forms of community labor and solidarity (Cowan 1954). Calpulli members use *faena* to describe their work as a form of gifted labor based on a system of collective reciprocity with territory. In various Mexican towns and Indigenous communities, under this rubric, communal bodies administer, nurture, and guarantee sovereignty over territory as well as collective resources like water and forests, in addition to other elements that range from old buildings to liturgical objects and even pre-Hispanic vestiges. These days, faenas are still organized in Coatlinchan for community projects like cleaning the cemetery and drinking-water network, and town authorities still demand certificates of participation in order to issue official documents like proof of residence needed for various bureaucratic processes. However, fewer and fewer residents actually participate in them. Many purposefully avoid the organizing committees or simply prefer alternative modes of contributing to the town, such as cash donations. Calpulli members complain about this, stressing that cash is not a substitute for the ways each individual and family is meant to invest bodily energy to sustain the community and its relationship to territory.

When I interviewed him in his home in 2009, Juan Manuel Tochintecutli described the faena not as a donation but as a form of restoration: "Coatlinchan looks just like any small town; we are poor, our fields are barren, and the city is taking us over. Everything has been taken from us, but in fact there are indescribable treasures lying just under our feet, latent, left there for us by our ancestors. We just have to learn to find them. That is what we are doing in the Calpulli; we are treasure hunters now." For Juan Manuel Tochintecutli, forms of communal social organization and labor from both the pre-Hispanic and more recent pasts, as well as the actual work the Calpulli performs to maintain ancestral sites, were a means to simultaneously recognize, recover, and heal the community and its territory. He described this as treasure hunting, looking to unearth that which lies latent, waiting to be uncovered to restore the town's legacy as an ancient altepetl. For Juan Manuel Tochintecutli, the Calpulli's work physically walking and engaging territory through vestiges and forgotten pathways from the past, investing bodily energy and gifting it to the collective, were ways to recover and reinvigorate this territory and the community's sovereignty over it. Although, to my knowledge, none of the members of the group described themselves as "Indigenous" (like many in Mexico, they equate being Indigenous with speaking an Indigenous language as a mother tongue), they seek to access ancestral lifeways by engaging in embodied relationships with territory. Indigeneity for them might better be described as a way of being related to territory that is not fixed in relation to time or conditioned by language or biology. It can be rekindled and reconstructed by incarnating an intimate relationship to territory and, in turn, ensuring its reproduction.

In some way or another, the stone's removal and lingering absence are connected to many forms of loss and disintegration that materialize in the physical traces that remain present in the town's landscape and in substances like water, sand, and ancient artifacts and maps that have been historically extracted from Coatlinchan. These enduring marks affect how town residents understand, experience, and embody "lo nuestro," its potential loss as well as its possible res-toration. Don Chava and others' description of these tangible traces as "scars" reveals the enduring presence of these absences and the ways in which they bind people to territory and to each other through the shared experience of their loss. These scars are part of a broader body that, like any organism, might recover from a wound inflicted by an act of violence but remains irrevocably altered and physically affected in both negative and generative ways. In con-temporary contexts, Tlacuaches' scars are also markers of healing, revival, and reclaiming "lo nuestro" as an ancestral and telluric form of politics that can be accessed, reconstituted, and deployed to face new kinds of risks: scarcity and dispossession.

Juan Manuel Tochintecutli and Daniel Ayatitlicui passed away tragically in 2014. In their absence, many in Coatlinchan, and especially Calpulli members, sustain their conviction that Coatlinchan's essence endures hidden inside terri-tory and that, with the right kind of research and work, it can be unearthed and restored. In this context, Tlakuanikoatl Ocelotl Xicome's description of the map as treasure evokes the immense worth that recovering ancient structures and the map, even in facsimile form, has for the larger project of revitalization that he and others in Coatlinchan are so deeply invested in. In this sense, in this place marked by histories of dispossession, Tlakuanikoatl Ocelotl Xicome's framing of the map as treasure transcends mere evocation. Coatlinchan's terri-tory is understood as treasure-laden, containing knowledge but also sources of worth and value historically produced, stored, and removed from circulation by the humans and more-than-humans who live there and care for "lo nuestro."

5

Treasure

In early 2011, I received a call from Dulce, a young woman who alternates between supervising her family's sewing workshop, selling colorful foam figurines and silver jewelry online, and tending to her mother's stationery store. I first met Dulce in 2005, when she had just finished high school and was one of the youngest and most energetic members of the Grupo Cultural. As time went by, we became friends, sharing many meals and conversations in her home. The entire family, four generations living in a single compound, rejoiced, making fun of my efforts to attend as many town events as possible and my often naive questions. Once I left Coatlinchan, Dulce kept in touch. She called or messaged periodically, keeping me up to date, mostly announcing the deaths of people I had spent time with who were already elderly when I lived there. This time, out of breath, she disclosed: "Guess what? Last night we overheard helicopters flying over the old Nextlalpan ranch. The watchman saw how [Enrique] Peña Nieto came to take everything. The workers are all from here and they saw—well, actually they found a pot of gold *centenarios* when they demolished one of the old walls. . . . The taxi drivers saw it all too. But Peña's people came and immediately took the treasure away and closed everything off. Then, the helicopters left and when the workers came back the next morning there was nothing there."

Dulce had been present in 2009 when the Grupo Cultural had invited me to tag along on a visit to the dilapidated ruins of Nextlalpan, an old dairy ranch. The state government had just bought it to build the Centro Cultural Mexiquense Bicentenario, a huge complex with several exhibition spaces and auditoriums. As it was under construction, she had expressed skepticism regarding the state government's narrative whereby Coatlinchan was selected for the center for its historical importance. "That's bullshit," she said, rolling her eyes. In addition to promising easy access given its proximity to the highway, the old ranch was one of the only privately owned plots large enough for such a project in a region known for land conflicts. Dulce speculated that the state government had purposely selected the ranch to avoid negotiating with the adjoining ejidos, notoriously active opponents to land expropriations, specifically in the planning of the controversial New Mexico City International Airport (NAICM). Like Dulce, many Tlacuaches were skeptical about the government's intentions and related the project to other kinds of state-sponsored extractivism, including the stone's forced removal decades earlier. During meetings with the authorities, town residents time and again brought up the stone's theft as an example of dispossession linked to governmental abuses. They threatened to sabotage construction if municipal and state governments didn't pay for access to the road where the complex was being built, arguing that it belonged to Coatlinchan because it had been given to the community in exchange for the stone (chapter 3).

I visited Dulce months after her call, just after Enrique Peña Nieto, then governor of the Estado de México, had won Mexico's presidential election. As we discussed the news, she brought up the story of the Nextlalpan treasure: "See! That's where all our gold went, to his campaign!" Dulce's mom, Concha, chimed in: "It was a whole lot of treasure too! They say there were even gold ingots, not just Centenario coins." They both then complained about how their town had been robbed of what was rightfully theirs: "lo nuestro." This dispossession had resulted from illicit appropriation and encroachment: the workers—town residents and thus the legitimate owners of the treasure found inside Coatlinchan's territory even if the surface was privately owned—had unearthed the gold through their labor, but Peña Nieto and his people, outsiders as well as cyphers for the Mexican state, had taken it away and turned it into political capital on a national scale. Concha continued half-jokingly: "We just get duped. Time and again, the government takes what is ours. Just like with the Piedra." The town's very recent dispossession in the form of stolen treasure was, in her eyes, equivalent to the stone's 1964 theft.

Stories of buried treasure are part of everyday conversations among Tlacuaches. People gossip about how the wealthier individuals in town serendipitously found pots of gold hidden inside old houses or stashed by nineteenth-century bandits in nearby hills and caves. Many stories of stolen treasure like the one Dulce related preserve a sense that outsiders have historically dispossessed the town of "lo nuestro." Tlacuaches use the concept of treasure to refer to that which they consider theirs, oftentimes stored or hidden underground. Treasure features prominently in the town's territory and built environment, somehow always both self-replenishing and at risk of being pillaged. It is coveted because it's never quite finite, emerging from unknown sources, omnipresent and powerful and at the same time situated and fragile. Often guarded by ghosts who refuse capitalist logics that might otherwise allow individuals to accrue wealth and profit from the community unhampered, treasure is produced, sustained, cared for, and kept in place through the complicity between the living, the dead, and a host of non- and more-than-human entities, working together to incarnate its substance and avoid its capture. Treasure tales, in this sense, are also morality tales: they tend to end in death and suffering for those who disturb it. Tlacuaches' attention to the gruesome details of the violence with which treasure's removal is reprimanded shows a certain delight in these tales' telling, demonstrating a tacit knowledge that hidden treasure does not belong to individuals, including to those who might have buried it in historical time, nor to whomever ultimately finds it. Such stories recall Gastón Gordillo's account of the lingering and spatialization of memories of violence in places in the Argentinian Chaco that "bring to light the historical nature of space and the tensions and ruptures that have constituted it" (2009, 344). In these places, treasure tales linger as one of progress's forms of rubble, haunted by affective charges of violence and dislocation that have vitality in the present (Gordillo 2014). In Coatlinchan, like in the Chaco, registers of treasure, then, work as telluric forms of resistance, reprimanding outside actors and individuals seeking to profit from and steal "lo nuestro."

It might seem that stories of stolen treasure have little to do with the absent stone. However, they merge with town residents' sense that the stone was part of a broader configuration that makes up "lo nuestro" and that its removal had effects much beyond the physical absence of the actual stone. Here, treasure tales merge with a history of theft and dispossession that marks the town as a site where valuable objects and resources—including the stone—have been taken by force.[1] In these narratives, hidden sources of wealth are located in specific places: large rocks, caves, freshwater springs, and old constructions from the town's layered past. In most cases, Coatlinchan's treasure tales feature forms of hidden wealth with easily recognizable exchange value like gold ingots and coins (centenarios) that could potentially circulate beyond the community. But there is also a sense that treasure is more than material wealth, restricting its ability to travel and translate easily into market economies. Treasure is made up of long-standing relations, knowledge, and intimacy with territory, which remain attached to Coatlinchan and are therefore ready to be engaged, used, and restored in the present. Hidden treasure bears witness to town residents' efforts to resist dispossession and store what they consider theirs even beyond their lifetimes, hidden out of sight by the living as well as dutifully kept in place by the dead and by beings that lurk in sites related to specific moments of historical violence: first during the Spanish invasion, then during the nineteenth- and early twentieth-century capitalist expansion, in the aftermaths of the Mexican Revolution, and, finally, in more recent times marked by the aftershocks of authoritarian state intervention.

As anthropologists since the 1940s and 1950s noted, treasure tales have been a common trope for explaining sudden wealth in Latin America in what George Foster called "static economies" (1964).[2] Although the "static" nature of campesino societies has been contested since then, more recent work in other parts of the region has set such stories of hidden treasure—mostly gold and silver (Taussig 1993, 2004; Collins 2015) but also body fat (Abercrombie 1998; Canessa 2000; Weismantel 2001)—in mines, in landscape, and even in human bodies as the result of colonial violence and more recent kinds of exploitation and appropriation. Contemporary stories of hidden treasure are riddled with inequalities that intensify with new forms of capitalist accumulation, escalating profits, and increasingly extractive economies largely reliant on poorly paid local labor and resource extractivism. In this sense, treasure might be thought of as a theopolitical formation that is specific to the aftermaths of the Americas' deep history of colonialism and the expansion of racial capitalism (McAllister and Napolitano 2020, 2021).

The prominence of treasure in Coatlinchan also points to different ways of understanding what makes up, sustains, and reproduces territory as well as what constitutes sovereignty over it. Understanding ancient artifacts as treasure complicates state institutions' and museums' focus on the material qualities of objects and monuments as separate and singular vestiges from the past that require intervention and "rescue," even expropriation, to ensure proper conservation and care. As treasure, such things are not only found under Coatlinchan's lands; they are made from and of its territory. They might be removed, even stolen, but they ultimately remain related to the ground they came from and to the people who live there. As such, they also reproduce, replicate, and might be restored and restituted there. Restitution does not necessarily imply their physical return but the proliferation of practices that engage, activate, decode, and reanimate their potential as telluric forces that guarantee the production and reproduction of "lo nuestro."

Bandits

Tales of avid treasure hunters lured to Coatlinchan have circulated since at least the nineteenth century. In some of the most well-known stories, the town figures as a site ripe for hiding stolen goods from the vigilant gaze of the authorities. This was recorded by writer Manuel Payno (1810–94) in his famous novel *Los bandidos de Río Frío* ([1891] 1996), in which Coatlinchan, located on the other side of the mountains from Río Frío and on the Camino Real—a road connecting Veracruz, Mexico's most important port, to the capital since viceregal times—features as one of the bandits' preferred hiding places. In addition to its strategic location, Coatlinchan's topography, with its uninhabited wooded hills crisscrossed by steep ravines and cliffs, made it an ideal hideaway for stolen bounty. In Payno's story, Coatlinchan is not merely a repository but also a source of treasure: the bandits visit the town to hide their loot as well as to steal gold and silver that had been concealed by the town's mayor in the local priest's bedroom rafters. Even in historical fiction, then, Coatlinchan figures as a place where treasure could be hidden from official networks but also produced and hoarded by the community.

To this day, townspeople complain about valuables that belonged to the town that, like the gold hidden in Payno's novel, were stored in the church and stolen by bandits. In February 2009, during morning Mass, Father Ezequiel, the priest then assigned to the town, mentioned the recent disappearance of several chalices and the silver accoutrements carried by the town's patron, San Miguel, for his feast day. As we exited the church and sat on a bench in the atrium, don Chava, who attended Mass with me that day, commented: "People have been stealing from Coatlinchan forever. When I was little, I was a choir boy and handled all the things that were used for Mass. There were tons of things! All shiny gold and silver! I know, because I used to have to polish them. But now, who knows where they all are." Don Chava related these losses to the stories he heard from his grandfather about the treasures hidden in nearby caves by the infamous Río Frío bandits: "They didn't just hide coins! They hid religious things like monstrances and vases, and many other things made out of gold and silver that my grandfather said people here found."

The search for objects stolen from the town parish and for treasures hidden by bandits became entwined with other things buried in Coatlinchan's territory from more remote pasts. During one of our many excursions to the monte, Jesús, a university student in his early twenties who was also a member of the Grupo Cultural, showed me a site near one of Coatlinchan's many ravines. There, the entrance to a cave known as San Bartolo could be accessed after climbing a steep pile of boulders that formed what was once a riverbed. Jesús knew of the cave because, as a kid, he had tagged along with his father, who, having read about the Río Frío bandits and their preference for caves, rock formations, and other topographical landmarks, went on expeditions with his friends hoping to find their stashes. They made maps and designed homemade metal detectors for these weekend outings, invigorated by the expectation of sudden fortune.

Pointing to the ground just at the cave's entrance, Jesús related excitedly, "They began digging a hole right here! But after many hours, my dad got tired and went to rest. He fell asleep under a tree. When he came back, his friends were acting suspicious. He was convinced they had found treasure but didn't say anything because they didn't want to share it." The next day, he went back and continued digging in case some of the treasure was still there. He didn't find any, but he did find what remained of a pre-Hispanic offering of broken ceramic vessels and figurines. Jesús told me: "My father still has the figurines and sherds [*tepalcates*] and always tells me they are the most valuable thing he owns. This is better than any treasure because it is ours. It belongs to us and makes us who we are." For both Jesús and his dad, the pre-Hispanic offering's worth constituted the timeless and generative potential of "lo nuestro."

Pots of Gold

Born in the 1920s, doña Lupe captivated her teenage granddaughter with stories from her youth during evening meals. One evening in 2009, as we all sat around the dinner table enjoying a bowl of lentil soup, she told us that when she was a child, only a decade after the revolution, the rich families of Coatlinchan would every so often spread their gold on their patios and expose it to sunlight. She was told by her mother that exposing gold to the sunrays made it multiply. This theory of multiplication by way of the sun, a telluric force that makes the earth productive and plants grow into food, made gold, like any other organism, thrive and reproduce into wealth in this specific place, subsequently available for extraction, circulating outward as capital.

Although it can be other things and substances, the most common kind of hidden treasure in Coatlinchan is gold. As Elizabeth Ferry has shown, gold's material qualities—its color, shine, and brightness but also its historical legacies—have associated it with a sort of intrinsic value resulting in its hoarding to guarantee different forms of collective sovereignty (Ferry 2020, 2021). In Coatlinchan, gold takes on particular shapes related to specific moments when the state and other actors have threatened local forms of sovereignty. There are many stories of buried ingots and other objects made from precious metals like silver spoons and gold liturgical chalices, but in Coatlinchan, gold coins are the most common form of buried treasure. These coins are not just any coin. They are centenarios, first minted in 1921 to commemorate the centenary of Mexico's independence from Spain, coinciding with the reconciliation of the different factions that led the Mexican Revolution.[3] According to elders, in the 1920s, revolutionary fighters from the Carrancista faction came seeking refuge in the town and turned the sixteenth-century church and its cloister into military barracks, burning the local archive as well as pillaging households. Coatlinchan's elites, the ones that doña Lupe remembered spreading their gold in their patios and who were close to and profited from the hacienda economy, allegedly buried centenarios inside the thick adobe walls or under the heavy stone floors of their homes as a means to protect their wealth from revolutionary plunder. As one of the older adobe houses on the town's main square was being demolished to make way for an internet café in 2010, Dulce's mom told me that the house belonged to one of her cousins: "He says he wants to make money off renting locales instead of keeping the old house that is falling apart. After all, he lives in Mexico City. But surely, he wouldn't mind finding a pot of centenarios in the walls!"

Doña Luz liked to flaunt that the house next to hers belonged to the richest man in Coatlinchan. He was not born in the town but had lived there for decades. When he became a widower, he moved to Tezayuca in the nearby state of Hidalgo. Doña Luz was a friend of the family and was asked to check in on the property occasionally. Dressed always impeccably, with colorful ribbons braided in her hair that matched her embroidered aprons, she took pride in her home's proximity to wealth. Don Pascual, her neighbor, had become an important member of Coatlinchan's community, lending money to people in need as well as accepting the role of godfather to many of their children. When I interviewed him in his home in 2009, when he was already in his nineties, he told me that he had come to Coatlinchan a poor man and prospered there. "I owe everything to Coatlinchan," he said proudly. His entrepreneurship consisted in buying hay from townspeople who grew maize and other crops in community lands for their own consumption and selling it as fodder in the regional markets, making a substantive profit. According to doña Luz, his fortune was only indirectly based on this form of capitalist accumulation. She was convinced it was also derived from the gold centenarios he had found in the old house that he had purchased using these profits. His real fortune, then, was premised on another kind of appropriation of the town's collective wealth.

Yet, even as it could be transformed into private capital, Coatlinchan's treasure was always still part of "lo nuestro." Doña Luz often talked about the house next door as it featured prominently in her childhood memories and in her dreams. Her mother told her that it was built over a palace that used to belong to the sister of Netzahualcoyotl, the famous ruler of Texcoco in pre-Hispanic times. She pointed to a crumbling structure propped against one of the property's walls and told me it was once the largest tlatel in the area. Doña Luz was one of the informants who had helped the Calpulli locate dozens of these stone mounds in Coatlinchan, some in public places like the town's cemetery or on the street near the water depot but many, like the one she lived next to, hidden inside courtyards or incorporated into town residents' homes. She told me that, when she was a child, she and her siblings had found the entrance to an underground tunnel just next to the tlatel. "My mother said that when she was little, she and her brothers found a golden throne there and a ball made of solid gold. Neither was there anymore by the time we found the tunnel. It was empty. But I didn't really go back to look because I got so scared. It spooked us [espantaba]!" For years, the ball appeared in her dreams, haunting her, but when she tried to catch it, it always disappeared.[4]

Like Luz's, there are many stories told in Coatlinchan today about tunnels and underground passageways. This network connects ancient settlements marked by constructions aboveground like tlateles and the colonial church thought to be built atop a large ceremonial complex as well as sites in the town's territory where pre-Hispanic offerings have been found: the nearby hills known as the Cerro de la Cruz and Quetzaltepec, the San Bartolo cave I visited with Jesús, the spring that provided water for the town before it mysteriously dried up, and, finally, Santa Clara or the Cañada del Agua, the ravine where the stone once lay. Tunnels also connect sites where treasure lies hidden following historical moments when Coatlinchan was ransacked by foreign actors. At the same time, they operate as topographic forms of resistance, keeping wealth underground to protect it from plunder as well as evading the vigilance of the authorities. Belowground, this wealth accrues and reproduces and, in turn, secures the community's sovereignty within and over its territory.

Ancient tunnels like the one doña Luz described come up in conversation when town residents discuss any kind of project that might require digging into the ground, be it the expansion of one of Coatlinchan's sand mines, the restoration of the church's cloister, or the excavation of a new cistern for a family compound. Although most people are fascinated by these tunnels and tell stories linking them to hidden treasure, these underground passages are fundamentally feared. The tunnels that run under Coatlinchan are considered dangerous. Like in doña Luz's childhood memories, these tunnels "espantan," spooking those who get close to them, working to keep their whereabouts and contents inaccessible.[5]

Don Ricardo, a local history enthusiast in his sixties, owns one of the largest and oldest houses in town. He told me that he had dreamed of owning it since he was a kid, growing up hearing rumors that it was built over tunnels connecting various stashes of hidden gold. He dug many holes and tore down several old walls looking for these tunnels. Now, rumors surrounded his own wealth, given that he did not come from one of the town's elite families. Some maintained that he found hidden gold during these explorations, using it to purchase hundreds of bulls, which he fattens and then sells to the regional meat industry—a relatively new form of profit in Coatlinchan. Don Ricardo, however, assured me that he had given up the search empty-handed. In his youth, he wanted to study archaeology because of stories told by his parents and grandparents that the real treasure of Coatlinchan was the gold buried under the church in the secret tunnels. Given that the church was managed by the Texcoco Archdiocese, which would not allow town residents to alter the building, let alone dig up its surroundings, working as a professional archaeologist would have given him the proper credentials to unearth the long-lost treasure. Shrugging his shoulders, he told me: "Life just caught up with me. And so being an archaeologist was just another childhood fantasy. Here I am, all grown up, and I have never found treasure."

Despite his prosperity, Ricardo had endured difficult times. The tragic death of his young niece several years earlier had plunged his family into a prolonged sadness. During my visits to the house, Juan, his son-in-law, a construction worker by trade, was helping Ricardo out, laying cement blocks to build a new room for the family. He was a great storyteller and artist, making drawings and prints in his spare time. As he shoveled mortar, he lowered his voice: "The girl fell after many nights when she had reported seeing a little girl around her same age roaming the roof of the house." Juan was convinced that a ghost had lured the little girl to her death and that her life was the price for the treasure. Juan also told me that the presence of this spirit and the rumors regarding his father-in-law's pact kept him up at night. His own little girl, the youngest of Ricardo's grandchildren and barely four years old at the time, had told him recently that she, too, had seen a little girl walking on the roof.

In the treasure stories I heard, it was only through the willingness of beings imagined as ancestors or sometimes as vengeful spirits and even devils that Coatlinchan's hidden riches could be accessed and made to circulate beyond the community. Doña Micaela, who rents the locale of her shop in one of the older and clearly more affluent constructions in town, told me when I casually asked her about the house during a visit to buy a gift for a birthday party:

> It belonged to one of the rich men in town. Everyone knew he was a very cruel man. He was murdered and when they lifted the coffin to take him away, it didn't weigh anything, and they realized the body had disappeared. That's how everyone knew he had made a pact with the devil in exchange for gold. That's why he was so rich. The family tried to fill the box with stones, but everyone already knew. And after that, his family members started to suffer violent deaths: gunshots, car accidents, things like that.

This story and others cast Coatlinchan's treasures as the town's collective wealth that is intimately and inextricably bound to its territory. As such, it cannot be removed without risk and reprimand. Coatlinchan's treasure is contained underground, binding people and place and being kept in place for future generations.

The most common character in Coatlinchan's treasure tales is the infamous Charro Negro, a prominent figure in Mexican folklore, also related to historical moments of violence. In the wake of the Mexican Revolution, this elegantly clad male avenger on horseback began to haunt the national imaginary with the deafening sound of chains and cavalcading hooves. An ambivalent and cunning trickster, the Charro Negro, also associated with the Devil, offers pacts in exchange for individual fortune that result in personal tragedy and even death.[6] He almost always appears to people—mainly men—to show them hidden treasure in exchange for sacrifices, many times their lives. People are assumed to accept the pact given the immediate joys of fast and easy fortune or for the sake of their families' long-term well-being. Not unlike the Devil figures also registered by Gordillo in El Chaco (2004), the Charro is fundamentally malignant, but he uses his supernatural powers in complicity with humans, working to guarantee community reproduction: punishing excess (he often appears to drunks after nights of debaucherous libation) and individual gain over the collective good (Foster 1964; Schryer and Foster 1976; Taussig 1980; Nash 1993).

In Coatlinchan, the Charro haunts specific places known to be linked to the aftershocks of violence, namely the ruins of the old haciendas and ranches that were dismantled in the wake of the revolution and its redistributive land reforms.[7] He has also been known to appear near a tree stump that flanks the Delegación on the town's main square. Don Pablo, sitting on one of the Plazuela's cement benches, pointed out the old stump and explained: "The Carrancistas hung their enemies from that olive tree. My grandfather witnessed the whole thing. The bodies remained there for days, stinking, full of flies." Olive trees were planted and exploited for profit by the region's haciendas and are still prominent in the lands belonging to the Tecuac ranch. Such places are marked by the Charro's appearances and remembered, even generations later, as sites of violence inflicted upon townspeople caught between the various factions fighting a revolution imagined to restore collective land and sovereignty.

In addition to the old hacienda hauls and the places associated with revolutionary violence, another of the Charro's favorite stomping grounds was the ravine known as the Paraje de la Piedra. Around the same time that Payno was writing about Coatlinchan as a hiding place used by the bandits of Río Frío, Leopoldo Batres, who excavated in Coatlinchan and was the first to fully unearth the stone to prepare it for its possible removal, also recorded stories of hidden gold related to the stone (chapter 1). In fact, Batres (1903, 12) believed that the stone had lost its defining features because it was desecrated by Spanish priests who had cast it down as a false idol in the sixteenth century and defaced it, hoping to strip away the gold nails that allegedly held it together. This understanding of the stone's ultimate shape as the result of a combination of colonial iconoclasm and attempts to extract pre-Hispanic gold by colonial authorities reinforces the ways that it, too, operates as a theopolitical formation emerging from histories of conquest and colonial appropriation. Within this same logic, the Charro, known to roam the ravine when the stone was still there, lured residents there to dig for gold. Several elders recounted that the Charro was not as much seen as heard. However, the chains and notorious horse's hooves had stopped sounding once the stone was removed, as if the gold and hidden treasures the Charro guarded had vanished along with it.

Doña Flora, in her early nineties when I met her in her family home in 2008, attributed the stone's broken features to outsiders coveting this treasure: "During the revolution, people came here looking for the bandits' treasure and thought it was hidden in the stone, so they blew its arm off with gunpowder." In her understanding, it was not erosion or colonial iconoclasm but more recent searches for treasure that resulted in the stone's defacement. Other versions of this story circulate. I even heard town residents, noticeably the younger generations, speculate that what the Mexican state was really after in taking the Piedra was not the stone and its potential repurposing as a museum artifact or monument but the gold that was hidden inside.[8] This was the treasure that the Charro Negro was guarding. Doña Flora told me: "My grandfather was a montero. He spent many nights sleeping in the ravine, inside the stone's headdress where he had shelter and got some shut-eye. He told me he often woke up scared, his heart racing and limbs frozen, hearing the Charro's chains and hooves. Many times!" She was silent for a moment and then giggled as she added: "I guess the Charro doesn't have anything to guard there anymore now that the Piedra is gone, does he? Maybe he is haunting other places! Maybe *you* can hear him outside the museum in Mexico City!"

Stories of pots of centenarios and unearthed treasures still circulate in Coatlinchan, but these are no longer the only sources of sudden wealth available. Whether through corruption, the market for illicit substances, or various forms of privatization, Tlacuaches have found new ways to prosper outside the collective. Jokingly, Jesús once told me, "You think the piedra that is important for us is the one at the museum! Ha! No, *güera*, look around! It's another kind of piedra that rules our world!"[9] He meant "piedra," the street name for crack cocaine sold in pebble-shaped nuggets. Just weeks before he said this to me, a police raid had revealed a crack kitchen working from an abandoned building in the vicinity and three dealers had been shot and killed by rival gangs two blocks away from the Plazuela, where they were rumored to sell to Coatlinchan's youth.

For many in Coatlinchan, new sources of wealth are the result of either illicit economies or individual appropriation and theft of "lo nuestro." Ancient spirits and ghosts seem, however, to be abandoning Coatlinchan's hidden treasure in the hopes of redistributing it to the collective. Going back to Dulce's story of Peña Nieto's helicopters coming to steal Coatlinchan's hidden gold that opened this chapter, these outside looters suffered no reprimand by charros or incensed ghosts. The sense that Coatlinchan's riches are no longer the collective wealth of its residents—living or dead—contrasts with the treasure tales and town residents' efforts to revitalize ancestral localities and rescue ancient forms of relating to and controlling territory. The treasures that Coatlinchan's residents know to be hidden in old houses, stone mounts, topographical features and ancient carvings and artifacts, are also the sources of what makes Coatlinchan endure as a form of social, political, and economic organization anchored in territory. And this form, following the stone's removal and in the subsequent decades, is under threat, at least aboveground. It is in this context and in the aftershocks of theft that the absent stone, like treasure, is being replicated and mobilized to restore Coatlinchan and its residents' relationship to territory.

6

Replicas

For more than a decade, a mural greeted town residents and visitors as they entered the Delegación on their way to meet with town authorities or participate in important community events. The mural featured the stone standing upright at the center of the phrase "We Are History, We Make History," accompanied by a glyph representing the Acolhua people that the Coatlinchan altepetl belonged to in ancient times (figure 6.1). This same combination was painted on another mural covering a wall outside the "Tlaloc" public school, not far from the Delegación, alongside a billboard with a huge drop of water, part of a campaign run by communal authorities to manage water use and educate children to care for the life-giving liquid.

In a sense, the ways in which the stone has become part of the town's sense of "being" and "making history" have made it all but absent in Coatlinchan. It is constantly being replicated and reproduced in murals and signage on Coatlinchan's main civic buildings, on community authorities' letterhead, and on

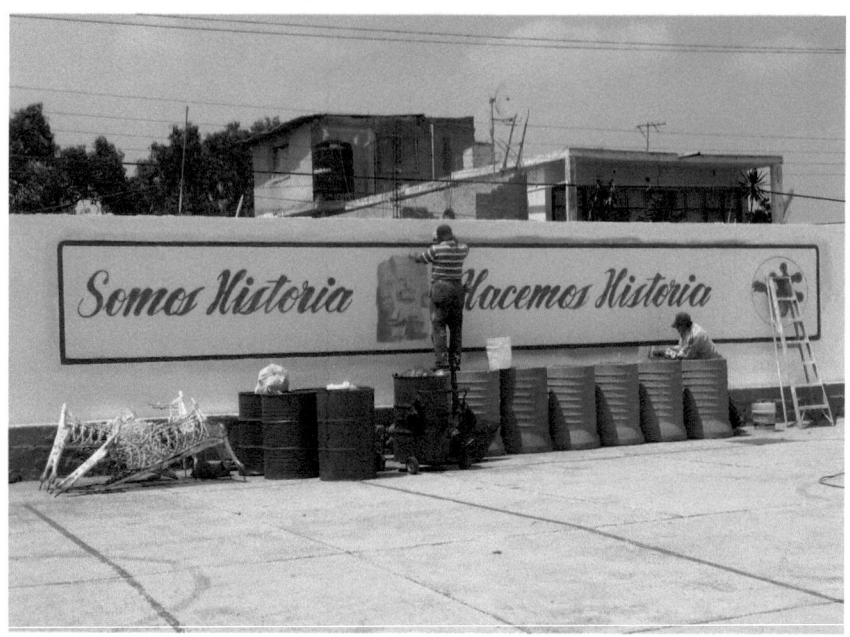

FIGURE 6.1. "Somos Historia, Hacemos Historia" (We Are History, We Make History) mural in the Delegación courtyard, 2010. Photograph by the author.

flyers, publications, and billboards printed to communicate with town residents (figure 6.2).

The proliferation of the stone's reproductions also goes beyond these official uses. They appear on storefront signage, as the logo of local taxi and minivan services (figure 6.3), and even on the *frontón* (handball court), known affectionately as "El Jorobado," which many say is a reference to the figure's hunched back. Over the past two decades, a familiar rendition, like the Delegación mural, has gotten painted over, only for a new one to appear. These depictions always show the stone as a bipedal figure, as it was repurposed for the museum. However, many transform the stone by appealing to humor, anthropomorphizing its features and making them wink, smile, or even wave (figure 6.4), or represent it performing gestures corresponding to whatever goods or trades are being advertised: an open mouth with a tooth being pulled out at a dentist's office, leaning on crutches with a desolate grimace and a bandage plastered over a wounded knee at a clinic, or happily blowing out candles on a birthday cake at the "Tlaloc" bakery.[1]

The town is also full of tridimensional replicas made of an array of materials and in different sizes, sometimes placed on pedestals or even inside fountains

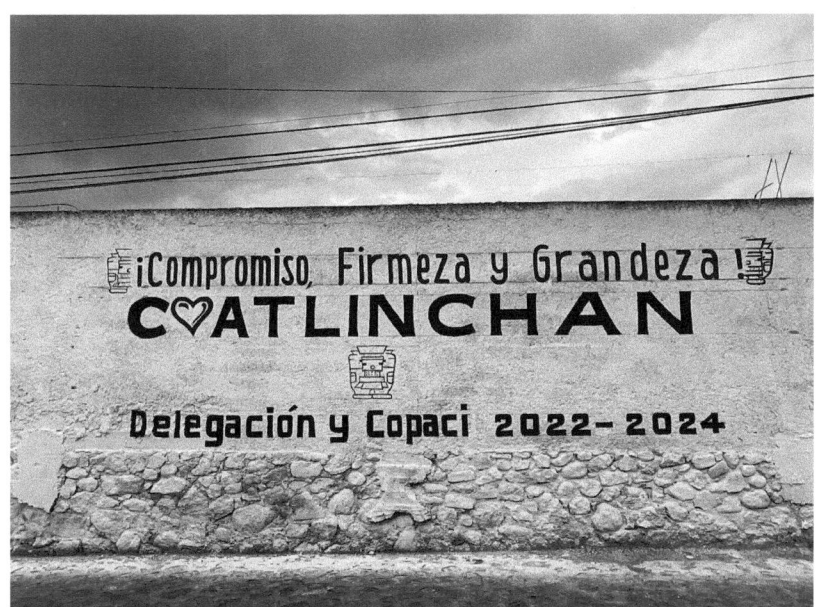

FIGURE 6.2. "Coatlinchan: ¡Compromiso, Firmeza y Grandeza!" (Coatlinchan: Commitment, Fortitude and Greatness). Mural with image of the stone, 2023. Photograph by the author.

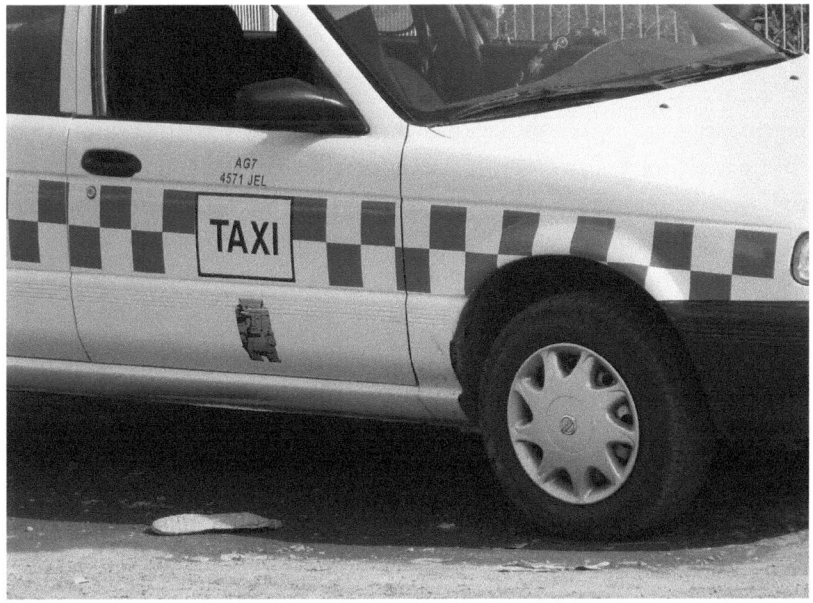

FIGURE 6.3. Taxi with logo of the stone, 2009. Photograph by the author.

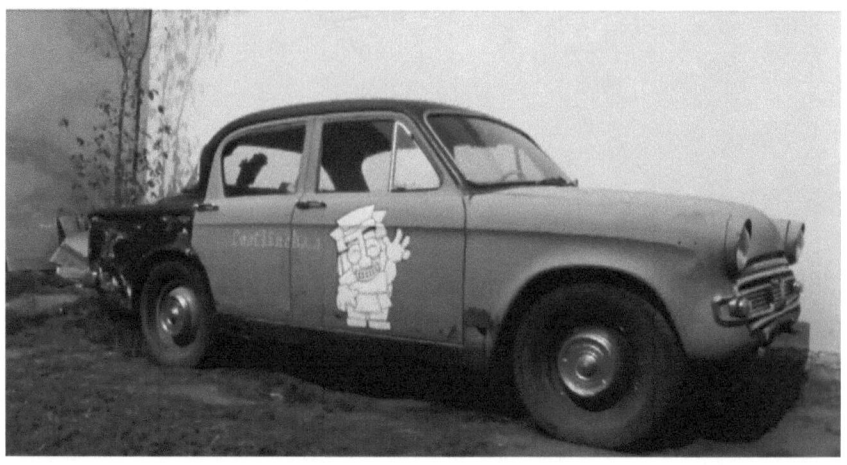

FIGURE 6.4. Sticker of a waving stone figure on an old car. Still from *The Absent Stone*, directed by Jesse Lerner and Sandra Rozental, 2013.

adorning gardens and patios. Smaller portable versions are kept inside homes or used to decorate window sills and awnings. Most Tlacuaches have at least one, if not several, miniatures standing upright as paperweights or displayed as decorative items in their living rooms, kitchens, and bedrooms, among other plastic and plaster figurines of smiling popular cartoon characters, emblazoned glassware, and memorabilia commonly distributed at christenings, weddings, and quinceaños. Standing alongside such collectables, these little replicas' arrangements as well as their scale and lightness contrast with the missing stone's lithic materiality, massive weight, and apparently static monumentality. Their prominence inside Tlacuache homes threads the stone back into town residents' everyday lives, domesticating it as one of myriad household objects. Through reproduction and multiplication, these replicas and representations are another kind of aftershock, attesting to how Tlacuaches experience but also confront and contest the stone's absence, creatively responding to its theft.[2] Replicas in Coatlinchan are true to the multiple meanings of the term *replicar* in Spanish: to reproduce and replicate, but also to fold over, to reverberate, and, finally, to contest.

In Coatlinchan, the proliferation of replicas and representations of the absent stone subverts state theft.[3] Prominent in Latin America, replicas and miniatures are historically given as offerings to ancestors or to "Earth Beings" (Allen 1997, 2016; Dean 2010; Cadena 2015, 2018; Angé and Pitrou 2016). Oftentimes, the ritual power of such miniatures is not inherent to their existence within

contexts of radical alterity but premised on their capacity to produce, reproduce, and maintain collectivities and their sovereignty over territories (Abercrombie 2016).[4] In Coatlinchan, reproductions and miniatures of the stone are
instantiating community and territory in more mundane contexts.[5] Making,
owning, and displaying these small-scale replicas has become a political act that
simultaneously refutes state theft and demarcates, produces, and claims back
sovereignty over territory and that which it contains. Multiplying and rescaling
the stone commemorates its loss while also opening up new opportunities for
relating to and deploying its absence as part of what "being" and "making" as a
community entails.[6] Their material qualities, size, scale, weight, manufacture,
and circulation allow for such transformations and associations.[7] At the same
time, these reproductions' multiplicity as well as the humor with which they
are made, arranged, and discussed complicate the state's interest in ancient artifacts as solemn, singular, and authentic material traces from the past that need
to be cared for and preserved in regulated ways, justifying their expropriation
and relocation to museums.[8]

Refuting Theft

Until very recently, replicas of the stone were not made in Coatlinchan. Residents bought them from shops and stalls in Mexico City, especially as they
became widely available as souvenirs made from inexpensive and lightweight
materials in the 1990s and 2000s. Most often these replicas are made of plaster,
plastic, fiberglass, or resin, about five to eight inches tall and painted in shades
of brown and gray to mimic the color and texture of stone. Very few of the
larger replicas inside homes are made of cement or of stacked stone blocks, but
these are also made elsewhere, commissioned from artisans from nearby towns
since there are no stone masons active locally (figures 6.5 and 6.6).

In 1991, the *mayordomía* gave out a clay pot in the shape of the stone with
a hand-painted "Coatlinchan 91" on its headdress as an acknowledgment for
contributions to the patron saint's annual festivities (figure 6.7). Even then,
these miniatures were commissioned from an artisan from Texcoco. Making
replicas in Coatlinchan would require artisanal labor and materials that, like
clay pots and stonework, have not been made for decades in a town where residents primarily work in the service economy.

As town residents become increasingly interested in Coatlinchan's history
and traditions, including crafts, a handful of Tlacuaches have begun making
miniature replicas themselves, an activity that is still more of a hobby than a
main source of income. Produced in home workshops by individuals who sell

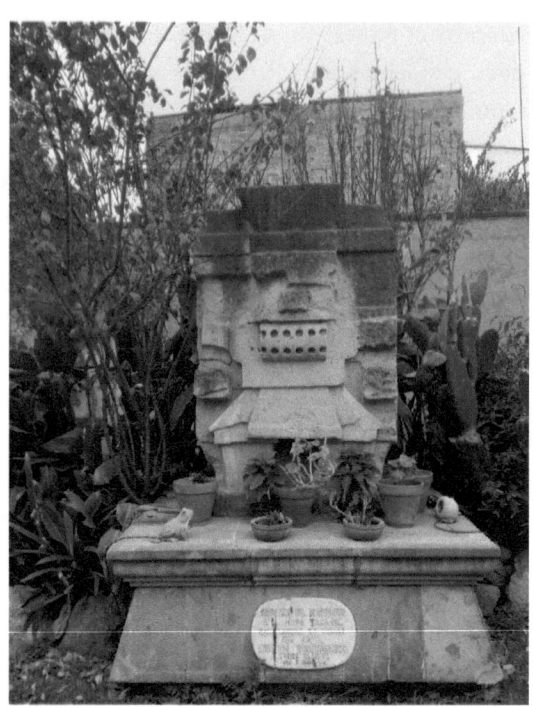

FIGURE 6.5. Replica of the stone in a garden, 2009. Photograph by the author.

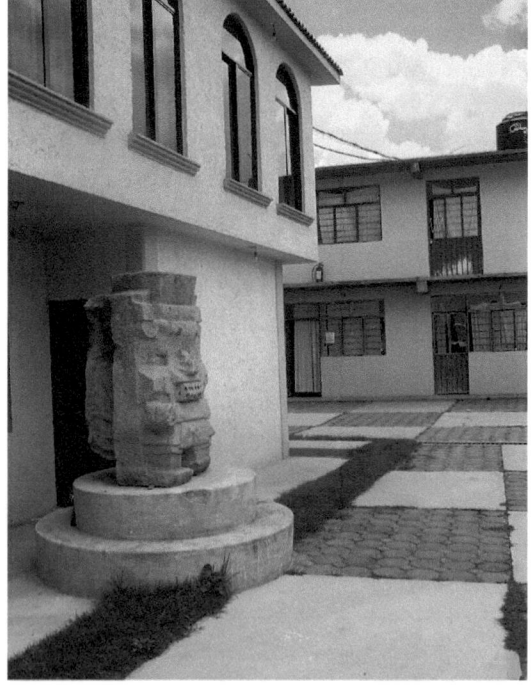

FIGURE 6.6. Replica of the stone outside an apartment complex, 2008. Photograph by the author.

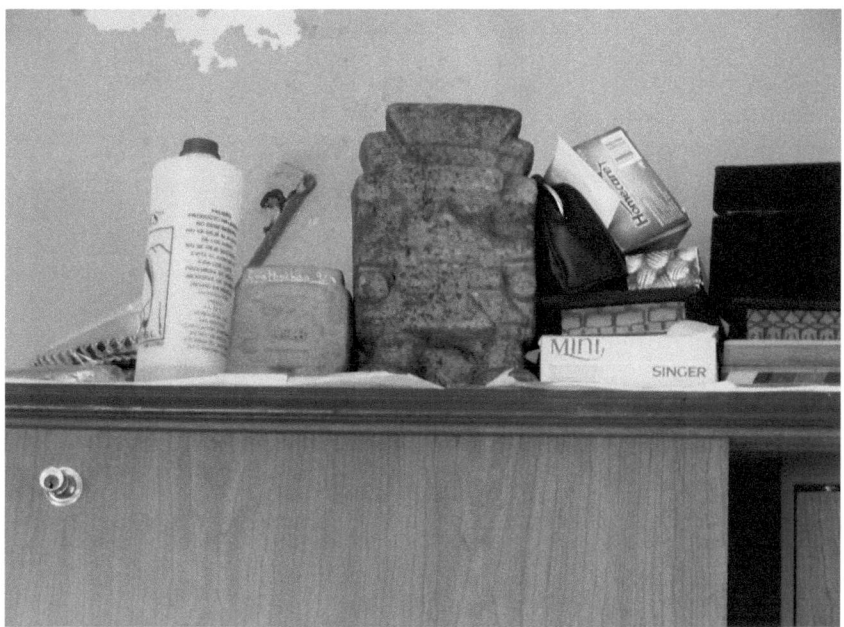

FIGURE 6.7. Miniatures inside a Tlacuache home, including the 1991 commemorative clay pot, 2006. Photograph by the author.

them at local fairs or through personal social media profiles, unlike the store-bought versions that tend to enhance the stone's anthropomorphic features like eyes and nose and even teeth or attempt to repair its broken features and limbs, the miniatures made in Coatlinchan render the stone faithfully, using handmade silicone molds to shape its broken and undefined features and even the protrusion on the stone's back. For Tlacuaches, replicating the stone faithfully, or as closely as possible, to show its state as a broken vestige from the pre-Hispanic past is a political act.

Several of the artisans now making replicas are active members of groups like the Grupo Cultural and the Calpulli Makoyolotzin, interested in local history and working to restore ancient lifeways. Don Chava, for example, started selling little resin replicas that he placed in round wooden fountains painted blue to mimic water. Tlakuanikoatl Ocelotl Xicome advertises his miniatures as "Replicas of the Piedra de los Tekomates wrongly known as Tlaloc," emphasizing the stone's local name while also asserting Coatlinchan as its place of origin and its residents as the authorities on its identification and uses. "The use of the *k* is more autochthonous," he explained. "We use *k* because its sound

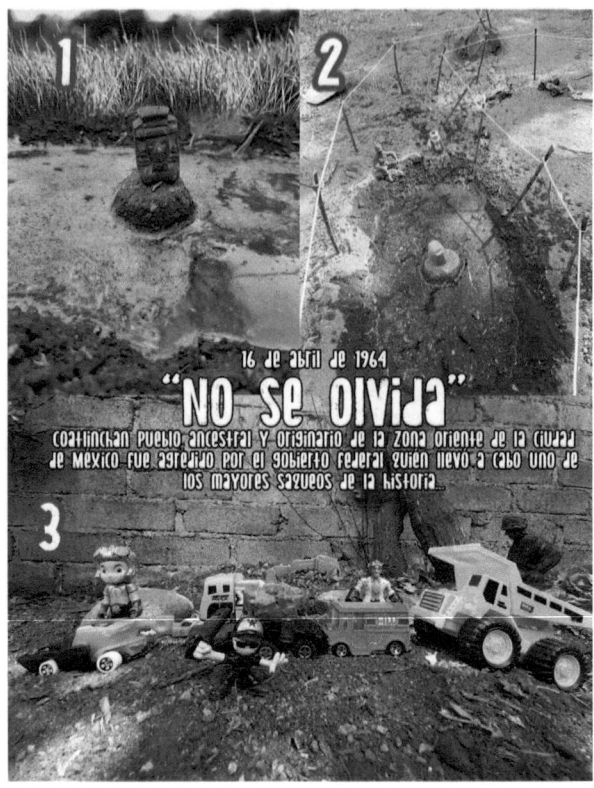

FIGURE 6.8. "Operación Coatlinchan: 16 de abril de 1964 'no se olvida,'" Facebook post, April 2021. Courtesy of Tlakuanikoatl Ocelotl Xicome (Marcelo Ortíz Sánchez).

is truer to Nahuatl, a language that would not have the Spanish-sounding *c*." Tlakuanikoatl Ocelotl Xicome thought about making replicas portraying the stone lying horizontally as it was before it was removed, but he reconsidered: "Most people want to buy a replica of the Piedra as they have come to know it, standing, monumental. Maybe our old people would recognize it lying down and want it like that, but even in their case, I am not so sure." For Tlakuanikoatl Ocelotl Xicome, replicas do not reproduce the stone as it was when it was embedded in their territory but rather its new life as a public monument outside the museum. He underscored that when the stone was still in Coatlinchan, town residents didn't need replicas or miniatures of it. "Why would they want a replica? They didn't need it; they had it right here in the *monte*." Replication, in this sense, is a response to theft, a kind of answering back that reclaims the stone, bringing it back to Coatlinchan.

In 2021, using the talents of his trade as a designer, Tlakuanikoatl Ocelotl Xicome marked the fifty-seventh anniversary of the stone's removal on his social media with a post using a series of photographs of his son's play, moving one of his little stone replicas on a toy truck (figure 6.8). He titled the post "Operación Coatlinchan," a reference to the military-sounding code name used by the Mexican government to remove it decades earlier (chapter 2). In the caption, he added "el 16 de abril de 1964 no se olvida" (April 16, 1964, is not forgotten), appropriating the slogan "el 2 de octubre no se olvida" commonly used to protest the state's involvement in the 1968 Tlatelolco student massacre during annual commemorations. Tlakuanikoatl Ocelotl Xicome replicated the slogan to denounce the stone's relocation as a state-sanctioned crime: "Coatlinchan, an ancestral and native town in the eastern zone of Mexico City, was assaulted by the federal government, which undertook one of the biggest looting events in history." By referring to Coatlinchan as "ancestral" and "native," the post also marked the stone's theft as a form of colonial violence. Even in the realm of children's play, replicas operate as political rebuttals and interventions.[9]

Don Félix displayed his collection of "mini piedras," as he liked to refer to them, in his family-run tortillería. As he showed them to me, he commented: "The Piedra is the pride of our town. We all know it is from here when we see it outside the museum. We know it is ours; we were here when they took it away." He then emphasized: "So, here it is, in *my* home, in Coatlinchan ... where it belongs." In other words, for don Félix, these "mini piedras" were not likenesses but little stones, materially instantiating the link between the stone, the community, and its territory, and thus, in some way, restoring it, albeit transformed into a monument of national significance, to its place of origin and to its rightful owners. For don Félix, as for many Tlacuaches I befriended, the town's relationship to the stone and more importantly to its absence had become even more significant in recent times in light of recent demographic pressures given Coatlinchan's proximity to ever-expanding Mexico City. Sitting in his courtyard on a hot afternoon by a small replica propped up against the wall next to an empty bird cage (figure 6.9), and with the mouthwatering smell of freshly baked corn dough in the air, he told stories of a time when Coatlinchan was a small town and he and his siblings ran in the milpas, chasing dust storms (*tolvaneras*). He lamented how much things had changed over the past decades, complaining that the landscape was increasingly overtaken by construction and corrals. Many new people had come to live in the town. He didn't know anyone anymore when he walked down the street or went to mass. "When I go into a store or to someone's house and I see they have a little piedra, I know it's people from here [*raza de acá*]." The replicas had become a form of recognition in times of disorienting social change.

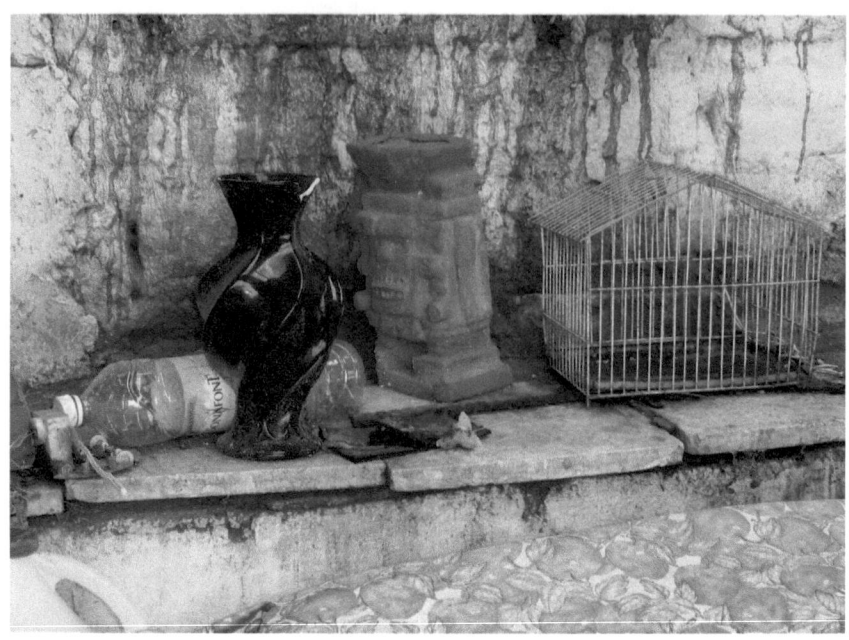

FIGURE 6.9. Replica of the stone in a courtyard, 2009. Photograph by the author.

Reproduction

"El Cherokee" was one of Coatlinchan's recent residents. He had lived in the Southwestern United States as well as on the border in Tijuana before moving to Coatlinchan in the early 2000s. His nickname was surely related to his style: his braided long hair and embroidered fringed suede jacket stood out in Coatlinchan's sea of men with gelled combed-back hair, norteño cowboy hats, jeans, and T-shirts. On weekends, he set up a stall on the Plazuela selling Native American and pre-Hispanic-inspired jewelry. When I approached his stall and struck up a conversation, he told me that he had moved to Coatlinchan because of the cheap rents but also because of his interest in pre-Hispanic history. He had heard of its importance as an ancient settlement, but it was only once he rented a place in the town that he found out it was also where "the Tlaloc" outside the museum came from. Hearing about how the stone was forcefully taken away, he decided to make a small replica as a form of restitution (figure 6.10). He carved it himself out of a soft pinkish rock he purchased in a quarry in Hidalgo. He told me: "These stones are not just random statues; they belong in the places where they were made by our ancestors. You can't just move them around without

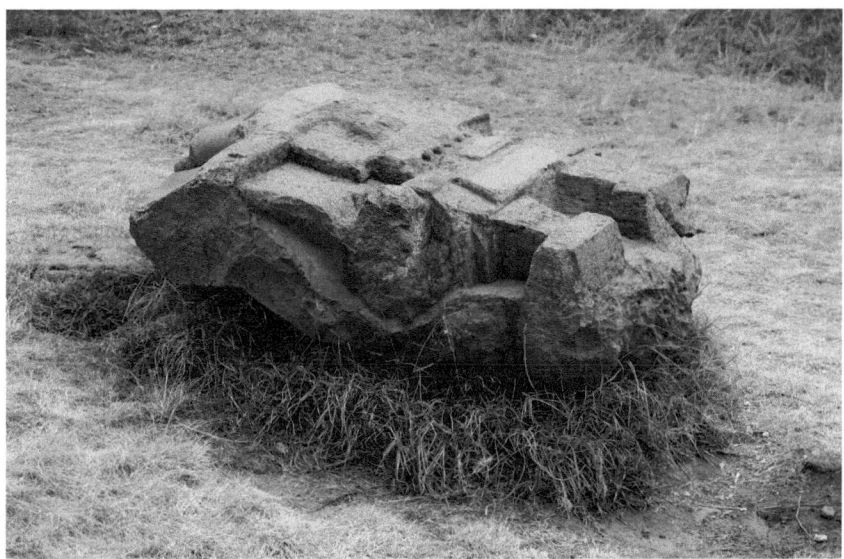

FIGURE 6.10. El Cherokee's replica in the ravine, 2006. Photograph by the author.

terrible consequences." The replica was his effort to restore, even if imperfectly, a broken equilibrium, sustained since ancient times in Coatlinchan's territory and disrupted by the stone's removal. He did not, however, anticipate that for Tlacuaches, its material and its maker also mattered.

Many town residents were critical of the replica because, like the man who made it, they considered it foreign. It was made of a different material and a fifth of the original's size, but more importantly it was from elsewhere. The replica was also misplaced: several meters away from where the Piedra had once lain, and it was facing the wrong direction. Commenting on its misplacement, don Chava noted: "We have always known that the Piedra lay east to west, the sun rising at its feet and setting on its headdress, just like the way we bury our dead." He pointed out that the relationship between the stone's position and local funerary customs would have been familiar to native town residents. The small hearth at the replica's feet marked the spot as a ritual site, but Chava underscored that it was only used by danzantes from other places who came to burn copal incense and make offerings there, not by the members of groups interested in reviving pre-Hispanic dances and ancestral practices who were from Coatlinchan. They, instead, placed their censers and offerings on the precise spot in the ground where they knew the stone had once lain. There, they had formed the stone's outline on the ground using small white pebbles. Chava

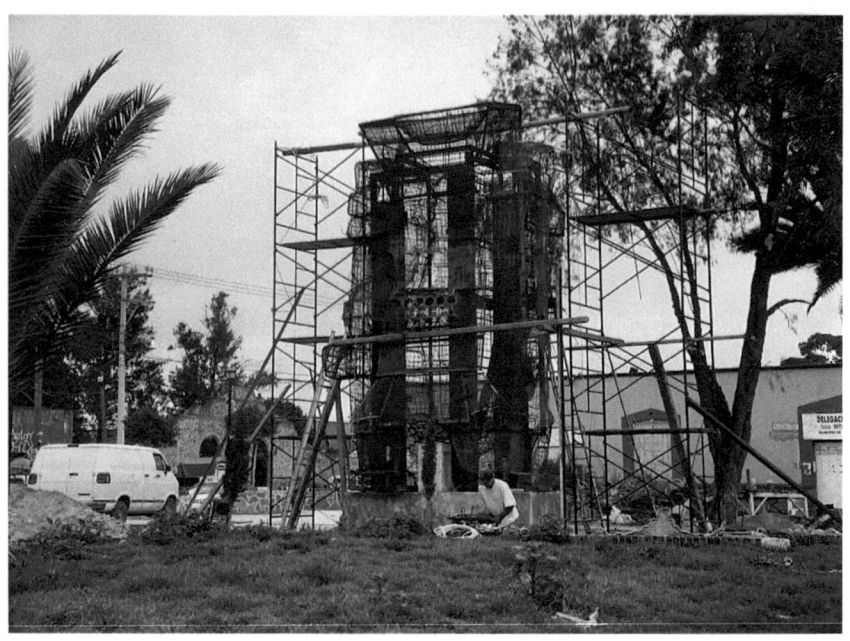

FIGURE 6.11. The one-to-one replica under construction in the Plazuela, Coatlinchan, 2006. Photograph by the author.

told me this was a way to imprint the place and make the stone present there even if it was far away. For him, El Cherokee's carving was certainly a generous gesture, but it was ultimately another kind of imposition by an outsider who did not know or understand, let alone share, town residents' attachments and relations to the stone and to the territory it was embedded in. Several people I met called this replica "la replica rosita," a term that signaled its pinkish hue but also belittled it as a camp copy that didn't do justice to the original. For elders, it also materialized the town's dispossession since they insisted that a one-to-one replica in the ravine had been part of the deal that town authorities had originally struck with the Mexican government back in 1964. The fact that they had to settle for this smaller "rosita" version made decades later represented yet another wound inflicted by the stone's theft.

In 2007, almost forty years after it had been promised, a one-to-one copy of the absent stone was built on the Plazuela, Coatlinchan's main square. Made out of poured concrete over a steel frame (figure 6.11), this replica looks exactly like the original, even standing inside a circular fountain similar to the one outside the museum. This one, however, was enhanced with other sculptural

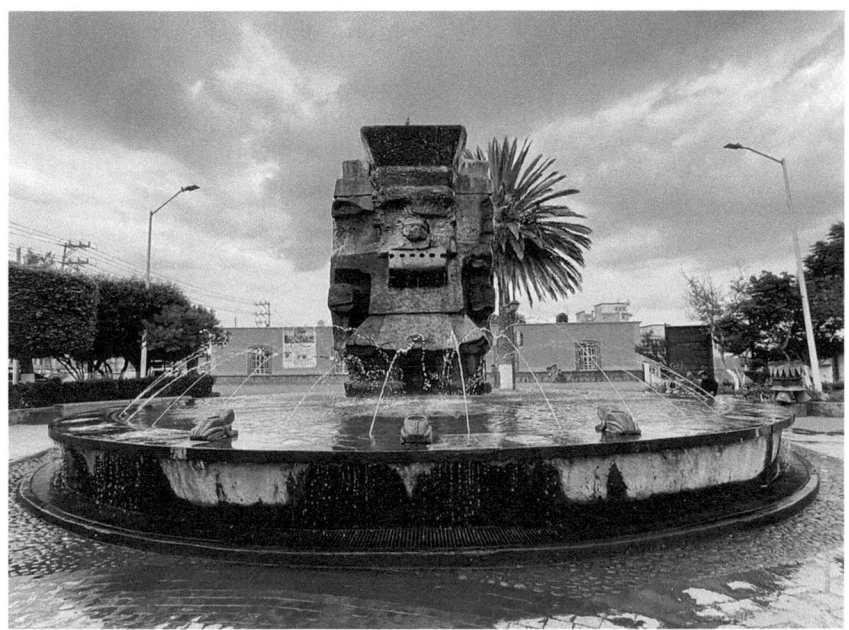

FIGURE 6.12. The replica as a working fountain in the Plazuela, 2021. Photograph by the author.

elements referencing Coatlinchan's pre-Hispanic legacy, including colorful glass mosaic glyphs of the various altepetl that made up the ancient Acolhuacan. The replica doubles as a fountain, with water sprouting from its headdress and features, cascading into a light-blue basin where a Tlaloc mask with goggle eyes and protruding fangs peers upward from the water's depth. As a working fountain, the replica recalls how the engineer Luis Becerril had envisioned the stone's ancient uses in the early twentieth century (chapter 1). Although town authorities only turn it on for special occasions, water accumulates in the replica's headdress, making it double as a pigeon bath (figure 6.12).

There are several versions of how this one-to-one replica came into being. They all, nevertheless, coincide in attributing its origin to the wills and desires of outsiders who, like El Cherokee, hoped to fill a void and imagined a replica as a stand-in, a kind of substitute for something that was no longer in Coatlinchan. Don Miguel, one of the town's representatives in the 1990s, told me it was a retired general from an elite Texcoco family who, having been posted at a nearby military base in the 1960s when the stone was taken from Coatlinchan, came up with the idea. This general had written a letter to town representatives during Miguel's administration suggesting that they ask the government for an exact copy of the stone. Up until his death in 2019, General Luis Antonio Morales visited Coatlinchan often. He had moved to the Condesa neighborhood in Mexico City, where he kept a stack of photocopies and newspaper clippings documenting the stone's 1964 relocation as well as a copy of the 1996 letter he had sent town authorities. During the replica's official unveiling in May 2007, attended by Enrique Peña Nieto, then Mexico's incoming president, Morales was given the podium and proudly proclaimed that it was this letter that had "infected" town representatives with the idea to build the replica, which also "enhanced" (*enaltecer*) the town. As a high-level military man, he was ashamed that the army had participated in dispossessing the town; he was, thus, especially satisfied that the town had not paid for the replica and that it was the government through the Texcoco Municipality that had picked up the check. In this version of the replica's origin, the desire and actual construction of the one-to-one copy were not imagined or actively sought by town residents. For Tlacuaches, although a welcome addition to the town, the replica, as designed by the Texcoco Municipality, was neither a substitute nor a form of restitution. They considered that it mostly served to reproduce the stone's new political role as a public monument in Mexico City and did not do justice to the myriad relations that the stone was, and continued to be, embedded in, in Coatlinchan.

Another version I heard was that the replica had not been commissioned by town representatives at all but that it was the Texcoco Municipality, headed at the time by the left-leaning opposition party, the Partido de la Revolución Democrática (PRD, Party of the Democratic Revolution), that, in 2005, decided to build the replica as part of a broader project to remodel its constituent towns. The municipality hired Óscar Ramírez, a Colombian sculptor who was working on several public statues in the region at the time, including an Emiliano Zapata on horseback in a suburb of Texcoco.[10] The PRD was strong in the area, even though the Estado de México was then a stronghold of the ruling PRI. The underlying goal of these remodeling projects was, then, to position Texcoco as an important and prosperous region and the PRD as a viable political alternative to the PRI. Municipal authorities had allegedly taken advantage of the situation to promote local tourism and show that, in ancient times, Texcoco, along with Tenochtitlan and Tlacopan, was part of the Triple Alliance that ruled the central valleys. Marking the region's pre-Hispanic importance became a way to recenter Texcoco, and the PRD, as a political force in local politics, extending the locality's ancient legacy into the present. Pre-Hispanic motifs were therefore prominent in town remodeling projects, with sculptures and decorative features recognizably inspired in the ancient

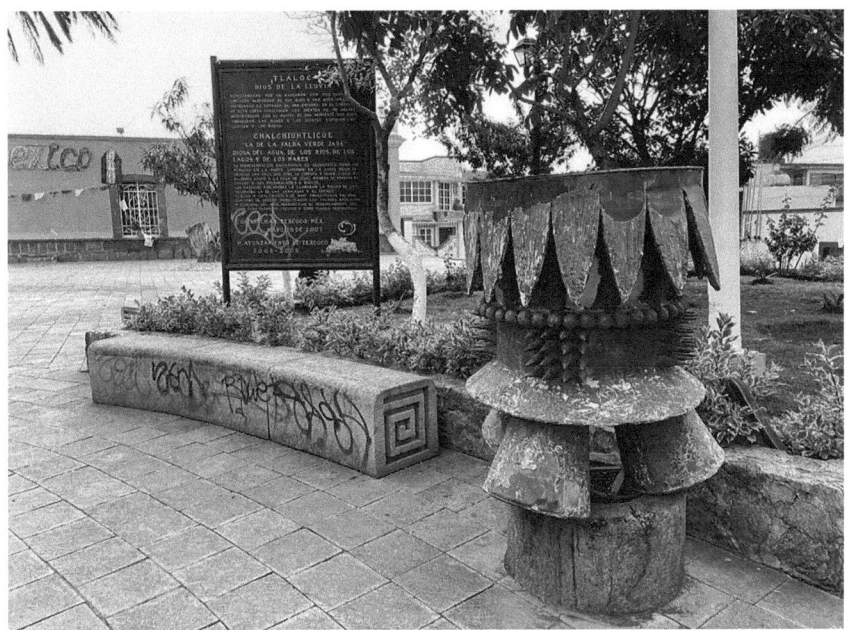

FIGURE 6.13. A replica of a Sala Mexica brazier in the Plazuela, with the plaque for the replica of the stone in the background, 2022. Photograph by the author.

civilizations that thrived in the area. In this sense, the design for Coatlinchan's Plazuela—including a generic feathered serpent that doubled as a planter and a wall enclosing the square flanked by two fiberglass copies of braziers displayed in the Sala Mexica of the Museo Nacional de Antropología, identical to but hardly as durable as the bronze copies standing outside the museum's main entrance—was not unique (figure 6.13).

The replica of the stone, however, set the Coatlinchan remodeling project apart. Built inside a fountain that substituted the town's old kiosk, the replica reproduced a vestige that was actually from Texcoco and specifically from Coatlinchan. The municipality and the PRD framed the replica as a way of "giving back" an ancestral object that had been stolen by a PRI-led government. As municipal authorities knew well, Coatlinchan had become one of the most populated towns in the area and could influence the outcome of the upcoming 2006 state and national elections. In this political climate, the PRD inscribed the square's remodeling explicitly as an effort to right the wrongs committed by the PRI. The replica became a way to denounce theft by the hand of the PRI and position the PRD as a benevolent warranter of justice. Ultimately, the strategy worked. Coatlinchan, a predominantly PRI-leaning town, voted for the PRD in the 2006 election and is now one of the strongholds of the Morena party, largely made up of former PRD politicians.

Back in 2007, one of the local schoolteachers who was part of the Grupo Cultural complained to me about the replica: "This is just for show. If it was for us, it would have been built in the ravine, where the stone originally lay just like they promised, and it would have been lying on its back, like when we were kids. But no, it is standing, and in the middle of a fountain, just like in the museum!" She continued: "They hired a Colombian, and sure, he is talented, but what does he know about Mexico, about our traditions? About our history?" For the teacher, the replica did not reproduce the stone as an embedded feature in Coatlinchan; it was a monument to the Mexican state's authoritarian and centralist policies that had been the perpetrators of the town's dispossession. It was a foreign imposition both because it was planned by the municipality and because it was manufactured by someone who, like El Cherokee, was himself a foreigner and thus had little connection to the town and its territory. Another of my friends in Coatlinchan shared the teacher's sentiment, insisting that the replica was facing north and not west, which had been the position the stone carving was pointed toward when it lay in the ravine. His phrasing in Spanish, "está norteada," evoked both the replica's erroneous orientation (looking north and far from the site where the carving originally lay) as well as its having lost its bearings, becoming lost and disoriented in a foreign place. This sense of the cement replica's disorientation recalls that of the replica "rosita" made by El Cherokee that don Chava also saw as being misplaced, not only because it was not in the actual place where the stone once lay but because its position was not entrenched in local funerary practices whereby bodies were placed in graves lying east to west.

In addition to the stone replica facing the wrong direction, town residents complained, municipal authorities had not taken a stance within ongoing debates on what entity the stone represented, placing a large bronze plaque next to the replica describing both "Tlaloc" and "Chalchiuhtlicue" and each of their attributes, while also referencing the local name "Piedra de los Tecomates," perhaps expecting readers to make up their own minds. The plaque offered a conciliatory synthesis: "Town residents from long ago called it La Piedra de los Tecomates: the one with the earrings and the headdress. Tlaloc and Chalchiuhtlicue are projected as a gender duality that symbolizes both the masculine and feminine values of water, personifying its unfolding as both a creative element and a destructive force" (figure 6.13). Most town residents I spoke with wanted the plaque to refer to the local name while also providing the most

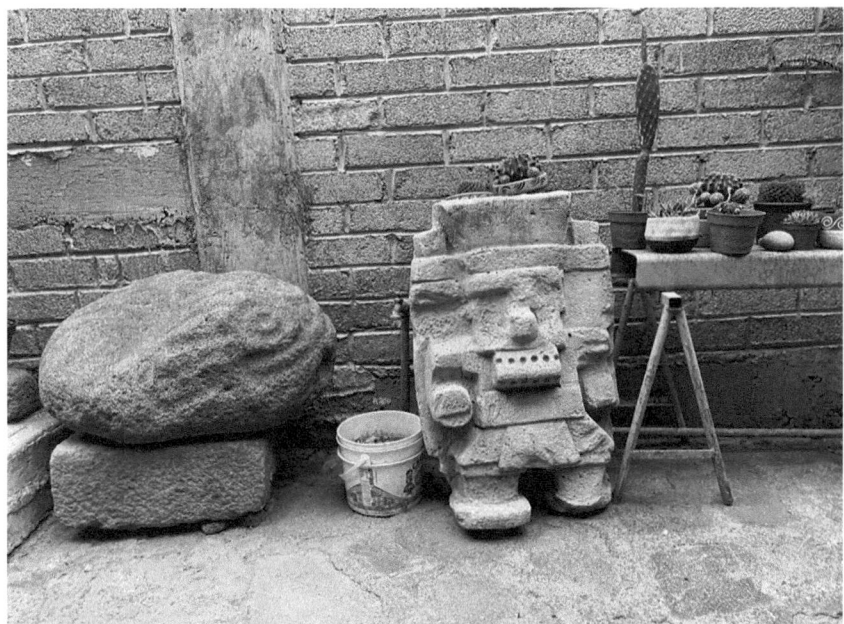

FIGURE 6.14. Miniature of the stone's replica by Óscar Ramírez and pre-Hispanic stone frog, 2020. Photograph by the author.

up-to-date "expert" interpretations settling this debate. Those more closely involved with the Calpulli insisted that this was an opportunity to officially dissociate the stone from its misattribution as the male storm god Tlaloc. Ultimately, the replica made by the municipality was not a restitution but another foreign imposition that didn't take local interests, perspectives, and practices into account.

Nevertheless, Tlacuaches appropriated even this replica to make it theirs: many of the little replicas that now adorn patios and gardens are in fact miniatures of the 2007 replica, made and sold by the sculptor who produced them as a side business in 2006–7, when he was working on the one-to-one copy. For these smaller versions, he flattened the back of the figure to accommodate its use as a standing architectural feature that could be placed against a wall or on a pedestal or fountain. These miniatures replicate the stone and the replica's new life as public monuments outside the museum and now in Coatlinchan's main square. Sometimes they even have a label or plaque, attesting to how the stone's new life as a museum artifact and the institutional language framing it as such have also been appropriated and domesticated in local contexts. Other replicas are displayed next to ancient objects found inside family compounds as equal instantiations of "lo nuestro" (figure 6.14).

Consecration

On March 7, 2007, two months before the cement replica's official unveiling, around forty Tlacuaches walked the perimeter of Coatlinchan's main streets, beating huehuetl drums and blowing into lavishly decorated conches. The air was thick with copal smoke. Participants carried flowers, seeds, seasonal fruit, jugs of water and pulque, miniatures of the stone, and vessels representing the storm god Tlaloc (figure 6.15). These were all arranged in a circular offering at the feet of the looming poured-concrete replica, then still under construction. Officiants, dressed in loincloths and huipiles adorned with daisy necklaces and turquoise headbands, removed the plastic tarp covering the replica so that it could witness the ritual. Town residents who were just passing by stopped to see what was going on. As soon as the ritual began, they unreservedly followed the officiants' instructions. Hands in the air, they faced each cardinal point and invoked the appropriate deities, guardians, and elements: Tezcatlipoca and earth to the north, Chalchiuhtlicue and water to the south, Quetzalcoatl and wind to the east, and Xipe Totec and fire to the west. When the time came to acknowledge the fifth point, the center, the entire crowd swooped to its hands and knees, touching the ground. Following the salutations, officiants invited all present to participate in a ritual dance intended to transform the replica from a cement likeness into the instantiation of an ancient water deity.

The municipal authorities and the sculptor charged with crafting the replica went to great lengths to ensure that the replica was as close as possible to the original: first by taking precise measurements of the stone now in Chapultepec and then using photographs of details to emulate its various colors, tones, and textures. Passing by the Plazuela during the replica's construction, Ramírez, who signs his work with the pseudonym "Margosk," and his team could be seen gathered under a tarp, peering over a large table where hundreds of large-format photographs were on display, zooming in on every detail of the "skin," as they all referred to the stone's surface. Regardless of their success in achieving extraordinary likeness, for many town residents, the replica still did not have the "essence" of Coatlinchan. In fact, the Texcoco Municipality's proposal to make the replica had been conditioned by Coatlinchan's representatives: they insisted a group of town residents oversee the process. The group was headed by several of the community's schoolteachers as well as the town's cronista, don Chava. Together, they recruited other residents equally interested in local history, many

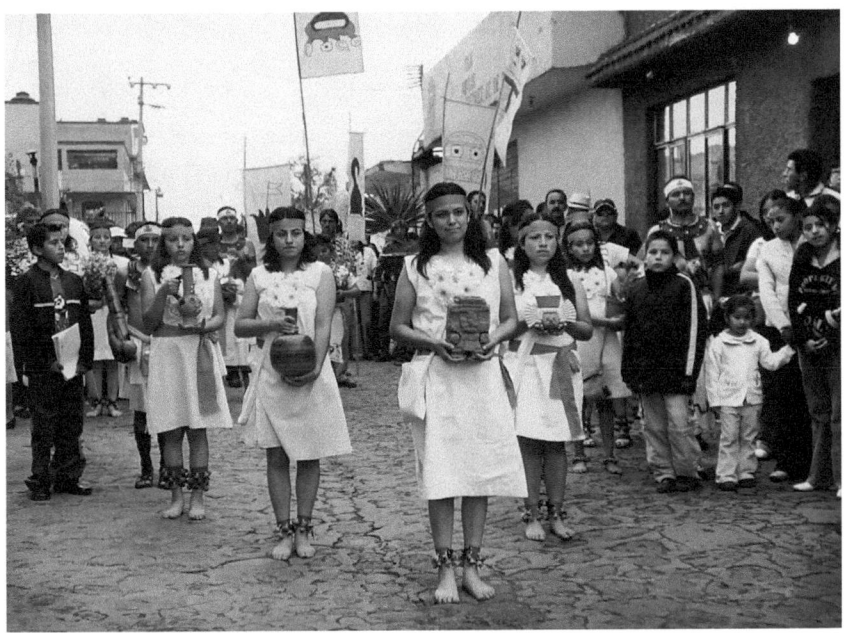

FIGURE 6.15. The consecration, March 7, 2007. Photograph by the author.

belonging to the Grupo Cultural and who would later form the Calpulli Ma-koyolotzin. Disagreeing with the project's political ambitions, the group had taken matters into its own hands. Members consulted scholarship on the pre-Hispanic past as well as teachers and ritual officiants from groups of neo-Aztec dancers in various localities in the Valley of Mexico to design a ritual that would ultimately invest the replica with Coatlinchan's "essence" and make it "nuestra."

Officiants referred to the ritual as a "consecration," using a familiar concept in a predominantly Catholic town. Rosa, who participated in the ritual, explained: "A saint image is just a statue made of wood until a priest blesses it with holy water or anoints it with oils in a church and then it becomes something else, it becomes *the* saint, right? Well, this is similar." Another of the ritual's officiants clarified: "Similar, but we don't have pre-Hispanic priests anymore. We just have the traces of the offerings and rites they performed and that is what we are trying to re-create." They used the term *consecration* to appeal to Coatlin-chan residents' familiarity with replication in the worship of the town's patron, San Miguel, since they were constantly involved in ritual work, processions, and offerings to transform generic replicas of the archangel into instantiations of the local saint, able to grant good health, abundant harvests, and general well-being. For participants, the replica's consecration was similar to the ritual work performed by Catholic priests to transform material objects into holy carriers of divine presence, as well as to more ancient forms of devotion.

This consecration was meant to invest the replica, conceived and built by outsiders, with what officiants referred to as "the essence" of Coatlinchan, subverting the replica's foreign origin and manufacture to bestow it with local meaning and potency.[11] Nevertheless, what exactly the replica reinstantiated became a subject of contention. Officiants placed a banner at the entrance of the Delegación serving as a backdrop for the consecration. Under the heading "The Essence of Xalxihuitlikue: Her Turquoise Sand Mantle, Her Mantle of Precious Stones," the event's organizers listed the day's activities while simultaneously recasting the stone's attribution. They hoped to correct what they considered a double error: the stone was not only not "Tlaloc," as the authorities had declared when it was forcefully taken from Coatlinchan and again in planning the replica; it was the female water deity, Chalchiuhtlicue, but spelled "Xalxihuitlikue." This alternative spelling was, like in Tlakuanikoatl Ocelotl Xicome's use of "k" for "Tekomates," understood as a purer rendition of its Indigenous name that would not have used the Spanish-sounding "ch" but "x," considered closer to the Nahuatl phoneme. The group was also hoping to change the way most Tlacuaches referred to the stone with the more popular names of "Tlaloc," and sometimes "La Diosa del Agua," or even as "La Piedra de los Tecomates." Given the coexistence of all these names, settling what or whom the replica reproduced became key to establishing its potential uses and significance.

The replica's materiality was also a subject of debate and ritual work. The "mezcla," or mix, as cement is colloquially called in Spanish, linguistically highlighting its materially composite nature, was a prefabricated mixture of materials also used to build roads and houses. Town residents had insisted that the sculptor enhance this material with sands from nearby riverbeds and ravines to make the hardened mixture visually emulate the texture and color of the basaltic boulders found in the local landscape, similar to the one that the ancient stone was carved out of. For Tlacuaches, it was this addition of materials harvested in the town's territory—and specifically in the ravine where the stone once lay—added to the mix of silicates, lime, and water that transformed the mixture, making it materially linked to Coatlinchan. This was another way of acknowledging the stone's telluric powers and relations. In a later conversation, some of the ritual's officiants mentioned that another element was necessary to invest the replica with essence: the night before the public consecration, officiants had put ancient artifacts found in Coatlinchan's territory as well as drops of their own blood in a secret compartment inside the replica. The presence of objects made by local ancestors and the substance running through contemporary Tlacuaches' veins achieved co-substantiality between the replica, the locality of Coatlinchan, and its residents, past and present.

One of the ritual's officiants told me in confidence: "Many people here would think I was crazy, or that I had joined some sort of cult." My interlocutor confessed he had placed an ancient obsidian blade found in his family's parcela into the fresh concrete mix before it hardened: "The idea was to give the replica the essence of Coatlinchan, of its history, of our ancestors, but the minute the blade touched the stuff, it began to boil! You wouldn't believe it, but I saw it with my own eyes." He then emphasized his surprise over the transformation of the mundane "stuff" and the supernatural effect that the ancient blade produced when it became part of the mix, recalling historical narratives of miracle-working saints in other times and latitudes known to cry or sweat (Bynum 2011; in Mexico, see W. Taylor 2010). The anxiety over the information he was sharing was justified in a town where the Catholic majority had violently expelled Protestant residents within living memory, burning down their homes and their place of worship in the 1940s in retaliation for their beliefs and practices that conflicted with Catholic teachings—many, in fact, tied to the power of objects and images in relation to the holy. His discomfort was likely also informed by a broader context of Mexico's long-standing colonial history involving campaigns against Indigenous idolatry.

Ultimately, the ritual was carefully planned to reclaim the replica and divest it of its intended political uses, foreign manufacture, and unhappy positioning. This was, for participants, in fact no longer a replica. It now had the same essence, materials, and powers as the original. The ritual's success can be measured by the ways many local groups periodically make offerings in exchange for rain and good harvests both to the stone outside the museum, which they visit every year in mid-April for Earth Day, and to the poured concrete replica on the Plazuela. Furthermore, neo-Aztec dancers from all over the Valley of Mexico come to Coatlinchan to dance and perform rain petition ceremonies at the cement replica's feet. There is also a linguistic slippage that signals the replica's successful metamorphosis: Tlacuaches for the most part call the replica "La Piedra," just as they call the many little replicas in their homes. In fact, for some, beyond the discursive association with its original, the stone's replicas might even be more potent because they are in and from Coatlinchan. Juan, one of the construction workers who built the 2007 replica and who lived most of his life in Coatlinchan even though he was born in Durango, told me: "First of all, this one is here, and the original is all the way in Mexico City, but more importantly, this one is even more original than the original! This one is more authentic than the one at the museum!" He added: "Its essence is from here, it was made by the labor of people from here, but more importantly, we did not include all the graffiti that is on the stone in the museum." He continued: "Letters were brought here by Spaniards, so in a way, we made the stone just like it would have looked before conquest. That is another reason why it is more authentic . . . more real than the real one." In other words, through their labor, the use of local materials, and ritual, as well as curated restoration, Tlacuaches had in a way decolonized the stone, making the replica "more original," and thereby contesting state theft by returning it to Coatlinchan in its intended preconquest form. Juan also highlighted that, although he and the sculptor were born elsewhere, they had both settled in Coatlinchan (he had moved here when he was twelve and Óscar Ramírez lived in the suburb of Coatlinchan known as Lomas de Cristo) and had therefore contributed to its authenticity by crafting it in the appropriate location. In a sense, following this labor and ritual work, the replica returned the stone to its original and rightful state and place.

Patrons

Although they do not necessarily work in the same ways, there are certain resonances between the stone's replicas and the proliferation of saint images and the town's patron, San Miguel. During one of our conversations on his patio in 2009, don Félix referred to the town's changing social composition, pointing out the parallels between the two in the midst of a recent urbanization and population boom: "Now Coatlinchan is full of strangers, many new residents who don't know San Miguel. They come here with their own saints, their own customs. They don't even know that the Piedra was from here. They piss in the fountain where the replica now stands. For us, for the people who are really from here, it is the Piedra de los Tecomates. That is how our grandparents knew it and told us about it. It is ours [nuestra]. It has another significance." For don Félix, having endured the stone's loss and reclaiming it through replicas reconstituted the essence of his town in the midst of social, economic, and even climatic upheaval that was threatening precisely that sense of close-knit proximity and territorial belonging that he also associated with the worship of the town's patron. For "strangers," the replica now standing in the Plazuela had little significance, but for native Tlacuaches, like the town's patron, the stone connected them spatially and temporally to Coatlinchan and to each other.

The proliferation and multiplication of replicas of the stone recall how images of San Miguel and other local saints are also used to demarcate the physical and social boundaries of the town through iteration and movement as well as through miniaturization. Saint images have been at the core of collective forms of territoriality, property, land tenure, and personhood first in early modern Spain and then in Latin America, where miraculous apparitions and saint images' wills to move or rather not to move have been central to the foundation and relocation of towns (Christian 1981; Abercrombie 1998; for Mexico, see J. Scheper Hughes 2010; W. Taylor 2010; López Caballero 2017). In this context, the replication of the stone and of San Miguel in Coatlinchan mirror each other as parallel theopolitical processes (McAllister and Napolitano 2021). Most native Tlacuaches, as in don Félix's rendering, keep both miniatures of the patron and of the stone in their homes. Although neither are made in Coatlinchan and are mostly bought from shops selling religious images or stalls catering to tourists in Mexico City's historic district, they equally participate in producing and reproducing Coatlinchan as an assemblage made up of people rooted and anchored in a specific territory, sustained and reproduced through theopolitical forces.

The image of the archangel, like that of the stone, is often painted on the facades of homes and featured on storefronts. For the patron's feast day in 2022, for example, the mayordomía in which Tlakuanikoatl Ocelotl Xicome participated had a mural that he designed painted on the wall that gives access to the Plazuela from the highway (figure 6.16). The mural features an opossum, San Miguel, the stone, and several other pre-Hispanic artifacts that the Grupo Cultural and the Calpulli researched in libraries, museums, and online, locating many known to have been found in Coatlinchan in both Mexican and foreign museum collections. Others had been found during their own research expeditions (chapter 4). Reproducing these figures on a wall welcoming visitors and townspeople alike made them stand on equal footing as town emblems.

There are, however, important differences. With the exception of members of the groups associated with pre-Hispanic revival, most Tlacuaches do not place replicas of the stone in altars or relate to them as devotional objects like they do representations of San Miguel. Also, San Miguel figures present in homes are not actual likenesses of the San Miguel images worshipped in the local church—they are generic plastic versions of the archangel that exist all over Mexico and Latin America. They become "from Coatlinchan" by being carried to the church and ritually consecrated or taken on procession and blessed by the town priest during the two San Miguel feast days on May 8 and September 28, and then, by being present and worshipped inside town residents' homes and everyday environments. When I was filming her, doña Luz scolded me for placing her replica of the stone too close to her altar featuring Christ figures, crosses, virgins, and an image of San Miguel. She remarked:

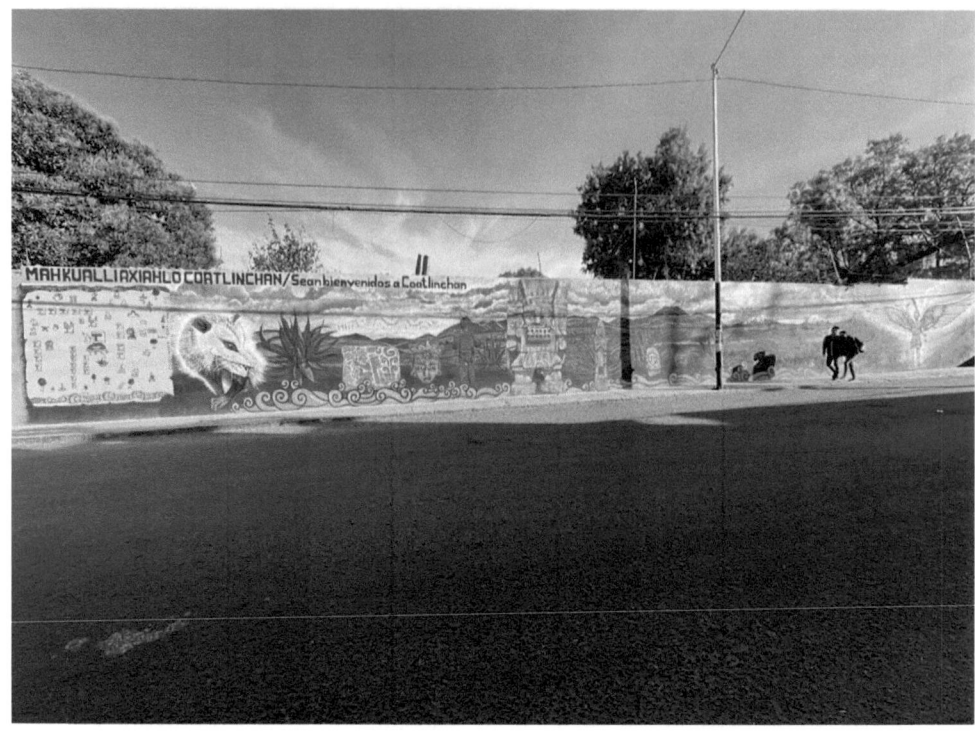

FIGURE 6.16. Mural designed by Tlakuanikoatl Ocelotl Xicome (Marcelo Ortíz Sánchez) at the entrance to the Coatlinchan Plazuela, 2023. Photograph by the author.

"Hey! The Piedra is not like San Miguel! We are not pagans here! The Piedra is part of our history, but we are devotees of San Miguelito!" Doña Luz was adamant about the distinction between a devotional object sanctioned and consecrated by the Catholic Church, of which she was a practicing member, and the replica of the stone that she held dear but was not the subject of her worship. Yet her unease over the place of the replica vis-à-vis the altar is also telling of a deep-seated anxiety over the material representations of saints and Indigenous deities characterized as "idols" given Mexico's colonial history.[12] The fact that doña Luz felt the need to demarcate these objects as being fundamentally different also points to their similarities. They were both made to be portable, mostly small and lightweight, but also made to be held and cradled in ways that mark them as vulnerable and in need of human care and bodily connection within Tlacuache homes (J. Scheper Hughes 2016).

Father Ezequiel, the priest assigned to Coatlinchan's parish during much of my fieldwork, also noticed the parallels between the replication of San

Miguel images and of the stone in the community. He pointed out that there are several "official" San Miguels that are all the patron of the town and coexist in the Church despite the fact that more Orthodox Catholic teachings would condemn this kind of multiplicity. The priest shared his frustration with Tlacuaches' religiosity, and specifically with their replication practices, which he attributed to "local confusion" with regard to Catholic teachings: "In Coatlinchan, there isn't one saint image that is the town's patron; there are, in fact, two in the church. People here insist that the two images of San Miguel are both the patron and thus should be placed on the main altar even though we were taught in seminary that each church should have only a single saint image as its patron." Why or how Coatlinchan came to have several San Miguels is unclear. The two images were allegedly made in different time periods: conservators from the INAH who worked on the local church's restoration in the early 2000s dated the smaller one to the late eighteenth century and the larger one to a later time period, probably the early twentieth century. Town residents already considered the smaller image older, and therefore it was thought to have accumulated more potency. Regardless, they treated both with great care and devotion. The mayordomos were charged yearly with dressing them the same for their feasts and taking them together, one after the other, in procession. The cortege headed by the two images walks the circumference of the four neighborhoods that make up the town center, accompanied by the deafening sound of firecrackers. Both are then taken to people's homes in the larger periphery of the town where residents pay for a mass or host the feast day meal. The San Miguels always travel together and are only very rarely separated, perhaps only for conservation work.

In recent years, the Calpulli found a third image that was stored in the church and in rather bad condition. It has since been restored (this is the image that Tlakuanikoatl Ocelotl Xicome chose for the 2022 mural on the wall giving access to the town).[13] According to the conservators consulted by the group, this might be the oldest of the three San Miguels. Because it is the smallest, and given its childlike features, town residents have begun to give it toys as votive offerings, dressing it with the same attire as the other two. The San Miguels' matching outfits are usually made of gold-embroidered satiny roman-style accoutrements reminiscent of colonial and renaissance sacred art. In 2021, however, the mayordomos decided to dress the three like ancient Aztec warriors, bearing a spear and a chimalli and wearing a feather headdress.

Back in 2009, Father Ezequiel somewhat dismissively described the multiplicity of San Miguels as the result of both flawed understandings of Catholic devotion and a defense mechanism in light of Coatlinchan's vertiginous social change:

On San Miguel's feast days, both of the San Miguel figures are taken out on procession, one behind the other, and town residents bring all the smaller San Miguelitos that have been traveling from house to house over the year to the church to be re-consecrated. People also have San Miguel images of all sizes in their homes, and they pray to them as if they were all the same. This tendency has increased in the last few years because San Miguel has become a symbol of Coatlinchan, and people here are uneasy with outsiders who have come to live here, bringing along their own practices and devotion to other saints associated with their places of origin.

Father Ezequiel's comment coincides with don Félix's sense of the new role taken on by San Miguel as well as the stone's replicas, in the face of the town's exposure to new residents, their customs, and their own devotional practices associated with foreign places. The priest also emphasizes that, as a foreigner himself (he was from nearby San Juan Teotihuacan), he had to respect the town's devotional practices, which he described as "local culture" even if they went against the Church's teachings.

Later during the same exchange, Father Ezequiel discussed the proliferation of stone replicas and the replication of San Miguels in tandem: "Well, it isn't idolatry or paganism or anything like that. The Piedra is part of local culture and so we respect it and encourage these types of practices." For the priest, both San Miguel's proliferation through multiple and traveling images and town residents' use of the stone's replicas were practices that strengthened community. He added: "Here people are almost as obsessed with the Piedra as with all their many San Miguels! They are everywhere!" This multiplicity attests to the socially, temporally, and spatially binding quality inherent to these figures' replication and to their movement in space. Saint images, like miniature piedras, conjure rather than merely point toward Coatlinchan as a community bound to a specific territory.

As the Mexican state removed the stone through a legal regime premised on the inalienability, stasis, originality, uniqueness, and authenticity of certain objects and substances, it simultaneously created the potential for replication as a form of telluric reterritorialization and theopolitical transformation. Regardless of the proliferation of stone replicas in Coatlinchan and its residents' ritual investment of the 2007 one-to-one copy with the town and the original's "essence," some Tlacuaches still insist that no matter how perfect and indistinguishable from the original, and no matter how many replicas and images of the stone exist in their town, no replica or set of replicas satiates the absence produced by the stone's removal. Don Chava was adamant: "Replicas are like photographs of dead people; they never really make present the person they portray."[14] In other words, replicas, despite their potency, do not restitute, or substitute, the absent stone. Nevertheless, in Coatlinchan, its replicas are mobilizing its absence as a present, tangible, and powerful telluric force and politics of connection and belonging.

7

Watershed

Agustín, a former soldier, left the army in his early thirties and returned to Coatlinchan to work in reforestation projects. I first met him in his mother's candy store. Both were generous in responding to my questions about Agustín's father, who had been one of the town representatives at the time of the stone's removal. I later found out that Agustín was also a friend and former school-mate of several members of the Grupo Cultural that later formed the Calpulli Makoyolotzin and he sometimes accompanied them on their expeditions. He loved hiking and, in his words, "being in nature." Equipped with sophisticated camping gear and gadgets, he accompanied Calpulli members wearing camou-flage and heavy leather boots from his army days, observing from a respectful distance when they made offerings or performed rituals. Walking a few steps behind him on one such expedition, I heard Agustín whistling a tune, inter-mittently uttering some of its lyrics: "¡Ay! qué bonito es mi pueblito . . . , qué lindo es Coatlinchan . . ." When I asked him about it, he explained it was a crowd-pleaser at community events when he was little. This was one of three songs written by José Chavarría Zamora, the town's late composer. Unlike the other two that had largely been forgotten and that spoke of loss in the wake of the stone's removal (chapter 3), this was an ode to Coatlinchan as a place of plenty and overall well-being: "Mi pueblito, lindo Coatlinchan" (My little town, lovely Coatlinchan). Agustín only remembered the chorus. The composer's son, the town's most prominent musician, told me he was still sometimes asked to play it at local events and provided me with the lyrics:

> ¡Ay! qué bonito
> es mi pueblito
> ¡Ay! qué precioso
> qué lindo es Coatlinchan
> donde nacimos
> yo y mi amorcito
> donde vivimos
> cantando con afán.
> Con sus mejillas bastante chapeteadas
> si nomás vieran
> qué rostros de mujer
> hasta parecen
> unas rojas manzanas
> que agua se hace la boca
> querérselas comer.
> ¡Ay! qué preciosa que linda es mi tierra
> donde sus hombres
> cultivan el maíz
> y muy contentos
> con lo que Dios socorre
> se goza de la vida
> alegre y muy feliz.

> (Oh! how pretty
> my little town is
> Oh! how precious,
> how lovely is Coatlinchan
> where my love and I
> were born
> where we live
> singing with joy.

With their red cheeks,
if you could only see
the women's faces,
they even look like
red apples
making your mouth water
wanting to eat them.
Oh! my lovely land
where men
grow maize
and are very pleased
with what God provides.
Life is good,
joyful and very happy.)

Nostalgically, Agustín related that the song was about a Coatlinchan that didn't exist anymore: it is about "ghosts," about "a disappeared place with fertile fields filled with maize. Hard to imagine, now!" Agustín was alluding to changes undergone in the past decades, as small agricultural towns like his, where residents lived off communal lands surrounded by lush hills and forests, had given way to what people called "the urban stain," a rather unsettling shorthand for rampant urbanization. In this context, the region's residents were witnessing their familiar landscapes and lifeways altered and ultimately swallowed up by this "stain." As it expanded, Coatlinchan went from having three thousand residents in the 1960s to more than twenty thousand today. In the process, its forests and fields were taken over by new neighborhoods, many built by outsiders who bought land cheap or by squatters who took up residence on lands abandoned by their owners because sowing them was no longer economically viable (chapter 4). More and more precarious houses with cement blocks and tin roofs with no access to basic services like water and electricity dot the once verdant hillside. Looking out onto this landscape, Agustín reminisced: "People here had it too good. They didn't have to work or care for what they had. The younger generations take everything for granted. They just sell off or abandon their parents' lands, lands their fore-fathers cared for and worked hard to sow. Just quick cash for them. But what they are selling is *lo nuestro*, it's our future." Given Agustín's new profession, he was especially interested in water and in rain as part of the equation leading to the demise of campesino lifeways: "Everything was green before; it rained for the entire rainy season. There was lots of maize and the hills were full of trees. And now, well, everything has been swallowed by cement. The urban stain. Just look!"

he exclaimed, pointing to the dry soil that felt almost like dust under our feet. "As if anything could grow in this!" And then, abruptly, he came back to the subject of our conversations in his mother's store when I first met him: "Coatlinchan became dry when the Piedra was taken away. That's when everything changed." For Agustín, the Coatlinchan portrayed in the song, the quaint pueblito praised for its abundance and fertility, disturbingly embodied in its alluring women and their mouth-watering apple-like cheeks, was disappearing. For Agustín, trained in ecological revitalization and forestry, the transformation undergone by Coatlinchan was certainly due to environmental factors, like climate change, deforestation, and soil degradation, as well as the demographic pressures leading to the over-exploitation of underground aquifers. But the underlying causes of these disruptions were the aftershocks of the stone's removal. Agustín is not alone in making this association, linking the loss of the stone to the end of a time of abundance, ecological plenty, and overall well-being in Coatlinchan. This is how many in Coatlinchan understand the effects of the stone's absence as bundled up with drought, declining soil fertility, and the loss of tightly knit sociality.

Even though town residents are, like Agustín, aware of other factors that might have contributed to these environmental disruptions, most Tlacuaches point to the stone's forced relocation as a watershed. I often heard people explain, with a hint of irony, the event as "la gota que derramó el vaso," an expression that, in keeping with watery metaphors, literally means "the drop making the glass spill." They refer to the stone's 1964 removal as just that drop, a tipping point that coincided with, and perhaps even provoked, a dramatic reconfiguration of Coatlinchan's climate and environment. Although the stone has been identified as a pre-Hispanic rain deity by scholars of ancient Mexico and is known in Coatlinchan to represent a deity associated with water, it isn't necessarily only because of this identification that it is understood as being responsible for rainfall or the lack thereof. The stone figures as an integral part of a system of telluric relations connecting humans, nonhumans, and more-than-humans to this place through water as well as through the forms of life on this earth that the liquid sustains both above and below the ground. Its removal is, therefore, experienced as an ecological disruption, yet one that might perhaps be reversed or at least partially restored.

Rain Stone

Many Tlacuaches remember that in the past, their forebearers were poor but could harvest what they needed from the soil of their community. Then, suddenly, when the stone was taken, it stopped raining and their fields became barren, almost around the same time that the springs that procured the town with drinking water dried up and wells had to be drilled deeper and deeper into the ground to quench residents' thirst. Despite the 1960s national press's insistence that town residents were "idolatrous" and "ignorant," opposing the stone's relocation because of their pagan beliefs in its meteorological powers (chapter 3), most of the elders I spoke with did not associate the stone's rainmaking to its being an incarnation of an ancient deity who might have been angered by its removal. Rather, their stories placed the stone's relocation as a process that limited its participation within networks of relations that worked together to guarantee water as well as their crops and livelihoods.

Maestra Lupe, for example, insists that people should refer to the stone as "La Señora del Agua" (The Lady of Water) and not as "La Piedra," based on her interviews with town elders who told her that the stone was female and that it was associated with the liquid.[1] One story she recorded and that was also told to me by other elders I met was that the stone was not a deity at all, nor a human-made rendition of one, but the remains of an actual human (coinciding with Becerril's account of local interpretations in the late nineteenth century; see chapter 1). It was a woman who had been turned to stone, punished by ancient deities for having broken a taboo by drinking pulque, a beverage reserved for the elite and only drunk for ritual purposes in ancient times. Her petrification was a cautionary tale made tangible in the solidity and enduring material of stone (Rozental 2008). Another story that circulated in Coatlinchan and that the teacher many times related was that the stone was an anthropomorphic feature within ancient hydraulic infrastructures, a kind of plug (*tapón*), placed strategically to regulate water contained deep underground. If removed, the water would drain from Coatlinchan's territory and go elsewhere.

Manuela, in her mid-nineties in 2009 when I spoke with her in her garden surrounded by pots of flowering plants, remembered her grandmother telling her to put her ear to the stone and listen for the sounds of the ocean and rivers that flowed underneath. With a certain sadness, she told me that, despite her many attempts, she never managed to hear the water's burbling (*borboteo*). She was nevertheless convinced that there was a connection between the stone and these underground flows. "That's why its removal caused drought," she insisted. "The stone was torn out of the depths of the earth. We were very poor here, but thanks to the stone, we always had plenty to eat, lots of maize, lots of fruit in our gardens, lots of water that came down from the mountains and flowed underground, but it stayed here, keeping our soil moist for plants and trees. Then they took the stone and that's when our fields dried up." She equated the town's loss with her own daily chores: "Fruit trees and flowers were just here in our gardens; we never had to water or tend to them. Now I have to spend my afternoons watering pots."

In many elders' memories, the stone had emerged as a physical manifestation of this timeless humidity above and below Coatlinchan's ground. Don Chava told me that his grandparents already knew of the Piedra's existence long before scholars showed up to identify it as a specific deity within the pre-Hispanic pantheon. He scoffed as he said: "They said they discovered it. But the stone was, well, just lying there!" They didn't even have to excavate it because it had already been unearthed by water. His grandfather had told him about a particularly strong rainy season—don Chava thought it was possibly around 1880— when the river that passed through the ravine overflowed. It was this powerful torrent—another telluric force—that was responsible for first revealing the stone buried in the mud. The monteros who worked in the hillside began to scrape the surface and soon uncovered its features: "They dug and dug, and little by little the stone grew and grew. They soon realized that it was an idol and that it had a face [tenía facciones]." In don Chava's narrative, the stone grew out of the earth, like a plant, following a surge of water. He explained that, once it was uncovered, the stone became a prominent feature in the locality, used pragmatically to satiate quotidian desires for shelter, recognition, and rest. It also became the subject of rituals associated with the preparation of lands to be sown as the rainy season began. The relationship between the stone and the life-giving liquid was mediated by Catholic devotion and theology, namely through saint worship organized around the agricultural calendar and where specific saints are also associated with fertility and water procurement.

Maestra Lupe published an account based on her interviews, mostly conducted with her extended kin, her aunts and uncles, in the 1970s and 1980s (Villarreal Galicia 2014). In these, she compiled their memories of Catholic Masses and festivities performed in the Santa Clara ravine. During these rituals, residents would alternatively ask for, or thank, the town's patron, San Miguel—whose devotion is also linked with water—as well as other saints that guaranteed fertility and agricultural plenty like San Juan, San Marcos, and San Isidro Labrador, with dedicated Masses officiated by the local priest in the months before the rains came, offering flowers, seeds, and fruit at the foot of a wooden cross that stood on the highest point of the surrounding hillside.[2]

In addition to these uses in Catholic ritual, the ravine was known to be inhabited by other beings and forces associated with water. Maestra Lupe transcribed an interview with her father, who told her of all sorts of "marvelous things" that he witnessed there when he went there to herd goats: "At night, the place looked like it was illuminated, as if light were coming from the ravine, like the light of a bonfire. Early in the morning, I would go and touch the stone, and it would be hot. . . . These were inexplicable things" (2014, 63). He told her other stories of the stone and the ravine related to temperature and climate: "Where the stone lay, it was never cold, there were never frosts, the February and March winds were not felt, it was also never too hot even in the hottest months, the rains in this place were soft, calm and warm, perhaps because of the three curtains of vegetation that wrapped the site" (2014, 63). Others spoke to Maestra Lupe about nonhuman or more-than-human beings, like the Charro Negro (chapter 5), who guarded the site but were also related to the elements and the environment. These generations, no longer alive when I lived in Coatlinchan, told the teacher about duendes, tlaloques, and chaneques, all trickster figures that had to be given candy and gifts in exchange for controlling the elements. Their main work involved procuring water, but just in the right amount, since they were also known to cause storms and flooding that could equally damage local crops and negatively affect residents' livelihoods if they were unhappy. In these interviews, Maestra Lupe reported people hearing the sound of children playing and giggling and the pitter-patter of small footsteps, a clear sign that these supernatural beings were present and caring for the place and all that lay within it, including the stone. As children, these beings represented life and renewal, but they were also mischievous, erratic, and sometimes had tantrums, easily satiated with sweets and toys, another offering people of older generations remembered leaving in the ravine. In many of Maestra Lupe's transcriptions, elders recalled the site being visited by *temperos* and *graniceros*, persons known for having been touched or struck by lightning (*rayo*) who mediated relationships with these guardians to control weather, especially rain and thunder.[3] Sparking much anthropological interest as present-day warranters of pre-Hispanic cosmologies as well as understandings of climate and the elements, these persons engaged the stone as part of a broader system of relations that conjured humans as well as more-than-humans to control water and climate and thus ensure survival in this specific place.[4]

Elders I met were mostly reluctant to discuss any kind of supernatural entity related to the stone or to the site, except for the Charro Negro that was often referenced, but that wasn't expressly related to Indigenous legacies. Some expressed annoyance with the government and the press's negative portrayal of the 1964 rebellion as the result of such beliefs that could be dismissed as "idolatry." Others insisted the stone itself had no ritual significance, except for the Catholic masses held on the hillside where there was a cross, and that, to their knowledge, all the talk about rain petition rituals happened after scholars came and said that it represented a water deity. Some simply referred to the stone as an element in the realm of play that was important in their childhood. "The site was perfect to play freeze tag," doña Luz remembered. Others described games they would play with the tecomates, the small orifices lining the stone's features that were used as targets into which to aim pebbles. Boys even played a game in which they would compete to see who could urinate in all twelve tecomates in one go, an elderly man told me, giggling. He smiled and ended: "I always won."

For others, the stone's orifices were known to alter substance, and very specifically water. A few elders told me that their parents and grandparents used the liquid accumulated in the tecomates after the morning dew and rainfall for medicinal purposes because of its known healing powers, curing parasites, healing wounds, and remedying the malady of fright (*espanto*). For many, the fact that the stone was always humid and that its twelve tecomates accumulated fresh water, even in the dry season, was a cause of wonder. Maestra Lupe reported elders telling her that water in the ravine itself had healing powers. In her own testimony, she remembered witnessing women going to collect water from both the stone's orifices and the nearby brook. They also collected plants that grew there that they would beat on the stone's surface and then use to perform ritual cleansings (*limpias*). The herbs arnica, papalo, pericon, estafiate, and San Juan flowers—as well as mushrooms—were used to cure various ailments. Her father recalled curanderas (healers) going to Santa Clara on specific dates and at specific times—especially at noon on September 23, coinciding with the day of San Marcos. In Catholic liturgy, this was the day that the Devil was let loose, when he would roll around in the plants, imbuing them with their powers (Villarreal Galicia 2014, 63–64).

Doña Luz remembered enjoying the ravine as a child because of its verdant vegetation but also because it felt cooler than the rest of the town's territory, especially in the hottest months, before the rains. The ravine was always green and shaded, she told me. She and her family and neighbors enjoyed the fresh air and organized weekend picnics, taking advantage of the cooler temperatures and beautiful landscape, resting from their daily chores and scorching heat. This was a place "to rest and be in the *monte*." The tree known as "Tecomate" that she had told me gave the ravine its nickname bore fruit used as water gourds as well as to cure respiratory illnesses but more importantly to prevent miscarriages. Since the stone was taken, doña Luz insisted, just like the rest of the ravine's vegetation, the healing tree that nurtured the town's health and reproduction, even regulating its fertility, had also disappeared. Like doña Luz, many elders recalled the ravine as a haven, a lush landscape that provided the town with both sustenance and well-being, always green, even in the dry season, and even connected to its residents' bodies and their own fertility. Flora, in her late nineties, reminisced that she often visited the site to gather wild mushrooms when the rains were just starting. Many mushrooms were used for food—she said they were "delicious, a real marvel!"—and others were consumed to cure illnesses, especially the ones named after San Juan, whose feast day marks the beginning of the rains. Doña María, another woman in her nineties, who sometimes visited Flora, described the site as "magical. Even the air smelled like flowers. Incredible things grew there." Both women shrugged their shoulders and with a saddened look commented: "None of that remains. It's all gone now!" These elements—rainfall, lush vegetation, surges of water, and abundance of healing and nourishing plants and fungi—all point to different forms of plenty and fertility. Life and reproduction came together in this particular place, and the stone was embedded in and part of this local ecosystem, nourishing and sustaining the soil and, through this process, the town and its residents. It was this ecosystem—located in territory and sustained through the complicity between humans and cunning more-than-human entities to control underground and celestial telluric flows and forces—that was disrupted with the stone's removal.

Sprouting Idols

The Cabeza del Penacho (Head with Headdress) is a large basalt boulder that lies half-buried in a local field, inscribed with ancient petroglyphs featuring an anthropomorphic figure wearing a headdress (figure 7.1).[5] Agustín was the first to tell me about it. He compared it immediately to the Piedra: "They didn't take it because they didn't know about it. Otherwise, it, too, would be in the museum." A few weeks after this conversation, I bumped into Agustín on the street outside his mother's store. He assumed I would have gone to see the Cabeza and was surprised that, given my interests in ancient things, I had not. He seemed worried: "You better hurry! You never know when someone will take it and then it will be gone!" The urgency in his tone suggested that despite their size and weight, ancient stone carvings, like hidden treasure in Coatlinchan, are always subject to potential theft and disappearance. I followed Agustín into his pickup truck that afternoon. We parked by what was once a riverbed crossing the town's territory. It was impossible to cross by car so we went on foot, climbing over boulders and piles of plastic bags and trash. The ditch was used to dispose of waste as well as animal carcasses, decaying in the intense sun. Barely enduring the stench, we walked less than a mile until we reached the spot where the Cabeza lay at the edge of a field on the other side of

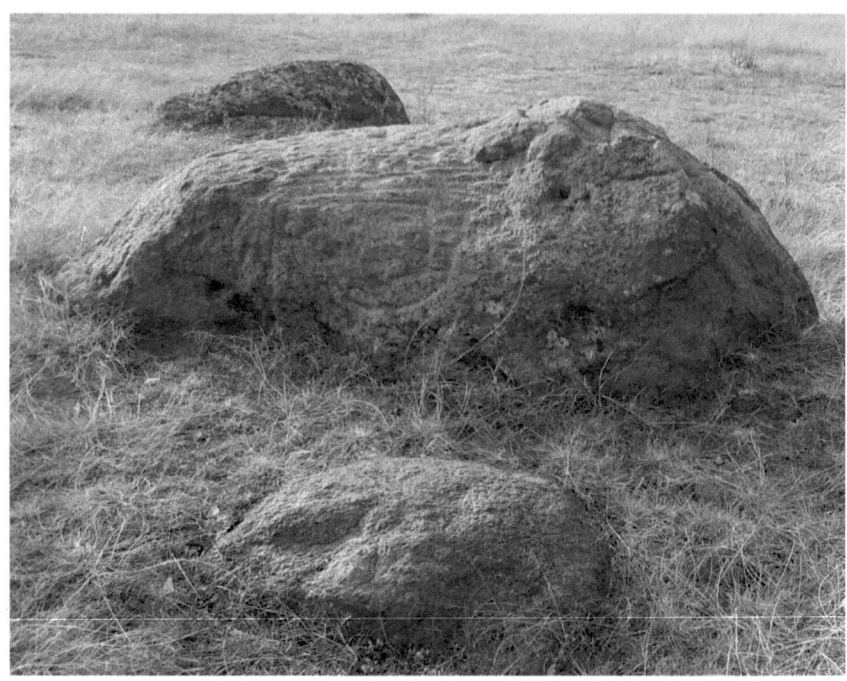

FIGURE 7.1. Cabeza del Penacho, Coatlinchan, 2014. Photograph by Jesús Curiel.

the dry riverbed. The area had been cleared and the plot prepared for sowing: the earth turned and sculpted mechanically into perfectly aligned rows. The outline of the petroglyph had been traced with white chalk, a practice common in archaeological surveys and in many places in Mexico where petroglyphs have become tourist attractions. Agustín commented: "At least people just traced its countour; other rocks around here are full of graffiti."

On our way there, he pointed out another large boulder on the side of the road, known as the Piedra del Toro for its bull-like shape (figure 7.2). That rock was covered in neon spray paint and tags of some of the gangs that operated in this part of the Estado de México. Although it doesn't have any pre-Hispanic carvings, this stone serves as an important landmark for town residents across many generations. For Agustín, its being covered in these tags showed a lack of respect for local history and culture, while also making the increasing presence of gang violence and organized crime in the area visible. Looking down at the Cabeza del Penacho, Agustín noted: "People respected this stone; they didn't cover it with tags [*pintas*] or blow it up. Now people dynamite big rocks like this so their tractors can maneuver, even if they have

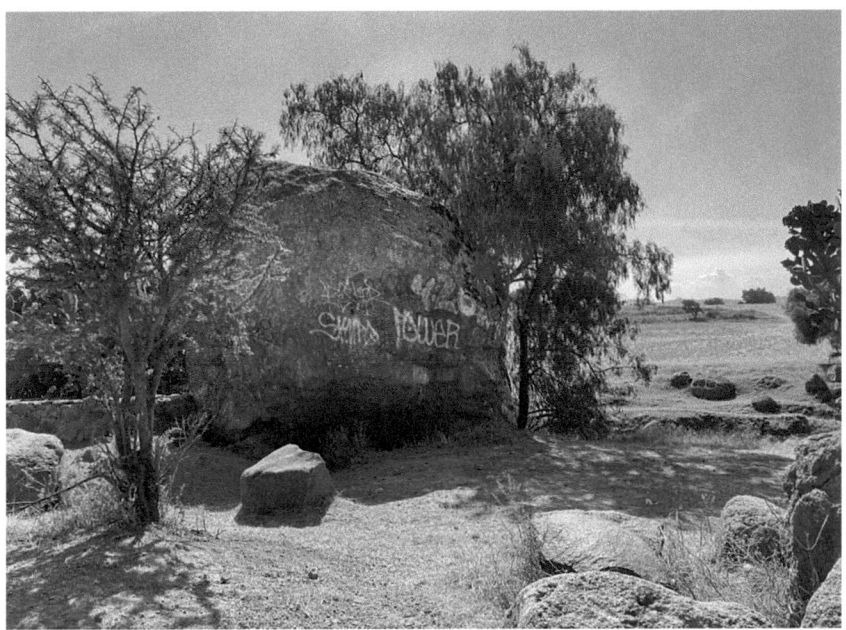

FIGURE 7.2. Piedra del Toro, Coatlinchan, 2022. Photograph by the author.

carvings [*figuras*]. They even blow up tlateles (stone mounds) to make way for their machines. My town has changed so much since they took the Piedra away! So many outsiders and delinquents who don't respect anything!" Agustín was worried that tlateles and rocks bearing traces of Coatlinchan's ancient history were being destroyed to build new neighborhoods and industrial farming complexes in what were once fertile fields: "It isn't just the tractors anymore; it is whole corrals to keep hundreds of bulls, or new neighborhoods that appear from one day to the next, just like that!" In the past two decades, many of Coatlinchan's remaining fertile lands had indeed been transformed from maize fields to plastic-covered corrals used to keep cattle fattened for the meat industry. For Agustín, this was another kind of destruction. In his rendition, the three stones—the Piedra that had been taken in 1964, the Cabeza that remained only precariously in Coatlinchan, and the Piedra del Toro covered in indices of the rising violence in the region—as well as the pre-Hispanic stone mounds that were being destroyed to make way for industrial agricultural and urbanization were related in ways that were part and parcel with the social, economic, political, and environmental change that Coatlinchan was experiencing.

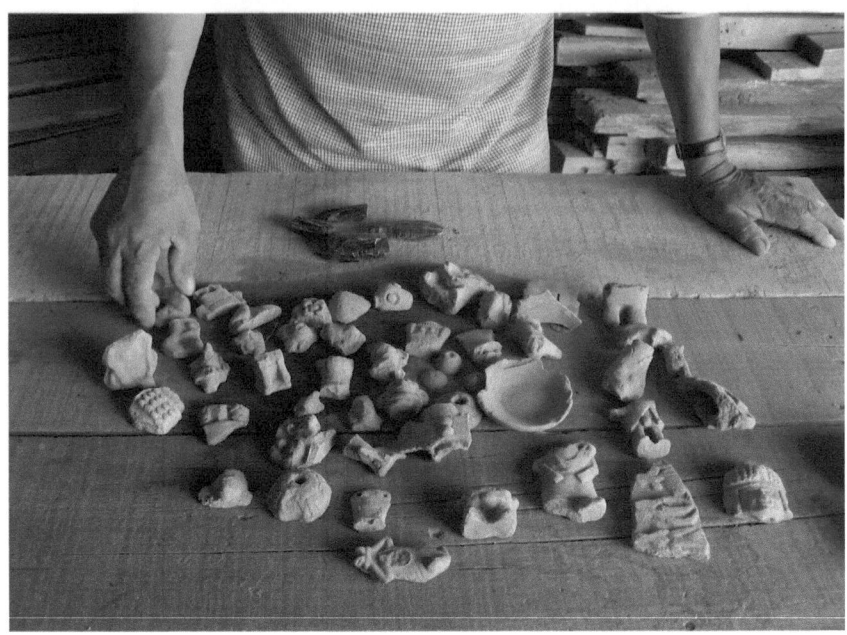

FIGURE 7.3. Ídolos and tepalcates found in Coatlinchan, 2010. Photograph by the author.

Just as in the lyrics of the song written around the same time, Agustín nostalgically told me about his childhood, when Coatlinchan was a small town where everyone knew one another, where everybody who lived in town was born and raised there. "Now there are all these strangers." I jokingly said that we all romanticize the past, but he insisted: "Before, you would see someone and know immediately just by looking at them what family they came from. Now, who knows who all these people are. Who knows where they come from." He then related this lost form of sociality to the loss of ancient artifacts, once prominent in Coatlinchan's fields. "The kids used to come out and play while their parents worked in the fields. They pushed the plows and went looking for *idolitos* and *tepalcates*. Now look around! No plows, no campesinos, no kids, and hardly any *ídolos* are left!" He described the types of objects he and others used to find: painted potsherds with blue, red, and black designs; pieces of polished shiny black and gray obsidian blades; little clay faces with beautiful headdresses and figures representing all kinds of animals like possums, deer, hummingbirds, snakes, and wild dogs as well as humans, standing and seated, many of the female figures with exposed breasts and pregnant bellies (figure 7.3).[6]

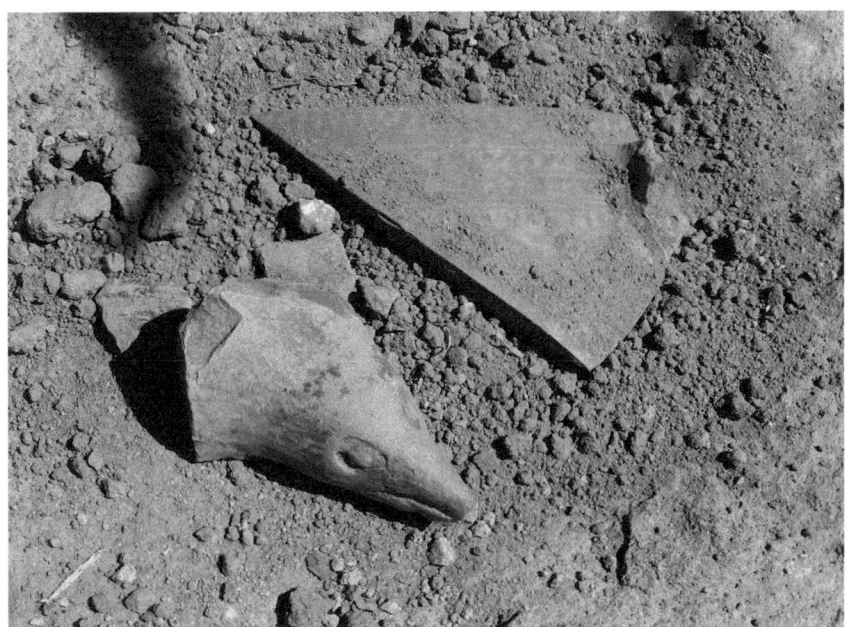

FIGURE 7.4. Pottery found in Coatlinchan, 2012. Photograph by the author.

These objects were often related to fertility because of what they represented but also because they sprouted from the ground, just like plants, maize, and other crops during the rainy season: "The best time to come looking for them was after the rains when the water cleared the dirt and they just appeared all over the place. Like magic!" Agustín looked down and pushed over a pile of dirt with his foot. Disappointed that there was nothing there, he sighed. "Before they were everywhere! You didn't have to look very hard. During the rainy season, they just turned up, hundreds, thousands of them! Now it doesn't rain much anymore and there are hardly any ídolos left to find." Agustín then hinted at the very different regimes of value that these objects circulated in when they were plentiful: "There were so many that people didn't even think they were anything out of the ordinary. Sometimes, they would even pass over them with their plows, shattering pots and figurines to pieces. Kids would collect the figurines that didn't break to sell for a few cents or candy. But now, there are almost none left and even so, people pass by with tractors so they wouldn't even see them if they were there."[7]

As Agustín and many Tlacuaches recall, ídolos were collected mostly by hand, by children who then sold them to the *idoleros* (figure 7.4). Translated literally as "idol people," the term *idolero* alludes both to foreigners and to outsiders from other parts of Mexico who came to Coatlinchan looking to dig for or buy ancient artifacts for private and museum collections.[8] Agustín, who now works to revert drought and soil erosion caused by deforestation, placed special emphasis on the destructive force of tractors and the distance industrial agriculture produced between people and the soil. He also linked this to the specific moment of the stone's removal: "Things have changed so much here since the Piedra was taken! We were all campesinos back then! Now it hardly rains. People drive pickup trucks and dream of going to the other side [of the border]."

Tlakuanikoatl Ocelotl Xicome, Agustín's former schoolmate who came of age at the same time, has many times told me that his own interest in Coatlinchan's ancient history was linked to his personal connection to what he calls "the idol trade." As he uncovered part of a stucco floor on one of the Calpulli's expeditions in 2010, he confessed: "An idolero, a gringo [from the United States], one of many who came to town on weekends to buy these things, got my great-great-grandmother pregnant and deceived her. He didn't marry her; he came and went and kept making false promises. And that's the story of my origin." After a pause, he went on: "When I was a kid, we all knew what they came for, so someone would yell, 'Hey! Here come the idoleros!' And we would all rush with our little bags full of figurines that we had collected behind our parents' plows when we accompanied them to work in the fields. We would sell a bag of ídolos for a peso, or each piece for a few cents . . . enough to buy some sweets or a soda." For Tlakuanikoatl Ocelotl Xicome, his ancestor's pregnancy by a man who did not honor his commitment mirrored the history of Coatlinchan in which residents were deprived of valuable things for far less than they were worth but also where Coatlinchan figured, much like in the song "Mi pueblito lindo Coatlinchan," as a land of fertility and abundance subject to others' plunder. For Tlakuanikoatl Ocelotl Xicome, the absence of pre-Hispanic objects brought about other losses that he was ambivalent about, namely that of people who came to Coatlinchan looking for them: "Idoleros no longer come to town," Tlakuanikoatl Ocelotl Xicome explained, "because there is so little left to take now." In a way, idoleros' presence, even if symbolic of unequal power relations and unjust exchange, even theft, marked Coatlinchan (and its residents' bodies) as fertile ground, reproducing valuable resources in the shape of pre-Hispanic figurines and potsherds but also other substances that, like water, used to be prominent in their territory. These elements had been the subject of rapacious extraction and were no longer available to be taken.

Almost every house in Coatlinchan contains some sort of display of broken potsherds, figurines, and finely carved obsidian blades placed in living rooms

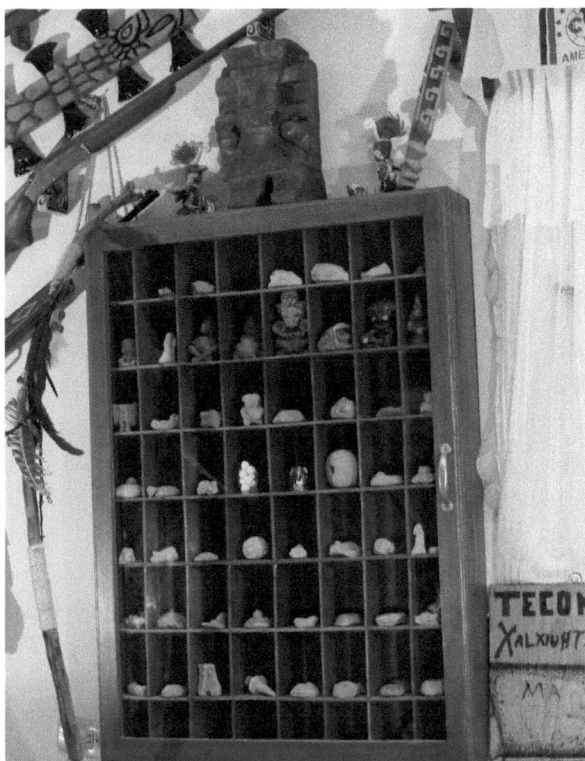

FIGURE 7.5. Cabinet in a resident's home, 2013. Photograph by the author.

and in more intimate spaces. Like their little replicas of the stone, Tlacuaches display these objects on shelves alongside family portraits, school diplomas, and commemorative objects from their kin's quinceañera parties and weddings. A few households flaunt cabinets made ex profeso to display their collections.

Some of these cabinets use humor in their arrangements, creating scenes in which the figures interact with other household collectibles. Others combine replicas of the absent stone and ancient pottery and figures found in Coatlinchan's territory (figure 7.5). Despite their discursive framing of these displays as "collections" and "mini-museums," town residents' collecting and display practices surrounding ancient potsherds and figurines both reproduce and deviate from such institutional frameworks. Although Tlacuaches worry about the possible consequences of their collections' status—namely that the INAH will come and take their collections away—they insist that their collections do in fact belong to them, as their rightful caretakers, a localized and powerful inheritance bequeathed to Coatlinchan's contemporary residents by ancestors who lived and thrived in their territory.

Doña Luz, for example, insisted that her collection of potsherds and ancient figurines was precious because having been so common in her youth, they had now become scarce. When she told me that there were hardly any ídolos left in her family's lands, I asked if this was because they had sold them to the idoleros. She corrected me: "It's because they took the Piedra and now it does not rain here anymore." For doña Luz, like for Agustín, it was not the idoleros' collecting practices, nor town residents' own participation in these artifacts' trade, that led to their scarcity. It was the stone's removal by the Mexican state that caused drought and led to their dearth. In a way, the state had not just taken an object from Coatlinchan; in so doing, it had altered Coatlinchan's environment, thwarting the abundance in rainfall and subsequently in ancient artifacts as well as maize and plants like the Tecomate tree that had stopped growing there.

The association between the recent absence of pre-Hispanic artifacts in Coatlinchan and decreasing rainfall and vegetation came up constantly, and increasingly so as predicting climate and therefore agricultural cycles is becoming more and more challenging. In May 2021, just as the rainy season began, Dulce, who was part of the Grupo Cultural when I began my fieldwork and is now in charge of a new group called Tlaloqueros that uses social media to document local history and promote community events, posted a photograph of decorated pottery sherds, barely visible in the mud in her family's compound after a downpour. She accompanied the image with the caption "when the past sprouts [brota] with the rain" and the hashtags #Tepalcates, #InTheGarden, #Ancestors. With these, Dulce, like don Chava, placed the ancient objects, in this case pottery fragments, that appeared with the rain as organic forms of life, sprouting out of the soil like plants, but also ancestors. Like many others in Coatlinchan and in this area of Mexico, Dulce lives in a compound where ancient artifacts are common. Her mother is especially keen on these objects, keeping cardboard boxes decorated with colorful and glittery wrapping paper, recycled paint cans, and buckets full of the tepalcates and "idolitos," as she calls them, that she and her family members have unearthed when digging in their plot to build a new addition for the growing family (figure 7.6).

Dulce's mother is very fond of her collection, often taking the little figurines out and showing them to her children and grandchildren, trying to make out their eroded or broken shapes, and speculating on their possible ancient uses. The whole family participates in these gatherings, coming up with different theories about how these objects might have been used and how they were relevant for the people who lived there long ago.

She relishes in bringing out her many containers filled to the brim with idolitos that she stores on shelves in her bedroom, carefully laying them out on the

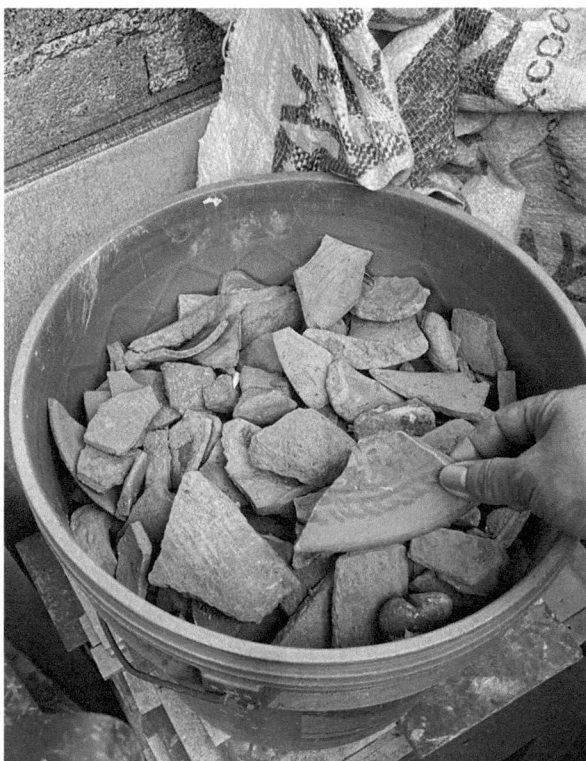

FIGURE 7.6. Pottery sherds stored in a bucket inside a home in Coatlinchan, 2022. Photograph by the author.

glass that covers the hand-knit doilies that decorate her dining room table. She has many times told me that she dreams of having a big glass cabinet specially made to display them but can't imagine designing one where they would all fit, not to mention paying for its manufacture. Recently having closed her stationery store, she adapted the display case she used to exhibit stuffed animals and other gifts and now uses it to show off the best of her collection. The best for her were often the most complete or intricately carved or molded pieces. Sometimes the value of her collection was connected to the find rather than to the object's shape or state of conservation. She loves to tell the story of each of her prized possessions. Even though she has thousands, mostly broken limbs from figurines and decorated pottery sherds, she knows exactly where and when she found each of them, carefully placing fragments made of similar materials or glazes in the palm of her hand, matching their shapes and designs to speculate on how they might have fit together (figure 7.7).

Her relationship to her collection is deeply sensorial, as she uses her fingers to gently rub off the dirt many of them still bare encrusted or just picks one

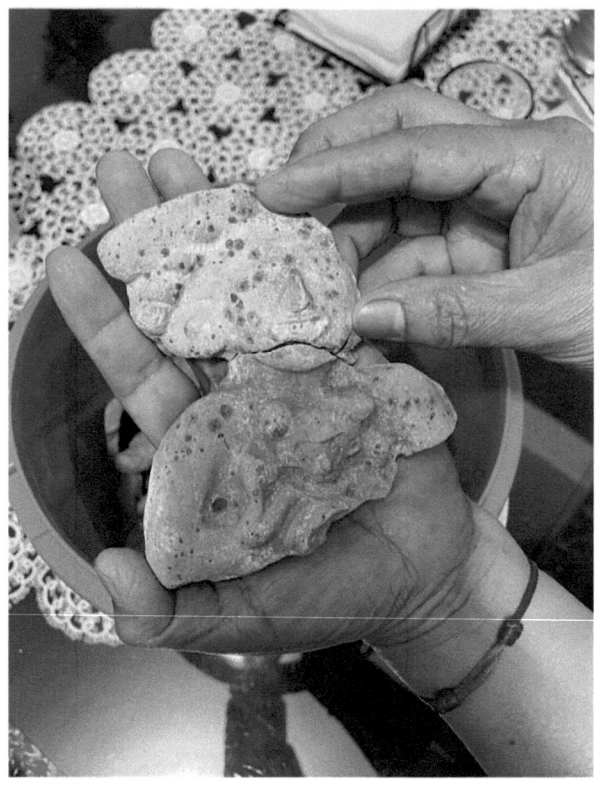

FIGURE 7.7. Putting pieces back together inside a resident's home in Coatlinchan, 2022. Photograph by author.

after another to caress their contours. Each time she invites me to Coatlinchan for a family birthday or special occasion, she presents a new find, often displayed next to an array of delicious dishes she has prepared, explaining how her whole family participated in looking for idolitos, how they clean and interpret them. Dulce once told me that collecting them was a way of bringing the family together, of reproducing what being family was all about.

It was her mother who taught Dulce and her siblings how to find tepalcates, digging in specific parts of the compound known to have been a former tlatel or going for long walks in the monte or in the plots of the ejido cared for by her kin. She insisted, as in the epigraph that begins this book, that these searches were also for stones—pretty, polished ones. Her mother had in turn learned these skills from her father, who was quite the collector as well as a skilled campesino. In fact, these two practices went hand in hand. Dulce's mom explained that it was important for her family to know what growing things from the soil was like for prior generations given that her own children and grandchildren have only known agricultural work from a distance, watching tractors sow

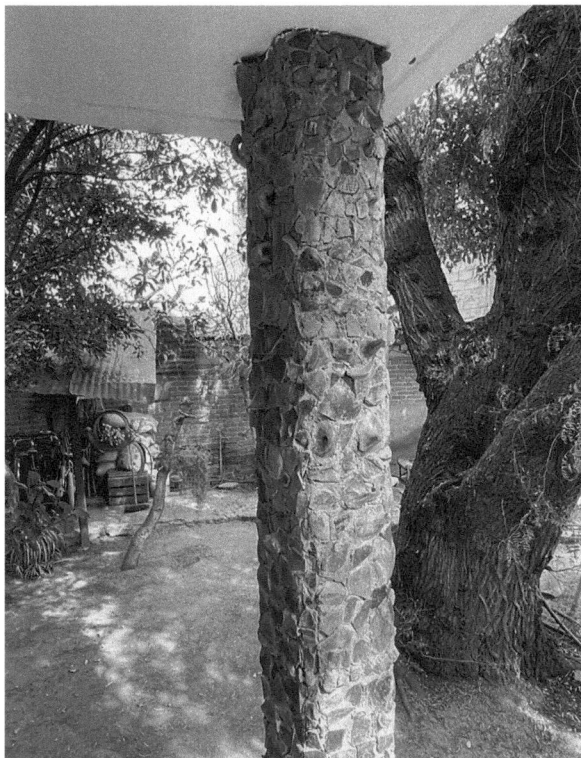

FIGURE 7.8. The renovated porch inside Conchita's home, 2022. Photograph by the author.

and harvest ejido lands to produce forage for the bulls. She displays some of her favorite ancient clay figurines and decorated pottery pieces on the same shelf with her father's portrait, straw hat, and "pizcador." The latter, and not the ancient things, was her "most valuable inheritance" (*herencia*), as she once described this object to me: an artisanally made cast iron tool that fits in the user's palm and is used for opening cornhusks. With her characteristic humor, she told me this tool was a "tepalcate," an unserviceable and broken relic from another time, since artisanal ironwork is no longer made in the region but also because only the older generations that were fast disappearing would know how to use it.

Over the past few years, the whole family has engaged in an architectural project using broken pottery pieces. With the help of her son, who studied architecture at the National Polytechnic University and who works for a construction company in Mexico City, Dulce's mom redesigned her porch. She asked her son to build her cement columns that she covered in ancient pottery sherds, using their shapes and designs to craft a mosaiclike assemblage (figure 7.8).

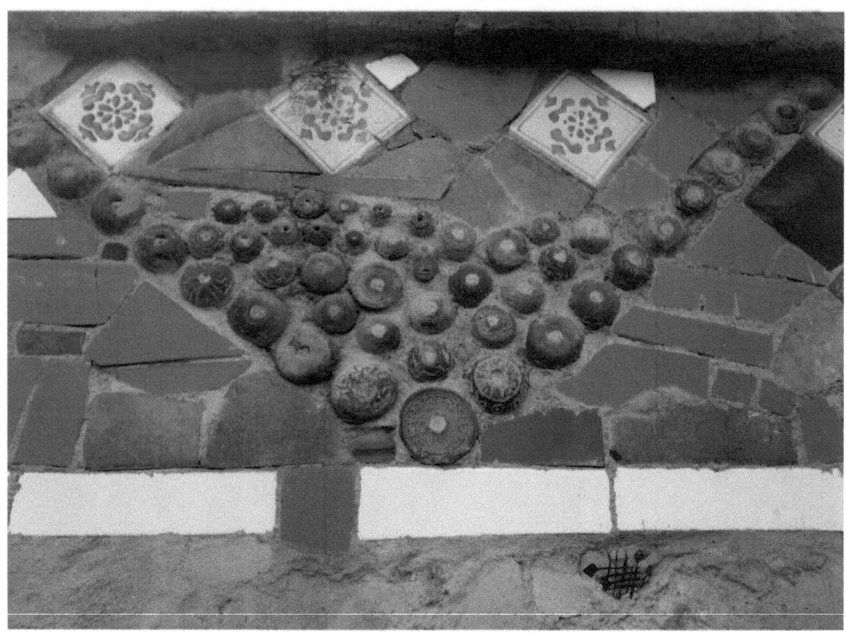

FIGURE 7.9. Malacates in a wall surrounding a courtyard inside a family compound in Coatlinchan, 2015. Photograph by the author.

The columns receive visitors into her home. From the driveway, they look like they are covered with terracotta-colored paint, but the sherds become visible once one gets closer, lured by the elaborate geometric designs and occasionally protruding earthen legs and handles. Others in Coatlinchan have made similar uses of their collections, crafting designs with tiles and ancient artifacts on patio walls and inside their homes, sometimes along with their initials (figure 7.9). These uses repurpose ancient artifacts as part of the town's built environment, making the past and its vestiges habitable in contemporary contexts.

Reproducing Territory

On the day we went looking for the Cabeza del Penacho, Agustín had barely begun to describe the absence of rain and of pre-Hispanic objects as consequences of the stone's removal when he suddenly stumbled and froze. "Here's one! I can almost hear it calling me!" Smiling enthusiastically, he picked up what looked like a round pebble covered in dry mud. He began rubbing it with his fingers and, little by little, the intricate details of a decorated clay spindle surfaced: a crouching monkey with elaborate geometric designs. Changing his tone, he proudly stated the many ways in which his find hinged on a series of relationships based on his status as native to Coatlinchan: "This *malacate* was made long ago by our *abuelos*.[9] They left it here for me to find. It belongs in my collection; that's why it showed itself to me." He then told me, "People who are not from here have to dig and scorch the earth, but for us, it's different. We know how to find them and they also find us." Later that day, we drove back to his home, where he showed me the rest of his collection carefully kept in a locked cabinet in his living room. Again hinting at these objects' fragile permanence in Coatlinchan, he explained: "I found these all over the place. Some in my family's *parcelas*, some in the *monte*. I am keeping them safe here. If I didn't keep them, somebody else would take them and then they would be lost forever." Between Agustín's keeping these objects safe under lock and key in his home and his sense that the clay spindle was calling out for him to find it on purpose after the rains, it became clear that, for him, these objects were in need of care to remain in place and participate in maintaining a certain ecological balance.[10]

Having retired many years ago, Maestra Lupe gives talks at various community events that are heavily attended by Tlacuaches interested in local history who appreciate and trust her status as a teacher trained in the Escuela Normal.[11] In April 2011, as part of an extensive program of cultural activities organized to mark the anniversary of the stone's removal, she gave a talk titled "The Faces of My Town." She spoke about the figurines so prominent in the town's lands that she referred to affectionately as "caritas" (little faces). She explained that these "little faces" were not just anthropomorphic ideal types: "These *are* the faces of our ancestors. They didn't have photographs like we have today. They just had clay and their imagination." She continued: "That is why they are most often just the faces, and we never find their bodies; what mattered was to leave behind a trace of what they looked like for us to remember them by." The teacher concluded her talk: "We must care for them, keep them, show them to our children just like we show them old pictures of our parents and grandparents." For the teacher, these were a tangible telluric imprint: they were the faces of town ancestors preserved in clay and kept in territory (figure 7.10).

Despite their status outside the law, many Tlacuaches like to talk about and show their collections. One woman I met showed me her prized finds lining a shelf in her kitchen: "This is a seated woman with a protruding belly button; and these are a series of monkey-faced figures." She classified the objects according to what she believed they revealed about Coatlinchan's place in a larger evolutionary history, sometimes using technical language to date and describe them. "These are very primitive," she said, "just clay shapes with very little detail

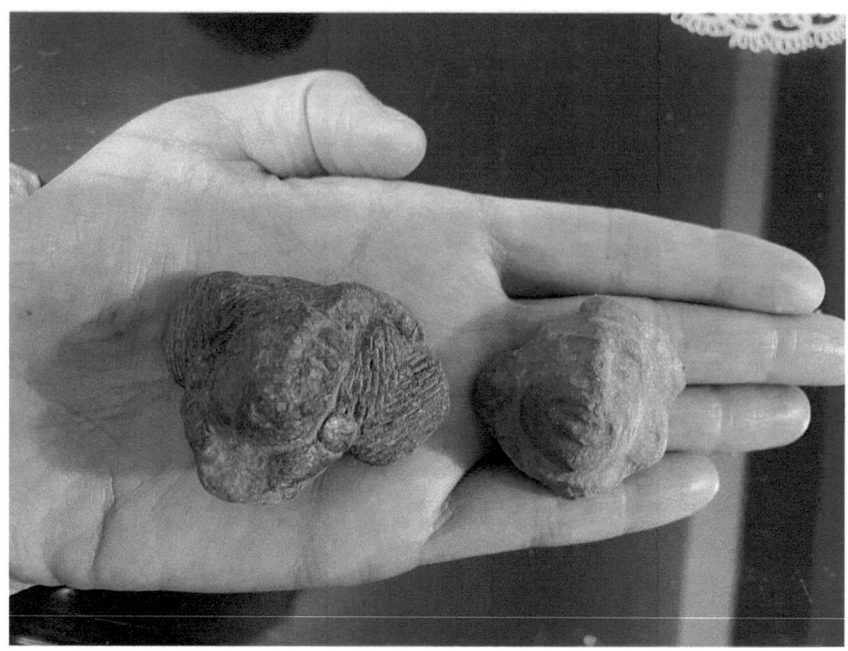

FIGURE 7.10. A woman holding caritas inside a Coatlinchan home, 2017. Photograph by the author.

and made with a pinching technique. These others are more Postclassic, with clear traits and intricate decorations. The monkey and humanoid faces with protruding chins are revealing of the history of those who made them who were making a portrait of their own ancestors, more primitive people." For her, the figurines were a legible archive through which to discern the history and origin of the peoples who once inhabited Coatlinchan as well as the material instantiations of that past. At the same time, her formalist reading reproduced the mid-twentieth-century Mexican state's nationalist and questionable accounts of race on Mexican soil. Regardless of whether or not this system of classification is based on Coatlinchan's actual history of settlement, her organization of objects into evolutionary sequences traced life and settlement in Coatlinchan from prehistoric times all the way through the Spanish conquest (some of the figurines are sculpted wearing Spanish-style hats and beards), echoing theories regarding the origins of American civilizations as well as crafting a history of settlement that connects the town's contemporary residents to its most ancient tangible remains. In these configurations, ancient pottery and "caritas" take on new life on contemporary surfaces.

Don Pablo showed me his collection, describing the objects one by one as a kind of mnemonic device, serving to remind him of his family's lands, plots in the ejido that he and his family had sown for generations. Like Dulce's mother, he pulled a figure out of a bucket full of hundreds and knew exactly which of his family plots he had found it in by name. He picked out another figure randomly, a small broken snake's head with bulging eyes, and again knew exactly where it came from. He took great pleasure in showing his collection, mapping the town's territory just as he described the sites of his finds as well as his family's, and his own relationship to them. Pablo's pleasure was also a source of worry: "Who knows if my grandkids will stay. Young people no longer want to work the land. They prefer video games or going to Mexico City, or even the US." Like Pablo, whose children and grandchildren all live in California, for many townspeople, these fragments do not represent an unknown past or a lost and ancient civilization and time. They are present-day indices of their deep-seated relationships to territory and earth that they, their parents, and grandparents had tilled and lived off for generations and that are currently under threat in times of social and ecological disruption.

Some Tlacuaches, more fearful of being reprimanded for their illicit ownership of ancient things, hide their collections under their beds or, like Agustín, in locked cabinets. Sometimes, the objects they display are ones they consider as having lesser quality or value. They use archaeology journals and visits to the Museo Nacional de Antropología to appraise their collections, comparing them to the ones displayed or written about as national treasures. Objects that resemble those in these sources are mostly hidden away, shown only to the trustworthy. By concealing them, Tlacuaches keep these artifacts as precious heirlooms that, like treasure, are hoarded as the collective wealth and material sustenance of the families of Coatlinchan. When a rumor circulated that I was asking questions about ancient things because I was looking to buy artifacts for the Centro Cultural Bicentenario then under construction, a friend gave me an off-handed warning: "We chased out at gunpoint the last person who came here asking about ídolos; she was an archaeologist. We were looted once. They took our Piedra, They're not going to loot us again."

Most residents insist that ancient objects cannot be translated into money, framing their collecting practices as a kind of salvage enterprise to stop the state's extraction as well as the black market trade of pre-Hispanic things. Tlacuaches often speak about this black market as something that only outsiders engage in, coming to Coatlinchan and taking artifacts to sell to collectors. Many have also expressed interest in setting up committees and collective associations to police and protect sites and tlateles from these rapacious practices. Some, however, confessed that in hard times, they or other town residents had to sell objects for money. These stories are always told as events in the past, before people realized the value of ancient artifacts for their own community or as mistakes tied to reprimandable practices that ultimately led to alienation or even expulsion. In a sense, they also serve as morality tales exemplifying what should not be done. A man who had recently died from cirrhosis, for example, was said to have left a large collection in a pulquería in a nearby town, where he went to feed his alcoholism and where the owner accepted these objects as payment. He nonetheless had to go elsewhere to be able to conduct this exchange. Rumors also circulate about specific town residents who engage in this black market, selling their finds to collectors in the United States who pay in dollars. More than once, often amid jokes, friends in Coatlinchan offered to sell me idolitos.

Even as Tlacuaches lament the recent scarcity of artifacts and their being always at risk, the town itself is full of fragments. A manhole on one of the town's main streets is decorated with old coins and ancient spindles with designs that have faded under the tires of passing cars and trucks. Painted sherds and little faces peek out from the adobe walls of old houses made from dried earth and hay. Stone skulls and sculptures are embedded in the walls of the sixteenth-century church that was surely the site where these objects were first referred to as dangerous idols. Inside the cloister, a figure associated with maize is carved into a stone repurposed from a pre-Hispanic construction, easily discernible at eye level within the wall that directly faces the entrance. A more recent renovation undertaken in the 1980s incorporated two small anthropomorphic figurines into the mortar, greeting visitors who come through the gates for daily prayers and masses. Through their efforts to keep these objects "safe" by hoarding them but also incorporating them into the spaces and structures they inhabit, and often also hiding them from state heritage institutions, Tlacuaches are claiming these traces as "lo nuestro," as central components of what makes up and sustains their community in this specific place. Their practices reveal these artifacts as deeply connected and coconstitutive elements that interact with, regulate, and reproduce territory as well as the networks that generate life there through environmental and ecological plenty.

Like Agustín, Tlakuanikoatl Ocelotl Xicome, Dulce, and others in Coatlinchan today, town residents are invested in mapping the town's ancient history onto its contemporary topography through their pre-Hispanic finds and collections. Unlike antiquarians, museum curators and private collectors who have coveted ancient artifacts for their unique aesthetic, economic, or symbolic value, Tlacuaches are interested in accumulating them to keep them within their territory. Although they know them to be valuable on the market, and occasionally profit from this value, they see their disappearance and loss as affecting many other elements that ensure their livelihoods and potential survival in this place. For Tlacuaches, keeping these objects safe, removing them from circulation after decades of having actively participated in their exchange, materializes present-day claims over territory and its resources in a region overtaken by increasing urbanization, drought, and economic hardship. Like Agustín, who hears clay spindles "calling him" and attributes his findings to magic, rain, the will of dead ancestors, and even the will of the objects themselves, most Tlacuaches I met experience these objects' plenty or scarcity as the result of both human and nonhuman agencies. The ethnographic richness of the ways in which Tlacuaches describe the deeply intertwined and mutually constitutive relationships between close social relations, artifacts, plants, and environmental elements such as rain allows for a rethinking of such objects' generative force and emergent potentials in sustaining community. As such, like the stone that was taken to the museum six decades ago, they cannot be wholly severed from territory or from the elements, like rain, that allow those relationships to emerge, blossom, and grow.

Conclusion

Isrrael Pixihua told me to meet him by the San Lázaro subway entrance. Amid stalls and vendors hustling to sell snacks and trinkets, people from all over the country congregate day in and day out in this place in Mexico City, manila folders in hand, on their bureaucratic pilgrimage to one of several government buildings in the vicinity. Isrrael Pixihua was part of a committee of town residents from Coatlinchan on such a pilgrimage, having secured an audience at the Cámara de Diputados, Mexico's lower court. "Don't forget to wear a hat, *güera*," he reminded me gently. It was late June 2023 and the rains that normally start in May, cooling and cleaning Mexico City's dusty air, had not begun. The line was long. The officers at the door, with the national coat of arms emblazoned in gold and silver on their chests, were sweating under their caps. Three hours passed under the midday sun. My companions did not seem affected by the heat in their white manta outfit, straw hats, and leather huaraches. Noticing my discomfort, Isrrael Pixihua calmly reassured me, "Don't worry, the south winds will be blowing change."

An active member of the Grupo Cultural Coatlinchan and then of the Calpulli Makoyolotzin, Isrrael Pixihua was one of the main protagonists of the film *The Absent Stone* (2013), which I codirected with Jesse Lerner. Since the film premiered in Coatlinchan in 2013, these groups had organized dozens of screenings, some during the yearly commemorations marking the stone's removal and some during other community-wide festivities. Now, they had decided to appropriate the film's title to campaign for restitution. Under an image of the stone standing on a bright blue background with splashing water and the hashtag #TlalocDevuelta (Tlaloc returned), they were gathering signatures for the return of "the absent stone" to its place of origin. The petition, addressed to Alejandra Frausto, then secretary of culture, and copied to President Andrés Manuel López Obrador, in keeping with the tradition of such missives, was presented on the Texcoco Municipality's official letterhead. It denounced the stone's theft in 1964 in the face of community opposition and emphasized that town residents had since then sustained their connections to the stone and to its ancient makers, demanding its return. By return, Isrrael Pixihua explained, they meant the stone's restitution to Coatlinchan, but not as it was before it was taken by the state. The stone would return renewed and reinvigorated by its new powers as a monument of national patrimonio, associated with the state that had taken it away. He and others in Coatlinchan had not come to a consensus of what such a return would look like, but they knew they wanted it back. Isrrael Pixihua and the members of the Calpulli hoped that it would be put back in the ravine, where it would be incorporated into a ceremonial center devoted to the ancient Acolhua; others spoke of making a site museum around it with other ancient things from the community.

Their request coincided with the current administration's campaign #MiPatrimonioNoSeVende (my heritage is not for sale), which instrumentalized the return of ancient artifacts from museum collections and auction houses worldwide as a central tenet of its proposed "Fourth Transformation." This radical change in Mexican politics promised to do away with historic forms of corruption and privilege in ways that equaled the transformative impact of independence from Spain, the Reform Wars, and the Mexican Revolution. The campaign was thus part of a larger project to return to the Mexican people that which had been stolen from them by both outsiders and national elites, most literally with the creation of the Instituto para Devolverle al Pueblo lo Robado (INDEP, Institute to Return the Stolen to the People).[1] Only a few weeks prior,

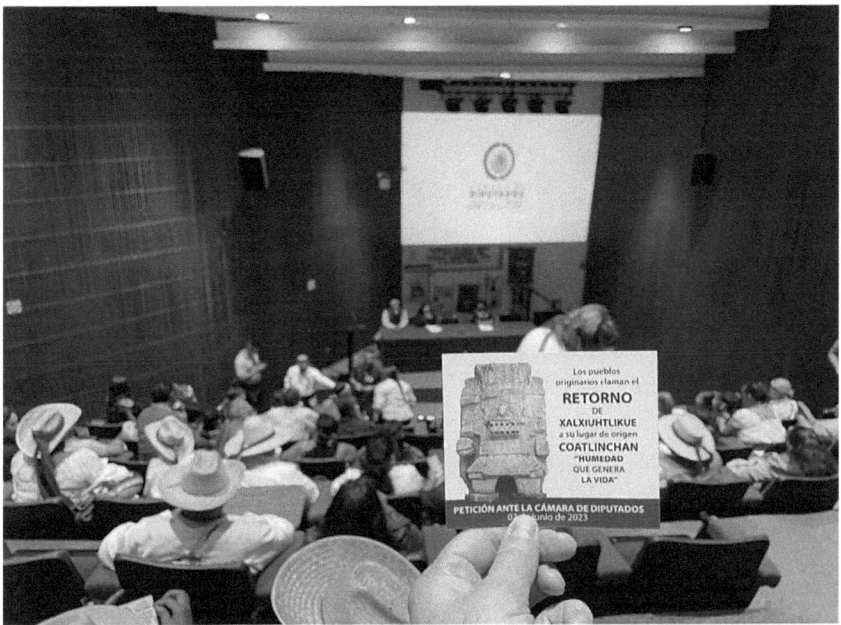

FIGURE C.I. Presentation for "El Retorno de Xalxiuhtlikue" at the Cámara de Diputados, June 2023. The badge shows the slogan "Humedad que genera vida" (life-making humidity). Photograph by the author.

in April 2023, the Mexican government had successfully repatriated an important Olmec work from a private collection in the United States. Greeting the plane transporting the object known as the Portal to the Underworld as it landed in Mexico City, Marcelo Ebrard, then foreign secretary, proclaimed that it was "of great significance for the idea that we have of ourselves. It was like an open wound not to have it. Returning it to Mexico restores something that explains to us where we come from." During his own speech at the court, Isrrael Pixihua appropriated Ebrard's words: "For us, not having the stone is an open wound." This wound, however, was not inflicted by a colonial power or by imperialist institutions but by the Mexican state now busy repatriating collections from abroad. Isrrael Pixihua spoke of this wound in the context of current ecological disruptions and climate change: "Bringing the stone back to Coatlinchan will reestablish the region's hydraulic equilibrium." Its return would restore a damaged ecosystem, bringing back "life-making humidity" (*humedad que genera vida*), a slogan printed on the badges worn by all the members of the committee (figure C.I). Restituting the stone to Coatlinchan offered the possibility of healing a scarring wound both because it would right a historical wrong inflicted by state theft and because it might guarantee survival in a threatened and threatening world.

Contesting the Monolith

Since its theft, social movements and artists have engaged the stone's repurposing as a stand-in for Mexico's authoritarian politics, state violence, and repression. In 1968, just four years after it was brought to Mexico City, photographer Toni Kuhn captured the rough texture of the stone plastered with flyers protesting state violence following the Tlatelolco student massacre.[2] In the image (which I am unable to reproduce here), taken at night, the stone's shape is barely discernible, its distinctive features and headdress camouflaged in darkness, with only its lower body and limbs illuminated. The three posters, however, were clearly legible. One showed a soldier beating a student. The other two denounced state violence with political slogans. One read, "They had no weapons but their blood," and the other, above and below a tank aiming straight ahead, said, "This is not a dialogue we understand." Curator and critic Alfonso Morales wrote about Kuhn's image as a new repurposing of the stone, meant to critique other monolithic formations in Mexico like family tradition, the PRI, and authoritarian presidentialism (Morales 2005, 206). Standing in for those other monoliths and for the postrevolutionary state as a whole, the photograph claimed the term *monolith* as a metaphor for the PRI's single-party rule over Mexico. This monolith, too, could be intervened, broken, transformed, and resignified by Mexican citizens clamoring for social justice and political change on the stone's surface.[3] Since then, other social movements, political parties, and unions have used the stone as a political platform and gathering point for meetings, protests, and marches. Although they enlisted the stone as an ally, these claims on its powers never questioned its repurposing as a monument outside the museum, an action that was indissociable from these politics.

But in December 2014, the city awoke to the stone wearing a large red skirt with the number "43," and another banner, covering the words "Museo Nacional de Antropología" on its pedestal with the demand "Take me back to Coatlinchan," next to the logo for the INAH, painted in black. The stone was recruited by the movement demanding justice for the disappearance of forty-three students from the Raúl Isidro Burgos Rural Teachers' College in Ayotzinapa in the state of Guerrero who were intercepted by local police when they commandeered buses to get to Mexico City to commemorate the anniversary of the 1968 Tlatelolco massacre. This time, the denunciation of the stone's place as a monument for the museum and as national patrimonio was central to its political repurposing. Written in chalk on the sidewalk in front of the fountain were the words "Fue el Estado" (It was the State), a phrase that, together with "Vivos se los llevaron, vivos los queremos" (They were taken alive, we want them back alive), were the key slogans of the protests denouncing the state's responsibility in the students' disappearance. These actions collapsed two moments in Mexican history characterized by state violence and forced disappearance—the 1960s Dirty War and that of today—to draw a parallel between the stone's forced removal from Coatlinchan and the contemporary Mexican state's authoritarian practices and endemic political and military corruption and violence (Aguayo 2015). The museum's maintenance staff removed the banners and chalk marks, but they reappeared the next day and on various occasions since.

The call to return the stone to Coatlinchan also recently permeated the Mexican contemporary art scene. In late April 2023, TONO, a Mexico City–based art festival, collaborated with the record label NAAFI to bring the third act and the finale of the opera *Atlacoya: Agua triste del Lago de Texcoco* to the stage.[4] The opera, based on the story of the Coatlinchan stone's forced relocation, was conceived and produced by Alberto Bustamante (Mexican Jihad) and Lauro Robles (DJ Lao), and its script was written and directed by performance artist Pepx Romero.[5] Romero, who made headlines after infiltrating the Museo Nacional de Antropología to film himself, dressed in a bright yellow suit, licking and kissing the ancient artifacts on display, framed the opera as a part of his broader interest denouncing the illicit trade and traffic of Mexican patrimonio, calling for its restitution.[6]

The venue for the opera was an old factory in the Azcapotzalco neighborhood, revamped for the occasion with stages and lighting features. Decked out in pleather and sequined outfits, the crowd was mostly in their twenties and thirties.[7] The lead was played by La Bruja de Texcoco, a talented trans musician, singer, and songwriter known for using traditional Mexican musical genres to queer, subvert, and reimagine gender binaries. That night she incarnated the stone majestic, wearing a shimmering turquoise pleated skirt with a neon train and several strings of obsidian, ceramic, jade beads, and replicas of ancient artifacts hanging heavily from her neck. The lyrics of the opera situated the stone's relocation within long-standing state and gender violence in modern Mexico:

Un Tlaloc que no es Tlaloc
Un hombre que no es un Hombre
Un hombre que es Mujer
Sus venas conectadas al drenaje

de lo que alguna vez fue
el imperio de las aguas flotantes
Ciudad antigua
Rompiendo el emplasto de asfalto
emerge el agua como un portento.

(Tlaloc that isn't Tlaloc
A man that isn't a Man
A man that is a Woman
Her veins connected to the sewage
of what was once
the empire of floating waters
An ancient city
Breaking the plastered asphalt
water emerges like a miracle.)

La Bruja traversed the space bearing a copal censer, blowing scented smoke into the air and singing sweetly. On the other side of the room, she encountered Pedro Ramírez Vázquez, played by Romero, on all fours amid piles of rubble, his underwear visible under a see-through plastic suit. La Bruja's melodic songs gave way to stern scolding (figure C.2).

She reprimanded the architect for having transplanted her from Coatlinchan, breaking her telluric relations to its mountains, lakes, and rivers, and placing her, alone and misidentified, amid the city's "veins of sewage" outside the modernist and nationalist nightmare of the Museo Nacional de Antropología. As soon as she finished her diatribe, a chorus of voices joined La Bruja, standing under a scaffolding that began gushing water onto the stage, demanding that the president give the stone back to Coatlinchan. As the act ended, the DJ began to play sets of electronic music and the audience broke into festive dance.

Restoring the Stone

For almost twenty years, I had heard people in Coatlinchan time and again denounce and lament the stone's theft, while also expressing a certain resignation and acceptance around its loss. Back in 2011, when Jesse and I were making our film, we decided to end it with a sequence that, at the time, seemed like a whimsical proposition. Working with the animation collective Viumasters, we used archival photographs, newsreels, and maps to cinematically reverse the stone's journey and return it to the ravine in Coatlinchan.[8] Upon arrival, it impulsively freed itself from the cage-like contraptions designed to transport it to Mexico

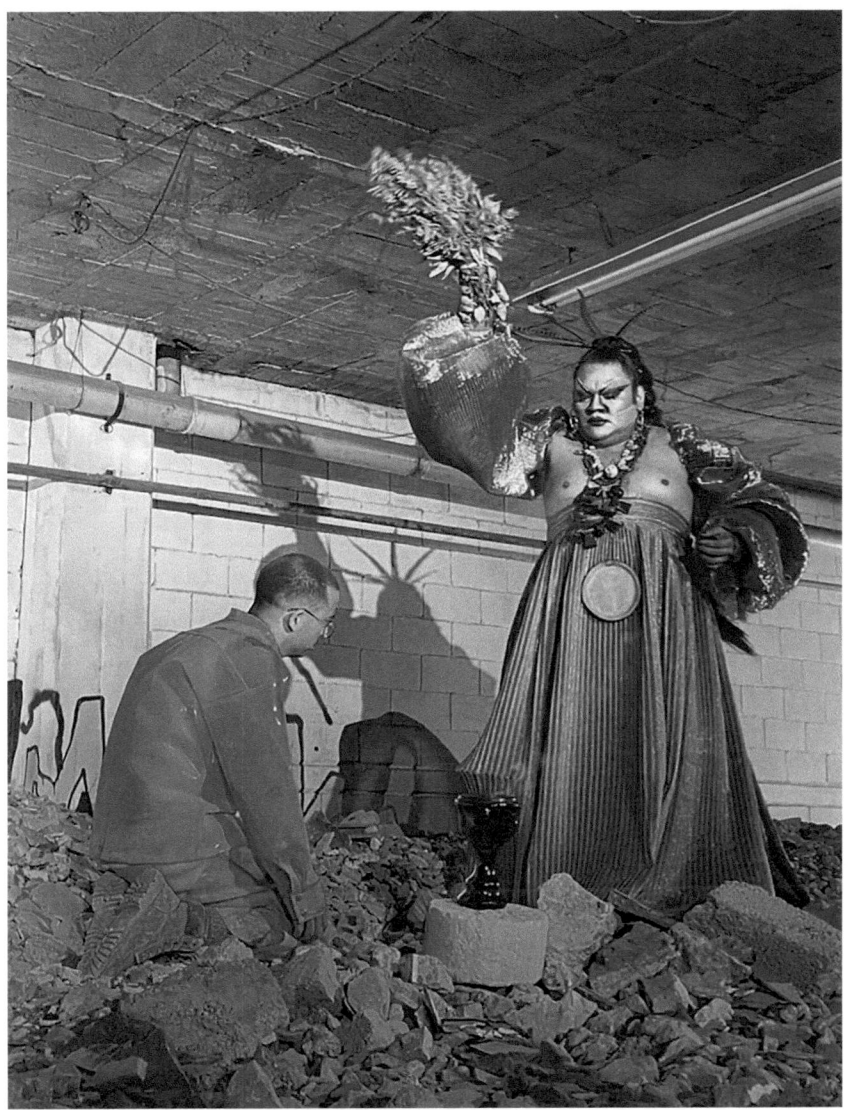

FIGURE C.2. La Bruja de Texcoco and Pepx Romero during the performance of *Atlacoya*, April 29, 2023. Photograph by the author.

City, returning to its horizontal position in the ravine amid the sound of intensifying raindrops. The sequence was loosely based on conversations with the groups we had worked with in Coatlinchan who longed for the stone's return, while recognizing what seemed like its impossibility.

Back then, the idea that the stone could someday return, or even that town residents had any right to demand its return, was simply unrealistic for most Tlacuaches, a fact they used their characteristic humor and reliance on double entendre to confront. In another sequence of the film, we recorded a multigenerational group of women sitting around a courtyard sipping pulque and sharing childhood recollections about the stone. One of them burst out: "They should bring it back!" An outspoken elderly woman laughed and, to everyone's amusement, retorted: "Nah, they can't! Back then, Mexico City was a maiden [virgin]. But since then, with so many subways drilled into it . . ." Using humor, she equated the stone's extraction with the irreversible effects of rape, while framing the impossibility of its return as a question of engineering obstacles, denying the town's political claim and the state's responsibility to return the stolen stone despite her wish that things were otherwise. But in the decade since this retort, as museum collections are being restituted to source communities and monuments made to commemorate figures and events associated with colonialism, racism, and gender violence are being questioned and even torn down all over the world, the panorama has changed. In Mexico, social movements, Indigenous rights activists, and feminist collectives have intervened and also cast down statues and monuments commemorating national, mostly white and male, historical figures and events, many located on the Paseo de la Reforma near the Piedra de los Tecomates.

In 2018, during one of the city's most massive protests in recent memory, feminist groups took over the avenue to sprinkle pink glitter and mark statues and pedestals with purple and pink spray paint and tags, condemning the state's apathy in countering escalating violence against women. The most visible of these interventions was at the Ángel de la Independencia, perhaps the most emblematic of the avenue's monuments because of both its original purpose commemorating national independence and its use as a site for massive gatherings for nationalist celebrations. The pedestal and column supporting the winged victory, which doubles as the city's official logo, was tagged with 565 slogans decrying "Estado asesino," "policias violadores," "vivir en México es un asesinato," and "la patria asesina," among other accusations. A conservative outcry denounced these actions as "vandalism," asking women to "behave" and use more "adequate" means to make their voices heard. Almost immediately after the marches, the city government announced that, in collaboration with the INAH, the Ángel would be closed off, cleaned, and restored to its original state (Minera 2020; Álvarez 2022).

This sparked much anger among feminist movements and several progressive sectors of civil society who pointed to the inherent contradiction in the government's interest and quick actions to "restore stones" and its lack of investment and care for the quotidian violence suffered by women. A movement among professional restorers, the Restauradoras con Glitter, came forth to defend the interventions (Sigüenza Salas 2021; Buentello García and Quinn Rice 2023). Proposing that the inscriptions be preserved as "uncomfortable markers" of the violence endured by women in Mexico, they insisted that the removal of these markers and restoration of the monuments' "pristinity" be postponed until gender violence was attended to and eradicated. Their official statement offered an alternative definition of patrimonio, challenging the concept's preservationist and patriarchal undertones: "We understand patrimonio as a medium that is not static, where multiple ideas, questions and consensuses can be manifested. Given this dynamism, sociocultural processes that emerge in and around patrimonio also generate meaning and identity. Our job is to ensure that patrimonio can participate in these social processes that, like society, are always in flux" (Restauradoras Con Glitter 2019).

For these Restauradoras—as for many contemporary critical archaeologists— patrimony is first and foremost a process, one that includes the ways that monuments and objects are made meaningful, cared for, and deployed in contemporary contexts, even if this means their transformation, perhaps even their destruction.[9] They invite us to experience objects and artworks through dynamic adaptations and changes—intentional, accidental, and environmental— rather than insisting they be preserved in timeless suspension (2022).[10]

For the residents of territories that have been victims of and continue to grapple with the Mexican state's seizure of monuments for its own ends, patrimony's open-endedness, as a process defined by relations and mutability, is also a politics that defies the state and offers new possibilities for replication, for restorative work and collective action. Actions by social movements and artists to repurpose and actively reconfigure Mexico's patrimonio resonate with Coatlinchan's residents' own claims to "lo nuestro" and their efforts to both thrive in the aftershocks of state-enforced dispossession, perhaps even through that dispossession, and to heal from it. Tlacuaches' efforts to return the stone through both legal and ritual channels, hoping to restore relations broken and harmed by the stone's relocation, offer important and eloquent alternatives to state patrimonio discourses and rapacious practices.

Restitution

In Coatlinchan, town residents are working toward the stone's return, but theirs is more than a call for straightforward restitution. As this book has shown, the stone's theft and subsequent absence generated creative and vibrant processes that have made patrimonio and the stone itself reproduce and multiply in myriad forms: replicas and copies as well as other matter contained in territory, including sprouting ancient artifacts and pottery sherds, treasure troves, colonial maps and documents, and telluric matter like sand, soil, and water. These aftershocks complicate preservationist understandings of patrimonio that hinge on the conservation and valuing of originals in conditions that might well guarantee their endurance over time but are based on violent forms of extractivism, expropriation, and disregard for their attachments to and relations with people, places and their environments.

Coatlinchan residents' engagement with ancient objects, their practices of collecting, keeping, displaying, and storytelling with them, are premised on their knowledge of how these objects work in interaction to produce and sustain community, participating in preventing contemporary environmental, political, and social collapse. These relations are oriented very differently from the grass metaphor evoked by the local teacher in architect Ramírez Vázquez's memory of the stone's removal, in which the grass on one side of a lake was equivalent to the grass on the other side or the center of the lake, justifying the state's modernizing and universalizing intention of transforming all pre-Hispanic objects, including Coatlinchan's stone, into the homogeneous and modern patrimonio of all Mexicans alike. For Tlacuaches, far from generic grass growing on one side or another of a lake, the Piedra and other ancient artifacts cannot be separated from telluric relations working together to make *their* grass, as also *their* crops and people, grow and thrive in *their* territory. This stone, even if physically absent in Coatlinchan, continues to be connected to its residents, to their bodies, and to their territory, despite state theft.

In April 2024, almost a year after Isrrael Pixihua's speech and the delivery of the formal petition to the Cámara de Diputados, the Observatorio Meteorológico managed by the Comisión Nacional del Agua (CONAGUA, National Water Commission) in Tacubaya, not far from where the Piedra stands on Reforma, registered a record high of 34.2 degrees Celsius (93.6 Fahrenheit), the hottest it has been in the Valley of Mexico in more than thirty years. The following months were unusually hot and the water reservoirs of the Cutzamala system that quench the thirst of Mexico City and the Estado de México, pumping water over more than three hundred miles of pipes climbing more than one thousand meters in altitude, were at an alarming low.[11] The infamous "día zero" was on everyone's lips as water intermittency, and now scarcity, have become part of the everyday.[12]

In this context, and while spending hours looking for *pipas* (water tanker trucks) to procure water for my own Mexico City home, I visited my friends in Coatlinchan.[13] Isrrael Pixihua laughed scornfully when I asked him for news concerning the petition to return the stone. He showed me a PDF of the INAH's official response to the group on his phone:

> In response to your letter Control number: 729-2023, addressed to Lic. Alejandra Frausto Guerrero, Secretary of Culture and forwarded to this Coordinación, in which you request support and intervention in order to return the Coatlinchan monolith to the Municipality of Texcoco in the Estado de México, which is currently located at the entrance of the Museo Nacional de Antropología on the Paseo de la Reforma in Mexico City and under the custody of the INAH. In this regard, we would like to make the following clarifications: the monolith in question's transfer took place on April 16, 1964, in compliance with a direct instruction from the Federal Government, at that time represented by Adolfo López Mateos and requested to the head of the SEP, Mr. Jaime Torres Bodet. Therefore, this order was not a request by this Institute. We also want to point out that, in accordance with our functions as a governmental body charged with the research, conservation, protection and dissemination of Mexico's prehistoric, archaeological, anthropological, historical and paleontological patrimonio, it has been precisely thanks to the place where it is currently located that we have been able to ensure the care and proper maintenance of the artifact [*pieza*] in question, including the restoration work carried out from 2011 to 2016, coordinated by Sergio González García with the participation of experts from various institutions. Finally, in correspondence with Article 4 of the Political Constitution of the United States of Mexico, it is by housing it in a place with great affluence, that we have been able to guarantee the access to culture and the enjoyment of these goods, as well as the full exercise of the cultural rights of national and foreign visitors who visit the Museo Nacional de Antropología. In view of the foregoing, it is not possible for this Coordinación to agree to what has been requested.[14]

Isrrael Pixihua noted that this dismissal of the town's request absolved the INAH from any responsibility in the stone's theft because it had allegedly not directly participated in its relocation back in 1964. He criticized the government functionary's insistence on complying with the INAH's mission to care for and

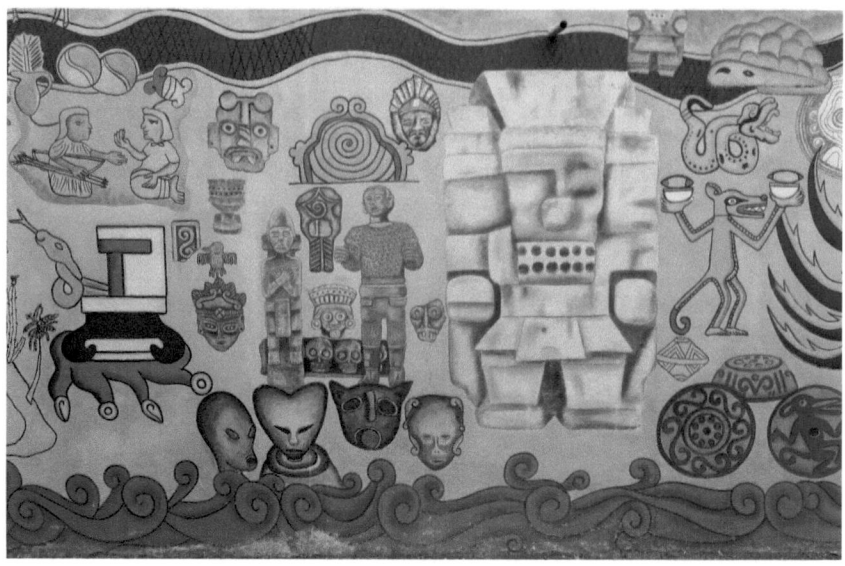

FIGURE C.3. Tlakuanikoatl Ocelotl Xicome (Marcelo Ortíz Sánchez), mural outside the artist's home, 2024. Photograph by the author.

preserve patrimonio as a fundamental cultural right of both Mexican citizens and foreigners as museumgoers, given the stone's theft and its subsequent exposure to the corrosive effects of fumes generated by ongoing Mexico City traffic and acid rain in its location outside the museum. "Pues si, así piensan ... Pero están equivocados. No quitaremos el dedo del renglón" (Well, that's how they think ... But they are wrong. We will not stop insisting), he assured me.

Meanwhile, Tlakuanikoatl Ocelotl Xicome was busy in his garden, assisted by his teenage son and daughter, painting the back wall of his home with a new mural that featured the stone standing amid all the ancient artifacts he and his friends had been able to locate that come from Coatlinchan's territory in museum collections both in Mexico and abroad, as well as some they had found during their own explorations (figure C.3).

He had just showed me another painting hanging on his wall inside his living room: a watercolor of the stone as a telluric force covered in landscape, gushing water from the tecomates, watering maize, magueys, and flowers blossoming from its earthen body (figure C.4). Inscribed with colorful pre-Hispanic glyphs and symbols, the stone bore the moon and the sun, in the shape of a stone carving of Tonatiuh similar to the central feature of the Aztec Calendar Stone, in each of its arms. Tlaloc's goggle eyes and fangs adorned its

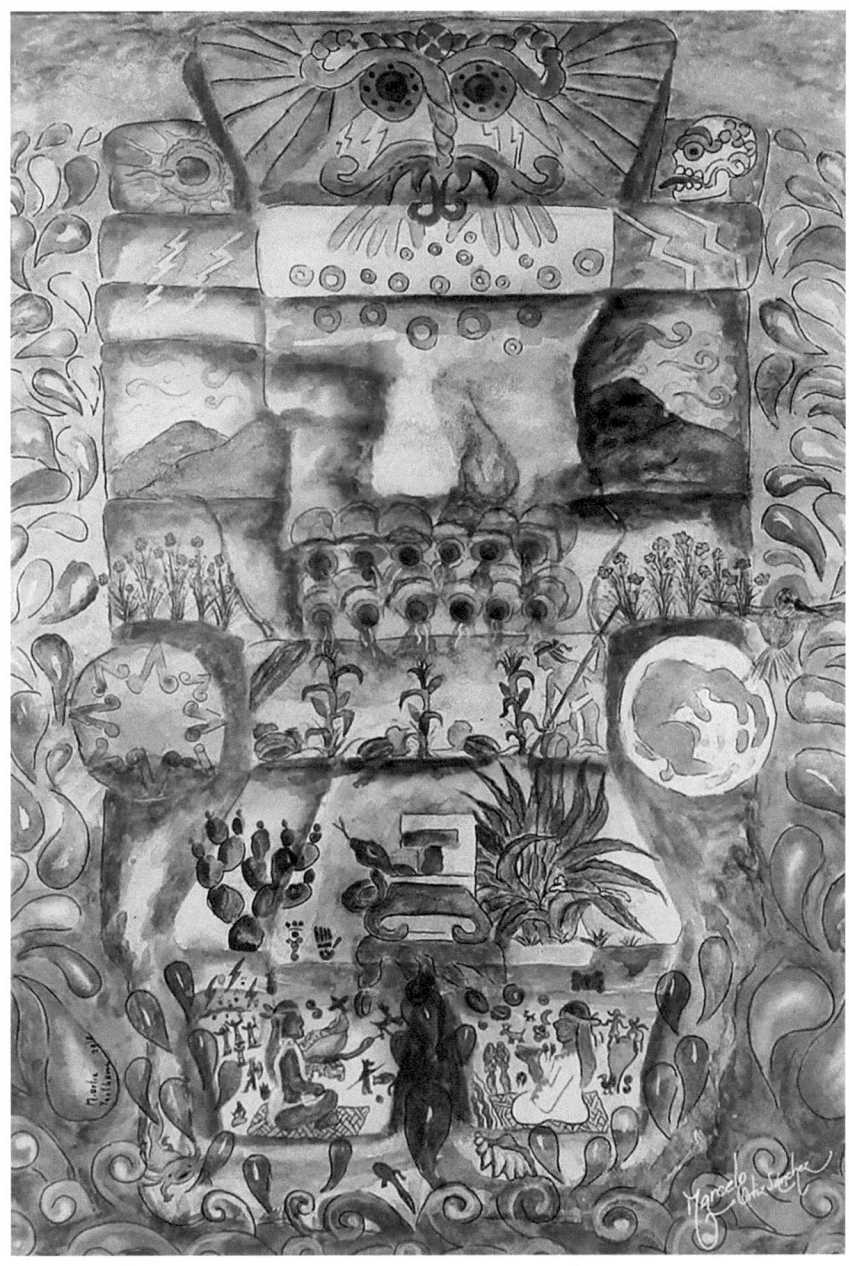

FIGURE C.4. Tlakuanikoatl Ocelotl Xicome (Marcelo Ortíz Sánchez), "Tlakuiloyotl." From *Sepan cuantos, historia del Señorio de Coatlinchan*, 2018. Watercolor. Courtesy of the artist.

headdress, sprouting drops of water and lightning. The Coatlinchan altepetl glyph formed its uterus. The ancestors of the ancient Acolhuacan depicted in the Xolotl Codex sustained its feet, submerged in agitated waters along with aquatic creatures like conches, axolotes, and tadpoles.

Without turning around, and continuing with his steady brushstrokes, Tlakuanikoatl Ocelotl Xicome declared: "We haven't heard anything more since we received the INAH's answer. They just stamped the petition to certify they received it and sent us a standardized response. And that was that." He paused and then, pacing his words to the measured and slow rhythm of his paintbrush, reflected: "But you know . . . I have a feeling . . . I know it in my gut . . . I or at least my children or maybe my grandchildren will live to see the stone back in the *cañada* . . . It will return . . . I don't know when or how, but they will have to bring it back."

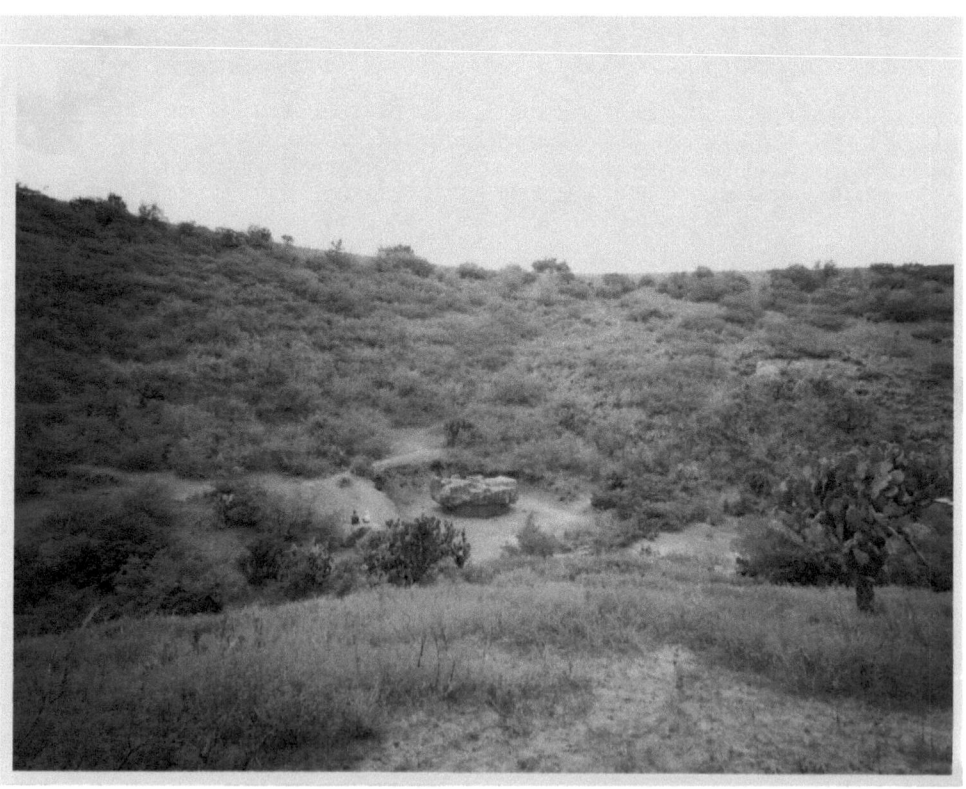

FIGURE C.5. The stone in situ in Coatlinchan, 1963. Courtesy of Acervo Arquitecto Pedro Ramírez Vázquez.

Acknowledgments

This is a book about but also made of relations: relations between and that make up humans, as well as non- or more-than-humans, that in one way or another came together to build its materials and arguments. Because it has been long in the making, spanning almost two decades of research, writing, and rewriting, there is no way that I can do justice here to all the relations that contributed to its coming into being.

My deepest gratitude goes to a nonhuman ally. The Piedra de los Tecomates from Coatlinchan has relentlessly insisted that I stretch, reimagine, and question my own understandings of and relationships to museums and their collections as well as to the things that extend our personhood beyond our lifetimes and that actively make the worlds and territories we cohabit. The Piedra has stubbornly remained in my daily trajectories and interactions as well as in my dreams and nightmares for more than two decades, and I suspect it still has much to teach me beyond this book.

I am forever indebted to the Tlacuache families and friends in Coatlinchan who so warmly opened their homes and shared their stories with me during the fourteen months that I lived there and over the years that I have been consistently visiting them. Challenging a common practice in anthropological writing, many asked to be named as a condition for their participation in my research. Some Tlacuaches have published their own books and memoirs; authored poems, paintings, and murals; or made films and videos available on YouTube, which I cite and discuss throughout the book. I therefore mostly use people's real names, except for the handful who explicitly asked me to use a pseudonym. I dedicate this book to all the Tlacuaches who contributed to its making.

The Galicia González family, especially Dulce and Mamá Conchita, provided a home and refuge filled with humor and delicious meals, multigenerational conversations, and key insights that gave shape to many of this book's arguments. I am also thankful to Guadalupe Villarreal and her daughter Zaira as well as to Don Panchito and Doña Concepción Garay, in whose home I lived for much of my stay. Salvador Suárez, "don Chava," as he is affectionately known, and his wife Coca were always generous with their time and gave me access to their collections of books and objects, teaching me much of what I know about Coatlinchan's history. Don Chava tended to his parcela as his grandfather and father had before him but was also a carpenter by trade. Despite his worsening arthritis, he built me a small desk on which I took notes every evening, very literally supporting my work during my time in Coatlinchan.

Don Chava was a founding member of the groups I write about here, the Grupo Cultural Coatlinchan and the Calpulli Makoyolotzin. The Calpulli, led by Isrrael Pixihua (Martínez) and Tlakuanikoatl Ocelotl Xicome (Marcelo Ortíz), following the tragic deaths of Juan Manuel Tochintecutli (Garay) and Daniel Ayatitlicui (Almaraz), as well as more recent associations like Moyanko, and the Tlaloqueros founded by Dulce Galicia and Jesús Curiel, became my guides, inspiration, and friends during these twenty years. This book is the result of time spent observing and participating in their meetings and events as well as of our many conversations and myriad walks in Coatlinchan's territory. I greatly admire the work that they are doing collectively and individually to reclaim their territory and vestiges from the past as "lo nuestro" and as central tenets for building more just and sustainable futures. Many other Tlacuaches were central to this research. Sadly, many, already elderly when I met them, passed away before this book was finished. I can only hope that I was able to capture some of their spirit and stories here.

Thinking in terms of relations is also inevitably about kinship. This book, in traditional Latin American anthropological form, has many madrinas and padrinos whom I was lucky to come across within vibrant intellectual communities in both New York and Mexico City, where it came into being. Although I never took a course with Debbie Poole, her mentorship, encouragement, and insights have been powerful influences, as have her incisive humor and generosity. Beyond her astounding contributions to the field, Debbie has always known how to live and how to listen, showing me that careful ethnography can be a window to understanding the world and how we might live in it better and more intensely. Debbie also provided a model for how to mentor, offering students and junior scholars shelter and guidance, often, along with Chacho and Lina, opening her home and providing support well beyond the call of duty. As she now goes through trying times, I strive to *acompañarla* as she did me and perhaps someday *llegarle a los talones.*

Elizabeth F. S. Roberts and Angela Garcia read and commented on an advanced draft during a book writing workshop with a view of the San Francisco Bay. Over the years, they have given me the strength, energy, and confidence to come back to a project I was about to abandon. Liz read and commented on the very first paper I wrote about this research in 2011 and has spent the past fourteen years being one of my closest interlocutors and this book's greatest champion. Her friendship and imaginative vision as well as her delight in excess and hilarity have provided wonderful company and motivation. Angela's creativity and her insistence that ethnography is a genre that requires careful attention to narrative and form, and, of course, her kindness, encouragement, and constant reinforcement, have inspired and helped me refine my arguments and writing.

This book would certainly not have seen the light of day, or would have taken another decade to write, were it not for my brilliant friends Miruna Achim and Jennifer Josten. Miruna's friendship as well as her companionship in teaching, stone obsessions, and volcanic explorations have become daily sources of discovery and surprise. This research began long before I met Miruna, but I hope she will see her influence and sensibility now on every page. Jennifer's insistence that she "needed" this book was a beacon that made me trust the process and navigate my own doubts and hesitations. Thank you for your thoughtful comments, critical reading, and editorial work; our many *pláticas* and *paseos* in Mexico's art worlds; and all your support during the difficult writing process. Jennifer also introduced me to Matthew Robb, now her husband, who is one of the most knowledgeable persons I know on the trajectories of all things Mesoamerican and whose incredible references and insights have given me much to think with and write about, and also joy.

Carlota McAllister provided deep friendship, lucid reflection, and revelatory humor as I tried to express and strengthen the book's arguments. Carlota helped me think through the telluric relations that bind ancient stones to contemporary territories and the people who live in and struggle to care for them. She also provided the book's subtitle, pointing to the many meanings of the word *réplicas* in Spanish. Carlota was part of another *madrin/padrinazgo*, a group of anthropologists across fields and latitudes struggling to write manuscripts in the midst of a global pandemic. Lindsay Bell, Risa Cromer, Ken McLeish, Emily Yates-Doerr, Carlota, and I met every month online for more than a year, reading and discussing chapter drafts, all with small children and puppies constantly interrupting, and then for an intensive weeklong writing retreat in Antigua, Guatemala. Six books, including this one, came out of our sustained discussions, generous readings, and unabiding solidarity.

Emily has been this project's *madrina* perhaps for the longest time, since she was also part of a broader network of relations and kin that nurtured its earliest drafts at New York University (NYU). Emily was central to the conversations and learning that took place at 25 Waverly Place, along with Sabra Thorner, my closest interlocutor and ally during those years, as well as Barbara Anderson, Ulla Berg, Lucas Bessire, Lily Defriend, Aaron Glass, Christopher Fraga, Amali Ibrahim, Rachel Lears, Will Thompson, April Strickland, Mercedes Duff, and others who have become my colleagues and friends. Being mentored by Emily Martin, Claudio Lomnitz, Renato Rosaldo, Fred Myers, Haidy Geismar, and Bruce Grant, and taking courses with Katherine Verdery, Barbara Kirshenblatt-Gimblett, Pablo Piccato, Bruce Altshuller, Rayna Rapp, Sally Merry, and Faye Ginsberg helped me refine my thinking and questions about property, heritage, art worlds, memory, museums, and collections.

No doubt, at NYU, Thomas Abercrombie was this book's most important coconspirator. Tom's interest in the pathways that bind people to the places they inhabit, or rather cohabit with, and his fascination with pilgrimage, saint images, miniature rocks, and other vibrant matters in the Americas, as well as his and Beth Penry's enthusiastic support, generosity and culinary abilities, helped me imagine and design this project. Tom sadly passed away in 2019, too soon to find out that, after a considerable hiatus and many doubts, I finally finished this book. The Ekeko he brought for me from the Alasitas market stands on my shelf, carrying bills from the Banco de la Fortuna and tiny pasta sacks, awaiting the next cigarette and mezcal libation (*se mexicanizó*), a constant reminder of the many ways that we are all made up of relations that linger and thrive much beyond human lifespans.

Tom also gifted me another of the book's padrinos, and now one of my most cherished friends and allies, when he suggested I invite Richard Kernaghan to comment on a paper I presented during a works-in-progress workshop just after I got back from the field. Over the years, we have navigated many rivers together, thinking in tandem about what constitutes territories, their surfaces, matters, and topographies. Richard's eloquent and beautiful writing has inspired what I write about but also how and why I write about it.

Jesse Lerner spent time with me in Coatlinchan as we made our film but also discussed many of the ideas and arguments that took shape here in written form. Jesse's attention to and interest in museums, as well as replicas and fakes, and his wonderful sense of humor, noticing the prominence of cartoon characters and unlikely juxtapositions of mass media icons in Coatlinchan's visual landscape, pointed me to their political relevance. It is with Jesse that the title, *The Absent Stone*, came to exist, first as our film and now as this book, hinting at the many ways in which absence is productive and powerful. Mariana Castillo Deball and Eduardo Abaroa's own interest in the Piedra de los Tecomates and their iconoclastic and critical artistic projects on scientific knowledge production and collecting, specifically on the Museo Nacional de Antropología, have been sources of stimulating conversations and creative collaborations.

Other colleagues have become close friends and have greatly influenced this book. Some, like Analiese Richard and François Richard (who are not related!), have read and commented on drafts. Many were part of academic communities in New York and across US academic institutions, while others are based in Mexico City, and some, the most long-lasting of my friends and interlocutors, have crossed the border back and forth, bridging my own academic trajectories: Tiana Bakić Hayden, Laura Roush, Gabriela Zamorano, and my comadre and compadre Alejandra Leal and Nitzan Shoshan.

My deepest gratitude goes to friends and colleagues in Mexico City, especially to the members of the Seminario Nación y Alteridad who first offered me an intellectual space upon my return to my hometown: Daniela Gleizer, Alejandro Araujo, Akuavi Adonon, and Paula López Caballero; and to the students and members of the seminars Taller de Etnografía de y sobre México, which I began with Carlos Mondragón a decade ago, and the Seminario Equilibrium de Estudios de la Ciencia y la Tecnología, co-organized with Miruna Achim, Analiese Richard, Violeta Aréchiga, Alberto Fragio, Juan Felipe Guevara, and Agustín Mercado, hosted by the Universidad Autónoma Metropolitana-Cuajimalpa, where I was full-time faculty for much of this book's writing.

I am also thankful to other ami-colegas who have inspired me and who have also read and commented on chapter drafts and ideas: Antonio Azuela, Mario Barbosa, Miriam Bertrán, Laura Cházaro, Seth Denizen, Vivette García Deister, Carlos López Beltrán, Haydeé López Hernández, Yaredh Marín, Ariana Mendoza, Mariana Mora, Erika Pani, Mario Rufer, Gabriela Torres-Manzuera, Pablo Yankelevich, and Claudia Zamorano. Historians Susan Deans-Smith, Emilio Kourí, Mauricio Tenorio, John Tutino, Mary Kay Vaughan, and Matthew Vitz, as well as my colleagues at the Centro de Estudios Históricos at the Colegio de México, have helped me understand the temporal and political dimensions of modern Mexico. I am also grateful to the Tepoztlan Institute Collective, especially Shane Dillingham, Laura González, Josie Saldaña, Adam Warren, and Elliott Young. Over the past few years, I have been privileged to meet and discuss this project with some of the most insightful scholars of the ancient Americas and the reworkings of Indigenous and modern art worlds: Luis Castañeda, Mary Coffey, Karen Cordero, Deborah Dorotinsky, Ana Garduño, Laura Filloy, Ramón Folch, Julio Garcia Murillo, Renato González

Mello, Rosario Granados, Aaron Hyman, Cristobal Jácome, Natalia Majluf, Mary Miller, Barbara Mundy, James Oles, Joanne Pillsbury, Ana Pulido Rull, Itzel Rodríguez Mortellaro, Adam Sellen, Aldo Solano, Lisa Trever, and Álvaro Vázquez Mantecón.

Anthropologists near and far, working on topics and questions close to mine, have provided great inspiration and encouragement: Sevil Baltalı Tırpan, Gisela Canepa, Marisol de la Cadena, Alanna Cant, Vladimir Caraballo Acuña, Pamela Cevallos, John Collins, Carolina Crespo, Alexandra Delano, Tarek Elhaik, Elizabeth Ferry, Olga González, Columba González, Gaston Gordillo, Richard Handler, Munira Khayyat, Ingrid Kummels, Lynn Morgan, Yael Navaro-Yashin, Diane Nelson, Hugh Raffles, Jason Ramsey, Joanne Rappaport, Isaias Rojas-Perez, Roger Sansi, Simon Uribe, and Rihan Yeh. I am also thankful to the anonymous reviewers and the editorial team at Duke University Press, and to Ken Wissoker, who had faith in this project from the day we met.

Pedro Ramírez Vázquez and Enrique del Valle Prieto spent many hours discussing their participation in building the museum and engineering the stone's transfer with me. For both, the event was something to be proud of and a remarkable moment in their careers, but they also understood that times had changed and that the underlying premises of the stone's relocation were now being questioned. Although they didn't always agree with me, they willingly participated in my research both on and off camera, came to screenings of the film that I made as part of this project, and gave me access to their incomparable archives. I reproduce many here with permission from their sons and heirs, Alex del Valle Prieto and Javier Ramírez Campusano. Karina Garcia, the archivist who cares for the architect's personal archive, also enriched my research. I was able to interview Mario Vázquez, Alfonso Soto Soria, and Íker Larrauri before they passed away and Raúl de la Rosa and Trinidad Irigoyen about the museum's design and collections, as well as the institution's directors over the span of time it took to write this book: Felipe Solís, Diana Magaloni, and Antonio Saborit. Thank you also to Mónica del Villar for having gotten me started on this path when she hired me as a translator for *Arqueología Mexicana*. Other institutions and their staff gave me access to their collections and archives. I am especially thankful to the staff at the many Instituto Nacional de Antropología e Historia (INAH) archives I consulted, including the Biblioteca Nacional de Antropología e Historia, the Archivo Histórico Institucional, the Archivo Histórico del Museo Nacional de Antropología, the Archivo Técnico de Arqueología, the Archivo Nacional de Monumentos Históricos, and the Fototeca Nacional, as well as to the archivists and staff at the Archivo General de la Nación, the Archivo General Agrario, and the Archivo Histórico del Estado de México in Toluca.

The research for this book was funded through a Henry M. MacCracken Fellowship, two research grants from the Center for Latin American and Caribbean Studies, and a Tinker Summer Travel Grant from New York University, as well as a Wenner-Gren Foundation Dissertation Fieldwork Grant. An Andrew W. Mellon Foundation / American Council of Learned Societies Early Career Fellowship supported a year of writing, along with an honorary fellowship at NYU's Humanities Initiative. My students at the Universidad Iberoamericana, the Instituto de Investigaciones Estéticas at the Universidad Nacional Autónoma de México (UNAM), the Humanities Department at the Universidad Autónoma Metropolitana-Cuajimalpa, and the Centro de Estudios Históricos at El Colegio de México have been my greatest teachers, asking the most thought-provoking questions and offering fresh and challenging perspectives. Special thanks go to Ricardo Fagoaga and Francisco Alvarado for their help getting references and archival materials ready for publication. Thank you also to my coaching team, Simonne Pollini and Teresa García Hubard. My friends Mauricio Alejo, Maria Antonieta Alcalde, Paula Arroio, Amando Basurto, Maja Bentzer, Rada Bogdacenco, Gabriela Cano, Narayani Lasala, Aline Rosenfeld, Pamela Saldaña, and Gabriela Palencia were this project's steadfast cheerleaders and doulas.

Finally, this book is the result of decades of love, care, solidarity, support, and engagement provided by my grandparents, aunts, uncles, *primas* and *primos*, and my extraordinary *suegro* and *suegra*, *cuñadas*, *sobrinos* and *sobrinas*, who put up with, but also encouraged and nourished, my obsessive personality and stubborn intuitions. None of the work that went into the past few years of research and writing would have been possible without my family and the childcare provided by Gloria Herrera Hernández. It is to my parents, Andrés and Vivian, to my sister, Tamara, to my partner, Ulises, who was its most enthusiastic, patient, and loving advocate, and to my children, Micaela and Sasha, whose curiosity and commentary have made every day fun-filled, fascinating, and magical, that this book is dedicated. *Gracias totales.*

Notes

1. The term most commonly used in Mexico to refer to the time before Spanish colonialism and to the peoples living in this territory in ancient times is *pre-Hispanic*. This term has been critiqued as Eurocentric, implying a clear temporal break following contact and conquest by Spanish peoples. I use this term as an imperfect adjective. I also use the term *Mesoamerican*, a term coined by anthropologist Paul Kirchhoff in the 1940s, suggesting shared traits and practices uniting peoples living in much of modern Mexico and Central America both before and after the European invasion (Kirchhoff 1943).

2. The museum's combination of modernist architecture, state-of-the-art engineering, and pioneering immersive museum design has mostly been discussed by its makers in commemorative catalogs published by the institution. Scholars from various disciplines have written on aspects of its history and on its ways of establishing continuity between Mexico's ancient past and the postrevolutionary state's ideological project; see García Canclini (1992); Florescano (1993); Dorotinsky Alperstein (2002); Alonso (2004); Navarrete Linares (2010); L. Castañeda (2014); Jácome (2014); Gorbach (2016); López Hernández (2018, 2019); Rufer (2021); and Achim, Deans-Smith, and Rozental (2021).

3. On the "Mexican Miracle," see Sherman (2000); Joseph and Buchenau (2013); and Alexander (2020). The Partido Revolucionario Nacional (PRN, National Revolutionary Party), founded in 1929, was renamed the Partido Revolucionario Mexicano (PRM, Mexican Revolutionary Party) under President Lázaro Cárdenas in 1938 and the PRI under President Miguel Alemán in 1946. It held power continuously until 2000 and then again from 2006 to 2012. Although an overarching history of the party has yet to be written, anthropologists and historians have analyzed its unique combination of authoritarian politics, corporatism, and co-optation of dissent (Claudio Lomnitz 1996, 1999, 2001; Camp 2011; Gillingham and Smith 2014).

4. On the Tlatelolco massacre and its effects, see Poniatowska (1971). For recent histories of the legacies of the student movement and state repression, see Vázquez Mantecón (2006); Gillingham and Smith (2014); and Rodríguez Kuri (2019).

5. Urban historians have discussed the avenue's design as an open-air museum commemorating moments of national significance as an "official" history lesson (Tenorio Trillo 1996a; Agostoni 2003; Martínez Assad 2005; Dixon 2009). On recent controversies regarding statues on the avenue, specifically the relocation and substitution of the Columbus monument, see Tenorio Trillo (2023); Valero Pie and Rabotnikof (2023); and Rozental (2024).

6. I have written elsewhere about the effects of the stone's placement on a busy street corner and restoration work undertaken in 2011 to remove hornet and bird nests and other marks resulting from its urban exposure (Rozental 2021).

7. Coatlinchan is one of 52 *delegaciones* within the Texcoco Municipality, one of 125 municipalities in the Estado de México. The town has the second largest population after the municipal capital Texcoco de la Mora. As its population grows, residents are hoping to become their own municipality.

8. In Spanish, *pueblo* refers both to a town as a physical, political, and administrative unit and to a more abstract entity that roughly translates as "the people." In Coatlinchan, residents use the term to refer to their town as a community of people related to each other as well as to the communal body that takes shape through collectively owned and administered territory and resources. For more on the term and its use in Mexico, see Eiss (2010). On its uses with regard to land tenure, see Kourí (2017).

9. The area has remained mostly barren since Lake Texcoco was gradually desiccated in viceregal times (Musset 1992; Candiani 2014) and finally disappeared in the early twentieth century (Vitz 2018; Soto-Coloballes 2019, Mendoza 2021).

10. Since the 1970s, the region's proximity to Mexico City made it ideal for anthropological explorations of continuity and change affecting communal forms of social organization and land tenure along what anthropologists define as "the folk-urban continuum" (Melville 2011). The Universidad Iberoamericana's field school based in Tepetlaoxtoc developed around the study of this area. For recent work on the area by Ibero anthropologists, see Magazine and Martínez Saldaña (2010) and Magazine (2019). For a more nuanced account of the effects of the region's urbanization and its residents' ambivalence toward this process, see Mendoza Fragoso (2022).

11. All translations of conversations and quotes from Spanish are my own, unless otherwise noted. I tried to remain faithful to the language and structure of people's speech to the best of my abilities.

12. George Kubler describes the church as one of the finest examples of early colonial architecture in the Americas (1962a, 397–98).

13. After having my research project approved during a community assembly in 2007, I lived in Coatlinchan for fourteen months in 2008–9 and have since returned for short and medium stays as well as day visits. During my time there, I lived with several families in different parts of town and of a variety of socioeconomic positions within its population. I also lived with a family that was not native to Coatlinchan and had recently arrived from Tepito. Over the course of my fieldwork, I attended as many town events as possible, participated in meetings and activities organized by the groups interested in local history, and attended community assemblies, events, and festivities. Ejido assemblies were restricted because there were land conflicts at the time and the authorities only allowed active *ejidatarios* to participate. I was able to participate in other communal bodies'

meetings, especially those related to local water use. I also attended masses and religious festivities. While living in Coatlinchan, I was invited into people's homes and work spaces and conducted periodic interviews with key informants whose testimonies and stories inspired this book's organization and arguments.

14. Jesse and I decided to work together on the film in 2009, after I had been living full-time in Coatlinchan for over a year. We proposed the project to community authorities during an assembly as an offshoot of the academic publications that would result from my work. The authorities consulted with several groups formed around a common interest in local history who received the project enthusiastically, agreeing to participate on camera and also as creative collaborators. They hosted the film crew, helped us select subjects and set up locations, organized the logistics of shoots, commented on the narrative structure of the film both during filming and during the editing process, and staged some of their practices and events for the production. Some of these stagings became important moments of ethnographic revelation that would not have been possible had it not been for the groups' collaboration in the film as well as for Jesse's and the camera's presence. I discuss several of these moments in the chapters that follow.

15. In Mexican Spanish, many words derive from Nahuatl. There are no native Nahuatl speakers in Coatlinchan today and have not been for at least two generations. Nevertheless, Nahuatl place-names and terms for many objects and practices, mostly related to agriculture and the preparation of food, continue to be in use.

16. In various parts of the world, stone is the prime material for tombs and funerary structures used to inscribe the world with human presence beyond our lifespans. Christopher Tilley (2004) explores this sense of permanence from a phenomenological perspective in his study of how Neolithic Breton Menhirs inscribe landscapes with the embodied experience and fixed identities of those who inhabited them in the past, while also affecting those who encounter them in the present and future. See also Díaz-Guardamino (2015). Roger Caillois (2014, 117) argues that thinking through and with stones reveals the relationships that intertwine human and nonhuman worlds. He is especially interested in stones and minerals that somehow go beyond their inert inorganic materiality, offering lifelike, almost animate images that do not represent or recall nature but that actually call it into being. For a different take on the ways stones are sites for rethinking the boundaries between life and nonlife, see Povinelli (1995; 2016, especially chapter 2), Reinert (2016); and Yusoff (2013, 2024).

17. Hugh Raffles looks to stone's unconformities as sites where this material's solidity is challenged by discontinuities and fissures that confront our own sense of them as "anchors in a world unmoored" (2020, 5). For Raffles, stones counterintuitively serve as sites that destabilize temporal continuity, as their materiality and the stories attached to them are marked by gaps, absences, recalcitrance, and even refusal. In his words, "the most solid, ancient and elemental materials are as lively, capricious, willful, and indifferent as time itself" (2020, 6).

18. Roger Sansi (2005, 2007) has written about other stones that cannot be severed from the people, saints, and shrines that consecrated them as part of Candomblé rituals, even if they are taken to museums.

19. Aveleyra, mostly known for his paleontological work and studies of prehistoric humans, also excavated and published on pre-Hispanic sites.

20. Andrea Ballestero explores the vibrant relations binding the elements of water and earth in underground aquifers as "elemental choreographies" (2019).

21. On the altepetl in Mesoamerican societies, see Lockhart (1992); Carrasco (1996); Fernández Christlieb and García Zambrano (2006); Navarrete Linares (2011, n.d.); Dehouve (2016); and Carballo and Robb (2017).

22. Recent work by feminist scholars of Latin America, notably geographers, has centered on the concept of "cuerpo-territorio" to emphasize the ontological, organic, intertwined, and mutually constitutive relations between bodies and territories as a response to colonial and patriarchal forms of violence and extractivism. See, for example, Gómez-Barris (2017); Marchese (2019); and Zaragocin and Caretta (2021). For a study of contemporary Indigenous claims to territory in Mexico from the perspective of legal anthropology, see Sierra Camacho, Hernández, and Sieder (2013); Mora (2017); and Adonon (2022).

23. Anthropologists have used other terms like *reverberations* (Navaro-Yashin et al. 2021) and *aftermaths* (McAllister and Nelson 2013; Kernaghan 2022a) to discuss the lasting effects of violence in different national contexts. Whereas *reverberations* recalls the movement of sound waves across time and space, Carlota McAllister and Diane Nelson point to the generativity of *aftermaths*, underscoring the term's origins as an agricultural concept linked to harvest (2013, 9–10).

24. *Montero* is used in Coatlinchan to describe people who make a living from the monte or hillside, mostly gathering wood for beams and coal and other forest resources for sale in local markets.

25. Ramírez Vázquez was known as "the architect politician" because of his administrative skills and his work heading several government agencies. For more on the architect's political career, especially his participation coordinating the 1968 Mexico City Olympics, see Rodríguez Kuri (2003, 2019) and L. Castañeda (2013b, 2014).

26. For the politics of nation making through archaeological practice and exhibition in Greece, see Hamilakis (2007) and Solomon (2021); in Israel, see Abu El-Haj (2001); and in Egypt, see Meskell (2000) and Reid (2002).

27. The concept of mestizaje was another fundamental tenet of this process; see Dawson (2004) and Tenorio Trillo (2009). For critical approaches to mestizaje as a racial politics, see Wade (2003); Moreno Figueroa (2010, 2022); and López Beltrán, García Deister, and Rios Sandoval (2014). For how the state produced the category of Indigenous people within this project, see Castillo Cocom (2004); Giraudo (2008); López Hernández (2013, 2024); Aguilar Gil (2018, 2023); and López Caballero (2021).

28. For a history of the national museum and its collections' origins in the early nineteenth century, see Morales Moreno (1994); Gorbach (2008); and Achim (2017).

29. Article 27 and its transformation of subsoil resources into national patrimonio was pictorially rendered in a mural by José Clemente Orozco; see Rodríguez Mortellaro (2015). The first laws claiming ancient artifacts as national property were drafted in 1827, soon after independence, to stop their international export as well as that of the most lucrative bases of colonial extraction: cochineal dye and silver ores (Lombardo de Ruiz and Solís Vicarte 1988). For a history of how the Mexican state came to regulate and claim what lies under the earth's surface as national property as a form of territorial sovereignty, see Bustamante (2024).

30. *Patrimony*—*patrimonio*'s closest English equivalent, which refers to inheritance passed down through the paternal line—is rarely used in Anglophone countries' and international legislation that refers to "heritage" or "cultural property." For a discussion of the contemporary uses of *heritage*, see Gnecco (2015). For a more in-depth discussion of this term's use in Mexico, see Rozental (2017b).

31. Renato González Mello (2017) analyzes how the concept and legal registers of patrimonio intersect with authorship and copyright law in cases related to artworks by certain Mexican artists.

32. As historians have noted, the appropriation of pre-Hispanic objects by the Mexican state and their removal from local contexts in ritual performances of nation making preceded the twentieth-century postrevolutionary state; see Tenorio Trillo (1996b); Bueno (2016); and Achim (2017).

33. Using Annette Weiner's (1992) work on "the paradox of keeping while giving" to describe inalienable possessions in Melanesia, Elizabeth Ferry (2005) explores how the concept of patrimonio was used by the members of Guanajuato's Santa Fe silver mining cooperative because of both patrimonio's inalienable status and the ways in which it circulated, consolidating kinship bonds and relations within the collective. For cases where pre-Hispanic artifacts and sites figure in local forms of sovereignty in the Yucatan, in Wixarika territories, and in the Central Valleys, see Breglia (2006) and Q. Castañeda (2009); Liffman (2011); and Morehart (2012), respectively.

34. These forms of distributed sovereignty were inherited from sixteenth-century Spanish traditions and laws as well as Catholic guilds and *cofradías*; see Christian (1981). For more on campesinos, pueblos, and corporate forms of property and personhood in Mexican history, see Chevalier (1970); Guerra (1985); and Owensby (2008). For a comprehensive study of the ejido as a legal, political, and moral category in Mexican history, see Torres-Mazuera (2016) and Kourí (2017, 2020).

35. Sahlins (2011) famously defined kinship as "the mutuality of being" between subjects who are intrinsic to one another's existence. Through kinship bonds, subjects participate in and coproduce each other's lives and are therefore indissociable from one another. I argue that the stone participates in such a "mutuality of being" by being related to and making territory in Coatlinchan.

36. Interview filmed for *The Absent Stone* in 2010 (Rozental and Lerner 2013).

37. See Martin (1989, 1991) on "sleeping metaphors."

38. Walter Benjamin's (2002) and Susan Buck-Morss's (1991, 2000) engagement with his writing opened a renewed interest in ruins and processes of ruination in anthropology, specifically as loci where colonial forms of power and violence persist into the present (Masco 2008; Stoler 2008, 2013; Navaro-Yashin 2009, 2012; Dawdy 2010; Schwenkel 2013; Yarrow 2017). See also Cristóbal Gnecco and Mario Rufer's (2023) edited volume on ruins as indices of violence in Latin America and beyond.

39. Crespo and Tozzini (2014) and Crespo (2022) describe similar cases in Argentina.

40. Residents of the neighboring towns of San Bernardino are known as "Ranas" or frogs; those from Chimalhuacan as "Pescaderos" or fish people, and those from Chicoloapan as "Chincolos" after a local bird. Others are known for their trades: those from Montecillo are "Tequesquiteros" after the sediments they collected from the former lakebed used to make nixtamal; those from Huexotla are "Tlacoyeros" after the traditional

food; and those from Cuautlalpan are "Comaleros" after the production of the earthenware used to make tortillas.

41. See, for example, the website koatlinchan.com's entry on the tlacuache and its relevance for the town, accessed August 2024, https://koatlinchan.jimdofree.com/el-tlakuache/.

42. Over the past decades, archaeologists have used ethnography to reflexively and critically explore "looting" or "huaquería" in Latin American contexts (K. Smith 2005, 2016; Antoniadou 2009; Field, Gnecco, and Watkins 2016; Londoño 2016; Barker 2018; Cevallos and Bedolla 2019; Cevallos 2023).

43. For examples of earlier histories of replicas, fakes, and forgeries of pre-Hispanic objects, see Sellen (2002) and Jennings and Sellen (2018).

44. For the first film festival held in Zapatista territories in 2018, *The Absent Stone* and Alonso Ruizpalacios's *Museo*, which fictionalized the museum's 1985 theft, were programmed back to back under the title "Ladrón que roba a ladrón" (a thief who robs a thief), riffing on the popular proverb that ends with "tiene cien años de perdón" (deserves a hundred years of pardon), implying that it is not a crime to rob a thief.

45. See Boone (1993). Following the acquisition of the Earl Stendahl papers, the Getty Research Institute, under the leadership of art historian Mary Miller, has carried out a Pre-Hispanic Art Provenance Initiative, hosting a series of conferences and editing several publications on the complicated histories and relations inscribed in collecting Mesoamerican art before and after the 1940s. See Turner and O'Neil (2024, forthcoming). See also Pre-Hispanic Art Provenance Initiative, Getty, accessed July 2024, https://www.getty.edu/projects/pre-hispanic-art-provenance-initiative/.

46. Recent decades have produced expanding scholarship on repatriation and restitution of museum collections and their effects in various disciplines. See, for example, Yalouri (2001); Barkan and Bush (2002); Fforde, Hubert, and Turnbull (2002); Peers and Brown (2003); Henare (2005); Clifford (2013); Anderson and Geismar (2017); Peers, Gustafsson Reinius, and Shannon (2017); Hicks (2020); and Turnbull and Pickering (2022).

47. On replication and itinerancy of patrimonial things in Latin American contexts, see also Rozental, Collins, and Ramsey (2016).

CHAPTER 1. A CURIOUS THING

1. Butler worked in Mexico for forty-four years and was the son of William Butler and Clementina Rowe, founders of the American Methodist Missions in India and Mexico (G. Anderson 1999).

2. Quoted in Sánchez (1886, 27). *Indian* is the term used during the viceregal period as well as during the nineteenth and early twentieth centuries to refer to people of Indigenous ancestry in Mexico. The term isn't capitalized in the original Spanish.

3. For more on Velasco's work and legacy, see Piolle Altamirano (2006); Ramírez Rojas (2017); and Olivares Sandoval (2020, 2021).

4. This was common practice associated with antiquarianism whereby albums with drawings and then photographs were used to compare objects and monuments that could not be transported, allowing them to circulate and become commensurable with each other across global networks (Podgorny 2008; Gänger 2014; Moser 2014). These

albums, like other scientific visual practices, worked to domesticate unwieldy things and facilitate their manipulation (Callon 1986; Latour 1987; Law 1987; Lynch and Woolgar 1990). Susan Stewart (1993) has similarly argued that reducing scale makes things otherwise unknown, unmanageable—and perhaps even out of control—visible and contained.

5. See Deborah Poole's (1997, 1998, 2005) insights into the politics of visuality and how photographs and what they showed about Indigenous people beyond the frame produced them as subjects within visual regimes and economies in the Americas. Feminist and STS scholars have also looked at how images separate subjects and objects, humans and nonhumans (Burri and Dumit 2008). Anthropologists have analyzed how ultrasounds produce the fetus as separate from the mother's body to justify anti-abortion politics; see L. Mitchell and Georges (1997, 2001) and J. Taylor (2008); and on these images' affect, see J. Grant (2017).

6. Antonio Peñafiel's book on ancient Mexican monuments includes Velasco's image with the caption "Xocaca." He states that the term was reported to him as the stone's local name but doesn't offer a translation (1890, vol. 1, plate 137). Neither "Xocaca" nor "Xicaca" appear in Nahuatl dictionaries. Nahuatl speakers I consulted speculate it might derive from "xico" and "ca" translated as "the place of the navel." People in Coatlinchan today do not use this name, nor do they recognize it as having been associated with the stone.

7. For more on Batres and the Díaz regime's interest in ancient vestiges and archaeology as a scientific discipline and nation-making practice, see Bueno (2016) and Valiant (2017).

8. In 1889, Batres had successfully relocated the monument known as the Diosa del Agua (Water Goddess) from Teotihuacan to Mexico City's Museo Nacional. The sixteen-ton stone was transported using a specially designed cart built by engineers and the railroad (Bueno 2010, 2016). Batres's venture into Coatlinchan and interest in the stone carving found there was likely inspired by this experience. Some scholarship on the Teotihuacan monument questions its identity as the Water Goddess; see Paulinyi (2006).

9. Jesús Sánchez (1886, 28–30) reported that the monument was 7 meters long, 3.80 meters high, and 1.50 meters thick, with a reservoir 50 centimeters deep inside its headdress. Batres (1903, 6) argued that these measurements were inaccurate: it was 7 meters long, 4.41 meters high, and 3.92 thick, and the basin was not 50 centimeters deep but 54. With this new data, Batres calculated the stone's weight at 150 tons.

10. See Batres (1904b) on Huexotla.

11. AGN, IPBA, caja 167, exp. 70, fol. 4.

12. AGN, IPBA, caja 167, exp. 70; BNAH, AHI, MNA Dirección, caja 7, exp. 670; BNAH, AHI, MNA Dirección, caja 1, exp. 41.

13. See Chavero (1904, 3). See also Rozental (2014a).

14. On the aesthetics of archaeology and the production of ancient sites and ruins, see Salas Landa (2018, 2024a).

15. This was the first written account that narratively connected the pre-Hispanic past and Mexico's nineteenth-century modernity. For more on its status in Mexican historiography, see Tenorio Trillo (1996b, 66–74).

16. Chavero explained: "It bears a headdress that is customarily placed on the goddess and that Mr. Butler compared to the calantica of certain Egyptian statues, but whose origin among us must be understood as coming from the two monoliths that sustained the platform at the Temple of the Cross, confirming its meaning as a deity of rains. The

top part of the headdress presents an excavation in the shape of a tub some 50 centimeters deep, used to deposit rain waters, just as the top vessel of the Tajín from Papantla. The immense monolith also has an instrument in its hands that looks like it made a sound when it was blown into, similar to the statue of Palemke. It is wearing a simple maxtli, while the one from Palemke bears an instrument that looks like it was used to measure water levels, a kind of nilometer" (1887, 663).

17. The terms *Aztec* and *Mexica* are often used interchangeably even though the former technically refers to the people coming from Aztlan that settled in the Valley of Mexico and formed the Aztec Empire and the latter refers to the population of the central valleys of Mexico that included other ethnic groups at the time of conquest.

18. Eduard Seler (1849–1922), a scholar of ancient Mexico working for the Königliches Museum für Völkerkunde, argued that Chalchiuhtlicue was the deity who wore a skirt of turquoise, symbolizing running waters, and this would explain the stone's location in the ravine; see Seler (1991, 87, 233–34, 248–49). Seler collected pottery sherds and figurines from Texcoco, Huexotla, and Coatlinchan in his earliest trip to Mexico, but he did not record the existence of the stone in the nearby ravine. He did, however, identify another object from Coatlinchan that he located in the Texcoco *jefatura*. His collections are now in the Berlin Ethnographic Museum (Seler 1991, 61–62, 155–57, 170); see also Rozental (2014a).

19. Zelia Nuttall (1857–1933) was an archaeologist and anthropologist who worked on Mexican antiquity and specialized in Mesoamerican ancient manuscripts; see Chiñas (1988); Grindle (2023); Ruiz Martínez (2016); and Rodriguez (2022). The other two scholars mentioned are Charles P. Bowditch (1842–1921) of Harvard University and the Peabody Museum, and Nicolás León (1859–1929), an established naturalist at the Museo Nacional.

20. BNAH, AHI, MNA Dirección, caja 7, exp. 428.

21. In a letter from October 1964, Heizer wrote the then director of the Museo Nacional de Antropología Ignacio Bernal, asking about the calculations of the monolith's weight because they were much lower than his and Williams's estimates (AHMNA, vol. 460-18576).

CHAPTER 2. ENGINEERING TRANSFER

1. Timothy Mitchell (2002, 43) defines such infrastructure projects as assemblages of humans and nonhumans constantly in transformation, a kind of "techno-politics," that is "both intentional and not, and in which the intentional or the human is always somehow overrun by the unintended."

2. For a parallel account of the ways aesthetics and hydroelectric infrastructures worked to shape human–nonhuman relations and produce state power in Venezuela, see Blackmore (2018).

3. For critical archaeologists, excavations and the extraction of ancient structures and objects as part of their practice are inevitably acts of disruption and destruction, regardless of whether the intention is in fact conservation. See Meskell (2002); Dawdy (2010); Harrison (2011); González-Ruibal (2013, 2018); Olivier (2013, 2019); Weismantel and Meskell (2014); DeSilvey (2017); Haber (2017); Gnecco (2019, 2021); and Jofré (2022).

4. For more on this archaeological find and the ensuing debates and controversies, see Gillingham (2011). Mariana Botey (2014) has also written about the political implications of Cuauhtémoc's bones, for the state and for Indigenous sovereignty. For a take on how gender politics played into how Guzmán's career and work on the project unfolded, see Ruíz Martínez (2008) and Rosemblatt (2024).

5. The café prides itself in having been where Fidel Castro and Che Guevara met to plan the Cuban Revolution.

6. For more on Tlatelolco and its avant-garde architecture in the context of 1950s–1960s Mexico, see Noelle (2008); Castañeda (2014); Flaherty (2016); and Josten (2018).

7. I found references to this engineer alternatively as Asunción Escobar or Escalante. He was allegedly from Chimalhuacan, a town near Coatlinchan, but did not maintain ties with people in Coatlinchan, nor with the engineers and architects I was able to locate.

8. There is more and more scholarship showing the importance of local labor in shaping archaeological explorations and reconstruction in Mexico and beyond. See Salas Landa (2024b); Holley-Kline and Mikel (2024); and Holley-Kline (2025).

9. I thank Luis Castañeda for pointing me to this reference.

10. Ramírez Vázquez later built the new Basilica de Guadalupe, Mexico's most important Catholic shrine.

11. Gonzalo Garita, interview with the author, 2009.

12. "Tlaloc en Wall Street," *Pentágono*, April 1964.

13. *Conti-News: Revista de Llantas Continental*, 2004, 16.

14. Jesse Lerner and I copied the type design for the end credits of our film.

15. Nemesio Becerril Rivas, interview with the author, 2013.

16. In the short story "Tlaloc," Paco Ignacio Taibo II (2006) ingeniously threads the actual events of the carving's trajectory from Coatlinchan to Mexico City with a fictionalized narrative foregrounding Mexican migration to the United States. The story takes place in the 1980s and features a science fiction writer who befriends a union of doormen and janitors in Manhattan, whose members are overwhelmingly from Coatlinchan but migrated to New York in search of better livelihoods following the stone's relocation. Together, they decide to hire the world-famous magician David Copperfield to help return the stone to Coatlinchan using the rusting low-bed trailer that they find abandoned in a warehouse on the outskirts of Mexico City.

17. For a detailed account of the Mexica efforts to control and reroute water, see Mundy (2015), especially chapter 1. See also Palerm (1973) and Rojas Rabiela, Martínez-Ruiz, and Murillo Licea (2009).

18. On Rivera and the Cárcamo, see Noelle (2001) and Rivera, Adriá, and Aguirre (2012). For more on the Cárcamo murals and the Mexican welfare state, see De Coss Corzo (2019).

19. On hydraulic engineering and the Mexican Revolution, see Wolfe (2017).

20. I am thankful to Emily Carrion and Luis Gantus for helping me locate the issue before it was available online. It can now be accessed at http://revisteriaponchito.com/aventurasvidareal/106/.

21. I have elsewhere written on the comic book and its use of images to justify the state's use of force (Rozental 2022a).

22. On the Coahuila dam and the Tlaloc monument, see Maldonado Ortíz (1993).

23. *Crónicas del Zuaque*, no. 215 (August 2009): 9–10.

24. See the full episode here: "Cantinflas y sus amigos, | Capítulo 1 | Yellowstone Park | Thomas Edison | Museo Antropológico," Toons Time, uploaded September 10, 2023, https://www.youtube.com/watch?v=_7W_PxoKZuo.

25. Under the heading "Reseña histórica del saqueo," this account was published in a booklet distributed during community events by town representatives and local groups interested in community history and traditions (Ortíz Sánchez and Calpulli Makoyolotzin 2006).

CHAPTER 3. THEFT

1. "Hay mar de fondo en el caso Tláloc," *Novedades*, February 23, 1964.

2. Torres Bodet's speech was transcribed in a volume on the López Mateos presidency's public works for education. In his words, the museum allowed Mexico "to evoke its past, measure the size of its present and—in both thoughts and deeds—project itself onto the future" (Secretaría de Educación Pública 1964, 380).

3. The film was included in a DVD in the book published by the museum on its construction (Ramírez Vázquez 2008) and was then made available online. See "Documental: Monumento de Monumentos," Museo Nacional de Antropología, uploaded March 3, 2015, https://www.youtube.com/watch?v=xtOQ_oufbWM.

4. I have written elsewhere about the museum's collecting process. Some of its new collections, like the Coatlinchan stone, were taken from local communities and sites using patrimonio laws to justify their forced extraction; many were collected ex profeso by anthropologists and archaeologists conducting fieldwork all over Mexico; and many were also purchased from private collectors (Rozental, forthcoming).

5. Art historian Mary Coffey (2012) offers a powerful analysis of how the museum incorporated works made by artists associated with various artistic schools and factions that emerged in the wake of postrevolutionary muralism. These works show the institution's political work much beyond the building's architecture and its collections.

6. Ramírez Vázquez was keen on researchers studying and writing about his work and legacy. He set up a private archive where he stored documentation and photographs of his projects as well as models and memorabilia, mostly from the 1968 Mexico City Olympic Games. During my time working in this archive in the summer of 2005, and for several months in 2009 and 2010, I sat in during many of his sessions with his ghostwriter and had several one-on-one interviews with him as well as conversations with him and his son Javier (who now runs his firm and archive) and other staff members. I am especially thankful to Javier for his generosity and to Karina Garcia, who helped me navigate the archive.

7. In a letter to the director of the INAH, Eusebio Dávalos Hurtado, Ramírez Vázquez attached an interview conducted by a reporter on the progress of the museum where this is mentioned (AAPRV, MNA Papers, August 11, 1962).

8. AAPRV, MNA Papers, Meeting Minutes, n.d.

9. For more on the transfer and display of Olmec heads, see Castañeda (2013a).

10. De Robina tells this story in an interview; see *El buen restaurador ama lo antiguo* (Aguayo et al. 1997).

11. Interview quoted in Ponce (1985, 48).

12. The architect's Facebook page, administered by his firm, published a post on March 5, 2024, with sketches of the Maya monument standing in front of the museum's facade and a photograph in situ in the Nocuchich archaeological site in Campeche.

13. Ramírez Vázquez, interview with author, 2005.

14. This version is quoted in *Proceso* (Ponce 1985). Ramírez Vázquez (2008) offered a similar version in his memoir.

15. Ramírez Vázquez, interview by the author, 2009.

16. Years after the stone's relocation, Alberto Beltrán (1969), one of the artist members of the Taller de Gráfica Popular, drew a parody in the magazine *Crucero*, speculating on the Aztecs' efforts to move the stone in ancient times whereby eagle warriors were deployed to Coatlinchan because its "primitive and progress adverse" residents opposed its removal.

17. The earliest documentation of these etchings are photographs taken by Martin Horst in the 1930s showing German tourists sitting on the stone with markings "IA" on an arm, "MR" on another, "LIZE" on its side. and "AG" on its headdress. Several have mostly faded and are no longer visible on the stone's surface. See "22 Ergebnisse für 'Lateinamerika-Aufenthalte 1934/1942 Mexiko tlaloc,'" Deutsche Digitale Bibliothek, accessed September 2024, https://www.deutsche-digitale-bibliothek.de/searchresults ?isThumbnailFiltered=false&query=Lateinamerika-Aufenthalte%2B1934%2F1942%2BM exiko%2Btlaloc&viewType=list&rows=40&offset=0. I am thankful to Bernd Hausberger for alerting me of these photographs' existence.

18. Town residents are not the only ones who claim these markings. On January 3, 2011, the Mexican newspaper *Reforma* ran a story on the stone's restoration underway at the museum. In the comments section of the paper's online portal, Bernardo Servin Massieu wrote: "The letters MA are chiseled on the top part of the monolith because of Dr. Russel Marker who was the pioneer of steroid hormones in Mexico that started with the transformation of diosgenin to progesterone using wild yams collected in the Metlac ravine near the town of Orizaba, Veracruz. When Marker left Syntex, he built a small factory near Texcoco, in the Estado de México, and his workers wanted to chisel the word Marker on the monolith in thanks for having bought them bicycles. They were only able to chisel the letters M and A because town residents realized what they were doing and made them flee fast and furiously." I later found out, thanks to historian of science Lajos Kovács, who has written about Marker, that he greatly rejoiced in telling this story (personal communication); see also Lehmann (1992) and Kovács (2024). In 2022, during a screening of *The Absent Stone* in Coatlinchan, a man from Coatepec who was in attendance volunteered that his father, Ezequiel Mecalco, had etched his initials EM on the stone's "nose" during a school excursion.

19. This reenactment was done for the film *The Absent Stone* (2013). Townspeople followed the band, joyfully singing along and throwing confetti and flowers.

20. "Traerán el monolito de Tlaloc al museo," *El Universal*, May 10, 1963.

21. Matthew Hull (2012) has argued that the ways documents are enacted as graphic and material artifacts through practices of inscription like signatures, stamps, and marginalia is as important as the information they communicate.

22. Many towns in Mexico have official cronistas named by local authorities or sanctioned by regional and state Consejos de la Crónica. In the past, few had academic

training, although more and more are studying history at the undergraduate and graduate level. They have been a key resource for historians and anthropologists, although they are rarely recognized as peers by the academy. Don Chava has published several of his crónicas; see, for example, Suárez Hernández (2008). He also gives presentations and talks for the Texcoco Consejo de la Crónica. See, for example, "Don Salvador Suárez Hernández, cronista de Coatlinchán, nos habla del monasterio de su comunidad," Facebook, June 10, 2020, https://www.facebook.com/CasaDelConstituyente/videos/don-salvador-su%C3%A1rez-hern%C3%A1ndez-cronista-de-coatlinch%C3%A1n-nos-habla-del-ex-monasteri/2668915566729998/.

23. Martin Horst traveled to various parts of Mexico in the 1930s and 1940s. His photographs from his visit to Coatlinchan in 1937 are in the Museum für Völkerkunde Dresden archives. See also note 17.

24. "Coatlinchan decidido a conservar su Tlaloc," *La Prensa*, February 24, 1964.

25. Nemesio Becerril Rivas was not driving the truck that day. The team of drivers who drove the low-bed in February allegedly refused to go again in April, so a new team was hired.

26. Formerly classified documents from the Dirección Federal de Seguridad have recently been made available as part of an effort to reckon with Mexico's Dirty War, among these, the files pertaining to town residents arrested and questioned in February 1964. In these files, several town residents are named and described as "extremely given to intoxicating drinks" (AGN, DFS, fichero 12, cajon 2, ficha F12-C2-906 and cajon 4, ficha F12-C4-3407).

27. "Coatlinchan despide al ídolo: Una escuela para un pueblo que agradece a las autoridades en un acto oficial," *La Prensa*, April 18, 1964.

28. "La Tournée de un Dios," *El Universal Gráfico*, April 17, 1964.

CHAPTER 4. SCARS

1. Anthropologists have long been interested in bodily inscriptions such as scars, tattoos, and piercings as interfaces that are both boundary making and enforcing. For an overview of this work, see Schildkrout (2004). For a broad range of examples, see Gennep (1909); Lévi-Strauss (1963); T. Turner (1980); and Gell (1993).

2. The value and symbolism of scars are at the heart of Janice Boddy's (1982) arguments for understanding female genital circumcision within the cultural context of the people, especially women, who practice it. On medical anthropologists' interest in scars following surgeries, see Cohen (1999); N. Scheper-Hughes (2007, 2019); and Yates-Doerr (2022). Elizabeth F. S. Roberts (2012) shows how C-section scars are valued because of how they mark people within complicated histories of race, class, and citizenship in contemporary Ecuador.

3. A bridge nearby bears the date 1914, when the hacienda was still active, a few years before its lands were expropriated following the Mexican Revolution.

4. Batres recorded that the stream that once flowed through this ravine was also known as Santa Clara (see figure 1.5).

5. For examples of projects using digital repatriation and the debates surrounding this as a form of return, see Hennessy (2010); Geismar (2012); Bell, Christen, and Turin

(2013); Hennessy et al. (2013); Geismar and Müller (2022); and J. Anderson and Atalay (2023). For creative alternatives through artistic practices, see Thorner (2019).

6. For an ethnography of a similar communal water system in the nearby town of La Purificación Tepetitla, see Ennis-McMillan (2001).

7. In 1930, after a 1921 petition in which 293 heads of household requested a land grant from the Banco Hipotecario de Crédito Territorial Mexicano, Coatlinchan was granted its ejido. The haciendas of Tepetitlan and Chapingo, two of the largest agricultural enterprises thriving in the Valley of Mexico at the time, were seized in 1917. Some of their lands were sold to individuals and became the privately run agricultural ranches Nextlalpan, Tecuac, Tlalmimilolpan, el Nopal, Junipero, and Tejocote. The rest were given to villages as communal property. Coatlinchan's land grant comprised 1,364 hectares. The village then negotiated an expansion in 1939, increasing its territory by 1,113.24 hectares taken from the Tecuac, Tlalmimilolpan, and Tepetitlan ranches. A second expansion was granted in 1952 with an extra 237.20 hectares taken from Tecuac (consulted in the Carpeta Básica, Ejido San Miguel Coatlinchan).

8. Whereas before, town residents were mostly landless and provided labor for the agricultural haciendas, the study recorded an overall sense, especially among elders, that Coatlinchan had become less cohesive after it was given the land grant. Certainly, there had been inequality based on whether one was a mere worker or was part of the higher echelons of hacienda life (as a male caretaker or female domestic worker or nanny), but most of the people interviewed said that, in the past, they all struggled more or less equally to make ends meet. They explained that once the ejido was set up, inequality and a class system premised on who had access to a *parcela* and who did not emerged (Martínez de Verburg and Verburg Moore 1964). The use rights of parcelas (generally measuring 1.5 hectares) were given to individuals, but the land continued to be collectively owned by the communal body of ejidatarios. For more on the allocation of individual titles within the ejido system, see Torres-Mazuera (2012a, 2012b, 2016).

9. Gabriela Martínez de Verburg and John Verburg Moore (1964, 41) mention that the ejido had grown marginally in terms of ejidatario families, from 293 in the original grant in 1930, to 302 in 1943 and 327 in 1958, and had physically fragmented the town's territory since the land grant did not comprise lands located in the same place but rather in four different sites. Some ejidatarios owned lands in two or more different areas of the ejido, some even 5 or 7 kilometers away from the town center. The first land grant was made up of plots of 1.5 hectares, but the second reduced them to a third of that, creating rivalries among ejidatarios. Almost half of the ejidatarios exploited their land in *mediera*, renting it to third parties and splitting the profits. A small group also owned private plots of up to 25 and 30 hectares, known as ranchos (1964, 42, 44). The ejido authorities were not interested in regulating the unequal distribution of land within the ejido since most ejidatarios profited not from tilling the soil but from other activities like the credits given by the ejidatario bank.

10. These practices were technically forbidden by laws regulating the ejido but existed de facto. In other cases, the owner sold land rights and the ejido authorities cast a blind eye, and in several cases the medieros continued working the land and refused to return it to its rightful owner. A single comisariado ejidal had 24 hectares of ejido lands to his name (Martínez de Verburg and Verburg Moore 1964, 50).

11. Between 1943 and 1963, 74 ejidatarios (24.5%) had less than half a hectare of land, 57 (18.87%) had between a half and 1 hectare, 118 (39.07%) had between 1 and 1.50 hectares, 38 (12.59%) had between 1.50 and 2 hectares, and 15 (4.97%) had more than 2 hectares of land (Martínez de Verburg and Verburg Moore 1964, 49).

12. The study was published at a time when the model developed by Eric Wolf in the 1950s to describe Latin American peasant communities, specifically using Mexican and Latin American examples, as "closed corporate communities" was also being challenged. Wolf (1957) had attempted to historicize what seemed like timeless forms of community organization showing their foundations in pre-Hispanic societies, as well as Spanish colonial models such as guilds, Repúblicas de Indios, and Cofradías. Yet Wolf's model's assumed communal forms of organization were rooted in both Indigenous and colonial systems of governance that were being more and more questioned. Marvin Harris's 1964 study of the cargo system and race in the Americas was perhaps the most emphatic critique, exposing the modes of production and exploitation of labor inherent to the closed-corporate community model, what Wolf would later admit was "a kind of pump siphoning off surpluses into the hands of moneylenders and external merchants" (1986, 327). Yet even in these critiques, inequality and exploitation were imagined as originating outside the community and having to do with landed property. The OAS study placed the source of inequality in internal rivalries and community members' own conflicting claims and corruption but still focused on land and resources as properties that could be owned, exchanged, and exploited, even if unequally above the ground.

13. One of these constructions, across the street from the town cemetery, even houses two of the saint images—San Miguel and San José—that used to be worshiped in the Tepetitlan hacienda chapel before it was dismantled and its lands expropriated for the ejido.

14. For more on the 1992 reforms and their effects on Mexican rural communities, see Nuijten (1998, 2003) and Torres-Mazuera (2012a, 2012b, 2016).

15. For an analysis of the conflicts over land in San Salvador Atenco, see Kuri Pineda (2010); Moreno Sánchez (2010, 2014); and Ramonetti Liceaga (2016).

16. I found many documents (tribute rolls and censuses) pertaining to the history of eighteenth- and nineteenth-century Coatlinchan in the national archives. In a 1777 census, 1,422 persons were living in the locality, including the hacienda. There were 389 families classified in casta and racial categories: 290 Indians; 44 Spaniards; 23 castizos; 6 mestizos; 12 mestindios; and 14 mulatos, lobos, and others (AGN, BN, vol. 152, exp. 9; AGN, P, 1776, vol. 1206, exp. 12; 1777, vol. 403, exp. 26).

17. Martha Maass Escandón inherited Tecuac from her father, the general. In a phone interview in 2013, she told me she wanted to restore the hull but didn't have the resources to do so. She nevertheless paid for a guard and the grounds' basic upkeep.

18. Jeffrey R. Parsons, the archaeologist who surveyed ancient settlement patterns in the central valleys, documented some of these tlateles in his early fieldwork. He never published the photographs he took of them in the 1970s and 1980s, but shortly before his death in 2022, he told me he was interested in going back to Coatlinchan to photograph them and evaluate their state of conservation (personal communication, 2020).

19. Allison Caine (2022) has written about similar enterprises in the Andes, focusing on the relationships between climate change and other environmental disruptions and herding practices.

20. For anthropological studies of the emergence of the Mexicanidad movement and its spread in and beyond Mexico, see Peña Martínez (2002, 2012); González Torres (2005); Torre (2007, 2008); Peña Martínez and Torre (2012); and Torre and Gutiérrez Zúñiga (2017).

21. Tlakuanikoatl Ocelotl Xicome writes about the map and its relevance for the community in the website he designed about Coatlinchan's history and regional importance: https://koatlinchan.jimdofree.com/historia-del-lugar/ (accessed January 2025).

22. Historians speculate that the map, painted on a 42 × 46 cm sheet of amate paper, was made in the early colonial period. The first written record of its existence dates from 1880, when it was cataloged as part of the private holdings of Alfredo Chavero, the prominent scholar of pre-Hispanic Mexico who was also one of the first to identify the Coatlinchan stone as the female water deity, Chalchiuhtlicue (chapter 1). The map is currently part of the Museo Nacional de Antropología's manuscript collections. Little is known about the map's history or how and when it left Coatlinchan. Like many of its kind, it was thought to have been made as part of a land dispute, but other documents supporting the case have not yet been found. Recent scholarship points to its representation of internal boundaries and to the positions of the various towns and sites as evidence that it was likely made for internal altepetl use (Pulido Rull 2020). These studies concur, however, that the document was probably removed from Coatlinchan sometime during the viceregal period and was privately owned until it was purchased by the museum in the late nineteenth century.

23. The Calpulli's approach resonates with anthropological and art historical studies that have investigated the relationship between ancient maps and contemporary landscapes and even more so with scholarship concerned with the pragmatic uses of such documents on the part of the Indigenous communities throughout and beyond the viceregal period, as evidence for court cases to ensure property over land and natural resources (Lockhart 1992; López Caballero 2003; Hamann 2011; Mcdonough 2017; Pulido Rull 2020). These uses have endured well into the present as many communities in contemporary Mexico refer to ancient maps to sustain more recent territorial disputes (Ruiz Medrano and Davidson 2011; Hermann Lejarazu 2019). Such uses point to a vernacular understanding of continuity between historical territories and communities represented and their present-day iterations as well as to such a continuity's recognition and legibility in both viceregal Spanish and modern Mexican law.

24. Ayoyotes are also known as *huesos de fraile* and are a percussion instrument used in pre-Hispanic dance and made up of the shells from the ayoyote or chachayote (*chachayotl*) tree, tied to dancers' ankles and wrists.

CHAPTER 5. TREASURE

Some of the materials and arguments of chapter 5 appeared in the author's earlier publications: in an edited volume on heritage in Latin America (Rozental 2017c) and in a dossier on the legacies of Kubler's understanding of continuity and change pertaining to ancient Mesoamerican conceptions of territory (Rozental 2020).

1. Treasure tales are also common in other parts of the world with long histories of conquest and dispossession. For an account of treasure tales as residues or "secretions"

of such histories in Greece, see C. Stewart (2003, 2012). Anya Bernstein (2011) has also written about the emergence of treasure in Buddhist communities in southern Siberia as the result of the violence and ruptures that followed the Russian Revolution and subsequent Soviet secularization campaigns. For another example of treasure stories and their contemporary valence in Mexico, see Cruz Martínez, Viañez Reyes, and Pedrosa (2021).

2. See also Schryer and Foster (1976).

3. Centenarios became an instrument for financial speculation given that their value is not the fifty pesos symbolically printed on the coin, nor a value pegged to Mexican currency, but determined by the price of gold as it fluctuates on global financial markets. Ferry (2020) has written about gold as a "speculative substance" that is also an ambiguous moral and political actor in both world and national financial markets.

4. For dreams as sources for history, see Koselleck (2004). In anthropology, Charles Stewart (2003, 2012) has written extensively on dreams as forms of historicity in Greece. Richard Kernaghan (2022a, 2022b) uses dreams and their tellings to explore the aftermaths of war in Peru as well as their potential for ethnographic writing.

5. For an account of how pre-Hispanic ruins haunt and possess people in contemporary Oaxaca, see Leathem (2019).

6. Given the prominence of this figure in twentieth-century Mexican folklore, it is surprising that there isn't much written about him in Mexican and Mexicanist anthropology, probably because he is a figure that is most prominent in mestizo communities and even in urban peripheries rather than Indigenous contexts. María Ana Portal and Vania Salles's (1998) study of Charro Negro stories in Xochimilco and Tlalpan as well as Johannes Neurath's (2005) interest in the figure as a mestizo trickster in Wixarika cosmologies and ritual are important exceptions.

7. In his rich ethnography of the hauntings caused by the Maoist regime's violent destruction of prior local collective forms of sovereignty and collectivity in China, Erik Mueggler (2001, 3) similarly argues that "wild ghosts" resulting from "unreconciled fragments of the past" erupted into the present.

8. The sense that archaeologists are in fact interested in hidden gold rather than in the vestiges of ancient societies is a common trope in Mexico, where excavations are generally viewed with suspicion by locals. Few professional archaeologists write about this. For an exception, see Adela Amaral's (2019) discussion on stories of buried gold during her fieldwork excavating remnants of maroon life in Amapa, Veracruz.

9. *Güera* is a term used in Mexican Spanish that literally means blonde but is used as both a racial and a class marker. See Leal Martínez (2016).

CHAPTER 6. REPLICAS

An earlier, shorter version of chapter 6 was published in the *Journal of Latin American and Caribbean Anthropology* (Rozental 2014b).

1. In 2006, the Museo Nacional de Antropología published a children's coloring book in which a cartoon version of the stone served as a guide through its galleries (see Francisco Javier González y García, "Guía para niños del Museo Nacional de Antropología," accessed April 2024, https://www.behance.net/gallery/33218475/Guia-para-ninos -Museo-Nacional-de-Antropologia). I noticed the same cartoon on bumper stickers and

painted on signage in Coatlinchan. Miguel Linares, a local designer who published the first website dedicated to the town's history and who passed away very young, told me then that he had drawn the cartoon long before the museum had and that the latter had appropriated his design without crediting his work or paying him royalties.

2. Esra Özyürek (2004, 2006) analyzes how people in Istanbul subvert the official monumentalization of Kemal Atatürk's image in public space by collecting miniatures that depict the statesman in more human contexts, manufactured, purchased, and displayed in private. On the cult of Atatürk, see Navaro-Yashin (2020).

3. I have written elsewhere about these replicas' iteration and movement not resulting in a loss of "aura" as Walter Benjamin's (1969) account of the consequences of technological reproduction have been interpreted to anticipate (Rozental 2016). This reading recenters the creative possibilities of reproduction whereby objects do not lose aura, but rather open up to new forms of authenticity. I am very grateful to Richard Kernaghan for his helpful comments on Benjamin and the ways in which technological reproduction produces new configurations of proximity and distance rather than loss.

4. Scale is not something Thomas Abercrombie (1998, 2016) discusses directly, beyond signaling, like Catherine Allen (1997, 2016) in her account of miniatures' ritual work in the Andes, that miniaturization allows for otherwise unwieldy things like mountains, but perhaps also massive stones, to become easily manipulatable and therefore also acted through and on. Art historians have paid attention to how ancient civilizations used miniatures within ritual and political realms as substitutes for things like topographical features, too large to control or move or too distant and remote to access. In her study of stone cults in the Andes, Carolyn Dean (2010, 97–99) documents "echo stones," shaped like mountains either naturally or through human alteration, using mimesis to both visually resemble but also embody that which they represent (2010, 56). Dean highlights the relationship between miniatures and power.

5. In *The Shape of Time* (1962b), George Kubler argues that the history of objects should be understood as an open-ended sequence made up of "prime objects" and their reworkings; he calls these their "replica mass" (1962b, 39). Art objects, then, have an inherent reproductive power through their repetition, which is central to how they take shape in social landscapes.

6. Dean (2010, 40) explores "presentational stones" in Inca landscapes as making absence present, not as intermediaries or representations but as immediates that were not substitutive. Along similar lines, ethnographer and artist Pamela Cevallos is creatively reworking the power of replicas and processes of replication of ancient material culture along with residents of La Pila in Ecuador, as practices that participate in the reproduction of the community. See Cevallos (2023) and Cevallos and Bedoya (2019).

7. Interested in collections, Susan Stewart (1993) used psychoanalytic as well as Marxist and poststructuralist theory to think through human (Western) fascination with miniatures. Her arguments are centered on longing and the ways miniaturization is connected to forms of nostalgia and desire experienced in the aftermath of loss. Stewart does not really consider miniatures as being important in and of themselves; they are relevant because of what they point to, what is projected onto them, and the pasts they remind us of.

8. See Laurajane Smith's discussion on the importance of monumentality, authenticity, and aesthetics in what she calls "authorized heritage discourse" or AHD (2006).

9. Alessandro Angelini (2016) writes about miniaturization and play as a form of politics in Brazil, where favela residents use avatars and building replicas to reenact as well as transform contexts of street and gang violence.

10. The sculptor was also connected to Higinio Martínez, the municipal president of Texcoco at the time and a powerful PRD regional leader through family relations (his daughter was partnered with Martínez's son).

11. Scholars have explored rituals of consecration, and the powers of objects described as "fetishes" mostly in African and African diaspora religions. See, for example, Sansi (2007) and Matory (2018). William Pietz (1985, 12) shows that such objects were related to very specific and situated events of colonial encounter that became "fixed" or territorialized.

12. The Catholic Church's distrust of images and the proliferation of devotional images as possible vectors of idolatry is not a new phenomenon, nor is it confined to Mexico's colonial legacy. It has, in fact, been at the heart of theological debates in Europe since medieval times. See Bynum (2011, 37–61).

13. For an analysis of potency and the dilemmas of saint image and devotional objects's restoration, see Wharton (2011) and Peleggi (2022).

14. James Siegel (1983, 3) equates the circulation of images of corpses in Java with the power of photographs to work against memory. See also Barthes (1993) on his mother's portrait and Kernaghan and Zamorano's edited dossier on the obtuse as a productive category for ethnography (2022).

CHAPTER 7. WATERSHED

Parts of chapter 7 and its arguments were published in *Anthropological Quarterly* (Rozental 2016).

1. The teacher has given and recorded many interviews in which she explains the stone's local significance. See, for example, her 2020 participation in the program *A donde nos lleva el viento*: "Coatlinchan y su Chalchiuhtlicue," YouTube, November 5, 2020, https://www.youtube.com/watch?v=k0F4u0X2i00.

2. Don Chava gave a talk for the 2021 San Miguel feast day, presented via the Facebook page of the group "Coatlinchan, cultura, historia y tradición," in which he explained that San Miguel was associated with fire and water given that his two-sided blade sword represented light and lightning, two elements related to controlling weather.

3. In Coatlinchan, there seem to not have been any graniceros, or climate ritual specialists, for at least two generations, but those from the nearby villages of Santa Catarina del Monte and Tequesquinahua were known to come, and still come to this day. Timoteo Hernández, or don Timo, as he is affectionately known, and his father, who passed away shortly after my fieldwork, were often invited by Calpulli members to participate in their work. They were both present during the 2007 consecration of the cement replica and were also invited to many of the rituals officiated in the ravine to appease its guardians over the following years. Don Timo is the subject of the feature documentary *Granicero* (2011), directed by Gustavo Gamou.

4. Graniceros have been the subject of many studies by Mexican anthropologists interested in these figures' role as mediators between human and nonhuman realms and as contemporary representatives of the survival and endurance of pre-Hispanic ontologies.

See, for example, Bonfil Batalla (1968); Glockner (2012); and, more recently, Lorente Fernández (2008, 2009, 2011, 2017).

5. The stone is also referred to as the Rostro de Contla (Contla Face) after the toponym of the place where it is located. This name also comes from the Nahuatl word for orifice or vessel, "comitl," the same root as "tecomate."

6. Ídolos are figures with identifiable human or animal features, and the term *tepalcates*—from the Nahuatl word *tepalcatl*—is used colloquially to describe earthenware or broken pottery, sometimes also used to mean "junk."

7. In the *Social Life of Things*, Arjun Appadurai (1986) argues that objects moved across various "regimes of value" within their biographies to destabilize the gift/commodity binary that had until then dominated anthropological thinking on material culture. In an edited volume, Fred Myers (2001, 6) and others stress the importance of ethnographically rendering the "multiple, coexisting, and variously related regimes of value" that different kinds of objects circulate across. As Myers shows in the introduction to the volume, "the value possessed by objects is subject to slippage and is therefore problematic. It must be sustained or reproduced through the complex work of production" (Myers 2001, 6).

8. I have written elsewhere about the collections of artifacts and potsherds from Coatlinchan that made their way to international museum collections, namely those gathered by Marshall H. Saville for the American Museum of Natural History in New York and by Eduard Seler for the Berlin Ethnographic Museum (Rozental 2014a).

9. *Malacate* is from the Nahuatl word *malacatl*, meaning spindle, bobbin, spiral, or spindle whorl. *Abuelos* can be translated as grandfathers or grandparents, but here it's used to mean ancestors.

10. Vladimir Caraballo Acuña (2022) has written about people who work scavenging for emeralds in Colombia who have a similar narrative, whereby they find the stones "sin querer la cosa."

11. The Escuela Normal is the school set up by the Ministry of Education to centrally train teachers for communities all over Mexico.

CONCLUSION: #TLALOCDEVUELTA

1. See Rozental (2022b).

2. The photograph is part of a series of images by Kuhn denouncing Mexican authoritarianism during the 1960s, including images of broken windows and equipment destroyed by police violence. It was published accompanying my chapter in Eduardo Abaroa's *Total Destruction of the Museo Nacional de Antropologia* (Rozental 2017a) and in the volume of Mexican photography edited by Alfonso Morales (2005). I was unable to secure the rights to reproduce it here.

3. For example, Carlos Monsiváis, a chronicler and critic of twentieth-century Mexico cultural politics, wrote: "The Revolution a monolith, a homogenous whole, indivisible" (1977, 337). I have written elsewhere about the uses of this term in Mexican literature and literary criticism (Rozental 2017a, 84).

4. Although the most recent and certainly most gender conscious and activist work, the opera was not the first artistic engagement that questioned the stone's place outside the museum. Several prominent contemporary artists used its forced relocation to

denounce state violence and Mexican authoritarian politics, notably Mariana Castillo Deball and Eduardo Abaroa. For more on Abaroa's installation and its work to detonate the monolith, see Rozental (2017a).

5. I am thankful to Allegra Cordero di Montezemolo and Laura Gutiérrez for introducing me to Alberto and to Pepx. Bustamante and Lao had wanted to work on the state uses of pre-Hispanic motifs and art in Mexican national identity formation after having heard a talk by art historian Maria Teresa Uriarte. Having attended a screening of *The Absent Stone* as university students, they became interested in the debates regarding the stone's gender identity. During the pandemic, they spent time in Texcoco and its surroundings, where they researched Nahua cosmologies and rain petition rituals and presented the project to La Bruja de Texcoco and Pepx (Bustamante, personal communication, 2024).

6. Pepx Romero, interview with the author, 2023. The INAH emitted an official document condemning Romero's actions: "The INAH expresses its respect for creative freedom, its gratitude to the voices that reject the illicit sale of cultural property abroad, but also its disagreement with conduct that is not permitted by the regulations of the institutions charged with the care and preservation of patrimonial things." See "Comunicado sobre performance en el Museo Nacional de Antropología," Secretaría de Cultura, April 6, 2022, https://www.gob.mx/cultura/prensa/comunicado-sobre-performance-en -el-museo-nacional-de-antropologia?idiom=es-MX.

7. The performance had a write-up in the *New York Times* (Anaya 2023).

8. Viumasters was a Mexico City–based collective of young animators Esteban Azuela, Carlos Gamboa, Güicho Nuñez, Amaranta Verdugo, and Mara Soler.

9. These critical archaeologists include Buchli and Lucas (2001); Meskell (2002); Dawdy (2010); González-Ruibal (2013, 2018); Olivier (2013, 2019); Weismantel and Meskell (2014); Haber (2017); DeSilvey (2017); Gnecco (2019, 2021); and Jofré 2022, among others.

10. For more on the Restauradoras con Glitter, see Rozental (2024) and Paulara et al. (2024).

11. See Espinoza (2024).

12. For a transdisciplinary account of the effects of water scarcity in Mexico City using bioethnography, see Huberts et al. (2023).

13. Since the late 1970s, many Mexico City neighborhoods have depended on privately owned and run trucks for water procurement when public infrastructures fail. These trucks, known as pipas, carry cylindrical tanks full of water, many times illegally siphoned from groundwater sources. In times of water scarcity, pipa prices soar and they become a coveted and fraught luxury.

14. Letter from Dr. Martha Lorenza López Mestas Camberos, head of the Coordinación de Arqueología, to Verónica Esmirna Venegas Silva, tercer delegada, and Luz Alicia Ocampo Rodríguez, quinta delegada, both from the Ayuntamiento de Texcoco, and Isrrael Martinez Trujano and Marcelo Ortiz Sánchez, Calpulli Makoyolotzin, June 27, 2023, Oficio 401.5S.1-2023/1097.

References

ARCHIVES

Acervo Arquitecto Pedro Ramírez Vázquez (AAPRV)
    Museo Nacional de Antropología (MNA) Papers
Archivo General de la Nación (AGN)
    Bienes Nacionales (BN)
    Dirección Federal de Seguridad (DFS)
    Fondo Archivo Fotográfico Hermanos Mayo
    Instrucción Pública y Bellas Artes (IPBA)
    Padrones (P)
    Tierras (T)
Archivo Histórico del Museo Nacional de Antropología (AHMNA)
Biblioteca Nacional de Antropología e Historia (BNAH)
    Archivo Histórico Institucional (AHI)
    Museo Nacional de Antropología (MNA) Dirección
Fototeca Nacional (FN)
Hemeroteca Nacional (HN)

PUBLISHED SOURCES

Abercrombie, Thomas A. 1998. *Pathways of Memory and Power: Ethnography and History Among an Andean People*. Madison: University of Wisconsin Press.
Abercrombie, Thomas A. 2016. "The Iterated Mountain: Things as Signs in Potosí." *Journal of Latin American and Caribbean Anthropology* 21, no. 1: 83–108. https://doi .org/10.1111/jlca.12184.
Abu El-Haj, Nadia. 2001. *Facts on the Ground: Archaeological Practice and Territorial Self-Fashioning in Israeli Society*. Chicago: University of Chicago Press.
Achim, Miruna. 2017. *From Idols to Antiquity: Forging the National Museum of Mexico*. Lincoln: University of Nebraska Press.

Achim, Miruna, Susan Deans-Smith, and Sandra Rozental. 2021. *Museum Matters: Making and Unmaking Mexico's National Collections*. Tucson: University of Arizona Press.

Adonon, Akuavi. 2022. *Vía tsotsil: Prácticas jurídicas en los Altos de Chiapas: Propuesta para descolonizar la mirada sobre el Derecho*. Mexico City: Universidad Autónoma Metropolitana.

Agostoni, Claudia. 2003. *Monuments of Progress: Modernization and Public Health in Mexico City, 1876–1910*. Calgary: University of Calgary Press.

Aguayo, Fernando, Graciela de Garay Arellano, and Lourdes Roca, dirs. 1997. *El buen restaurador ama lo antiguo: Testimonio del arquitecto Ricardo de Robina*. Documentary film. Mexico City: Instituto Mora.

Aguayo, Sergio. 2015. *De Tlatelolco a Ayotzinapa: Las violencias del Estado*. Mexico City: Ediciones Proceso.

Aguilar Gil, Yásnaya Elena. 2018. *¿Nunca más un México sin nosotros?* San Cristóbal: CIDECI, Universidad de la Tierra Chiapas.

Aguilar Gil, Yásnaya Elena. 2023. *Tëkëëk piky: Antología*. Mexico City: Centro de Estudios para el Cambio en el Campo Mexicano.

Alexander, Ryan. 2020. "Myth and Reality of the Mexican Miracle, 1946–1982." In *The Oxford Handbook of Mexican History*, edited by William Beezley. New York: Oxford University Press. https://doi.org/10.1093/oxfordhb/9780190699192.013.32.

Allen, Catherine J. 1997. "When Pebbles Move Mountains: Iconicity and Symbolism in Quechua Ritual." In *Creating Context in Andean Cultures*, edited by Rosaleen Howard-Malverde, 73–84. New York: Oxford University Press.

Allen, Catherine J. 2016. "The Living Ones: Miniatures and Animation in the Andes." *Journal of Anthropological Research* 72, no. 4: 416–41. https://doi.org/10.1086/689293.

Alonso, Ana María. 2004. "Conforming Disconformity: 'Mestizaje,' Hybridity, and the Aesthetics of Mexican Nationalism." *Cultural Anthropology* 19, no. 4: 459–90. https://doi.org/10.1525/can.2004.19.4.459.

Álvarez, Marina M. 2022. "Monumentality and Anticolonial Resistance: Feminist Graffiti in Mexico." *Public Art Dialogue* 12, no. 2: 178–94. https://doi.org/10.1080/21502552.2022.2112349.

Amaral, Adela. 2019. "Contesting Temporalities in a Runaway Slave Town: Mexico, 1769 to the Present." *Journal of Contemporary Archaeology* 6, no. 1: 47–63. https://doi.org/10.1558/jca.33824.

Anand, Nikhil, Akhil Gupta, and Hannah Appel, eds. 2018. *The Promise of Infrastructure*. Durham, NC: Duke University Press.

Anaya, Suleman. 2023. "In Mexico City, Club Kids Take the Stage: How a Group of Underground Queer Artists Came Together to Create a New Kind of Opera." *New York Times*, April 28.

Anderson, Gerald H., ed. 1999. *Biographical Dictionary of Christian Missions*. Cambridge: William B. Eerdmans.

Anderson, Jane, and Sonya Atalay. 2023. "Repatriation as Pedagogy." *Current Anthropology* 64, no. 6: 670–91. https://doi.org/10.1086/727786.

Anderson, Jane L., and Haidy Geismar, eds. 2017. *The Routledge Companion to Cultural Property*. New York: Routledge.

Angé, Olivia, and Perig Pitrou. 2016. "Miniatures in Mesoamerica and the Andes: Theories of Life, Values, and Relatedness." *Journal of Anthropological Research* 72, no. 4: 408–15. https://doi.org/10.1086/689259.

Angelini, Alessandro M. 2016. "Favela in Replica: Iterations and Itineraries of a Miniature City." *Journal of Latin American and Caribbean Anthropology* 21, no. 1: 39–60. https://doi.org/10.1111/jlca.12174.

Antoniadou, Ioanna. 2009. "Reflections on an Archaeological Ethnography of 'Looting' in Kozani, Greece." *Public Archaeology* 8, nos. 2–3: 246–61. https://doi.org/10.1179/175355309X457259.

Appadurai, Arjun, ed. 1986. *The Social Life of Things: Commodities in Cultural Perspective.* New York: Cambridge University Press.

Azuela, Antonio. 2011. "Property in the Post-Post-Revolution: Notes on the Crisis of the Constitutional Idea of Property in Contemporary Mexico." *Texas Law Review* 89, no. 7: 1915–42. https://www.corteidh.or.cr/tablas/r27179.pdf.

Azuela, Antonio. 2019. "When Land Is Inalienable: Territorial Transformations and Peasants' Property Rights in Mexico." In *Property Rights from Below: Commodification of Land and the Counter-Movement,* edited by Olivier De Schutter and Balakrishnan Rajagopal, 186–202. New York: Routledge.

Báez, Lourdes. 1998. "Encuentros peligrosos: Contaminación y ciclo de vida entre los Nahuas de la Sierra Norte de Puebla (México)." *Mitológicas* 13, no. 1: 19–34. https://www.redalyc.org/pdf/146/14601302.pdf.

Bakhtin, Mikhail Mikhaïlovich. 2010. *The Dialogic Imagination: Four Essays.* Austin: University of Texas Press.

Ballestero, Andrea. 2019. "Aquifers (or, Hydrolithic Elemental Choreographies)." *Cultural Anthropology Online.* https://culanth.org/fieldsights/aquifers-or-hydrolithic-elemental-choreographies.

Barad, Karen. 2007. *Meeting the Universe Halfway: Quantum Physics and the Entanglement of Matter and Meaning.* Durham, NC: Duke University Press.

Barkan, Elazar, and Ronald Bush. 2002. *Claiming the Stones, Naming the Bones: Cultural Property and the Negotiation of National and Ethnic Identity.* Los Angeles: Getty Research Institute.

Barker, Alex W. 2018. "Looting, the Antiquities Trade, and Competing Valuations of the Past." *Annual Review of Anthropology* 47, no. 1: 455–74. https://doi.org/10.1146/annurev-anthro-102116-041320.

Barthes, Roland. 1993. *Camera Lucida.* Translated by Richard Howard. London: Vintage Classics.

Batres, Leopoldo. 1903. *¿Tlaloc? Exploración arqueológica del Oriente.* Mexico City: Secretaría de Justicia e Instrucción Pública.

Batres, Leopoldo. 1904a. *El Sr. Lic. Chavero y El monolito de Coatlinchan.* Mexico City: Imprenta de Fidencio S. Soria.

Batres, Leopoldo. 1904b. *Mis exploraciones en Huexotla, Texcoco y Montículo de "El Gavilan."* Mexico City: Inspección y Conservación de los Monumentos Arqueológicos de la República Mexicana.

Batres, Leopoldo. 1905. *Contestación a la dúplica del Sr. Lic. Alfredo Chavero en la controversia del monolito de Coatlinchan.* Mexico City: Imprenta de Fidencio S. Soria.

Becerril, Luis G. 1903. "La Piedra de Nezahualcoyotl o de 'los tecomates.'" *Memorias de la Sociedad Científica "Antonio Alzate"* 20: 69–71.

Bell, Joshua A., Kimberly Christen, and Mark Turin. 2013. "After the Return: Digital Repatriation and the Circulation of Indigenous Knowledge Workshop Report." *Museum Worlds* 1, no. 1: 195–203. https://doi.org/10.3167/armw.2013.010112.

Beltrán, Alberto. 1969. "El traslado de Tlaloc en tiempo de los Aztecas, reconstrucción de los hechos." *Crucero*, June 14.

Benjamin, Walter. 1969. "The Work of Art in the Age of Mechanical Reproduction." In *Illuminations*, edited by Hannah Arendt, 217–53. New York: Schocken Books.

Benjamin, Walter. 2002. *The Arcades Project*. Cambridge, MA: Belknap Press of Harvard University Press.

Bernal, Victoria. 2013. "Please Forget Democracy and Justice: Eritrean Politics and the Powers of Humor." *American Ethnologist* 40, no. 2: 300–309. https://doi.org/10.1111/amet.12022.

Bernstein, Anya. 2011. "The Post-Soviet Treasure Hunt: Time, Space, and Necropolitics in Siberian Buddhism." *Comparative Studies in Society and History* 53, no. 3: 623–53. https://doi.org/10.1017/S0010417511000272.

Bittman Simons, Bente. 1978. *El mapa de Coatlinchan: Pictografía de Acolhuacan: Glosas del mapa de Coatlinchan*. Mexico City: Biblioteca Nacional de Antropología e Historia.

Blackmore, Lisa. 2018. "Colonizing Flow: Hydropower and Post-Kinetic Assemblages in the Orinoco Basin." In *Natura: Environmental Aesthetics After Landscape*, edited by Jens Andermann, Lisa Blackmore, and Dayron Carrillo Morell, 171–97. Zurich: Diaphanes.

Boddy, Janice. 1982. "Womb as Oasis: The Symbolic Context of Pharaonic Circumcision in Rural Northern Sudan." *American Ethnologist* 9, no. 4: 682–98. https://doi.org/10.1525/ae.1982.9.4.02a00040.

Bonfil Batalla, Guillermo. 1968. "Los que trabajan con el tiempo: Notas etnográficas sobre los graniceros de la Sierra Nevada de México." *Anales de Antropología* 5, no. 1: 239–70.

Boone, Elizabeth Hill, ed. 1993. *Collecting the Pre-Columbian Past*. Washington, DC: Dumbarton Oaks Research Library and Collection.

Botey, Mariana. 2014. *Zonas de disturbio: Espectros del México indígena en la modernidad*. Mexico City: Siglo Veintiuno Editores.

Boyer, Dominic. 2013. "Simply the Best: Parody and Political Sincerity in Iceland." *American Ethnologist* 40, no. 2: 276–87. https://doi.org/10.1111/amet.12020.

Boyer, Dominic, and Alexei Yurchak. 2010. "American Stiob: Or, What Late-Socialist Aesthetics of Parody Reveal About Contemporary Political Culture in the West." *Cultural Anthropology* 25, no. 2: 179–221. https://doi.org/10.1111/j.1548-1360.2010.01056.x.

Breglia, Lisa. 2006. *Monumental Ambivalence: The Politics of Heritage*. Austin: University of Texas Press.

Brighenti, Andrea. 2006. "On Territory as Relationship and Law as Territory." *Canadian Journal of Law and Society* 21, no. 2: 65–86. https://doi.org/10.1017/S0829320100008954.

Brown, Michael F. 2003. *Who Owns Native Culture?* Cambridge, MA: Harvard University Press.

Brown, Michael F. 2004. "Heritage as Property." In *Property in Question: Value Transformation in the Global Economy*, edited by Katherine Verdery and Caroline Humphrey, 49–68. Oxford: Berg.

Brulotte, Ronda L. 2012. *Between Art and Artifact: Archaeological Replicas and Cultural Production in Oaxaca, Mexico*. Austin: University of Texas Press.

Buchli, Victor, and Gavin Lucas. 2001. *Archaeologies of the Contemporary Past*. London: Routledge.

Buck-Morss, Susan. 1991. *The Dialectics of Seeing: Walter Benjamin and the Arcades Project*. Cambridge, MA: MIT Press.

Buck-Morss, Susan. 2000. *Dreamworld and Catastrophe: The Passing of Mass Utopia in East and West*. Cambridge, MA: MIT Press.

Bueno, Christina. 2010. "Forjando Patrimonio: The Making of Archaeological Patrimony in Porfirian Mexico." *Hispanic American Historical Review* 90, no. 2: 215–45. https://doi.org/10.1215/00182168-2009-133.

Bueno, Christina. 2016. *The Pursuit of Ruins: Archaeology, History, and the Making of Modern Mexico*. Albuquerque: University of New Mexico Press.

Buentello García, María Eugenia Desirée, and Jasmine Quinn Rice. 2023. "Gender Debates on the Stage of the Urban Memorial: Glitter, Graffiti, and Bronze." *Landscape Research* 48, no. 5: 647–61. https://doi.org/10.1080/01426397.2022.2120604.

Burri, Regula Valérie, and Joseph Dumit. 2008. "Social Studies of Scientific Imaging and Visualization." In *The Handbook of Science and Technology Studies*, edited by Edward J. Hackett, 297–317. Cambridge, MA: MIT Press.

Bustamante, Andrés. 2024. "Excavating Mexico: Archaeology and the Subsoil Politics of State Formation, 1821–1944." PhD diss., Yale University.

Bynum, Caroline Walker. 2011. *Christian Materiality: An Essay on Religion in Late Medieval Europe*. New York: Zone Books.

Cadena, Marisol de la. 2015. *Earth Beings: Ecologies of Practice Across Andean Worlds*. Durham, NC: Duke University Press.

Cadena, Marisol de la. 2018. "Earth-Beings: Andean Indigenous Religion but Not Only." In *The World Multiple: The Quotidian Politics of Knowing and Generating Entangled Worlds*, edited by Keiichi Omura, Grant Jun Otsuki, Shiho Satsuka, and Atsuro Morita, 20–36. New York: Routledge.

Caillois, Roger. 2014. *La lécture des Pierres*. France: Xavier Barral.

Caine, Allison. 2022. "Herding at the Edges: Climate Change and Animal Restlessness in the Peruvian Andes." *Ethnos* 89, no. 5: 1–21. https://doi.org/10.1080/00141844.2022.2142266.

Callon, Michel. 1986. "Some Elements of a Sociology of Translation: Domestication of the Scallops and the Fishermen of St. Brieuc Bay." In *Power, Action and Belief: A New Sociology of Knowledge?*, edited by John Law, 196–233. London: Routledge and Kegan Paul.

Camarena, Cuauhtémoc, and Teresa Morales. 2006. "Community Museums and Global Connections: The Union of Community Museums of Oaxaca." In *Museum Frictions:*

Public Cultures/Global Transformations, edited by Ivan Karp, Corinne A. Kratz, Lynn Szwaja, and Tomás Ybarra-Frausto, 322–44. Durham, NC: Duke University Press.

Camp, Roderic Ai. 2011. "The Revolution's Second Generation: The Miracle, 1946–1982 and Collapse of the PRI, 1982–2000." In *A Companion to Mexican History and Culture*, edited by William H. Beezley, 468–79. Oxford: Blackwell.

Candiani, Vera S. 2014. *Dreaming of Dry Land: Environmental Transformation in Colonial Mexico City*. Stanford, CA: Stanford University Press.

Canessa, Andrew. 2000. "Fear and Loathing on the Kharisiri Trail: Alterity and Identity in the Andes." *Journal of the Royal Anthropological Institute* 6, no. 4: 705–20. https://doi.org/10.1111/1467-9655.00041.

Caraballo Acuña, Vladimir. 2022. "'Como sin querer la cosa': Insinuaciones e indeterminación en los encuentros entre esmeralderos y esmeraldas en Colombia." *Revista Colombiana de Antropología* 58, no. 1: 235–59. https://doi.org/10.22380/2539472X .2046.

Carballo, David M., and Matthew H. Robb. 2017. "Lighting the World: Teotihuacan and Urbanism in Central Mexico." In *Teotihuacan: City of Water, City of Fire*, edited by Matthew H. Robb, 12–19. San Francisco: Fine Arts Museums of San Francisco, de Young.

Cardona Peña, Alfredo, ed. 1964. *Aventuras de la vida real: Una deidad en el asfalto*. Mexico City: Editorial Novaro.

Carrasco, Pedro. 1996. *Estructura político territorial del Imperio tenochca: La triple alianza de Tenochtitlan, Tetzcoco y Tlacopan*. Mexico City: El Colegio de México.

Castañeda, Luis M. 2013a. "Doubling Time." *Grey Room* 51 (Spring): 12–39. https://doi .org/10.1162/GREYa00105.

Castañeda, Luis M. 2013b. "Pre-Columbian Skins, Developmentalist Souls: The Architect as Politician." In *Latin American Modern Architectures: Ambiguous Territories*, edited by Patricio del Real and Helen Gyger, 107–28. New York: Routledge.

Castañeda, Luis M. 2014. *Spectacular Mexico: Design, Propaganda, and the 1968 Olympics*. Minneapolis: University of Minnesota Press.

Castañeda, Quetzil E. 2009. "Heritage and Indigeneity: Transformations in the Politics of Tourism." In *Cultural Tourism in Latin America: The Politics of Space and Imagery*, edited by Michiel Baud and Annelou Ypeij, 263–95. Boston: Brill.

Castillo Cocom, Juan. 2004. "Lost in Mayaland." *Journal of Latin American Anthropology* 9, no. 1: 179–87. https://doi.org/10.1525/jlca.2004.9.1.179.

Cevallos, Pamela. 2023. "Réplicas y regresos, activar el pasado desde el arte contemporáneo." *Índex, revista de arte contemporáneo*, no. 16, 103–18. https://doi.org/10.26807/cav .v9i16.532.

Cevallos, Pamela, and María Elena Bedoya. 2019. "Réplicas en tránsito: Patrimonio y crítica institucional desde La Pila (Ecuador) hasta el Museo de América (España)." *Terremoto*, March 18. https://terremoto.mx/revista/replicas-en-transito-patrimonio-y -critica-institucional-desde-la-pila-ecuador-hasta-el-museo-de-america-espana/.

Chavero, Alfredo. 1887. *México a través de los siglos: Historia general y completa del desenvolvimiento social, político, religioso, militar, artístico, científico y literario de México desde la antigüedad más remota hasta la época actual*. Vol. 1, *Historia antigua y de la conquista*. Mexico City: Ballescá y Compañía.

Chavero, Alfredo. 1904. *El monolito de Coatlinchan: Disquisición arqueológica, presentada al XIV Congreso de Americanistas*. Mexico City: Imprenta del Museo Nacional.

Chevalier, François. 1970. *Land and Society in Colonial Mexico: The Great Hacienda*. Berkeley: University of California Press.

Chiñas, Beverly N. 1988. "Zelia Maria Magdalena Nuttall (1857–1933)." In *Women Anthropologists: A Bibliographical Dictionary*, edited by Ute Gacs, Aisha Khan, Jerry McIntyre, and Ruth Weinberg, 269–74. New York: Greenwood.

Christian, William A. 1981. *Local Religion in Sixteenth-Century Spain*. Princeton, NJ: Princeton University Press.

Clifford, James. 2013. *Returns: Becoming Indigenous in the Twenty-First Century*. Cambridge, MA: Harvard University Press.

Coffey, Mary K. 2012. *How a Revolutionary Art Became Official Culture: Murals, Museums, and the Mexican State*. Durham, NC: Duke University Press.

Cohen, Lawrence. 1999. "Where It Hurts: Indian Material for an Ethics of Organ Transplantation." *Daedalus* 128, no. 4: 135–65. https://doi.org/10.1111/1467-9744.00527.

Colin Varela, Alfredo E. 1964. *Tláloc, Lopez Mateos y la SRH: La nueva política hidráulica de México, realizaciones de un régimen de gobierno*. Mexico City: Impresora de Industria y Comercio.

Collins, John F. 2015. *Revolt of the Saints: Memory and Redemption in the Twilight of Brazilian Racial Democracy*. Durham, NC: Duke University Press.

Construcción Mexicana. 1964a. "Histórica escultura de 167 toneladas transportada sin moverla." *Construcción Mexicana* 5, no. 4: 18–20.

Construcción Mexicana. 1964b. "Remolque, diseñado en México, para trasladar 167 toneladas." *Construcción Mexicana* 5, no. 5: 32–34.

Coombe, Rosemary J. 1998. *The Cultural Life of Intellectual Properties: Authorship, Appropriation, and the Law*. Durham, NC: Duke University Press.

Cottom, Bolfy. 2008. *Nación, patrimonio cultural y legislación: Los debates parlamentarios y la construcción del marco jurídico federal sobre monumentos en México, siglo XX*. Mexico City: Porrúa.

Covarrubias, Miguel. 1957. *Indian Art of Mexico and Central America*. New York: Alfred A. Knopf.

Cowan, George M. 1954. "La importancia social y política de la faena mazateca." *América Indígena* 14, no. 1: 67–92. https://doi.org/10.22201/iis.01882503p.1956.1.59837.

Crespo, Carolina. 2022. "Restitution of Indigenous Ancestors, Uncomfortable Heritage, and Ways of Seeing Violence in Argentina." *European Review of Latin American and Caribbean Studies* 113: 143–61. https://doi.org/10.32992/erlacs.10896.

Crespo, Carolina, and María Alma Tozzini. 2014. "Memorias silenciadas y patrimonios ausentes en el Museo Histórico de el Hoyo, comarca andina del paralelo 42, Patagonia Argentina." *Antípoda: Revista de Antropología y Arqueología* 19, no. 1: 21–44. https://doi.org/10.7440/antipoda19.2014.02.

Cruz Atienza, Victor, Shri Krishna Singh, and Mario Ordaz. 2017. ¿Qué ocurrió el 19 de septiembre de 2017 en México?" *Revista Digital Universitaria* 18, no. 7: 1–9. https://doi.org/10.22201/codeic.16076079e.2017.v18n7.a10.

Cruz Bárcenas, Arturo. 2014. "Tláloc sigue enterrado aquí; se llevaron a Chalchiuhtlicue: Guadalupe Villarreal." *La Jornada*, April 5.

Cruz Martínez, Xochiquetzalli, Marcela Viañez Reyes, and José Manuel Pedrosa. 2021. *El tesoro de la cueva de Tlapanalá, o los héroes que tiemblan en el umbral del infierno.* Morelia: Escuela Nacional de Estudios Superiores, Unidad Morelia.

Dawdy, Shannon Lee. 2010. "Clockpunk Anthropology and the Ruins of Modernity." *Current Anthropology* 51, no. 6: 761–93. https://doi.org/10.1086/657626.

Dawson, Alexander Scott. 2004. *Indian and Nation in Revolutionary Mexico.* Tucson: University of Arizona Press.

Dean, Carolyn J. 2010. *A Culture of Stone: Inca Perspectives on Rock.* Durham, NC: Duke University Press.

De Coss Corzo, Julio Alejandro. 2019. "Waterworks: Labour, Infrastructure and the Making of Urban Water in Mexico City." PhD diss., London School of Economics and Political Science (LSE).

Dehouve, Danièle. 2016. "Altepetl: El lugar del poder." *Americae* (online), November 1. https://americae.fr/dossiers/altepetl/altepetl-lugar-poder/.

Denizen, Seth. 2018. "Baroque Soil: Mexico City in the Aftermath." In *Political Geology: Active Stratigraphies and the Making of Life,* edited by Adam Bobbette and Amy Donovan, 71–105. Cham: Palgrave Macmillan. https://doi.org/10.1007/978-3-319 -98189-5_371-104.

Denizen, Seth. 2019. "Five Soils and a Letter: Profiles in the Political Ecology of Mexico City." PhD diss., University of California, Berkeley.

DeSilvey, Caitlin. 2017. *Curated Decay: Heritage Beyond Saving.* Minneapolis: University of Minnesota Press.

Diaz-Guardamino, Marta. 2015. "Stones-in-Movement: Tracing the Itineraries of Menhirs, Stelae and Statue-Menhirs in Iberian Landscapes." In *Things in Motion: Object Itineraries in Anthropological Practice,* edited by Rosemary A. Joyce and Susan D. Gillespie, 101–22. Santa Fe, NM: School for Advanced Research Press.

Dixon, Seth. 2009. "Symbolic Landscapes of Identity: Monumentality, Modernity and Memory on Mexico City's Paseo de la Reforma." PhD diss., Pennsylvania State University.

Dorotinsky Alperstein, Deborah. 2002. "Fotografía y maniquíes en el Museo Nacional de Antropología." *Luna Córnea,* no. 23: 60–65.

Eiss, Paul. 2010. *In the Name of El Pueblo: Place, Community and the Politics of History in Yucatán.* Durham, NC: Duke University Press.

Ennis-McMillan, Michael C. 2001. *La Purificación Tepetitla: Agua potable y cambio social en el somontano.* Mexico City: Universidad Iberoamericana.

Espinoza, Kimberly. 2024. "Day Zero in Cutzamala Mexico." *Libertad Latina,* April 2. https://latinarepublic.com/2024/04/02/day-zero-in-cutzamala-mexico/.

Fernández Christlieb, Federico, and Angel J. García Zambrano, eds. 2006. *Territorialidad y paisaje en el altepetl del siglo XVI.* Mexico City: Fondo de Cultura Económica and Instituto de Geografía de la Universidad Nacional Autónoma de México.

Ferry, Elizabeth. 2005. *Not Ours Alone: Patrimony, Value, and Collectivity in Contemporary Mexico.* New York: Columbia University Press.

Ferry, Elizabeth. 2020. "Speculative Substance: 'Physical Gold' in Finance." *Economy and Society* 49, no. 1: 92–115. https://doi.org/10.1080/03085147.2019.1690254.

Ferry, Elizabeth. 2021. "'Deep in the Earth a Shining Substance': Sequestration and Display in Gold Mining and Central Banks." *Journal of Cultural Economy* 14, no. 4: 416–34. https://doi.org/10.1080/17530350.2020.1818603.

Fforde, Cressida, Hilary Susan Howes, Gareth Knapman, and Lyndon Ormond-Parker, eds. 2023. *Repatriation, Science and Identity*. London: Routledge.

Fforde, Cressida, Jane Hubert, and Paul Turnbull, eds. 2002. *The Dead and Their Possessions: Repatriation in Principle, Policy, and Practice*. London: Routledge.

Field, Les W., Cristóbal Gnecco, and Joe Watkins, eds. 2016. *Challenging the Dichotomy: The Licit and the Illicit in Archaeological and Heritage Discourses*. Tucson: University of Arizona Press.

Fine-Dare, Kathleen S. 2002. *Grave Injustice*. Lincoln: University of Nebraska Press.

Flaherty, George F. 2016. *Hotel Mexico: Dwelling on the '68 Movement*. Berkeley: University of California Press.

Florescano, Enrique. 1993. "La creación del Museo Nacional de Antropología y sus fines científicos, educativos y políticos." In *El patrimonio cultural de México*, edited by Enrique Florescano, 145–64. Mexico City: Consejo Nacional para la Cultura y las Artes.

Foster, George M. 1964. "Treasure Tales, and the Image of the Static Economy in a Mexican Peasant Community." *Journal of American Folklore* 77, no. 303: 39–44. https://doi.org/10.2307/538017.

Foucault, Michel. 2007. *Security, Territory, Population: Lectures at the Collège de France, 1977–78*. London: Palgrave Macmillan.

Gamou, Gustavo, dir. 2011. *Granicero*. 52 min. Jacaranda Correa.

Gänger, Stefanie. 2014. *Relics of the Past: The Collecting and Study of Pre-Hispanic Antiquities in Peru and Chile, 1837–1911*. Oxford: Oxford University Press.

García Canclini, Néstor. 1992. *Culturas híbridas: Estrategias para entrar y salir de la modernidad*. Buenos Aires: Editorial Sudamericana.

García Ramos, Salvador. 1982. *Tlaloc: El dios de la lluvia*. Mexico City: GV Editores.

Garrigan, Shelley E. 2012. *Collecting Mexico: Museums, Monuments, and the Creation of National Identity*. Minneapolis: University of Minnesota Press.

Geismar, Haidy. 2012. "Museum + Digital =?" In *Digital Anthropology*, edited by Heather A. Horst and Daniel Miller, 266–87. London: Berg.

Geismar, Haidy, and Katja Müller. 2022. "Postcolonial Digital Collections: Instruments, Mirrors, Agents." In *The Routledge Companion to Media Anthropology*, edited by Elisabetta Costa, Patricia G. Lange, Nell Haynes, and Jolynna Sinanan, 258–71. London: Routledge.

Gell, Alfred. 1993. *Wrapping in Images: Tattooing in Polynesia*. Oxford: Oxford University Press.

Gennep, Arnold van. 1909. *Les rites de passage: Étude systématique des rites de la porte et du seuil, de l'hospitalité, de l'adoption, de la grossesse et de l'accouchement, de la naissance, de l'enfance, de la puberté, de l'initiation, de l'ordination, du couronnement des fiançailles et du mariage, des funérailles, des saisons, etc.* Paris: E. Nourry.

Gillingham, Paul. 2011. *Cuauhtémoc's Bones: Forging National Identity in Modern Mexico*. Albuquerque: University of New Mexico Press.

Gillingham, Paul, and Benjamin T. Smith, eds. 2014. *Dictablanda: Politics, Work, and Culture in Mexico, 1938–1968*. Durham, NC: Duke University Press.

Giraudo, Laura. 2008. *Anular las distancias: Los gobiernos posrevolucionarios en México y la transformación cultural de indios y campesinos*. Madrid: Centro de Estudios Políticos y Constitucionales.

Glockner, Julio. 2012. *Los volcanes sagrados: Mitos y rituales en el Popocatépetl y la Iztlaccíhuatl*. Mexico City: Santillana.

Gnecco, Cristóbal. 2015. "Heritage in Multicultural Times." In *The Palgrave Handbook of Contemporary Heritage Research*, edited by Emma Waterton and Steve Watson, 263–80. London: Palgrave Macmillan.

Gnecco, Cristóbal. 2019. *El señuelo patrimonial: Pensamientos post-arqueológicos en el camino de los incas*. Tunja: Universidad Pedagógica y Tecnológica de Colombia.

Gnecco, Cristóbal. 2021. "Patrimonialización como despojo: Tiempos otros y tiempos de otros." *Mélanges de la Casa de Velázquez* 51, no. 2: 319–24. https://doi.org/10.4000/mcv.15558.

Gnecco, Cristóbal, and Mario Rufer, eds. 2023. *El Tiempo de las ruinas*. Bogotá: Universidad de los Andes.

Goldstein, Donna M. 2013. *Laughter Out of Place: Race, Class, Violence, and Sexuality in a Rio Shantytown*. Berkeley: University of California Press.

Gómez-Barris, Macarena. 2017. *The Extractive Zone: Social Ecologies and Decolonial Perspectives*. Durham, NC: Duke University Press.

González Mello, Renato. 2017. "When the State Is the Estate: Copyright and Patrimony in Mexico." *Art Journal* 76, no. 1: 170–76. https://doi.org/10.1080/00043249.2017.1332915.

González-Ruibal, Alfredo. 2013. "Embracing Destruction." In *Destruction: Archaeological, Philological and Historical Perspectives*, edited by Jan Driessen, 37–51. Louvain: Presses Universitaires de Louvain.

González-Ruibal, Alfredo. 2018. *An Archaeology of the Contemporary Era*. Oxford: Routledge.

González Torres, Yólotl. 2005. *Danza tu palabra: La danza de los concheros*. Mexico City: Plaza y Valdés.

Gorbach, Frida. 2008. *El monstruo, objeto imposible: Un estudio sobre teratología mexicana, siglo XIX*. Mexico City: Universidad Autónoma Metropolitana, Unidad Xochimilco.

Gorbach, Frida. 2016. "Commemorate, Consecrate, Demolish: Thoughts About the Mexican Museum of Anthropology and Its History." In *Entangled Heritages: Postcolonial Perspectives on the Uses of the Past in Latin America*, edited by Olaf Kaltmeier and Mario Rufer, 109–22. New York: Routledge.

Gordillo, Gastón. 2004. *Landscapes of Devils: Tensions of Place and Memory in the Argentinean Chaco*. Durham, NC: Duke University Press.

Gordillo, Gastón. 2009. "Places That Frighten: Residues of Wealth and Violence on the Argentine Chaco Frontier." *Anthropologica* 51, no. 2: 343–51.

Gordillo, Gastón. 2014. *Rubble: The Afterlife of Destruction*. Durham, NC: Duke University Press.

Gordillo, Gastón. 2018. "Terrain as Insurgent Weapon: An Affective Geometry of Warfare in the Mountains of Afghanistan." *Political Geography* 64 (May): 53–62. https://doi.org/10.1016/j.polgeo.2018.03.001.

Gordillo, Gastón. 2020. "Gravity: On the Primacy of Terrain." In *Voluminous States: Sovereignty, Materiality, and the Territorial Imagination*, edited by Franck Billé, 159–72. Durham, NC: Duke University Press.

Gordillo, Gastón. 2021. "The Power of Terrain: The Affective Materiality of Planet Earth in the Age of Revolution." *Dialogues in Human Geography* 11, no. 2: 190–94. https://doi.org/10.1177/2043820621100123.

Grant, Bruce. 2009. *The Captive and the Gift: Cultural Histories of Sovereignty in Russia and the Caucasus*. Ithaca, NY: Cornell University Press.

Grant, Jenna. 2017. "Fixing Things, Moving Stories." In *The Ethnographic Case*, edited by Emily Yates-Doerr and Christine Labuski, 245–50. Manchester: Mattering Press.

Grindle, Merilee. 2023. *In the Shadow of Quetzalcoatl: Zelia Nuttall and the Search for Mexico's Ancient Civilizations*. Cambridge, MA: Belknap Press of Harvard University Press.

Guerra, François Xavier. 1985. *Le Mexique de l'Ancien Régime à la Révolution*. Paris: L'Hartmattan.

Haber, Alejandro. 2017. *Al otro lado del vestigio: Políticas del conocimiento y arqueología indisciplinada*. Popoyán: Universidad del Cauca.

Hamann, Byron E. 2011. "Inquisition and Social Conflicts in Sixteenth-Century Yanhuitlan and Valencia: Catholic Colonizations in the Early Modern Transatlantic World." PhD diss., University of Chicago.

Hamilakis, Yannis. 2007. *The Nation and Its Ruins: Antiquity, Archaeology, and National Imagination in Greece*. Oxford: Oxford University Press.

Harris, Marvin. 1964. *Patterns of Race in the Americas*. New York: Walker.

Harrison, Rodney. 2011. "Surface Assemblages: Towards an Archaeology in and of the Present." *Archaeological Dialogues* 18, no. 2: 141–61. https://doi.org/10.1017/S1380203811000195.

Harvey, Penny, and Hannah Knox. 2015. *Roads: An Anthropology of Infrastructure and Expertise*. Ithaca, NY: Cornell University Press.

Haugerud, Angelique. 2013. *No Billionaire Left Behind: Satirical Activism in America*. Stanford, CA: Stanford University Press.

Heizer, Robert F., and Howel Williams. 1963. "Geologic Notes on the Idolo de Coatlinchán." *American Antiquity* 29, no. 1: 95–98. https://doi.org/10.2307/278639.

Henare, Amiria J. M. 2005. *Museums, Anthropology and Imperial Exchange*. Cambridge: Cambridge University Press.

Hennessy, Kate. 2010. "Repatriation, Digital Technology, and Culture in a Northern Athapaskan Community." PhD diss., University of British Columbia.

Hennessy, Kate, Natasha Lyons, Stephen Loring, Charles Arnold, Mervin Joe, Albert Elias, and James Pokiak. 2013. "The Inuvialuit Living History Project: Digital Return as the Forging of Relationships Between Institutions, People, and Data." *Museum Anthropology Review* 7, nos. 1–2: 44–73. https://scholarworks.iu.edu/journals/index.php/mar/article/view/2039.

Hermann Lejarazu, Manuel. 2019. "El entorno simbólico-territorial del Mapa de Teozacoalco: Representación del paisaje y sus linderos." *Anales de Antropología* 53, no. 2: 11–27. https://doi.org/10.22201/iia.24486221e.2019.2.67126.

Hernández Bravo, Fernando, dir. 1964. *Monumento de monumentos*. Instituto Nacional de Antropología e Historia, Mexico City.

Hicks, Dan. 2020. *The Brutish Museums: The Benin Bronzes, Colonial Violence and Cultural Restitution*. London: Pluto Press.

Holley-Kline, Sam. 2025. *In the Shadow of El Tajín: The Political Economy of Archaeology in Modern Mexico*. Lincoln: University of Nebraska Press.

Holley-Kline, Sam, and Allison Mickel. 2024. "Introduction: Archaeological Labor in Historical Contexts." *Bulletin of the History of Archaeology* 34, no. 1. https://doi.org/10.5334/bha-726.

Hoobler, Ellen. 2006. "'To Take Their Heritage in Their Hands': Indigenous Self-Representation and Decolonization in the Community Museums of Oaxaca, Mexico." *American Indian Quarterly* 30, nos. 3–4: 441–60. https://doi.org/10.1353/aiq.2006.0024.

Huberts, Alyssa, David Palma, Ana Cecilia Bernal García, Faith Cole, and Elizabeth F. S. Roberts. 2023. "Making Scarcity 'Enough': The Hidden Household Costs of Adapting to Water Scarcity in Mexico City." *PLoS Water* 2, no. 3. https://doi.org/10.1371/journal.pwat.0000056.

Hull, Matthew S. 2012. *Government of Paper: The Materiality of Bureaucracy in Urban Pakistan*. Berkeley: University of California Press.

Jácome, Cristóbal Andrés. 2014. "Palimpsestos constructivos: La impronta del pasado prehispánico en la modernización mexicana." *CAIANA: Revista de Historia del Arte y Cultura Visual del Centro Argentino de Investigadores de Arte (CAIA)*, no. 4: 1–14. https://caiana.caiana.com.ar/dossier/2014-1-04-d07/.

Jennings, Justin, and Adam T. Sellen, eds. 2018. *Real Fake: The Story of a Zapotec Urn*. Ottawa: Royal Ontario Museum.

Jofré, Ivana Carina. 2022. "Interrumpiendo el discurso patrimonial: Crítica y resistencia al neoextractivismo minero en Argentina." *Heterotopías* 5, no. 9: 1–26. https://revistas.unc.edu.ar/index.php/heterotopias/article/view/38162.

Joseph, Gilbert M., and Jürgen Buchenau. 2013. *Mexico's Once and Future Revolution: Social Upheaval and the Challenge of Rule Since the Late Nineteenth Century*. Durham, NC: Duke University Press.

Josten, Jennifer. 2018. *Mathias Goeritz: Modernist Art and Architecture in Cold War Mexico*. New Haven, CT: Yale University Press.

Kernaghan, Richard. 2022a. *Crossing the Current: Aftermaths of War Along the Huallaga River*. Stanford, CA: Stanford University Press.

Kernaghan, Richard. 2022b. "El trueno lejano: Imágenes que persisten en el río Huallaga." *Encartes* 5, no. 9: 59–85. https://doi.org/10.29340/en.v5n9.226.

Kernaghan, Richard, and Gabriela Zamorano Villarreal. 2022. "Obtuso es el sentido: Visualidad y práctica etnográfica." *Encartes* 5, no. 9: 1–27. https://doi.org/10.29340/en.v5n9.274.

Kirchhoff, Paul. 1943. "Mesoamérica: Sus límites geográficos, composición étnica y caracteres culturales." *Acta Americana: Revista de la Sociedad Interamericana de Antropología y Geografía* 1, no. 1: 92–107.

Khayyat, Munira. 2022. *A Landscape of War: Ecologies of Resistance and Survival in South Lebanon*. Berkeley: University of California Press.

Kohl, Philip L., and Clare P. Fawcett, eds. 1995. *Nationalism, Politics, and the Practice of Archaeology*. Cambridge: Cambridge University Press.

Koselleck, Reinhart. 2004. *Futures Past: On the Semantics of Historical Time*. New York: Columbia University Press.

Kourí, Emilio. 2017. "Sobre la propiedad comunal de los pueblos, de la reforma a la revolución." *Historia Mexicana* 66, no. 4: 1923–60. https://doi.org/10.24201/hm.v66i4.3422.

Kourí, Emilio. 2020. "On the Mexican Ejido." *Humanity: An International Journal of Human Rights, Humanitarianism, and Development* 11, no. 2: 222–26. https://doi.org/10.1353/hum.2020.0013.

Kovács Lajos. 2024. "The Campfire Stories of Russell Marker, a Pioneer of Chemistry." *Notes and Records* 78, no. 3: 467–92. https://doi.org/10.1098/rsnr.2023.0022.

Kubler, George. 1962a. *The Art and Architecture of Ancient America: The Mexican, Maya and Andean Peoples*. New York: Viking-Penguin.

Kubler, George. 1962b. *The Shape of Time: Remarks on the History of Things*. New Haven, CT: Yale University Press.

Kuri Pineda, Edith. 2010. "El movimiento social de Atenco: Experiencia y construcción de sentido." *Andamios* 7, no. 14: 321–45. https://doi.org/10.29092/uacm.v7i14.110.

Larkin, Brian. 2013. "The Politics and Poetics of Infrastructure." *Annual Review of Anthropology* 42 (October): 327–43. https://doi.org/10.1146/annurev-anthro-092412-155522.

Latour, Bruno. 1987. *Science in Action: How to Follow Scientists and Engineers Through Society*. Cambridge, MA: Harvard University Press.

Latour, Bruno. 1993. *We Have Never Been Modern*. Cambridge, MA: Harvard University Press.

Law, John. 1987. "Technology and Heterogeneous Engineering: The Case of Portuguese Expansion." In *The Social Construction of Technological Systems: New Directions in the Sociology and History of Technology*, edited by Wiebe E. Bijker, Thomas P. Hughes, and Trevor Pinch, 111–34. Cambridge, MA: MIT Press.

Leal Martínez, Alejandra M. 2016. "La ciudadanía neoliberal y la racialización de los sectores populares en la renovación urbana de la ciudad de México." *Revista Colombiana de Antropología* 52, no. 1: 223–44. https://doi.org/10.22380/2539472X9.

Leathem, Hilary Morgan. 2019. "Manifestations That Matter: A Case of Oaxacan Ruin Possession." *Archaeological Review from Cambridge* 34, no. 2: 93–100. https://doi.org/10.17863/CAM.59741.

Le Guin, Ursula K. 1987. "Three Rock Poems." In *Buffalo Gals and Other Animal Presences*, 55–60. New York: Capra.

Lehmann, Pedro A. 1992. "Early History of Steroid Chemistry in Mexico: The Story of Three Remarkable Men." *Steroids* 57, no. 8: 403–8. https://doi.org/10.1016/0039-128X(92)90084-M.

Lejeal, Léon. 1905. "Alfredo Chavero: El Monolito de Coatlinchan." *Journal de la Société des Américanistes*, no. 2: 295–96.

Lerner, Jesse. 2001. "Brígido Lara: Post-Pre-Columbian Ceramicist: Making the Old Anew." *Cabinet* 2. https://www.cabinetmagazine.org/issues/2/lerner.php.

Lévi-Strauss, Claude. 1963. *Structural Anthropology*. Translated by Claire Jacobson and Brooke Grundfest Schoepf. New York: Basic Books.

Liffman, Paul M. 2011. *Huichol Territory and the Mexican Nation: Indigenous Ritual, Land Conflict, and Sovereignty Claims*. Tucson: University of Arizona Press.

Lockhart, James. 1992. *The Nahuas After the Conquest: A Social and Cultural History of the Indians of Central Mexico, Sixteenth Through Eighteenth Centuries.* Stanford, CA: Stanford University Press.

Lombardo de Ruiz, Sonia, and Ruth Solís Vicarte. 1988. *Antecedentes de las leyes sobre monumentos históricos (1536–1910).* Mexico City: Instituto Nacional de Antropología e Historia.

Lomnitz, Cinna. 1988. "The 1985 Mexico Earthquake." In *Natural and Man-Made Hazards,* edited by Mohammed I. El-Sabh and Tadepalli Satyanarayana Murty, 63–79. Dordrecht: Springer Netherlands.

Lomnitz, Cinna. 1990. "Gravity Waves in Earthquakes?" *Engineering Geology* 29, no. 1: 95–97. https://doi.org/10.1016/0013-7952(90)90084-E.

Lomnitz, Cinna, and Heriberta Castaños. 2006. "Earthquake Hazard in the Valley of Mexico: Entropy, Structure, Complexity." In *Earthquake Source Asymmetry, Structural Media and Rotation Effects,* edited by Roman Teisseyre, Eugeniusz Majewski, and Minoru Takeo, 347–64. Berlin: Springer.

Lomnitz, Claudio. 1996. "Ritual, rumor y corrupción en la formación del espacio nacional en México." *Revista Mexicana de Sociología* 58, no. 2: 21–51. https://doi.org/10.2307/3540967.

Lomnitz, Claudio. 1999. "Modes of Citizenship in Mexico." *Public Culture* 11, no. 1: 269–93. https://doi.org/10.1215/08992363-11-1-269.

Lomnitz, Claudio. 2001. *Deep Mexico, Silent Mexico: An Anthropology of Nationalism.* Minneapolis: University of Minnesota Press.

Lomnitz, Claudio. 2005. "Sobre reciprocidad negativa." *Revista de Antropología Social* 14: 311–39. https://www.redalyc.org/pdf/838/83801412.pdf.

Londoño, Wilhem. 2016. "Fact and Law: Guaquería and Archaeology in Colombia." In *Challenging the Dichotomy: The Licit and the Illicit in Archaeological and Heritage Discourses,* edited by Les W. Field, Cristóbal Gnecco, and Joe Watkin, 41–56. Tucson: University of Arizona Press.

López Austin, Alfredo. 1996. *Los mitos del tlacuache: Caminos de la mitología mesoamericana.* Mexico City: Universidad Nacional Autónoma de México.

López Beltrán, Carlos, Vivette García Deister, and Mariana Ríos Sandoval. 2014. "Negotiating the Mexican Mestizo: On the Possibility of a National Genomics." In *Mestizo Genomics: Race Mixture, Nation, and Science in Latin America,* edited by Peter Wade, Carlos López Beltrán, Eduardo Restrepo, and Ricardo Ventura Santos, 85–106. Durham, NC: Duke University Press.

López Caballero, Paula. 2003. *Los títulos primordiales del centro de México.* Mexico City: Consejo Nacional para la Cultura y las Artes.

López Caballero, Paula. 2017. *Indígenas de la nación: Etnografía histórica de la alteridad en México (Milpa Alta, siglos XVII–XXI).* Mexico City: Fondo de Cultura Económica.

López Caballero, Paula. 2021. "Inhabiting Identities: On the Elusive Quality of Indigenous Identity in Mexico." *Journal of Latin American and Caribbean Anthropology* 26, no. 1: 124–46. https://doi.org/10.1111/jlca.12535.

López Hernández, Haydeé. 2013. "De la gloria prehispánica al socialismo: Las políticas indigenistas del Cardenismo." *Cuicuilco* 20, no. 57: 47–74.

López Hernández, Haydeé. 2018. *En busca del alma nacional: La arqueología y la construcción del origen de la historia nacional en México (1867–1942)*. Mexico City: Instituto Nacional de Antropología e Historia.

López Hernández, Haydeé. 2019. "Los indios del Museo Nacional de Antropología: Una mirada paralela." *Dimensión Antropológica* 76, no. 26: 163–94. https://revistas.inah .gob.mx/index.php/dimension/article/view/15481.

López Hernández, Haydeé. 2024. *Retrato del Mezquital: Antonio Rodríguez y la imagen del otomí en la modernización del Estado Mexicano a mediados del siglo XX*. Mexico City: Instituto Nacional de Antropología e Historia.

Lorente Fernández, David. 2008. "Deidades de la lluvia, graniceros y ofrendas terapéuticas en la Sierra de Texcoco." *Anales de Antropología* 42: 167–201. https://doi.org/10 .22201/iia.24486221e.2008.0.19003.

Lorente Fernández, David. 2009. "Graniceros, los ritualistas del rayo en México: Historia y etnografía." *Cuicuilco* 16, no. 47: 201–23.

Lorente Fernández, David. 2011. *La razzia cósmica: Una concepción nahua sobre el clima: Deidades del agua y graniceros en la Sierra de Texcoco*. Mexico City: Centro de Investigaciones y Estudios Superiores en Antropología Social and Universidad Iberoamericana.

Lorente Fernández, David. 2017. "Tesifteros, los graniceros de la Sierra de Texcoco: Repensando el don, la experiencia onírica y el parentesco espiritual." *Dimensión Antropológica* 70: 101–50. https://revistas.inah.gob.mx/index.php/dimension/article/view /11738.

Lynch, Michael, and Steve Woolgar, eds. 1990. *Representation in Scientific Practice*. Cambridge, MA: MIT Press.

Mackie, Edith, and Sheldon Dick. 1935. *Mexican Journey: An Intimate Guide to Mexico*. New York: Dodge Publishing.

Magazine, Roger. 2019. "Dos visiones de la región de Texcoco: Periferia urbana y centro moral." In *Periferias: Antropología en los límites de la ciudad y la cultura*, edited by María Ana Portal Ariosa and Antonio Zirión Pérez, 149–74. Mexico City: Universidad Autónoma Metropolitana, Unidad Iztapalapa, and Editorial Gedisa.

Magazine, Roger, and Tomás Martínez Saldaña, eds. 2010. *Texcoco en el nuevo milenio: Cambio y continuidad en una región periurbana del Valle de México*. Mexico City: Universidad Iberoamericana.

Maldonado Ortíz, Carlos. 1993. "La Presa de la Amistad: Un mar artificial entre dos países." *México Desconocido*, no. 199. https://escapadas.mexicodesconocido.com.mx /atractivos/presa-de-la-amistad/.

Marchese, Giulia. 2019. "Del cuerpo en el territorio al cuerpo-territorio: Elementos para una genealogía feminista latinoamericana de la crítica a la violencia." *EntreDiversidades: Revista de Ciencias Sociales y Humanidades* 6, no. 2: 9–41. https://doi.org/10 .31644/ED.V6.N2.2019.A01.

Marcus, George E. 1988. "Parody and the Parodic in Polynesian Cultural History." *Cultural Anthropology* 3, no. 1: 68–76. https://doi.org/10.1525/can.1988.3.1.02a00060.

Martin, Emily. 1989. "The Cultural Construction of Gendered Bodies: Biology and Metaphors of Production and Destruction." *Ethnos* 54, nos. 3–4: 143–60. https://doi .org/10.1080/00141844.1989.9981390.

Martin, Emily. 1991. "The Egg and the Sperm: How Science Has Constructed a Romance Based on Stereotypical Male-Female Roles." *Signs: Journal of Women in Culture and Society* 16, no. 3: 485–501. https://doi.org/10.1086/494680.

Martínez Assad, Carlos. 2005. *La patria en el Paseo de La Reforma*. Mexico City: Fondo de Cultura Económica and Universidad Nacional Autónoma de México.

Martínez de Verburg, Graciela, and John A. Verburg Moore. 1964. *San Miguel Coatlinchán: Estudio sobre un ejido marginal en el Estado de México*. Mexico City: Organización de los Estados Americanos.

Masco, Joseph. 2008. "'SURVIVAL IS YOUR BUSINESS': Engineering Ruins and Affect in Nuclear America." *Cultural Anthropology* 23, no. 2: 361–98. https://doi.org/10.1111/j.1548-1360.2008.00012.x.

Mateos Higuera, Salvador. 1945. "Colección de estudios sumarios de los códices pictóricos indígenas: Códice de Coatlinchan, Texcoco." *Tlalocan* 2, no. 1: 35–36. https://revistas-filologicas.unam.mx/tlalocan/index.php/tl/article/download/391/387.

Matory, James Lorand. 2018. *The Fetish Revisited: Marx, Freud, and the Gods Black People Make*. Durham, NC: Duke University Press.

McAllister, Carlota, and Valentina Napolitano. 2020. "Introduction: Incarnate Politics Beyond the Cross and the Sword." *Social Analysis* 64, no. 4: 1–20. https://doi.org/10.3167/sa.2020.640401.

McAllister, Carlota, and Valentina Napolitano. 2021. "Political Theology/Theopolitics: The Thresholds and Vulnerabilities of Sovereignty." *Annual Review of Anthropology* 50, no. 1: 109–24. https://doi.org/10.1146/annurev-anthro-101819-110334.

McAllister, Carlota, and Diane M. Nelson. 2013. "Aftermath: Harvests of Violence and Histories of the Future." In *War by Other Means: Aftermath in Post-Genocide Guatemala*, edited by Carlota McAllister and Diane Nelson, 1–49. Durham, NC: Duke University Press.

Mcdonough, Kelly S. 2017. "Plotting Indigenous Stories, Land, and People: Primordial Titles and Narrative Mapping in Colonial Mexico." *Journal for Early Modern Cultural Studies* 17, no. 1: 1–30. https://doi.org/10.1353/jem.2017.0003.

Melville, Roberto. 2011. "The Influence of The People of Puerto Rico Project on Mexican Anthropology." *Identities* 18, no. 3: 229–33. https://doi.org/10.1080/1070289X.2011.635285.

Mendoza Fragoso, Ariana. 2021. "La huida de la sirena: Una narrativa del desastre de la desecación y el despojo en los pueblos ribereños al noreste de la Ciudad de México." *Revista de Antropología y Sociología: Virajes* 23, no. 2: 23–58. https://doi.org/ 10.17151/rasv.2021.23.2.3.

Mendoza Fragoso, Ariana. 2022. "Vivir a la orilla, vivir en el fango: La producción destructiva en la ribera nororiental del Lago de Texcoco, México." PhD diss., Centro de Investigaciones y Estudios Superiores en Antropología Social.

Meskell, Lynn. 2000. "The Practice and Politics of Archaeology in Egypt." *Annals of the New York Academy of Sciences* 925, no. 1: 146–69. https://doi.org/10.1111/j.1749-6632.2000.tb05588.x.

Meskell, Lynn. 2002. "Negative Heritage and Past Mastering in Archaeology." *Anthropological Quarterly* 75, no. 3: 557–74. https://doi.org/10.1353/anq.2002.0050.

Meskell, Lynn. ed. 2008. *Archaeologies of Materiality*. Oxford: Blackwell.

Minera, María. 2020. "De zombis y monumentos." *Revista Código*, March 12. https://revistacodigo.com/feministas-monumentos/.

Mitchell, Lisa M., and Eugenia Georges. 1997. "Cross-Cultural Cyborgs: Greek and Canadian Women's Discourses on Fetal Ultrasound." *Feminist Studies* 23, no. 2: 373–401. https://doi.org/10.2307/3178405.

Mitchell, Lisa M., and Eugenia Georges. 2001. *Baby's First Picture: Ultrasound and the Politics of Fetal Subjects*. Toronto: University of Toronto Press.

Mitchell, Timothy. 2002. *Rule of Experts: Egypt, Techno-Politics, Modernity*. Berkeley: University of California Press.

Mohar Betancourt, Luz María. 1994. *Mapa de Coatlinchan: Líneas y colores en el Acolhuacan*. Mexico City: Instituto Nacional de Antropología e Historia and Benemérita Universidad Autónoma de Puebla.

Monsiváis, Carlos. 1977. "Notas sobre la cultura mexicana en el siglo XX." In *Historia general de México*, vol. 4, edited by Daniel Cosío Villegas, 303–476. Mexico City: El Colegio de México.

Mora, Mariana. 2017. *Kuxlejal Politics: Indigenous Autonomy, Race, and Decolonizing Research in Zapatista Communities*. Austin: University of Texas Press.

Morales, Alfonso. 2005. "La Venus se fue de juerga: Ámbitos de la fotografía mexicana, 1940–1970." In *Imaginarios y fotografía en México 1839/1970*, edited by Emma Cecilia García Krinsky, 180–267. Barcelona: Lunwerg Editores.

Morales Moreno, Luis Gerardo. 1994. *Orígenes de la museología mexicana: Fuentes para el estudio histórico del Museo Nacional, 1780–1940*. Mexico City: Universidad Iberoamericana.

Morehart, Christopher T. 2012. "What if the Aztec Empire Never Existed? The Prerequisites of Empire and the Politics of Plausible Alternative Histories." *American Anthropologist* 114, no. 2: 267–81. https://doi.org/10.1111/j.1548-1433.2012.01424.x.

Moreno Figueroa, Mónica Gabriela. 2010. "Distributed Intensities: Whiteness, Mestizaje and the Logics of Mexican Racism." *Ethnicities* 10, no. 3: 387–401. https://doi.org/10.1177/1468796810372305.

Moreno Figueroa, Mónica Gabriela. 2022. "Entre confusiones y distracciones: Mestizaje y racismo anti-negro en México." *Estudios Sociológicos De El Colegio De México* 40: 87–118. https://doi.org/10.24201/es.2022v40.2084.

Moreno Sánchez, Enrique. 2010. "El aeropuerto y el movimiento social de Atenco." *Convergencia* 17, no. 52: 79–96. https://www.scielo.org.mx/scielo.php?script=sci_arttext&pid=S1405-14352010000100004.

Moreno Sánchez, Enrique. 2014. "Atenco, a diez años del movimiento social por el proyecto del aeropuerto. Análisis socio-urbano y político." *Estudios Demográficos y Urbanos* 29, no. 3: 541–78. https://doi.org/10.24201/edu.v29i3.1471.

Moser, Stephanie. 2014. "Making Expert Knowledge Through the Image: Connections Between Antiquarian and Early Modern Scientific Illustration." *Isis* 105, no. 1: 58–99. https://doi.org/10.1086/675551.

Mrázek, Rudolf. 2002. *Engineers of Happy Land: Technology and Nationalism in a Colony*. Princeton, NJ: Princeton University Press.

Mueggler, Erik. 2001. *The Age of Wild Ghosts: Memory, Violence, and Place in Southwest China*. Berkeley: University of California Press.

Mundy, Barbara E. 2015. *The Death of Aztec Tenochtitlan, the Life of Mexico City*. Austin: University of Texas Press.

Musset, Alain. 1992. *El agua en el valle de México, siglos XVI–XVIII*. Mexico City: Centro de Estudios Mexicanos y Centroamericanos.

Myers, Fred R., ed. 2001. *The Empire of Things: Regimes of Value and Material Culture*. Santa Fe, NM: School of American Research Press.

Nash, June C. 1993. *We Eat the Mines and the Mines Eat Us: Dependency and Exploitation in Bolivian Tin Mines*. New York: Columbia University Press.

Navaro-Yashin, Yael. 2009. "Affective Spaces, Melancholic Objects: Ruination and the Production of Anthropological Knowledge." *Journal of the Royal Anthropological Institute* 15, no. 1: 1–18. https://doi.org/10.1111/j.1467-9655.2008.01527.x.

Navaro-Yashin, Yael. 2012. *The Make-Believe Space: Affective Geography in a Postwar Polity*. Durham, NC: Duke University Press.

Navaro-Yashin, Yael. 2020. *Faces of the State: Secularism and Public Life in Turkey*. Princeton, NJ: Princeton University Press.

Navaro-Yashin, Yael, Zerrin Özlem Biner, Alice von Bieberstein, and Seda Altuğ, eds. 2021. *Reverberations: Violence Across Time and Space*. Philadelphia: University of Pennsylvania Press.

Navarrete Linares, Federico. 2010. "Ruinas y Estado: Arqueología de una simbiosis mexicana." In *Pueblos indígenas y arqueología en América Latina*, edited by Cristóbal Genecco and Patricia Ayala Rocabado, 65–84. Bogotá: Universidad de los Andes.

Navarrete Linares, Federico. 2011. *Los orígenes de los pueblos indígenas del Valle de México: Los altépetl y sus historias*. Mexico City: Universidad Nacional Autónoma de México.

Navarrete Linares, Federico. n.d. "El Altépetl." *Noticonquista*. Accessed March 17, 2025. http://www.noticonquista.unam.mx/amoxtli/765/744.

Neurath, Johannes. 2005. "Máscaras en mascaradas: Indígenas, mestizos y dioses indígenas mestizos." *Relaciones: Estudios de Historia y Sociedad* 26, no. 101: 22–50.

Noelle, Louise. 2001. "Integración plástica y funcionalismo: El edificio del Cárcamo del Sistema Hidráulico Lerma y Ricardo Rivas." *Anales del Instituto de Investigaciones Estéticas* 23, no. 78: 189–202.

Noelle, Louise. 2008. *Mario Pani*. Mexico City: Universidad Nacional Autónoma de México.

Noguera, Eduardo. 1964. "El monolito de Coatlinchan." *Anales de Antropología*, 1, no. 1: 131–43.

Nuijten, Monique. 1998. "In the Name of the Land: Organization, Transnationalism and the Culture of the State in a Mexican Ejido." PhD diss., Wageningen University.

Nuijten, Monique. 2003. "Illegal Practices and the Re-Enchantment of Governmental Techniques: Land and the Law in Mexico." *Journal of Legal Pluralism and Unofficial Law* 35, no. 48: 163–83. https://doi.org/10.1080/07329113.2003.10756570.

Olivares Sandoval, Omar. 2020. "Velasco, José Maria." *Grove Art Online*. Oxford: Oxford University Press. https://doi.org/10.1093/gao/9781884446054.article.T088452.

Olivares Sandoval, Omar. 2021. "The Axolotl Scientific Images of José María Velasco and Their Role in Nineteenth-Century Evolutionary Thinking." *Nuncius* 36, no. 1: 1–24. https://doi.org/10.1163/18253911-bja10005.

Olivier, Laurent. 2013. "The Business of Archaeology Is the Present." In *Reclaiming Archaeology: Beyond the Tropes of Modernity*, edited by Alfredo González-Ruibal, 117–29. London: Routledge.

Olivier, Laurent. 2019. "The Future of Archaeology in the Age of Presentism." *Journal of Contemporary Archaeology* 6, no. 1: 16–31. https://doi.org/10.1558/jca.33674.

Ortíz Sánchez, Marcelo (Tlakuanikoatl Ocelotl Xicome), and Calpulli Makoyolotzin. 2006. *Coatlinchan, su morada de la serpiente, donde mora la sabiduría, lugar donde habita gente sabia*. Mexico City: n.p.

Owensby, Brian Philip. 2008. *Empire of Law and Indian Justice in Colonial Mexico*. Stanford: Stanford University Press.

Özyürek, Esra. 2004. "Miniaturizing Atatürk Privatization of State Imagery and Ideology in Turkey." *American Ethnologist* 31, no. 3: 374–91. https://doi.org/10.1525/ae.2004.31.3.374.

Özyürek, Esra. 2006. *Nostalgia for the Modern: State Secularism and Everyday Politics in Turkey*. Durham, NC: Duke University Press.

Palerm, Ángel. 1973. *Obras hidráulicas prehispánicas en el sistema lacustre del Valle de México*. Mexico City: Instituto Nacional de Antropología e Historia.

Pasztory, Esther. 2002. "Truth in Forgery." *RES: Anthropology and Aesthetics* 42: 159–65. https://doi.org/10.1086/RESv42n1ms20167576.

Paulara, Daniela Pascual Cáceres, and Elena Taylor Muñoz. "Restauradoras con Glitter contra la criminalización de la protesta." *Memorias Disidentes: Revista de Estudios Críticos del Patrimonio, Archivos y Memorias* 1, no. 2: 207-12. https://dialnet.unirioja.es/servlet/articulo?codigo=9744426.

Paulinyi, Zoltán. 2006. "The 'Great Goddess' of Teotihuacan: Fiction or Reality?" *Ancient Mesoamerica* 17, no. 1: 1–15. https://doi.org/10.1017/S0956536106060020.

Payno, Manuel. (1891) 1996. *Los bandidos de Río Frío*. Mexico City: Porrúa.

Peers, Laura. 2017. "The Magic of Bureaucracy: Repatriation as Ceremony." *Museum Worlds* 5, no. 1: 9–21. https://doi.org/10.3167/armw.2017.050103.

Peers, Laura, and Alison K. Brown, eds. 2003. *Museums and Source Communities: A Routledge Reader*. London: Routledge.

Peers, Laura, Lotten Gustafsson Reinius, and Jennifer Shannon. 2017. "Introduction: Repatriation and Ritual, Repatriation as Ritual." *Museum Worlds* 5, no. 1: 1–8. https://doi.org/10.3167/armw.2017.050102.

Peleggi, Maurizio. 2022. "When Shrines and Images Grow Tired: Toward a Theory of Devotional Conservation. *Res: Anthropology and Aesthetics* 77–78: 157–166. https://doi.org/10.1086/719600.

Peñafiel, Antonio. 1890. *Monumentos del arte mexicano antiguo: Ornamentación, mitología, tributos y monumentos*. Vol. 1. Berlin: A. Asher.

Peña Martínez, Francisco de la. 2002. *Los hijos del sexto sol: Un estudio etnopsicoanalítico del movimiento de la mexicanidad*. Mexico City: Instituto Nacional de Antropología e Historia.

Peña Martínez, Francisco de la. 2012. "Profecías de la mexicanidad: Entre el milenarismo nacionalista y la new age." *Cuicuilco* 19, no. 55: 127–43. https://revistas.inah.gob.mx/index.php/cuicuilco/article/view/396.

Peña Martínez, Francisco de la, and Renée de la Torre. 2012. "Presentación [Dossier: La mexicanidad y el neoindianismo hoy]." *Cuicuilco* 19, no. 55: 123–26. https://revistas .inah.gob.mx/index.php/cuicuilco/article/view/395.

Petrović, Tanja. 2018. "Political Parody and the Politics of Ambivalence." *Annual Review of Anthropology* 47, no. 1: 201–16. https://doi.org/10.1146/annurev-anthro-102215-100148.

Pietz, William. 1985. "The Problem of the Fetish, I." *RES: Anthropology and Aesthetics* 9, no. 9: 5–17. https://doi.org/10.1086/RESv9n1ms20166719.

Piolle Altamirano, María Elena. 2006. *José María Velasco: Paisajes de luz, horizontes de modernidad*. Mexico City: DGE Equilibrista.

Podgorny, Irina. 2008. "Portable Antiquities: Transportation, Ruins, and Communications in Nineteenth Century Archeology." *História, Ciências, Saúde-Manguinhos* 15, no. 3: 577–95. https://doi.org/10.1590/S0104-59702008000300002.

Pomar, Juan. 1963. "La presencia del monolito de Coatlinchan puede permitir la creación de un tipo diferente de museo." *El Día*, December 30.

Ponce, Armando. 1985. "Veintiún años después: El Tláloc llegó al Museo de Antropología como último recurso, tras frustrados intentos con otras piezas." *Proceso*, September 14.

Poniatowska, Elena. 1971. *La noche de Tlatelolco: Testimonios de historia oral*. Mexico City: Ediciones Era.

Poole, Deborah. 1987. "Landscapes of Power in a Cattle-Rustling Culture of Southern Andean Peru." *Dialectical Anthropology* 12, no. 4: 367–98. https://doi.org/10.1007/ BF00245529.

Poole, Deborah. 1997. *Vision, Race, and Modernity: A Visual Economy of the Andean World*. Princeton, NJ: Princeton University Press.

Poole, Deborah. 1998. "Landscape and the Imperial Subject: U.S. Images of the Andes, 1859–1930." In *Close Encounters of Empire*, edited by Gilbert M. Joseph, Catherine C. LeGrand, and Ricardo D. Salvatore, 107–38. Durham, NC: Duke University Press.

Poole, Deborah. 2005. "An Excess of Description: Ethnography, Race, and Visual Technologies." *Annual Review of Anthropology* 34, no. 1: 159–79. https://doi.org/10.1146/ annurev.anthro.33.070203.144034.

Portal, María Ana, and Vania Salles. 1998. "La tradición oral y la construcción de una figura moderna del mundo en Tlalpan y Xochimilco." *Alteridades*, no. 15: 57–65. https://www.redalyc.org/articulo.oa?id=74745550006.

Povinelli, Elizabeth A. 1995. "Do Rocks Listen? The Cultural Politics of Apprehending Australian Aboriginal Labor." *American Anthropologist* 97, no. 3: 505–18. https://doi .org/10.1525/aa.1995.97.3.02a00090.

Povinelli, Elizabeth A. 2016. *Geontologies: A Requiem to Late Liberalism*. Durham, NC: Duke University Press.

Pulido Rull, Ana. 2020. *Mapping Indigenous Land: Native Land Grants in Colonial New Spain*. Norman: University of Oklahoma Press.

Quintero Wier, José Ángel. ed. 2020. *Las lenguas del diablo: Lengua, cosmovisión y re-existencia de los pueblos de Abya Yala*. [Mexico City]: Tumbalacasa & Arte a 360 grados.

Raffles, Hugh. 2020. *The Book of Unconformities: Speculations on Lost Time*. New York: Pantheon Books.

Ramírez Rojas, Fausto. 2017. *José María Velasco: Pintor de paisajes*. Mexico City: Fondo de Cultura Económica and Universidad Nacional Autónoma de México.

Ramírez Vázquez, Pedro. 2008. *Museo Nacional de Antropología: Gestación, proyecto y construcción*. Mexico City: Instituto Nacional de Antropología e Historia.

Ramonetti Liceaga, Ariadna. 2016. "(Re) inventar la tradición: Actos políticos de resistencia y significaciones rituales en la región de Atenco, Estado de México." *Textual* (Chapingo) 68: 65–79. https://www.redalyc.org/articulo.oa?id=688378275005.

Reddy, Elizabeth. 2023. *¡Alerta! Engineering on Shaky Ground*. Cambridge, MA: MIT Press.

Rehak, Jana Kopelent, and Susanna Trnka. 2019. *The Politics of Joking*. London: Routledge.

Reid, Donald Malcolm. 2002. *Whose Pharaohs? Archaeology, Museums, and Egyptian National Identity from Napoleon to World War I*. Berkeley: University of California Press.

Reinert, Hugo. 2016. "About a Stone: Some Notes on Geologic Conviviality." *Environmental Humanities* 8, no. 1: 95–117. https://doi.org/10.1215/22011919-3527740.

Restauradoras con Glitter. 2019. "Postulado restauradoras con glitter." https://web .archive.org/web/20190906081447/http://gastv.mx/postulado-restauradoras-con -glitter-primerolasmujeresdespueslasparedes//.

Restauradoras con Glitter. 2022. "Conservación como acción política: La alteridad que somos." *CR: Conservación y Restauración*, no. 22, 55–72.

Richard, François G. 2018. *Reluctant Landscapes: Historical Anthropologies of Political Experience in Siin, Senegal*. Chicago: University of Chicago Press.

Rivera, Diego, Miquel Adriá, and Cynthia Aguirre. 2012. *El agua, origen de la vida en la tierra: Diego Rivera y el Sistema Lerma*. Mexico City: Arquine.

Roberts, Elizabeth F. S. 2012. "Scars of Nation: Surgical Penetration and the Ecuadorian State." *Journal of Latin American and Caribbean Anthropology* 17, no. 2: 215–37. https://doi.org/10.1111/j.1935-4940.2012.01223.x.

Rodríguez, Julia E. 2022. "Under the Mexican Sun: Zelia Nuttall and Eclipses in Americanist Anthropology." In *Invisible Labour in Modern Science*, edited by Jenny Bangham, Xan Chacko, and Judith Kaplan, 39–50. London: Rowman and Littlefield.

Rodríguez Kuri, Ariel. 2003. "Hacia México 68: Pedro Ramírez Vázquez y el proyecto olímpico." *Secuencia* 56: 37–73.

Rodríguez Kuri, Ariel. 2019. *Museo del universo: Los juegos olímpicos y el movimiento estudiantil de 1968*. Mexico City: El Colegio de México.

Rodríguez Mortellaro, Itzel. 2015. "El paisaje subterráneo y *Las riquezas nacionales* (1940–1941) de José Clemente Orozco." In *Coloquio Internacional de Historia del Arte Estética del paisaje en las Américas*, 309–23. Mexico City: Universidad Nacional Autónoma de México.

Rojas Rabiela, Teresa, José Luis Martínez-Ruiz, and Daniel Murillo Licea. 2009. *Cultura hidráulica y simbolismo mesoamericano del agua en el México prehispánico*. Mexico City: Instituto Mexicano de Tecnología del Agua and Centro de Investigaciones y Estudios Superiores en Antropología Social.

Rosemblatt, Karin Alejandra. 2024. "Investigating Cuauhtemoc's Bones: Politics, Truth, and Mestizo Nationalism in Mexico." In *Empire, Colonialism, and the Human Sciences: Troubling Encounters in the Americas and Pacific*, edited by Adam Warren, Julia E. Rodriguez, and Stephen T. Casper, 211–36. Cambridge: Cambridge University Press.

Rowlands, Michael. 2004. "Cultural Rights and Wrongs: Uses of the Concept of Property." In *Property in Question: Value Transformation in the Global Economy*, edited by Katherine Verdery and Caroline Humphrey, 207–26. New York: Berg Books.

Rozental, Sandra. 2008. "Becoming Petrified: The Making of Archaeological Personhood." In *These Ruins That You See*, edited by Mariana Castillo Deball, 193–223. Mexico City: Sternberg Press.

Rozental, Sandra. 2014a. "Coatlinchan in Fragments: Where Do They Belong?" *Ixiptla* 1: 34–53.

Rozental, Sandra. 2014b. "Stone Replicas: The Iteration and Itinerancy of Mexican Patrimonio." *Journal of Latin American and Caribbean Anthropology* 19, no. 2: 331–56. https://doi.org/10.1111/jlca.12099.

Rozental, Sandra. 2016. "In the Wake of Mexican Patrimonio: Material Ecologies in San Miguel Coatlinchan." *Anthropology Quarterly* 89, no. 1: 181–219. https://doi.org/10.1353/anq.2016.0007.

Rozental, Sandra. 2017a. "Kit to Detonate a Monolith." In *Total Destruction of the National Anthropology Museum*, edited by Eduardo Abaroa, 76–94. Mexico City: Athenée Press.

Rozental, Sandra. 2017b. "On the Nature of Patrimonio: Cultural Property in Mexican Contexts." In *The Routledge Companion to Cultural Property*, edited by Jane Anderson and Haidy Geismar, 237–57. London: Routledge.

Rozental, Sandra. 2017c. "Unearthing Patrimonio: Treasure and Collectivity in San Miguel Coatlinchan." In *Entangled Heritages: Postcolonial Perspectives on the Uses of the Past in Latin America*, edited by Olaf Kaltmeier and Mario Rufer, 137–53. London: Routledge.

Rozental, Sandra. 2020. "The Pre-Hispanic in Landscape: Ethnography with the Mapa de Coatlinchan." *Latin American and Latinx Visual Culture* 2, no. 4: 91–96. https://doi.org/10.1525/lavc.2020.2.4.91.

Rozental, Sandra. 2021. "A Monolith on the Street." In *Museum Matters: Making and Unmaking Mexico's National Collections*, edited by Miruna Achim, Susan Deans-Smith, and Sandra Rozental, 265–88. Tucson: University of Arizona Press.

Rozental, Sandra. 2022a. "Los fragmentos de un traslado: Los desbordes de las imágenes." *Encartes* 5, no. 9: 86–115. https://doi.org/10.29340/en.v5n9.227.

Rozental, Sandra. 2022b. "Restituir el patrimonio del pueblo." *Revista de la Universidad*, 10, December, 34–39. https://dialnet.unirioja.es/servlet/articulo?codigo=8703958.

Rozental, Sandra. 2024. "La némesis de Colón: Replicar la estatua de Amajac en Reforma." In *Las luchas por la memoria contra las violencias en México*, edited by Alexandra Delano and Benjamin Nienass, Mexico City: El Colegio de México.

Rozental, Sandra. Forthcoming. "The Collecting State or How to Fill 30,000 Square Meters of the New Museo Nacional de Antropología." In *Collecting Mesoamerican Art 1940–1964*, edited by Andrew Turned and Megan O'Neil. Los Angeles: Getty Research Institute.

Rozental, Sandra, John F. Collins, and Jason Ramsey. 2016. "Matters of Patrimony: Anthropological Theory and the Materiality of Replication in Contemporary Latin America." *Journal of Latin American and Caribbean Anthropology* 21, no. 1: 7–18. https://doi.org/10.1111/jlca.12194.

Rozental, Sandra, and Jesse Lerner, dirs. 2013. *The Absent Stone.* The American Egypt, Mexico City.

Rubenstein, Anne. 1998. *Bad Language, Naked Ladies, and Other Threats to the Nation: A Political History of Comic Books in Mexico.* Durham, NC: Duke University Press.

Rufer, Mario. 2014. "Paisaje, ruina y nación: Memoria local e historia nacional desde narrativas comunitarias en Coahuila." *Cuicuilco* 21, no. 61: 103–36. https://revistas.inah.gob.mx/index.php/cuicuilco/article/view/6178/7017.

Rufer, Mario. 2017. "The Ambivalence of Tradition: Heritage, Time, and Violence in Postcolonial Contexts." In *Entangled Heritages: (Post)Colonial Perspectives on the Uses of the Past in Latin America*, edited by Olaf Kaltmeier and Mario Rufer, 175–97. New York: Routledge.

Rufer, Mario. 2021. "Conjuring Violence Away with Culture: The Featherwork National Emblem in the Sala Purépecha of the Museo Nacional de Antropología." In *Museum Matters: Making and Unmaking Mexico's National Collections*, edited by Achim Miruna, Susan Deans-Smith, and Sandra Rozental, 243–64. Tucson: University of Arizona Press.

Rufer, Mario. 2023. "Zanjas, ruinas y espectros: Relatos del país donde no hay sombra." In *El tiempo de las ruinas*, edited by Cristóbal Gnecco and Mario Rufer, 17–203. Bogotá: Universidad de los Andes.

Ruiz Martínez, Apen. 2008. "Eulalia Guzmán y la imposibilidad de excavar en suelo nacional." *Cuicuilco* 15, no. 43: 137–57. https://revistas.inah.gob.mx/index.php/cuicuilco/article/view/4273/4228.

Ruiz Martínez, Apen. 2016. *Género, ciencia y política: Voces, vidas y miradas de la arqueología mexicana.* Mexico City: Secretaría de Cultura and Instituto Nacional de Antropología e Historia.

Ruiz Medrano, Ethelia, and Russ Davidson. 2011. *Mexico's Indigenous Communities: Their Lands and Histories, 1500–2010*, Boulder: University of Colorado Press.

Ruizpalacios, Alonso, dir. 2018. *Museo.* Manuel Alcalá, Mexico.

Sahlins, Marshall. 1963. "Poor Man, Rich Man, Big-Man, Chief: Political Types in Melanesia and Polynesia." *Comparative Studies in Society and History* 5: 285–303. https://doi.org/10.1017/S0010417500001729.

Sahlins, Marshall. 1972. *Stone Age Economics.* London: Routledge.

Sahlins, Marshall. 2011. "What Kinship Is (Part One)." *Journal of the Royal Anthropological Institute* 17, no. 1: 2–19. https://doi.org/10.1111/j.1467-9655.2010.01666.x.

Salas Landa, Mónica. 2018. "(In)Visible Ruins: The Politics of Monumental Reconstruction in Postrevolutionary Mexico." *Hispanic American Historical Review* 98, no. 1: 43–76. https://doi.org/10.1215/00182168-4294456.

Salas Landa, Mónica. 2024a. *Visible Ruins: The Politics of Perception and the Legacies of Mexico's Revolution.* Austin: University of Texas Press.

Salas Landa, Mónica. 2024b. "Shedding Light on Labor: Photography, Archaeology, and the Making of Monumentality in Tajín, Mexico." *Bulletin of the History of Archaeology* 34, no. 1. https://doi.org/10.5334/bha-698.

Sánchez, Jesús. 1886. "Estatua colosal de la diosa del agua." *Anales del Museo Nacional de México* 1, no. 3: 27–30. https://revistas.inah.gob.mx/index.php/anales/article/view/6448.

Sansi, Roger. 2005. "The Hidden Life of Stones: Historicity, Materiality and the Value of Candomblé Objects in Bahia." *Journal of Material Culture* 10, no. 2: 139–56. https://doi.org/10.1177/1359183505053072.

Sansi, Roger. 2007. *Fetishes and Monuments: Afro-Brazilian Art and Culture in the 20th Century.* New York: Berghahn Books.

Scheper Hughes, Jennifer. 2010 *Biography of a Mexican Crucifix: Lived Religion and Local Faith from the Conquest to the Present.* New York: Oxford University Press.

Scheper Hughes, Jennifer. 2016. "Cradling the Sacred: Image, Ritual, and Affect in Mexican and Mesoamerican Material Religion." *History of Religions* 56, no. 1: 55–107. https://doi.org/10.1086/686768.

Scheper-Hughes, Nancy. 2007. "The Tyranny of the Gift: Sacrificial Violence in Living Donor Transplants." *American Journal of Transplantation* 7, no. 3: 507–11. https://doi.org/10.1111/j.1600-6143.2006.01679.x.

Scheper-Hughes, Nancy. 2019. "A Finger in the Wound: On Pain, Scars, and Suffering." *Representations* 146, no. 1: 32–58. https://doi.org/10.1525/rep.2019.146.1.32.

Schildkrout, Enid. 2004. "Inscribing the Body." *Annual Review of Anthropology* 33: 319–44. https://doi.org/10.1146/annurev.anthro.33.070203.143947.

Schryer, Frans J., and George M. Foster. 1976. "A Reinterpretation of Treasure Tales and the Image of Limited Good." *Current Anthropology* 17, no. 4: 708–13. https://doi.org/10.1086/201805.

Schwenkel, Christina. 2013. "Post/Socialist Affect: Ruination and Reconstruction of the Nation in Urban Vietnam." *Cultural Anthropology* 28, no. 2: 252–77. https://doi.org/10.1111/cuan.12003.

Secretaría de Educación Pública. 1964. *Obra educativa en el sexenio, 1958–1964.* Mexico City: Secretaría de Educación Pública.

Seler, Eduard. 1991. *Collected Works in Mesoamerican Linguistics and Archaeology.* Vol. 2. Culver City: Labyrinthos.

Sellen, Adam. T. 2002. "Storm-God Impersonators from Ancient Oaxaca." *Ancient Mesoamerica* 13, no. 1: 3–19. https://doi.org/10.1017/S095653610213104X.

Sherman, John W. 2000. "The Mexican 'Miracle' and Its Collapse." In *The Oxford History of Mexico*, edited by Michael C. Mejer and William H. Beezley, 575–609. Oxford: Oxford University Press.

Siegel, James T. 1983. "Images and Odors in Javanese Practices Surrounding Death." *Indonesia*, no. 36, 1–14. https://doi.org/10.2307/3351023.

Sierra Camacho, María Teresa, Rosalva Aída Hernández, and Rachel Sieder, eds. 2013. *Justicias indígenas y estado: Violencias contemporáneas.* Mexico City: Facultad Latinoamericana de Ciencias Sociales, Sede México and Centro de Investigaciones y Estudios Superiores en Antropología Social.

Sigüenza Salas, Irma. 2021. "Cuando la revolución es en femenino, es vandalismo: La Revolución de la Brillantina y la pugna por la memoria." *Sociología y tecnociencia: Revista digital de sociología del sistema tecnocientífico* 11, no. 1: 55–77. https://doi.org/10.24197/st.1.2021.55-77.

Smith, Kimbra. 2005. "Looting and the Politics of Archaeological Knowledge in Northern Peru." *Ethnos* 70, no. 2: 149–70. https://doi.org/10.1080/00141840500141139.

Smith, Kimbra. 2016. "Like the Chameleon Who Takes on the Colors of the Hills: Indigeneity as Patrimony and Performance in Coastal Ecuador." *Journal of Latin American and Caribbean Anthropology* 21, no. 1: 19–38. https://doi.org/10.1111/jlca.12188.

Smith, Laurajane. 2006. *Uses of Heritage*. London: Routledge.

Solomon, Esther, ed. 2021. *Contested Antiquity: Archaeological Heritage and Social Conflict in Modern Greece and Cyprus*. Bloomington: Indiana University Press.

Soto-Coloballes, Natalia Verónica. 2019. "Proyectos y obras para el uso de los terrenos desecados del antiguo lago de Texcoco, 1912-1998." *Estudios de Historia Moderna y Contemporánea de México* 58: 259–87. https://doi.org/10.22201/iih.24485004e.2019.58.70695.

Stengers, Isabelle. 2005. "Introductory Notes on an Ecology of Practices." *Cultural Studies Review* 11, no. 1: 183–96. https://doi.org/10.5130/csr.v11i1.3459.

Stewart, Charles. 2003. "Dreams of Treasure: Temporality, Historicization and the Unconscious." *Anthropological Theory* 3, no. 4: 481–500. https://doi.org/10.1177/1463499960334005.

Stewart, Charles. 2012. *Dreaming and Historical Consciousness in Island Greece*. Cambridge, MA: Harvard University Press.

Stewart, Susan. 1993. *On Longing: Narratives of the Miniature, the Gigantic, the Souvenir, the Collection*. Durham, NC: Duke University Press.

Stoler, Ann Laura. 2008. "Imperial Debris: Reflections on Ruins and Ruination." *Cultural Anthropology* 23, no. 2: 191–219. https://doi.org/10.1111/j.1548-1360.2008.00007.x.

Stoler, Ann Laura, ed. 2013. *Imperial Debris: On Ruins and Ruination*. Durham, NC: Duke University Press.

Strathern, Marilyn. 2005. *Partial Connections*. Walnut Creek, CA: AltaMira Press.

Suárez Hernández, Salvador. 2008. "El Acolhuacan desde Tzontecomatl a Nezahualcoyotl." In *Crónicas de Texcoco*, vol. 1, edited by Alejandro Contla, 141–49. Mexico City: Consejo de la Crónica Municipal de Texcoco.

Summers, Lachlan. 2023. "Mexico City Is Two Hours from Mexico City." PhD diss., University of California, Santa Cruz.

Summers, Lachlan. 2025. "Touched by Deep Time: Earthquake Sickness in Mexico City." *Cultural Anthropology* 40, no. 3: 463–92. https://doi.org/10.14506/ca40.3.04.

Taibo, Paco Ignacio, II. 2006. *Sólo tu sombra fatal*. Mexico City: Porrúa.

Taussig, Michael. 1980. *The Devil and Commodity Fetishism in South America*. Chapel Hill: University of North Carolina Press.

Taussig, Michael. 1993. *Mimesis and Alterity: A Particular History of the Senses*. London: Routledge.

Taussig, Michael. 2004. *My Cocaine Museum*. Chicago: University of Chicago Press.

Taylor, Janelle S. 2008. *The Public Life of the Fetal Sonogram: Technology, Consumption, and the Politics of Reproduction*. New Brunswick, NJ: Rutgers University Press.

Taylor, William B. 2010. *Shrines and Miraculous Images: Religious Life in Mexico Before the Reforma*. Albuquerque: University of New Mexico Press.

Tenorio Trillo, Mauricio. 1996a. "1910 Mexico City: Space and Nation in the City of the Centenario." *Journal of Latin American Studies* 28, no. 1: 75–104. https://doi.org/10.1017/S0022216X00012645.

Tenorio Trillo, Mauricio. 1996b. *Mexico at World's Fairs: Crafting a Modern Nation.* Berkeley: University of California Press.

Tenorio Trillo, Mauricio. 2009. "Del mestizaje a un siglo de Andrés Molina Enríquez." In *En busca de Molina Enríquez: Cien años de Los grandes problemas nacionales,* edited by Emilio Kourí, 33–64. Mexico City: El Colegio de México.

Tenorio Trillo, Mauricio. 2023. *La historia en ruinas: El culto a los monumentos y a su destrucción.* Madrid: Alianza Editorial.

Thorner, Sabra G. 2019. "The Photograph as Archive: Crafting Contemporary Koorie Culture." *Journal of Material Culture* 24, no. 1: 22–47. https://doi.org/10.1177/1359183518782716.

Tilley, Christopher. 2004. *The Materiality of Stone: Explorations in Landscape Phenomenology.* New York: Berg.

Torre, Renée de la. 2007. "Estética azteca de las danzas concheras: Tradiciones exóticas o memorias re-descubiertas." *Versión: Estudios de Comunicación y Política,* no. 20: 147–86. https://versionojs.xoc.uam.mx/index.php/version/article/view/315.

Torre, Renée de la. 2008. "Tensiones entre el esencialismo azteca y el universalismo New Age a partir del estudio de las danzas 'conchero-aztecas.'" *Trace* 54: 61–76. http://journals.openedition.org/trace/480.

Torre, Renée de la, and Cristina Gutiérrez Zúñiga. 2017. *Mismos pasos y nuevos caminos: Transnacionalización de la danza conchero azteca.* Mexico City: El Colegio de Jalisco and Centro de Investigaciones y Estudios Superiores en Antropología Social.

Torres-Mazuera, Gabriela. 2012a. "El ejido posrevolucionario: De forma de tenencia sui generis a forma de tenencia ad hoc." *Península* 7, no. 2: 69–94. https://doi.org/10.22201/cephcis.25942743e.2012.7.2.44081.

Torres-Mazuera, Gabriela. 2012b. *La ruralidad urbanizada en el centro de México: Reflexiones sobre la reconfiguración local del espacio rural en un contexto neoliberal.* Mexico City: Universidad Nacional Autónoma de México.

Torres-Mazuera, Gabriela. 2016. *La común anomalía del ejido posrevolucionario: Disonancias normativas y mercantilización de la tierra en el sur de Yucatán.* Mexico City: Centro de Investigaciones y Estudios Superiores en Antropología Social.

Tovar Santana, Alfonso. 1993. *Cómo llegó Tlaloc a Chapultepec.* Mexico City: Instituto Politécnico Nacional.

Trnka, Susanna. 2011. "Specters of Uncertainty: Violence, Humor, and the Uncanny in Indo-Fijian Communities Following the May 2000 Fiji Coup." *Ethos* 39, no. 3: 331–48. https://doi.org/10.1111/j.1548-1352.2011.01196.x.

Trouillot, Michel-Rolph. 1995. *Silencing the Past: Power and the Production of History.* Boston: Beacon Press.

Turnbull, Paul, and Michael Pickering, eds. 2022. *The Long Way Home: The Meaning and Values of Repatriation.* New York: Berghahn Books.

Turner, Andrew, and Megan O'Neil. 2024. *Collecting Mesoamerican Art Before 1940: A New World of Latin American Antiquities.* Los Angeles: Getty Research Institute.

Turner, Andrew, Megan O'Neil, and Mary E. Miller. Forthcoming. *Collecting Mesoamerican Art, 1940s to 1960s: Museums, Markets, and Modernism in the United States and Mexico.* Los Angeles: Getty Research Institute.

Turner, Terence S. 1980. "The Social Skin." In *Not Work Alone: A Cross-Cultural View of Activities Superfluous to Survival*, edited by Jeremy Cherfas and Roger Lewin, 112–40. London: Temple Smith.

Uribe, Simon. 2017. *Frontier Road: Power, History, and the Everyday State in the Colombian Amazon*. Hoboken, NJ: Wiley.

Vaillant, George Clapp. 1950. *The Aztecs of Mexico: Origin, Rise and Fall of the Aztec Nation*. New York: Doubleday.

Valero Pie, Aurelia, and Nora Rabotnikof. 2023. "¿Qué hacer con el pasado? Tiempo, memoria e historia en los debates contemporáneos en México en torno a la estatua de Cristóbal Colón." *Historia y Grafía*, no. 60: 73–108. https://doi.org/10.48102/hyg.vi60.445.

Valiant, Seonaid. 2017. *Ornamental Nationalism: Archaeology and Antiquities in Mexico, 1876–1911*. Leiden: Brill.

Vázquez León, Luis. 2003. *El leviatán arqueológico: Antropología de una tradición científica en México*. Mexico City: Centro de Investigaciones y Estudios Superiores en Antropología Social.

Vázquez Mantecón, Álvaro. 2006. "La visualidad del 68." In *La era de la discrepancia: Arte y cultura visual en México, 1968–1997*, edited by Olivier Debroise, 37–40. Mexico City: Universidad Nacional Autónoma de México.

Verdery, Katherine. 1994. "Elasticity of Land: Problems of Property Restitution in Transylvania." *Slavic Review* 53, no. 4 (1994): 1071–1109. https//:doi.org/10.2307/2500847.

Verdery, Katherine. 2003. *The Vanishing Hectare: Property and Value in Postsocialist Transylvania*. Ithaca, NY: Cornell University Press.

Villarreal Galicia, Guadalupe. 2014. *La piedra de los tecomates "Chalchiuhtlicue": Por siempre en Coatlinchan*. Texcoco: Los Libros de la Capilla.

Vitz, Matthew. 2018. *A City on a Lake: Urban Political Ecology and the Growth of Mexico City*. Durham, NC: Duke University Press.

Wade, Peter. 2003. "Repensando el mestizaje." *Revista Colombiana de Antropología* 39 (January–December): 273–96. https://doi.org/10.22380/2539472X.1243.

Weiner, Annette B. 1992. *Inalienable Possessions: The Paradox of Keeping-While-Giving*. Berkeley: University of California Press.

Weismantel, Mary. 2001. *Cholas and Pishtacos: Stories of Race and Sex in the Andes*. Chicago: University of Chicago Press.

Weismantel, Mary, and Lynn Meskell. 2014. "Substances: 'Following the Material' Through Two Prehistoric Cases." *Journal of Material Culture* 19, no. 3: 233–51.

Wharton, Glenn. 2011. *The Painted King: Art, Activism, and Authenticity in Hawai'i*. Honolulu: University of Hawai'i Press.

Williams, Howel, and Robert F. Heizer. 1965. "Sources of Rocks Used in Olmec Monuments." In *Sources of Stones Used in Prehistoric Mesoamerican Sites*, edited by Robert F. Heizer, 1–40. Berkeley: University of California Press.

Wolf, Eric R. 1957. "Closed Corporate Peasant Communities in Mesoamerica and Central Java." *Southwestern Journal of Anthropology* 13, no. 1: 1–18. https://doi.org/10.1086/soutjanth.13.1.3629154.

Wolf, Eric R. 1986. "The Vicissitudes of the Closed Corporate Peasant Community." *American Ethnologist* 13, no. 2: 325–29. https://doi.org/10.1525/ae.1986.13.2.02a00080.

Wolfe, Mikael D. 2017. *Watering the Revolution: An Environmental and Technological History of Agrarian Reform in Mexico*. Durham, NC: Duke University Press.

Wright, Norman Pelham. 1947. *Mexican Kaleidoscope*. London: W. Heinemann.

Yalouri, Eleana. 2001. *The Acropolis: Global Fame, Local Claim*. New York: Berg.

Yarrow, Thomas. 2017. "Remains of the Future: Rethinking the Space and Time of Ruination Through the Volta Resettlement Project, Ghana." *Cultural Anthropology* 32, no. 4: 566–91. https://doi.org/10.14506/ca32.4.06.

Yates-Doerr, Emily. 2022. "Bloodwork: Circulatory Disorders, Immunity, and the Scarring of Systems." *Anthropology of Work Review* 43, no. 2: 106–16. https://doi.org /10.1111/awr.12240.

Yusoff, Kathryn. 2013. "Geologic Life: Prehistory, Climate, Futures in the Anthropocene." *Environment and Planning D: Society and Space* 31, no. 5: 779–95. https://doi .org/10.1068/d11512.

Yusoff, Kathryn. 2024. *Geologic Life: Inhuman Intimacies and the Geophysics of Race*. Durham, NC: Duke University Press.

Zaragocin, Sofia, and Martina Angela Caretta. 2021. "Cuerpo-Territorio: A Decolonial Feminist Geographical Method for the Study of Embodiment." *Annals of the American Association of Geographers* 111, no. 5: 1503–18. https://doi.org /10.1080/24694452.2020.1812370.

Zendejas, Sergio. 1994. "Sobre la otra cara del ejido: El ejido como ámbito de organización de prácticas políticas de grupos locales." *Regiones: Revista Interdisciplinaria en Estudios Regionales* 2, no. 4: 37–50.

Zepeda, Gabriela. 2000. "Guardianes y moneros: Patrimonio arqueológico y supervivencia campesina en el sur de Nayarit." MA thesis, Centro de Investigaciones y Estudios Superiores en Antropología Social.

Index

Page numbers in italics indicate figures.

contract (*actas*): as evidence of exchange, 100, 101; contested as fraudulent, 102

corruption: in the *ejido*, 129; of local authorities, 103–4, 138; of the state, 214, 217

Covarrubias, Miguel: on stone as unfinished work, 50

criminalization: of local claims and attachments, 18; of local residents, 111, 95, 246n26, 209

cronista (local historian), 102, 119, 245n22

Cuerpo-territorio (body-territory): as feminist concept of Latin American scholars, 238n22

CUFAC (Construcción Urbana Francisco Alonso Cué): employment of engineers by, 55, 59; role in relocation, 60, 71. *See also* transfer

Curiel, Jesús (Coatlinchan resident), 152, 154, 157–158, *196*

curfew: imposed on Coatlinchan, 87, 100; *See also* military

custodianship: by local residents, 90, 97

Cutzamala system, 222

dams: in Coatlinchan 122, as public works, 53, 54, 76, 77; Aswan, 58; Infiernillo, 67, 75; Presa de la Amistad, 84, *85*; Presa Miguel Hidalgo, 84; replicas of stone at, 83–84

dance: as ritual offering, 143. See also *danzantes*; neo-Aztec dancers; Mexicanidad, La

danzantes, 143, 169

Dávalos Hurtado, Eusebio, 100

decolonization: of the stone, through replicas, 180

defacement: of the stone, by treasure hunters, 157

deforestation: as a cause of environmental disruption, 190, 200

Delegación (municipal building): mural in, 159, *160*

delegados. See community representatives

Delta Industrial Mexicana (DIMSA). *See* DIMSA

desde que se llevaron La Piedra (phrase), 6, 9

devotion: Catholic vs. pre-Hispanic, 182, 184. *See also* Catholicism

Díaz, Porfirio, 36, 104

día zero (day zero), 223

Día, El (newspaper), *12*

DIMSA (Delta Industrial Mexicana): advertisements by, 73

Dirty War, 217, 246n26

dispossession: aftershocks of, 221; of *lo nuestro*, 148–49; replica as monument to, 174; stone's removal as, 149

dreams: Ayatitlicui's (Daniel), of ancient spirits, 143; as historical and ethnographic sources, 250n4; Luz's (doña), of golden ball, 154

drought: attributed to deity's wrath, 82; linked to stone's removal, 190, 191, 202; in Mexico City, 213

drug trade, 129, 138, 158

duendes (trickster figures), 193

Dulce (Coatlinchan resident), see Galicia González, Dulce

dynamite, 124, 137; stolen by residents, 109, 110

Earth Day: visits to museum on, 179

earthquakes: aftershocks and, 13; as explanation for stone's location, 33; in Mexico City (1985), 23; and stone, local beliefs about, 8; in Valley of Mexico, frequency of, 13–14

Ebrard, Marcelo: on repatriation of Olmec monument (from Chalcatzingo), 215

Ecatepec: as Ulises Figueroa's hometown, 125

ecology: disruption of, 190, 211, 215; of the ravine, 195

Edelman and Associates, 69

Edzná (archaeological site): stela from, 94

Egypt: antiquities of, as comparison, 16, 33, 241n16; Aswan Dam and monument relocation in, 58

ejido: land grant 17, 101, 113; *comisariado ejidal*, 100, 122, 136; corruption in, 129–130; land sales and, 134; OAS study of, 132–33. See also agrarian reforms

engineering/engineers: as protagonists in relocation, 54–55, 76; calculations by, 35, 51, 55–56; continuity with pre-Hispanic technology, 76; early interest in, 31; homegrown/Mexican, 53, 66, 76; role in hydraulic infrastructure, 54, 77; role in relocation, 2, 4, 16, 24

erratic block: stone as, 51

Esquila, La. *See* Piedra, La

espanto (fright): 154, 155; water as cure for, 194

essence: as local knowledge and history, 125–26, 142–44, 146; replica invested with, 176–80

"Estatua colosal de la diosa del agua" (Sánchez) (report), 33, *34*

Estado de México (State of Mexico): Coatlinchan as part of, 6, 236n7; gang violence in, 196; Peña Nieto as governor of, 148; political context of, 172; water scarcity in, 222

Ezequiel, Father (priest): on multiplicity of San Miguel, 183, 184; on theft of church valuables, 151

healing: Calpulli's work as, 139; medicinal plants, 194, 202; of scarring wound, 216; scars and, 117, 120; water for, 194

Heizer, Robert: study of the stone's weight, 48, 49, 242n21; study of heavy transport by, 50–51

helicopters: at Nextlalpan, 147–48

Heredia, Guillermo de: architectural drawings, 37, *37*

highways: as public works, 53

history: murals and, 159, *160*

hole (*hoyo*): left by the stone, 118, 120, 122, 126; left by mine (Las Joyas), 129

Holy Week: mass in ravine during, 123, 126

humedad que genera vida (life-making humidity): as slogan for restitution campaign, 215, *215*

humor, 10, 11, 14, 20, 25; in collections, 201; in depictions of the stone, 10, 160; as response to loss, 220; in storytelling, 205

hydraulic imaginary: concept of, 76, 84

hydraulic infrastructure, 54, 76, 77; Dolores sump (Cárcamo de Dolores), 77; Lerma River Basin, 77

iconoclasm: colonial, 34, 43; double gestures of, 44

idolatry: colonial campaigns against, 41, 179; local beliefs as, 45, 184, 191, 193

"idol trade": history of, 200

ídoleros (idol people): as collectors and traders, 142, 199–200, 202

ídolos/idolitos (figurines): abundance and scarcity of, 199, 202; as ancestral faces (*caritas*), 207; collections of, 198, 201; sprouting with the rain, 199, 202; stone described as, 32, 34, 40. *See also* collecting/collections

Impacto (magazine), 104, *106*

inalienable possessions: Weiner's theory of, 239n33

Indigeneity: as relationship to territory, 145

indigenismo: history of, 238n27; as origin of La Mexicanidad movement, 139

Indigenous peoples: colonial views of, 50, 240n2; lifeways of, 41

INAH (Instituto Nacional de Antropología e Historia), 21–23, *22*, 100; and Mapa de Coatlinchan, 140, 141; official response to petition, 223–24; and restoration of monuments, 221; and residents' collections, 201; restoration of San Miguel images by, 183

INDEP (Instituto para Devolverle al Pueblo lo Robado): creation of, 214

infrastructural technology: stone's relocation as, 54

infrastructure: as exchange for the stone, 101, 103; as producing nation-states, 54; as public works, 54, 76

Instituto de Geología, 47

IPN (Instituto Politécnico Nacional), 58, 123

Isrrael Pixihua. *See* Pixihua, Isrrael (Martínez)

Iztaccihuatl, 7, 42

Japan: as rumored location of stone, 8, 9

Juan (Coatlinchan resident): on authenticity of replica, 179–80; on ghosts and treasure, 155

"k": used for more autochthonous spellings, 165, 178

Kenworth (company), 75

Kernaghan, Richard: on aftermaths of violence, 238n23; on dreams and ethnographic writing, 250n4; on "the obtuse" as an ethnographic category, 252n14

King Kong. *See* Piedra, La

King, Martin Luther, Jr., 66

Kubler, George: on Coatlinchan church architecture, 236n12; on prime objects and their "replica mass," 251n5

Kuhn, Toni: photograph of stone by, 216

labor: local, use of in excavation, 63, *63*, 64. *See also faena* (communal labor)

land: community, 189, 190; community donation of, 103; degradation of, 190; *ejido*, 101, 113, 132–134; ownership patterns, 132; sale of, 134–135, 189

Las Joyas (sand mine), 129, 130

Latour, Bruno: on purification and translation, 32

Lazo, Carlos: as engineer on relocation project, 75

Lejeal, Léon: on uncertainty of stone's identity, 46

Le Guin, Ursula K.: on rocks as place, (epigraph), 6

León, Nicolás, 46, 242n19

León-Portilla, Miguel: opposition to stone's removal, 96

Lerner, Jesse: as codirector of *The Absent Stone* (film), 9, *92*, *162*, 214, 218

limpias (ritual cleansings): in the ravine, 194; ritual by Calpulli, 143

Linares, Miguel (Coatlinchan resident) on design of stone cartoon, 250–51n1

Panchito, don (Coatlinchan resident): stories of his father and Porfirio Diaz interest in the stone, 104

Paraje de la Piedra, El. *See* ravine (cañada/barranca)

Partido de la Revolución Democrática. *See* PRD

Paseo de la Reforma (Mexico City): history of monuments on, 5, 236n5; feminist protests on, 220; stone's location on, 56, 222, 236n6

Pascual, don (Coatlinchan resident): wealth of, 153

patria (fatherland): greatness of, 112; *la patria asesina* slogan, 220; as root of *patrimonio*, 16

patriarchal claims/tenets: of *patrimonio*, 17, 18

patrimonio: as dynamic process, 221; as justification for removal, 89, 90, 122; legal handling of, 55, 60; laws, 16–17, 23, 50, 87, 89–90; as priceless, 60, 63, 64; restitution of, 214, 217; state discourses of, 84, 221

Payno, Manuel: *Los bandidos de Río Frío*, 151

Paz, Octavio, *30*

Pedro, don (Coatlinchan resident). *See* García, Pedro

Pellicer, Carlos: opposition to stone's removal, 96; proposal for Tlaloc Museum, 129

Peña Nieto, Enrique (president and state governor): alleged theft of treasure by, 147–48, 158; at unveiling of replica, 172

petrification: of woman, as origin of stone, 191

petroglyphs, 50; Cabeza del Penacho, 195, *196*

photography/photographs: of army presence, 111, *112*; Batres's use of, in excavation, 37; of birthday cake replica, 93, *93*; glass-plate negative postcard of the stone, 34, 37; of local guide, *105*; role in separating stone from landscape, 34, 37; use of, in creating replicas, 176; in Ramírez Vázquez's office, 92; of rebellion's destruction, 104, *106*

Piedra de los Tecomates, La, 8, 10, 45; on replica plaque, 174. *See also* Piedra, La; *tecomate*

Piedra del Toro: description of, 196, *197*

Piedra, La (The Stone): absence of, effects of, 6, 9–11, 15–16, 23, 25, 117, 120, 159, 162; appropriation of, for protests, 216; as bewitched (*encantada*), 107–8; community's attachment to, 90, 106; as "curious thing," 32; as distinct from its location, 32, 34, *36*; early accounts and studies of, 32–40; excavation of (by Batres), *36*; gender of, as contested, 8, 10, *30*, 32, 41–46, 48, 191, 217–18; geological composition of, 49; graffiti and markings on, 97, 245nn17–18;

as *lo nuestro* (what is ours), 9, 107; names for, 2, 8, 10, 33, *35*, 45, 47; orientation of, 166, 169, 174; relocation of (1964): arrival in Mexico City, 1–2, 11; community resistance to, 86–89, 104–11; engineering of, 53–87; official narrative of, 6, 89–91; as theft, 87, 90, 149; as watershed moment, 190; return of, campaign for, 214, 216–17; size and weight of, 1, 31, 33, 56, 60, 241n9; as stand-in for authoritarian politics, 216; supernatural and meteorological powers of, 8, 78, 82, 84, 86; as telluric entity, 12–13, *225*; and treasure, 149, 157–58; as unfinished work, 50, 51. *See also* Chalchiuhtlicue (deity); monolith; replicas; restitution; Tlaloc (deity)

piedra (crack cocaine), 158

Piña Chan, Román, 95

pipas (water tank trucks), 223

Pixihua, Isrrael (Martínez) (Coatlinchan resident): on campaign for stone's return, 214; on community museum, 128; on Figueroa's installation, 125–26; migration to US, 128, 129; Nahuatl name of, 125; pilgrimage to Cámara de Diputados, 213; on state's response, 223–24; speech by, 215

pizcador (corn-husking tool), 205

plataforma. *See* trailer (low-bed)

Plazuela (Coatlinchan): description, 7, 157; as site of drug dealing, 158; replica of stone in, 170–74

plows (*yuntas*), 199, 200, 204

Poole, Deborah: on photography and the politics of visuality, 241n5; on theft and resistance to the state, 21

Portal to the Underworld (Olmec monument): repatriation of, 215

Postclassic period, 45, 141, 208

Postcolonial: 23

postrevolutionary Mexican state: appropriation of pre-Hispanic past, 16, 76–77, 235n2, 239n32; authoritarianism, 5, 216; infrastructure projects, 134; muralism and, 244n5

pottery sherds. *See* tepalcates

pre-Hispanic past: appropriation of by the state, 239n32; artifacts and monuments of, 1, 10, 53, 73, 152, 202; continuity with modern state, 16–17, 54, 76; as latent and recoverable, 139, 142; revival of cosmologies and practices, 139, 143, 169, 181, 193; shrines, 44; stone's connection to, 165; term, critique of, 235n1; *tlateles* (stone mounds), 137, 142, 197

Prensa, La (newspaper), 105, 111, *112*, 113

preservation. *See* conservation

Presa de la Amistad (dam), 84, *85*

Presa Miguel Hidalgo (dam), 84

PRI (Partido Revolucionario Institucional), 135, 173, 174; monolith as metaphor for, 216, 253n3; single-party rule by, 5

PRD (Partido de la Revolución Democrática): role in Plazuela and replica at Coatlinchan, 172, 173, 174

Proceso (magazine), 95

procession: stone's relocation as, 71; of San Miguel images, 183, 184

progreso (progress): as justification for exchange, 99, 101

property rights: local claims to, 90

protests: against state violence, 216; feminist, 220; *replicar* as protest, 14, 162

Protestants: expulsion from Coatlinchan, 179

public works: construction of, 53; dams as, 53, 54, 76, 77; highways as, 53; role in nation-building, 54, 76

pulque, 191

purification (Latourian concept): applied to the stone, 32

quarry: Coatlinchan as, 49, 50; of pink replica in Hidalgo, 168

quinceaños, 162

Quintana, Miguel: role in hiring truck driver, 75

Quetzaltepec (hill), 154

Quezada, Abel, *30*, 83

racial capitalism: treasure and, 150

Raffles, Hugh: on stones' unconformities, 237n17

rain: accompanying stone's arrival, 75, 78, 82; decrease in, 130, 132, 189, 190, 199, 202, 206; connection to sprouting of artifacts, 192, 199, 202, 207, 211; petition rituals 179, 193. *See also* drought

rainmaking: stone's connection to, 190, 191; stone's powers of, 78, 82, 220

Ramírez, Oscar (pseudonym, "Margosk"), 176; miniatures made by, 175, *175*; as sculptor of Plazuela replica, 172, 180.

Ramírez Campusano, Javier: on his father's connection to the stone, 93

Ramírez Vázquez, Pedro: on community consent and resistance, 89; connection to stone, 93; on foreign manufacturing, 66; on graffiti, 97; on the "grass of a lake" metaphor, 19, 113, 222; on local residents' motivations, 96; personal

archives of, 60, 244n6; role in relocation, 16, 18, 23, 55, 60, 64, 75, 78, 90, 100; as architect of museum, 16; stone model of, 92, *92*

Raúl Isidro Burgos Rural Teachers College (Ayotzinapa), 216

ravine (*barranca*): as barren, 122, *122*; as Santa Clara 36, *38*, 121, *122*, 154, 194, 246n4; Catholic rituals in, 192; Charro Negro in, 157; childhood memories of, 121, 126; contemporary state of, 118, 122; as desired location for stone's return, 214, 218, 226; as empty vessel, 121; Figueroa's installation in, 124, *125*; healing plants in, 194; names for, 121, 154, 194; as scar, 119; as sacred site, 144; as site of play, 194; as site of treasure, 154, 158, as *tecomate*, 121

raza de acá (people from here), 167

rebellion: community resistance as, 104, *106*, 107. *See also* borlote; sabotage

reforestation, 187

Reform Wars, 214

regeneration: scars and, 120

relics: *pizcador* as, 205

repatriation: scholarship on, 23, 240n46, digital, 125, 246n5; of Olmec monument (Chalcatzingo), 215; state campaign for, 214

replicas: artisans of, 163, 165; authenticity and, 179–80, 251n3; on birthday cake, *93*; by "El Cherokee" (in ravine), 168, *169*, 170; at dam sites, 83–84, *85*; humorous depictions of, 160, *162*; materials of, 163, 170, 178; on murals and signage, 159, *160*; as offerings, 162, *177*; one-to-one copy (in Plazuela), *170*, *171*, 172, *173*–74; orientation of, 169, 174; as political act, 163, 165, 167; as response to theft, 162–63, 166; ritual consecration of, 176, *177*, 178–79; by Óscar Ramírez ("Margosk"), 172, *175*; San Miguel images and, 180, 183; scars as form of, 120; scholarly discussion of, 115, 251n5, 251n6; as souvenirs, *118*, 163, *165*. *See also* miniatures

repurposing: of the low-bed trailer, 75, 76, 243n16

rescue, narrative of: by corporations (Goodrich-Euzkadi), 70; by engineers and scholars, 47, 58; by the state (official discourse), 4, 16, 90–91, 150; town residents' rejection of, 90

resistance: telluric, 149

Restauradoras con Glitter: on *patrimonio* as a process, 221

restoration: of ancient statue by locals, 44; Calpulli's work as, 139, 142, 146